PRAISE FOR ANN RULE AND . . .

EVERYTHING SHE EVER WANTED

"ANN RULE HAS BECOME A MASTER OF THE TRUE-CRIME GENRE." —*Chicago Tribune*

"Yet another true crime triumph for Ann Rule . . . a magnificently constructed book."

—*Washington Post Book World*

"Ann Rule draws a chilling picture of a female sociopath who believes she deserves everything and manipulates and destroys the lives of all those who love her. . . ." —*Atlanta Journal/Constitution*

"Ms. Rule . . . now turns her devastatingly accurate insight to the twisted mind of a modern-day Southern belle. A measure of how well she succeeds is the feeling that came over me after reading just a few paragraphs about Pat Allanson. I wanted to reach into the book and strangle her."

—*The New York Times Book Review*

IF YOU REALLY LOVED ME

"An absolute masterpiece of reporting . . . No writer in America has ever probed the dark heart of a killer so deeply." —*Edna Buchanan, author of Contents Under Pressure*

"Bone chilling . . . a truly staggering case . . . Rule does an admirable job of drawing out the drama and the nuances." —*Washington Post*

"A real page-turner . . . a passport into perversion."

—*Seattle Times/Seattle Post Intelligencer*

For orders other than by individual consumers, Pocket Books
grants a discount on the purchase of **10 or more** copies of
single titles for special markets or premium use. For further
details, please write to the Vice President of Special Markets,
Pocket Books, 1230 Avenue of the Americas, 9th Floor,
New York, NY 10020-1586.

For information on how individual consumers can place
orders, please write to Mail Order Department, Simon &
Schuster Inc., 100 Front Street, Riverside, NJ 08075.

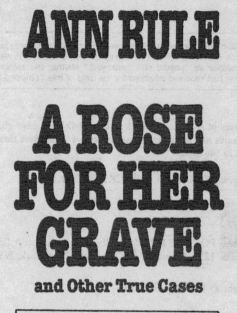

ANN RULE

A ROSE FOR HER GRAVE

and Other True Cases

Ann Rule's Crime Files: Vol. 1

POCKET BOOKS

New York   London   Toronto   Sydney   Singapore

The names of some individuals in this book have been changed. Such names are indicated by an asterisk (*) the first time each appears in the book.

An *Original* Publication of POCKET BOOKS

POCKET BOOKS, a division of Simon & Schuster Inc.
1230 Avenue of the Americas, New York, NY 10020.

ISBN: 0-671-79353-5

First Pocket Books printing August 1993

19 18 17 16 15 14 13 12 11 10

POCKET and colophon are registered trademarks of Simon & Schuster Inc.

Cover art by Kam Mak

Printed in the U.S.A.

This book is dedicated to women, to the friends I cherish and to the friends I will never know. Too many times I have to write about the tragedies that befall my sisters. *A Rose for Her Grave* is no exception. I am continually amazed at the strength women have shown in the face of catastrophe, particularly the survivors who pick up their lives and go on after losing a child to a conscienceless killer.

I salute all women who have had dreams, for themselves, for their children and for those they love. Their dreams were—and are—as different as the dreamers. Some came true; many did not. Some women found love and some found betrayal. Some were victims and some were heroines.

Some were both.

This book is dedicated to women in the Armed Forces and to the hundreds I worked with and knew. I became interested in womanhood because that holiday season, I found that I enjoyed the group, the companion-ship and so the several women I met, shown in the several questioning personalities survived two major tribulations and persisted after being a military man from being a soldier.

There are all women who have had illusions about love, for those that they've had, that make up the difference? Some deeper feelings and the brighter, hand-to-hand love we've known and were wives. So thick...

others will battle.

Acknowledgments

In a book that covers as many cases as *A Rose for Her Grave* does, there are dozens of people to thank. My research begins, quite literally, with a blank page or a short newspaper clipping. If it were not for those who consented to share their experiences, their impressions, their information and their emotions with me, I would be stuck with my blank page.

The names that follow are not in any particular order and they certainly are not alphabetized—but I am tremendously grateful to everyone listed:

King County Detectives Sue Peters, Randy Mullinax, Mike Hatch and Stan Chapin; King County Senior Deputy Prosecuting Attorneys Marilyn Brenneman and Susan Storey; Donna and Judy Clift, Ben and Marta Goodwin, Brittany Zehe, Hazel and Merle Loucks, Jim and Marge Baumgartner; Judge Frank Sullivan, Lori Merrick and Lynn Harkey, Todd Wheeler, Timothy Bergman, and Jeff Gaw; Chris Jarvis, *Journal American;* Richard Seven and Steve Clutter, *The Seattle Times;* Jack Hopkins, *The Seattle Post-Intelligencer;* Eric Zoeckler, *The Herald;* and Rose Mandelsberg-Weiss, *True Detective.*

Hank Gruber, Rudy Sutlovich, Dan Engle, John Boren, Billy Baughman, Gary Fowler, John Nordlund, Al Lima, Richard Steiner, Gene Ramirez and Don Cameron of the Seattle Police Department Homicide Unit; King County Medical Examiner Dr.

Acknowledgments

Donald Reay and Chief Deputy Medical Examiner Bill Haglund; Joe Belinc, Doug Englebretson and Glenn Mann of the Snohomish County Sheriff's Office; Private Investigator Jim Byrnes, formerly of the Marion County, Oregon, Sheriff's Office.

Jean and Warren McClure, Doreen Hanson, Hilda Ahlers, Don Hendrickson.

Gerry Brittingham, Leslie Rule and Donna Anders, my unflinching critics, researchers and friends.

Finally, to my faithful and hardworking agents Joan and Joe Foley (East Coast) and Mary Alice Kier and Anna Cottle of CINE/LIT (West Coast); to Emily Remes, who thank goodness, knows the law better than I do; to Liate Stehlik and Joe Gramm, editorial assistants; and to my editors, Bill Grose and Julie Rubenstein of Pocket Books, who envisioned this new series and prodded me every inch of the way until my blank pages became a real book.

And, once again, to the members of the oldest living literary group in Washington State: the inscrutable B. & M. Society.

Contents

Contents

Author's Note

I have always believed that true crime writing should not only absorb its readers but also educate them. There is no need to embroider spectacular cases; human behavior is in and of itself more fascinating than anything to be found in fiction. Those who have read my work before know that I do not stress blood and gore and grotesque details; I focus my research on the *whys* of murder more than on the *how*. Every day perfectly normal-appearing people commit crimes that seem inexplicable, leaving the rest of us to ponder, *"What* happened?" And there are the monsters, too, who make us ask, "Why did it take so long to happen?"

This series will, I hope, break new ground in the true crime genre. Each volume is designed to stand on its own, unveiling the details of aberrant and criminal behavior in the format that suits a particular case best, and yet the entire series will give the reader a deeper understanding of the psychopathology behind many types of crime.

Among the fourteen hundred murder cases I have covered, there are many that I will never forget. They have become so much a part of my life that the families of the victims are still my friends and so are the detectives who caught the killers. I cannot really tell you why these cases are as real to me today as they were the first time I delved into the police files and visited the places where the human beings involved once walked. It may be because these stories are, in a shadowy, frightening way, classics.

In Volume 1 the title story covers the case of Randy Roth, a modern-day Bluebeard whose alleged crimes went unpunished for more than a decade. The Roth case is an original book-length piece written expressly for this anthology. Randy Roth's trial was held in 1992.

You will also find other true cases from my own archives. These have been revised and updated: "Campbell's Revenge," "The Hit Person: Equal Opportunity Murder," "The Runaway," "The Rehabilitation of a Monster," and "Molly's Murder."

I have selected each case for a special reason. Some I find extraordinary because of the insights they offer into bizarre and unpredictable human behavior. Others follow police investigators as they search for a killer, and provide examples of the most remarkable detective work I have encountered. Some demonstrate the almost space age advancements in forensic science, new techniques in blood work, computerized fingerprints, and in the identification of the most minuscule evidence imaginable. Even a decade ago detectives could never have foreseen these giant leaps in their fields. And some cases point out tragic gaps that still exist in our justice system.

I hope that you will find *Ann Rule's True Crime Cases* a series unlike anything you have read before.

With best wishes,

Ann Rule

A ROSE FOR HER GRAVE

and Other True Cases

A Rose for Her Grave

Bluebeard—La Barbe-Bleu—*the story of the wife killer of fairy tales and folklore, has been part of the world's popular culture since 1697. There is a murderous husband in every version of the story from* Tales of Mother Goose *to similar stories in European, African, and Asian folklore. The essentials of the oft told horror tale are the locked, forbidden room, the wife's curiosity, and her eleventh hour rescue.* Bluebeard *is such an antiquated story that it seems strange that it might be played out in real life in the 1980s and 1990s. Down through the centuries the most popular version has a cruel husband who leaves his bride with the keys to all the rooms in his home—but forbids her to open one room. The disobedient wife cannot resist the temptation to see what is in the room denied her. When that door swings open, she is transfixed with horror to see the bodies of her husband's former wives. The wicked husband discovers her treachery when he finds one telltale spot of blood on the key to that room.*

Knowing that she will die, the doomed bride calls out piteously to her sister who is watching from the tower for sign of rescue, "Sister Ann, Sister Ann, do you see anyone coming?"

In fiction the frightened bride is rescued just in time. In real life it is not always so.

* * *

1

He was a man who hated women, truly *hated women. Unlike the serial killer who chooses, stalks, and physically destroys women he does not know, this man knew his victims only too well. The serial killer is "addicted to murder"; Bluebeard was addicted to his own greed. He was above all a man in complete control. He had to be, of course, because his plans required timing, charm, charisma, cunning, and a complete lack of conscience or empathy. He was handsome and boyish, and his victims never saw the danger in his eyes until it was far too late.*

His victims were many, but he did the greatest harm to women and children. He wanted a family. He insinuated himself into a number of close families and became something of a cross between the young uncle and the oldest son. But when he formed families of his own, he destroyed them. Utterly. Unlike the serial killer whose crimes invariably have aspects of sexual aberrance, Bluebeard was more stimulated by an expensive car than by the women who desired him. He only used their passion to gain those things he wanted more.

"A Rose for Her Grave" is the story of that man and of the King County detectives and prosecutors who sought to stop him from acting on his obsessions.

PART ONE

Janis

1

Janis Miranda was a little bit of a thing. She stood no more than an inch over five feet tall, and she weighed only 98 pounds. The few snapshots of her that remain are blurry. Even so, it was easy to see that she was pretty. She had long glossy brown hair and green eyes and a good figure that she kept by jogging and dancing. She admitted that jogging bored her, but she loved to dance. Oh, how she loved to dance. On the dance floor she could forget the sad times in her short life, too many failed dreams and too many broken promises. Her natural grace and a lot of practice drew admiring glances from other dancers, and she never lacked for partners.

Janis left home young. When she set off on her own, her mother, Billie Jean Ray, was living in Dallas, Texas, and her father was off in Little Rock, Arkansas —at least he was the last time his daughter had heard from him. He had gone off and left Billie Jean with all the responsibility of raising their four kids. As long as Janis could remember, Billy Jean had worked three jobs at a time. Her mother was more philosophical about her husband than Janis was. She saw how exhausted Billie Jean was most of the time, and she would never forgive her father for what she perceived as desertion. When he tried to make up later by sending Janis birthday cards and offering to send

5

small sums of money, she told him, "If you wanta help somebody, start sending checks to Mom. Once you've caught up with all that you owe her, *then* you can think about your children."

There had been many times when food was scarce, and Janis never forgot them. It wasn't easy for her to believe in men after her daddy took off. And yet her emotions were ambivalent; she longed for a good man even as she doubted that such an animal existed.

Nevertheless, Janis married young the first time. She had known Joe Miranda for a year or so and she was eighteen when she and Joe got married on April 17, 1971. Joe was in the army, and they were transferred to Augsburg, Germany, where their daughter, Jalina, was born on October 10, 1973. When they returned to Dallas, Janis worked at several jobs—first as a lab assistant and then for a security firm and a stockbroker.

The romance went out of their marriage too soon, and Joe and Janis separated in late 1975. Their divorce was final on September 16, 1976. There were no bitter recriminations; they simply went their separate ways, and twenty-four-year-old Janis got custody of Jalina. Somewhat reluctantly, according to Janis, Joe paid $250 a month toward Jalina's support. Janis tried to save most of that for her little girl's future. She found herself working as hard as her own mother had just to cover the necessities of life for herself and Jalina. She couldn't hope to get much help from her family; they were working to keep afloat themselves.

Janis Miranda was a young woman of moderate habits. Occasionally she would have a drink or two when she was out dancing, but that was all. Drinking was against her religion, and besides that, the music and the excitement that she always found at a dance were enough of a high for her. Janis fantasized sometimes that she could be a professional disco dancer, and she also loved to dance to the big band sound. She didn't use drugs—except for diet pills once in a while.

6

She was so tiny that her friends wondered why she felt the need to watch her weight, but she complained that every extra pound showed when you were short. If she went over 105 pounds, she worried.

Janis, with Jalina in tow, moved often, looking perhaps for some geographic solution to the melancholy that periodically washed her world in shades of gray. She went from Texas to California and then on up to Washington State. She didn't have anything in the way of earthly possessions, but she had what was most important—her daughter. Jalina's hair was a little darker than her mother's but just as thick and gleaming with highlights. Janis combed Jalina's hair back and caught it up with a ribbon, letting it cascade to her daughter's waist.

Mother and daughter were close—perhaps too close. Sometimes Janis confided too much in her child. She told Jalina almost everything. "That's more than a little kid should know," Janis's friends cautioned more than once. But Janis shook her head. "Jalina and I don't have any secrets between us."

During and after her marriage to Joe, Janis was a Jehovah's Witness. "She was heavy into religion," Joe remembered. "She was always looking for something to belong to. Her family broke up after a divorce, and Janis was kicked around a lot from family to family."

As an adult, Janis was close to her mother, sisters, and brother, and she had one other person she could count on—her friend Louise Mitchell. The women met at their church in Dallas in 1975. Louise was a little older and had kids of her own, but the two women hit it off right away. Janis's size could make her seem almost waiflike sometimes, as if she needed someone who gave a damn about her. Louise did. They had similar problems, and the two women sometimes combined their households to save expenses. They got along fine. They trusted each other so much that they shared a bank account on occasion. Then one or the other would move and their friendship would continue with long-distance calls and letters.

Janis still longed for a man who would truly love her, but now that would mean loving Jalina too. Janis was young and attractive, and most of the time she managed to show the world an upbeat attitude even when she was sad and scared underneath. Half of her believed in fate and in love at first sight. Half of her clung to her own autonomy and made her treasure her independence.

Pressed to reveal her real feelings, Janis admitted that she believed she would have a second chance at love.

Sometimes Janis leapt without thinking, making decisions based on emotion rather than on common sense. She seemed to change her mind as often as she changed her clothes. The one thing she was absolutely steadfast about was her daughter. Jalina always came first. Janis would have given up her life for her little girl.

Louise Mitchell had seen Janis discouraged and depressed, but not often. The only time she was really concerned was when they were living in California. Janis had looked upon the move to California as a whole new start, only to find that there was nothing magical there either. It was still hard to make a living and support Jalina, and sometimes she got so lonely.

When Louise moved to Seattle in 1979, Janis followed a few months later and found an apartment right across the street from Louise's place. She hadn't found happiness in Texas or in California, and she missed having her best friend around. They fell immediately back into their old habit of visiting together every day, either on the phone or over coffee.

Janis soon got a job working in the office at the Richmond Pediatric Clinic on North 185th in the north end suburb of Seattle. The move from Texas had taken everything she had saved, except for

Jalina's college money. She wouldn't touch Jalina's savings if she could help it. Janis had only her 1974 Pinto. She had no furniture at all and no clothes for cold weather. One of the other women working at the clinic loaned her a little television set, and she was surprised and shocked when she brought it over to see that Janis and Jalina slept on the floor of their small apartment in sleeping bags because they had no beds. They were using a suitcase for a table. But neither mother nor daughter seemed to feel bad about it; they were "camping out" until they could afford furniture.

Janis was a good worker, and everyone liked her at the clinic. She never complained about what she didn't have. She just worked harder to change things. "She took a job at K Mart in the evenings," Shirley Lenz, the clinic receptionist, recalled. "She wanted Jalina to have whatever she needed. Janis herself didn't even have a winter coat. She *had* to have two jobs to make it."

If only on a subconscious level, Janis Miranda waited for a prince to come along and rescue her. She knew that wasn't likely to happen. Still, she could hope. Every time she went to a dance, she wondered if it might turn out to be her lucky night. She joined Parents Without Partners and attended all their dances. She went to their Halloween party and then to the PWP Thanksgiving dance. Faces in the crowd began to seem like friends.

Janis went to a Parents Without Partners New Year's Eve dance on the last day of 1980. It was held at a dance hall over the Richmond-Highlands Ice Arena. As always, there were four times as many women attending as men. The women brought the chips and dip and cheese trays and leftover Christmas cookies, and the men brought themselves, fully aware that their very scarcity made them more desirable. Most of the celebrants were over forty. Janis didn't really expect New Year's Eve to be any different from the rest of her nights. She just wanted to dance. Jalina was safe with a baby-sitter, and Janis knew she looked especially pretty in one of her few good dresses.

When she heard a soft voice behind her asking for a dance, she turned around and got a pleasant surprise. She had danced with the man holding out his hand before, although they had never really talked. His name was Randy something. He wasn't very tall, but he had a wonderfully muscular physique, warm brown eyes, and a luxuriant mustache. He was handsome and he was young; he looked no more than twenty-five.

He couldn't dance more than rudimentary steps.

But that didn't matter. Suddenly they were talking as if they had known each other for a long time. He made no move to leave her side all evening. Maybe it was the thought that she wasn't really alone on New Year's Eve any longer; maybe it was her sense that the physical attraction between them was very strong. Whichever. Janis was both thrilled and fascinated with Randy Roth. He told her he had just celebrated his twenty-sixth birthday on the day after Christmas. He had been married once, but his divorce had been final on May 20. He said he had a little boy, Greg, who was three. He was raising his son by himself. She was touched by that; right away they had something in common. Janis looked at the picture Randy carried of his son and saw an adorable chubby-cheeked little boy. It was obvious to her that Randy loved his child as fiercely as she loved Jalina.

As 1981 arrived and the crowd whooped and whistled, Janis Miranda was already half in love. Inwardly she marveled at that; she was the woman who didn't trust men. She had been bruised in the wars of love too many times. But this man was different. Somehow special. When Randy Roth asked if he might call her, she agreed enthusiastically.

And then she held her breath until he *did* call. So many men said they would and then never did. Randy did. He seemed to be as interested in her as she was in him.

Her friend Louise and her co-workers at the clinic warned her to be cautious, but Janis just shook her head and smiled. The more time she spent with Randy, the more she thanked her lucky stars. He was the dearest, sweetest, most romantic man she had ever known. His own life hadn't been easy. He trusted her enough to confide in her about his service in the Marine Corps in Vietnam—but only to a point. She sensed he was holding some of the horror back so that he wouldn't upset her. All he seemed to care about was her happiness. She had never known anyone like that before.

"Janis came to work one morning just beaming," Shirley Lenz would recall later. "She was carrying a little bouquet of flowers and a note. Randy had left them on her car. She just couldn't get over that. She thought it was wonderful."

When Randy sent Janis a dozen red roses, she was even more enchanted with him. If she had sat down and written out exactly what she wanted in a man, her list would have described Randy Roth. Except for the fact that he was only a passable dancer, he was perfect. She told Louise that Randy had held a steady job as a diesel mechanic for Vitamilk Dairy for a long time and that he wanted the same things out of life that she wanted—a happy family, a home with a mother and a father to take care of both Greg and Jalina. Randy told her he was renting his house with an option to buy it. He had lived in the Lynnwood, Washington, area most of his life. Randy seemed solid to Janis, not like the fly-by-night guys she had met before.

Although Janis wasn't thrilled with working out and jogging, she accompanied Randy in those pursuits, puffing along behind him but grinning gamely. If Randy had wanted her to, she would have lifted weights and swum the English Channel. He was a stickler for physical fitness, and she wanted to be just the kind of woman he admired. When she saw how he detested smoking, she quickly quit. She hoped he would never find out that she had smoked.

Loving Randy's son, Greg, was easy for Janis. He was a sweet little boy who didn't even remember his real mother. Janis was ready to be Greg's mother if Randy wanted her to be.

Both Louise Mitchell and Shirley Lenz kept warning Janis to slow down. What did she really know about Randy? She just laughed and told them she knew enough to know she wanted to marry him and live with him for the rest of her life.

Shirley had never even met Randy, but he sounded like the perfect man for Janis. Maybe too perfect. She suggested to Janis that a perfect man would be willing to wait a few more months. Real love could stand the test of time. From Janis's description of their dating, it sounded as though they were racing toward a serious commitment.

Shirley's suspicions were right on target. One morning in February, Janis rushed in to work and showed her co-workers her left hand. She wore a ring with a tiny diamond on her third finger. "He's gonna take care of me!" she cried joyously. "Randy's gonna marry me and take care of me!"

Janis Miranda and Randy Roth were married in a civil ceremony in municipal court in Seattle on March 13, 1981. They took a short honeymoon to Victoria, British Columbia, on Vancouver Island. It was only three ferryboat rides away and a short drive from the Lynnwood-Everett area; culturally it was a world away. The historic Empress Hotel where they stayed seemed so grand and European, with its majestic structure and the afternoon high tea it was famous for. Janis was dazzled by the splendor and romance.

After the honeymoon Janis and Jalina moved into Randy's rented house at 4029 42nd Place West in Mountlake Terrace. At his urging, Janis quit her job and stayed home to be a mother to the two children of their new family. She felt a little guilty because Randy was bringing so much into the marriage, at least financially, and she had nothing to contribute but her love. Randy told her he had $250,000 worth of insurance on his life and that he had changed the policy so that she was the beneficiary.

Three weeks after they were married, Janis applied for a day-care license, had the house inspected, and opened a child-care center in their home. The first of her four toddlers came at 6:00 A.M., and Jan was busy all day. She even kept one child from 10:00 P.M. until 4:00 A.M. for a registered nurse who worked a night shift at a nearby hospital. Jan didn't earn very much —$1.25 an hour during the day and $1.50 at night— but she had children there sixteen hours a day for five days a week. Randy worked at Vitamilk from 7:30 A.M. until 5:00 P.M. He made $14.39 an hour, plus time and a half when he worked overtime. He led Janis to believe that he earned close to $30,000 a year.

Janis and Randy hadn't been married long when Janis told Louise that someone had stolen her car. Louise thought that was almost laughable. Seven-year-old Pintos were not exactly the most desirable targets for car thieves—not like Camaros or Pontiac Firebirds. Besides, Janis acted strange when she talked about it. Actually she didn't want to talk about it at all, and she avoided Louise's questions. She had insurance on the car, however, and she and Randy accepted a cash settlement. What was left of the Pinto turned up a couple of months later, stripped and abandoned.

In the beginning, Janis was deliriously happy in her marriage. Everybody who knew her was happy for her. It was Louise Mitchell who first became aware that things in the Roths' marriage might not be as blissful as they had been.

While Randy had been an ardent lover during his headlong pursuit of Janis, she confided to Louise that he had cooled off rapidly. Even their honeymoon had been a disappointment. Randy told Janis that intercourse was painful for him because of an infection that set in after he had had a vasectomy. Janis didn't understand male physiology, and she was puzzled. Still, she accepted his explanation although she was disappointed that the physical side of their marriage was so diminished.

Randy also had a private area of his life that Janis worried about. During their whirlwind courtship, he hadn't talked about other women, but she had been around enough to assume that he'd had lovers in his past, just as she had. She did not expect that he would continue to see his old girlfriends.

Janis was not happy to discover that Randy was still very close to Lily Vandiveer,* a married woman who had been Greg's baby-sitter. He often had lunch alone with her. Indeed, he sometimes still had her baby-sit with Greg—which was ridiculous, because Janis was available to care for Greg. Jalina told her mother that when Randy went to pick Greg up at Lily's house, he always made her stay in the car.

Randy laughed at Jan's questions about Lily. "She just wants my attention," he explained. "There's nothing romantic about it."

Jan wanted her husband's attention too, and she was not getting much of it. Before her second marriage was three months old, Janis Miranda Roth began to worry that Randy might be seeing other women. And then she berated herself for being so suspicious; it was her own lack of confidence, she reasoned, and nothing that Randy was doing. After all, hadn't Randy brought up the idea of their buying a house? A man who had fallen out of love with his wife wouldn't do that. She tried to tell herself that they were building a future together, that Randy was simply a man who did not desert his old friends.

Sometimes she had to try very hard to talk herself

*The names of some individuals in this book have been changed. Such names are indicated by an asterisk (*) the first time each appears in the book.

out of the jealous thoughts that crept into her mind. Everything was so different after their wedding. The romantic gestures that Janis had appreciated so much during their courtship had long since stopped. There were no more nosegays or love notes, no more roses. Janis no longer felt as if Randy saw her as the center of his universe. She rationalized that disappointment away too: Randy was working hard and so was she; roses cost money, and they were saving to buy the house; she would be foolish to expect their relationship to continue as it had before they were married.

Still, Randy's tender and impulsive gestures had ended so suddenly that it was almost as if he had thrown cold water in her face. One day she had been basking in his complete devotion; the next, she felt like a baby-sitter. Her husband seemed closed off to her, his face void of expression, his attitude toward her often almost one of annoyance.

She couldn't understand what had happened. Feeling disloyal, she confided again in Louise Mitchell, "Sometimes I wonder if I didn't get married too quickly."

"Does he hit you?" Louise asked.

"Nothing like that. He's just—just different."

Louise ventured her opinion that her friend's husband seemed to be wound up too tight. She felt that Randy was capable of violence, and she warned Janis to be careful.

Janis shook her head. No, it wasn't that. She didn't know for sure what was wrong. They could sit down and talk things out calmly, and they often did.

"I just worry about things," she admitted. "He lives so dangerously. He drives so fast. And he's so jealous of me. He's got no reason to be. I never even look at anyone else."

Like Jan, who had been slow to tell her family about her marriage, Randy didn't seem anxious to introduce her to his mother or his siblings. In fact, she had no idea where they lived, nor had she heard any details about them. She would have been shocked to realize how close by they lived. However, they did visit Randy's father, Gordon, and his stepmother, Sandy, in southwest Washington in July of 1981. They went camping during their vacation and drove down the coast pulling a trailer. They camped at Ocean Shores in Washington and then at a campground in Astoria, Oregon, before they arrived in the little town of Washougal where Gordon lived.

Gordon was built much like Randy, muscular and compact, and he was a strong man too. The elder Roth had a small farm near Washougal, and Randy helped his father harvest a crop of hay—something he had done often in the past. Janis liked her stepmother-in-law and Randy's step-siblings—Marcie, thirteen; John, nine; and J.R., seven. Jalina was thrilled to learn that Marcie had two horses, Stardust and Dusty.

Randy, Janis, Jalina, who was seven, and Greg, now three, camped at Beacon Rock State Park, about fifteen miles east of Washougal along the Columbia River gorge. Randy suggested that they hike up Beacon Rock itself. Although Janis was not an avid hiker, she was swept up in Randy's enthusiasm—at least until she saw Beacon Rock up close.

Beacon Rock was more of a mountain than a rock. It was a huge monolith that rose up out of the earth more than 500 feet into the sky. High up at its summit it looked forbidding and dangerous. There was only stone up there. Eight or nine stubborn fir trees clung to its inhospitable surface. Janis confided that she was terrified of heights, but Randy assured her there were easy hiking trails that even the children could manage. With his coaxing and soothing, Janis nodded nervously and said she would give it a try.

16

They took Marcie and John along, and trudged up the huge rock. The kids did just fine—maybe because their center of gravity was so low. The trail was well marked, and it had handrails and numerous switchbacks to ease the uphill climb. Even so, it wasn't for sissies. There were many other vacationers climbing along with them. Randy walked out on one shortcut about two hundred feet from the top, and Janis saw other people ducking under the handrails, but she hung back. She knew she would get dizzy if she looked down. She kept a close eye and grip on Jalina and Greg to be sure they stayed well back from the edge of the trail where the earth ended suddenly in nothing but a few scraggly shrubs and air.

Janis felt much better when they were back down on flat ground. She was relieved when they headed north to Seattle, leaving the looming bulk of stone behind them.

Back home, Janis and Randy went ahead with their plans to buy a house. In August they found a place they could afford—also in Mountlake Terrace. The community was Seattle's answer to the East Coast's Levittowns built during the post–World War II building boom. Just off the I-5 freeway, halfway between Seattle and Everett, it was the first town of any size to the north. Young couples flocked to buy the new homes that sprouted up as quickly as mushrooms, with only the color of the paint and other minor cosmetic differences distinguishing one from the other.

Randy's service in the marines allowed him to get a VA loan to buy the new house at 6207 229th S.W. It cost $59,950, and there was no down payment required—only closing costs. Randy's rent for the old house had been just $250 a month. Now their mortgage payments were almost $900 a month and it

17

would be years before they built up any real equity in the new house, but it was theirs, not a rental.

Janis was so excited about having her own home. Mountlake Terrace wasn't as popular an area as it had been three decades before; there were scores of newer subdivisions around Seattle and Everett now, and the newness had worn off. The house wasn't fancy, but it was a huge step up from an apartment with no beds or tables.

When they bought the little house, Janis felt slightly guilty that she had complained about Randy to Louise. Even though she had discovered that Randy had only a part-time job as a mechanic for Vitamilk, he was the one who had made their buying a house possible. Her baby-sitting chores didn't bring in enough money to make much of a difference.

"It doesn't seem right," Janis told Louise, mentioning again Randy's $250,000 insurance policy, the policy he had stressed was there to ensure that Greg and Jalina would always be taken care of. "Randy has all that insurance, and I don't have any. He wants us both to get a policy, and that seems fair to me. That way I'll be evening up the financial burden a little."

Randy had made an appointment with Darrel Lundquist, an insurance agent for Farmer's New World Life. Lundquist explained that both Randy and Janis were eligible for a VIP nonsmoking policy with a payoff value of $100,000 and that the premiums would be negligible, only $15.90 a month apiece. Since they were both under thirty and lived clean and healthy lives, they were just the kind of clients that insurance companies wanted.

"This way," Randy told Janis, "we will have mortgage insurance. If either of us should die, the other will be able to pay off the house and look after Jalina and Greg without worrying about losing our home."

It sounded reasonable to Janis. On September 26,

1981, identical insurance policies were issued to the Roths by Farmer's New World Life. They would go into effect in early November. Randy's beneficiary was, of course, his wife, Janis. He listed a neighbor couple, Ron and Nancy Aden, who had become close friends, as secondary beneficiaries. Janis listed Randy first and the Adens second. The Adens belonged to the Baptist church in Silver Lake that she and Randy attended, although Randy wasn't as faithful about attending services as Janis was.

Randy seemed to have a real talent for making friends. His longest friendship was with Nick Emondi,* whom he had known since 1977 when Emondi was only nineteen. They had been friends during the time Randy was married to his first wife, Donna Carlson Sanchez, Greg's mother. Donna had lived with Randy in the rented house he later shared with Janis. When Randy and Donna divorced, Nick had helped to move Donna over to eastern Washington. She had a little girl by her first marriage and apparently agreed to let Randy have custody of Greg. Beyond that, Jan knew practically nothing about Donna.

Randy and Nick Emondi punched the same time clock at Vitamilk Dairy, and they both were into fixing up cars and riding motorcycles. Randy seemed to be the leader and Nick the follower. "Randy liked to control me," Nick would recall years later. "He used the carrot-and-the-stick approach. He would either give you something or punish you so you'd do what he wanted."

Nick was married and had a small daughter. Janis and Carrie Emondi* were friendly, but it was mainly because of their husbands' long camaraderie.

Janis hadn't told her family in Dallas that she had married again—not at first. Maybe she was afraid they would question her impetuous decision after such a short courtship. Maybe she wanted time alone with Randy before they revealed their somewhat checkered family histories. She and Randy had been together for months before she broke the news. Once she told her mom, Billie Jean Ray, that she was married, she wrote to her often and seemed eager for Billie Jean and her sisters Cleda and Sharon and the rest of the family to accept and admire Randy.

On October 12, 1981, Janis sent a long letter to Billie Jean: "It was good to talk to you again," Janis began. She told her mother that Jalina was now four feet five inches tall and weighed 65 pounds. Janis explained that she was not working outside the home and that it was good to be there when Jalina came home from school.

She said that she was baby-sitting for a one-year-old and a four-year-old, and hoped to build up to more clients. Greg's fourth birthday was coming up, Janis noted, and he made his own bed and helped her with chores. "He's quite mature because Randy would not tolerate a 'sissy' boy." Janis's affection for Greg was obvious. "He is a good boy most of the time."

Janis's letter was cheerful as she described the aftermath of Greg's attempt to shave, when he cut himself, and how he had come home from playing with dog mess in his hair. "Kids are kids."

Janis told her mother that Greg told her she looked "pretty" as she fixed her hair and makeup every evening before Randy came home.

She told her mother that Randy was five feet seven and a half inches tall and weighed about 155 pounds, and that he was very strong; he was a former karate champion with trophies to prove it. "He doesn't do it much anymore: he'd get so involved that he couldn't sleep . . . "

Perhaps protesting too much, Janis wrote that Randy has *many* very good qualities. "Sometimes his drawbacks are due to the . . . years he spent in Vietnam. He used to have nightmares, some depression after his tour there. You probably wouldn't believe some of the things he had to do there. He isn't proud of them. But it's either you or the enemy. Also, if you don't do what you're told, then you go to the Stockade. If we ever had another war and Randy got drafted, I wouldn't let him go. . . . So many guys get messed up in 'Nam.' That was a dumb war. The world itself can make you a hard, cold person—but so can war. He had to learn to be human again—if you can understand that."

Janis hastened to assure her mother that Randy had never, used any type of drug, and when they went out, they drank very moderately. She had never seen Randy even tipsy, and he had never smoked.

As for her love affair with dancing, Janis wrote that she and Randy only went out dancing once every six weeks. She complained jokingly that she was getting old and that at twenty-nine she couldn't keep up the way she could when she was only twenty-five. "I don't take getting too old to disco lightly!"

Janis complimented Billie on getting a good job as a housekeeper for a wealthy couple and wrote nostalgically about the good old Texas home cooking, which she missed. She said Randy didn't care for vegetables much, and she tried to cook only the things he preferred.

Janis wrote about the weather and the beautiful—and hot—summer the Northwest had just had. Temperatures had soared over a hundred degrees.

She was annoyed with her sister Cleda for giving their father her mailing address—which she still listed as Louise Mitchell's house—because she didn't want him to write to her. "If he really ever cared about us, he would have sent you child support when he was working. When he has paid you a couple of thousand dollars of back child support, *then* I'll speak to him. . . . He forgot his responsibility to us and now I

21

forget mine to him, since I don't live a Christian life anymore." Janis wrote that she lived according to her own standards—as most people seemed to.

Although Janis was no longer a practicing Jehovah's Witness, she did attend church and she was living a Christian life. But she was very hard on herself.

"Think I'm bitter?" she wrote. "Damn right I am. I only appreciate those worth appreciating. (That's my own opinion.) It took me years and years to realize all this. . . . He didn't care if we had clothes or food to eat, now did he?"

Whatever her father had done to make amends, Janis felt it wasn't enough. He had once offered to take Jalina to ease her burden. That wasn't the answer. "I was the problem, not Jalina," she wrote, explaining that several times in her life, Jalina was the reason for her to keep trying. "She loves her Mama and I needed that."

It was a strangely ambivalent letter, sounding happy and confident, but with an undercurrent of . . . what? It was more than bitterness over a lost childhood. A kind of dread, perhaps.

It felt good, she wrote, reversing herself again, to know that it was no longer "I, alone" who was taking care of a family. Janis concluded, "I am the most secure and generally the happiest I've ever been, but sometimes I don't know if that's what I want. Sometimes playing housewife isn't always fun. Sometimes I miss my independency. . . . Randy's good to all of us—and fair—but I sometimes remember liking to be my own boss."

Janis Miranda Roth told her mother she had never had so much in the way of worldly goods, even though she and Randy longed for things they couldn't yet afford. They wanted a basement and a second bathroom and money was tight. Their house payments took $871 a month, and the rest went for groceries, utilities, and insurance. "This house is half mine, and if I choose to leave, I forfeit all rights . . . that's how the contract was written." Janis closed her letter, saying, "I DO LOVE RANDY VERY MUCH. However, sometimes I ASK MYSELF, IS LOVE REALLY WORTH IT? I don't know that answer yet. Bye."

Janis enclosed money for her mother's birthday. She didn't explain "Is love really worth" *what?* Billie Jean Ray never got another letter from Janis Roth.

Nor did anyone else.

2

On Halloween, Randy Roth and his friend Nick Emondi took Nick's daughter and Greg and Jalina out trick-or-treating. The men talked as they waited in the road while the excited children ran across the lawns giggling to knock on doors. Afterward Nick Emondi could not recall how they got into a conversation whose topic was macabre enough to fit right in with the foggy, dark Halloween night.

"Could you kill your wife?" Randy had asked Nick suddenly.

"What?" Nick was startled. "What do you mean?"

"I mean, under certain circumstances, if you had to?" Randy gave examples of situations where a man might kill his wife to save her from something far worse. "What if we were invaded?" Randy continued. "What if the Russians were coming and you knew she was going to be tortured or raped? Could you kill her first?"

Emondi shook his head, chilled at the thought.

"Jan asked me if I could kill her if something like that happened," Randy explained, as if they were carrying on the most normal conversation in the world.

Emondi changed the subject and tried to shrug off Randy's questions as Halloween spookiness, but he remembered the conversation for years.

Randy had an intensity about him, a way of speaking softly and staring at someone with his brown eyes fixed. Sometimes he came up with the weirdest thoughts.

Nick hadn't realized it, but Jan Roth had felt a chill for a long time, a sense of foreboding that drained the sunshine from her heart the way the northwest rains washed the sky of light. In the space of seven months she had gone from a bubbly bride to a woman with circles under her eyes who seemed always to be watching for something behind her, something creeping up on her.

When Louise Mitchell questioned her about what was wrong, Janis just bit her lip and looked away. Her marriage wasn't happy; that was patently clear to Louise. She *knew* Janis and had seen her put up with all manner of disappointments and still hide her pain from the world. This was something different.

Janis didn't talk about Randy the way she had. There was no joy in her at all. Finally she acknowledged quietly to her best friend that she had made a mistake. She had even begun to think of leaving her husband, although she had nothing but Jalina's college fund to see them through. Janis believed that if she left, she would have no claim at all on the property she and Randy now co-owned.

Louise felt her skin prickle with goose bumps. It almost seemed that Janis was afraid of Randy.

By November 1981 Nick Emondi saw the same

depression in his friend's wife. One morning Randy asked Nick to drive him to work. He said he was leaving "on a hunting trip" and didn't want to park his car at Vitamilk overnight. Nick obliged, using Randy's car, although he was puzzled. He had never known Randy to hunt. He felt sure that if Randy was staying away overnight, he wasn't going hunting for deer or elk.

After he dropped Randy off, Nick drove the car back to the little house in Mountlake Terrace. He stopped in to say hi to Jan and found a very sad and frightened woman.

"She said she was scared of dying," Emondi remembered later. "I just know she wasn't happy."

Why on earth would a perfectly healthy twenty-nine-year-old woman be afraid of dying? he wondered. Janis was still jogging and exercising. She was in great shape. She had every right to expect to be around for another fifty or sixty years. Nick Emondi couldn't cheer her up, and he left, perplexed.

On November 25 Janis asked Jalina to come into the master bedroom with her. She had something important to tell her, something that no eight-year-old child should ever have to deal with.

"Jalina," Janis said hopelessly, "you know I love you and I want to stay with you forever and ever. But if anything should happen to me—if I'm not here—I want you to know I have some money put away. It's for you."

Janis showed Jalina the hiding place she had selected. She pulled out a drawer in a cabinet built into the wall. There was a white envelope taped to the back of the drawer. She showed her daughter the thick clump of bills inside. "Remember, honey—if I'm gone, I want you to come in here and take this and hide it."

Jalina nodded, but she was worried. Why was her mother talking like that? It scared her.

* * *

Worried and frightened enough, Janis might have dipped into Jalina's money to get away from whatever she feared. Janis had promised Billie Ray that she and Jalina would come to Texas for either Christmas or New Year's, but she hadn't said one word about bringing Randy along.

As far as anyone knew, their marriage was still a going concern. Randy gave no indication to anyone that there were problems. On November 7, 1981, Randy's and Jan's identical VIP $100,000 insurance policies had gone into effect. They continued to work at fixing up their new home in Mountlake Terrace.

Janis made no move to leave her husband. It is likely she hoped that her fears were groundless and that things would go back to the way they had been at first. She had loved Randy so much when she married him, and she had loved their life together until all the affection and sharing trickled away.

Jan had no idea what she had done wrong. All the makeup and dressing up for Randy's homecoming and all her efforts to cook his favorite foods were met with a blank stare. Sometimes she thought he hated her. Sometimes she blamed Vietnam and what that terrible war had done to him.

More often she blamed herself.

Randy announced that they would be going down to visit his father and stepmother in Washougal for Thanksgiving dinner. Janis was enthusiastic about the trip when she told Louise about it. Although she didn't look forward to the long drive, she liked Randy's family. Gordon and Sandy Roth were having their own marital problems and had separated, but they lived just across S.E. 380th Avenue from each other; it was an amicable parting. Randy still felt comfortable visiting them in their separate homes. He and Janis would stay at the farm with Sandy, though; Gordon Roth's bachelor cottage was tiny.

Thanksgiving Day went well, the kids had a good

time, and no one in Washougal sensed any strain at all between the newlyweds. They all talked about Christmas and where they would spend the holiday.

On Friday morning, November 27, 1981, Randy and Janis prepared to go Christmas shopping. When the kids heard about their plans, they all clamored to go. But Randy said no. This was just for Jan and him; they needed some time to be together. The weather was chilly but sunny, and he wanted to get started at once. He turned down Sandy Roth's offer to make her usual pancake breakfast for company. Marcie Roth and her little brothers were disappointed about that. Sandy didn't bother making pancakes just for the kids. Jalina didn't care; she was excited about spending the day with Marcie and riding the horses.

Jan seemed happy to go shopping with Randy. In fact she seemed to be happy and enthusiastic about the Thanksgiving weekend in general; it was her first real holiday as Randy's wife. And now there was a Christmas coming up when she and Jalina wouldn't be alone anymore. If she still had doubts about her marriage and fears about something unknown waiting to destroy her happiness, she gave no indication of them.

But Randy and Janis didn't go Christmas shopping after all. As Randy explained later, they were barely down the road toward the huge shopping mall at Jantzen Beach on the Columbia River when Janis asked him if they could change their plans. "She suggested we climb Beacon Rock," Randy said. "She thought it would be romantic for us to climb up alone."

Janis wore jeans and a bright pink ski jacket with white fake fur trim; Randy wore his street clothes and a jacket. Neither had shoes meant for rough terrain. It didn't matter. It wasn't as if they would be going mountain climbing. Randy reminded Jan that Beacon Rock had a trail where they could walk side by side—at least as they started up. Last summer's climb hadn't been nearly as scary as she expected, had it?

Skamania County, Washington, is one of the state's least populated counties, with much of its land mass covered over with forests and mountains. The Gifford Pinchot National Forest sprawls across Skamania County and the Cascade Range, whose infamous Mount Saint Helens erupted on May 18, 1980, thrusts skyward from the land. Here is the Indian Heaven Wilderness and the Trapper Creek Wilderness. Skamania's small towns crouch along the great Columbia River at the bottom of the county: Underwood, Home Valley, Carson, North Bonneville, Skamania, and Stevenson, the county seat. Except for its natural wonders, Skamania is not a rich county; it is a world away from the industry of Seattle and of Portland, Oregon—its income even more depleted with the slump in the timber industry and the battle between the environmentalists and the loggers over the rights of the spotted owl.

With the exception of an occasional drunken shootout and one tragically memorable family mass murder, Skamania County has a markedly low homicide rate. Lawmen are far more likely to have to deal with highway accidents and mishaps suffered by tourists. It is true now, and it was true in 1981.

It was 11:23 on the morning of November 27 when case number 81-3885 began to unfold in the Skamania County Sheriff's Office. The day after Thanksgiving had been quiet for deputies on duty until Deputy E. L. Powell was instructed to respond to a "possible fall victim" at Beacon Rock. There was very little information available on the incident—if, indeed, there had been a fall. Powell asked that a team from Skamania County Search and Rescue respond. "Better roust Ray out, too," he said quietly into his radio mike. Ray was Undersheriff Ray Blaisdell. Peo-

ple didn't fall off Beacon Rock and walk away with a
sprained ankle. If the report was true, the news could
be bad. They had perhaps four hours of daylight to
locate a fall victim.

When Deputy Powell got to the Beacon Rock
trailhead ten minutes later, he was met by a worried-
looking young woman who said her name was Shelley
Anderson. She said her party of climbers—her husband, Steven Anderson, Merle Quarter, and Edward
Warfield, all from Vancouver, Washington—had noticed a man running up and down the trail, calling out
some name they couldn't understand. "Then he said,
'My God! My wife has fallen!' He wanted someone to
come down and call for help," she explained. "So I
said I would."

With only second-party information, Powell tried
to determine just where the fall victim might have
gone off the rock so that the ambulance crew and the
search and rescue team could concentrate their efforts. So far, he was told, they had been unable to
locate the woman. He figured that it would be best for
them to go into the area from the intersection of Little
Road and State Road 14.

Undersheriff Blaisdell arrived to take over the
scene, and he talked with the distraught man who said
his wife had fallen. He gave his name as Randolph
Roth and his address as Mountlake Terrace, Washington. Roth pointed out an area about 200 feet from the
top of Beacon Rock and said his wife, Janis, had slid
over and off at that point. They had been taking a
shortcut—one that they had taken on a climb earlier
in the summer—and he had climbed over the railing
and Jan had crawled under. His wife was in the lead,
Roth said. "She made a sharp right turn. . . . She
started to slide on something—dried pine needles,
loose dirt, leaves—something." He said he tried to
reach out for her, but he wasn't close enough to grab
her. As he watched in horror, he said, his wife
disappeared from sight. He climbed down as far as he

possibly could, trying to find her. He looked down from every vantage point possible, but was unable to find her. Roth said he thought maybe he could run down and come up from the bottom to find Jan, but that didn't work either. Desperate, he said he climbed back up and ran down the trail to find the hikers he had seen earlier and ask them for help. He led them up to the spot where he had last seen his wife. None of them spotted her either.

Far down below the spot where Janis Roth had fallen, searchers looked for her in vain. Bill Wiley, coordinator for Search and Rescue in the county and a master at rock-climbing, rappelled down the face 200 feet in his search for the victim. They were able to pinpoint the area where someone would land—but Janis wasn't there. She should have been. Wiley lowered a weighted rope to indicate the direction of fall. It didn't make any kind of sense; the woman could not have bounced so far off the predictable fall pattern.

Two helicopters, piloted by Jack Caseberg and Tom Nolan, were brought in from the 304th Air Squadron. It was a perilous situation for the searchers. The air currents around Beacon Rock were notoriously treacherous, with sudden wind shears that could tumble the copters themselves down the face of the giant monolith. The backwash of the rotors tugged at Bill Wiley, threatening to knock him from his precarious perch. A parajumper, who was also a highly trained paramedic, was lowered by a rope from the copter in a vain attempt to spot the missing woman.

Down in the parking lot by the sheriffs' cars, Randy repeated exactly what Jan had been wearing. Her new jacket was such a bright pink, he said, that she should be easy to spot. He was pale and sweaty as he paced frantically, his face a study in despair.

From time to time he mentioned small things. Climbing Beacon Rock had been "Jan's idea. It was her day. She could do what she wanted. I told her it was cold and asked her if she was sure. She was," he said hopelessly. "She wanted to be alone with me."

Minutes and then hours passed. A score or more searchers raced against sundown. Sandy Cobart, Bob Hoot, Corey Dowty, Connie Davis, Lester MacDonald, and Todd and Sandy McCaldey from the search and rescue team moved above the trail on the west side of Beacon Rock. Helping them were personnel from the Bonneville Fire Department: Greg Hodges, Jay Christiansen, Mike Southard, Doug McKenzie, and Jim Duff. The Anderson rock-climbing party stayed on to help search too.

Finally the aerial team and the ground searchers, working on a concentrated sweep together, caught a glimpse of pink in a dense clump of timber halfway down the rock. For the missing woman to have landed in the timber, she would have had to fall at a 45-degree angle from where her husband said she had gone off. Janis Roth lay 300 feet from the top on the west side of the mammoth rock. The chance that she had survived was almost minimal. The parajumper from Tom Nolan's helicopter was lowered on a swaying rope harness to where the victim lay while her husband waited for some word of her condition.

Blaisdell's radio crackled, and communication between the paramedics and the ground station was audible. The medics were requesting IV's!

Blaisdell turned to Randy Roth. "It's possible that she's still alive."

Randy Roth's face showed joy and relief. That was unmistakable. Policemen are by nature a suspicious lot. Blaisdell studied Randy intensely. The undersheriff figured that if there had been any foul play, Roth would have been stunned and horrified to learn his wife was alive. Randy Roth's expression revealed only elation that his wife still lived. Blaisdell worried that he might be building up for an emotional crash. It seemed incredible that anyone could have survived that fall with all the stone outcroppings along the way.

Fifteen minutes passed. The word that came over the radio was what Blaisdell had expected all along: the small woman in the pink jacket was dead; there was no longer any question of that. She had been carried to a level field where medics got only a flat line on their Life-Pak monitors. They found no signs at all of life. Blaisdell turned to Randy Roth and informed him of the tragic news.

Roth began to sob. "Then why did they ask for the IV's?" he demanded. "She *must* have been alive."

"I don't know," Blaisdell answered. And he didn't.

It took a quarter of an hour for the widower to regain any kind of composure. He walked away from Ray Blaisdell to where his car was parked. He was still crying, but he gradually got control of his emotions. When the undersheriff asked if there was anyone he could call, Roth said he would be all right by himself.

"Can I see her body?"

"Yes, that would be all right. If you could identify her . . ."

Janis Roth's shattered body had been carried from a field on the south side of Beacon Rock by Skamania County ambulance crewmen Terry Webber, Duane Hathaway, and Sonny Kadau. They had transported her first to the Pierce ranch and then to the fire hall to await transportation to Straub's Funeral Home in Camas.

"She doesn't look so good," one of the medics murmured to Randy, cautioning him.

Ashen-faced, Randy Roth leaned into the ambulance to view Janis's body. Silently he studied his wife as she lay in the ambulance. "She doesn't look so bad," he remarked quietly. "Her face doesn't seem as badly damaged as I expected." His tone was flat, washed of any emotion at all.

Later Randy remembered that he had to be absolutely sure that Jan was dead, absolutely beyond help, before he could let them take her body to the funeral home. If there was anything, anything at all, that could be done for her, he wanted it done.

But he could see there was nothing to be done. Jan was dead. He turned away, stumbling toward Blaisdell's patrol car. His voice was suddenly full of tears as he said, "I've seen a lot of deceased people when I was in the service, but I've never had to look at a loved one like this. She didn't smoke and she didn't drink. That's the reason I married her. I loved her very much."

He repeated that statement three times. Did he mean that literally? Was it so hard to find a clean-living women that Roth had fallen in love with his wife because she had those attributes? Probably not. He was hurting and he was crying and he probably didn't know exactly what he was saying. The men standing around turned away. What could anyone say? The poor man seemed overwhelmed with grief. Sonny Kadau handed him Janis's engagement ring and wedding band. When Roth asked about the gold necklace that Janis had been wearing, they told him she hadn't been wearing it; it had probably been ripped off as she plummeted 300 feet down Beacon Rock.

"Besides you," Blaisdell asked, "who are her next of kin?"

"She's got a daughter, Jalina. She's back at my mother's house in Washougal." Roth paused, trying to remember. "And she has a mother in Texas some-place, but I don't know her address. I never met any of her folks."

As it happened, the on-call ambulance driver from Straub's Funeral Home in Camas, the first good-sized town along the Columbia River, was ex-homicide detective Dick Reed. Reed had retired in 1979 after working for almost fifteen years in the Homicide Unit of the Seattle Police Department. As he viewed the body of the young woman and listened to the account of what had happened that day, he got what detectives call a "hinky feeling." A dozen years later he still remembered going to the fire hall to pick up the body of the fall victim.

"It bothered me. Something didn't add up. I suggested to Ray Blaisdell that he at least ask the husband to take a lie detector test, but Ray wasn't receptive at the time. He felt that it had been a terrible accident, that the husband was so grief-stricken that it had to be on the up-and-up."

Dick Reed drove Janis Roth's body back to Straub's Funeral Home. It was a little before 5:00 P.M. when he arrived. It wasn't long after that when Randy Roth himself came into the reception area. He was very definite about what he wanted. He paid in full as he insisted that "Jan" be cremated as soon as possible. "She would have wanted that. We've talked about it, and she hated the idea of being in the ground. We promised each other that if anything happened to either of us, the other would see to cremation."

It would not be an expensive procedure. Roth explained that he and Jan had also agreed that lavish funerals were a waste, that money should go to take care of the living. He paid Straub's $541. Ironically it cost him less to dispose of his dead wife's body than it would have to fly Jan and Jalina to Texas for Christmas.

Randy was a well-organized man, even in such bleak circumstances. His wallet was equipped with data he might need. He added the number of Janis's insurance policy to the papers he filled out at the funeral home.

The last time Sandy Roth had seen her stepson and stepdaughter-in-law, they were happily heading off for a day of Christmas shopping. She expected them home for supper any minute. Instead, Randy called and suggested that everyone come to Camas for pizza. They were all sitting in the restaurant before they noticed Janis wasn't with Randy. He evaded their questions about where she was. Finally and almost casually, he pushed a receipt of some kind across the table.

Sandy looked at it and froze, all color draining from her cheeks. She seemed incapable of saying anything. Marcie pulled it over and gazed without understanding at the piece of paper.

"What does this mean?" she asked Randy. "What's cremation . . . and who's Janis Miranda Roth?"

"You know," he answered.

"No, I don't know any Janis Roth."

"Yes, you do. Think about it."

Slowly the thirteen-year-old girl understood. She had never heard Janis called anything but "Jan." She looked at Jalina, but the little girl clearly didn't comprehend what Randy was saying. Marcie couldn't believe it either. It had to be one of Randy's sadistic jokes. Marcie looked at him. He wasn't crying; he wasn't upset in the least. He was gobbling his pizza hungrily.

It was so weird that it couldn't be real. Jan was probably going to walk in any minute with a breathless excuse. Marcie looked at the door as if she could will her new sister-in-law to appear. But the door was closed to keep the cold air out, and nobody appeared.

Feeling nauseated and scared, Marcie excused herself to go to the ladies' room. Jalina followed her, talkative and cheerful as always. She didn't realize that something awful might have happened. Marcie herself was only thirteen; how could she be expected to tell a little kid that her mother might be dead, that she might already be nothing but ashes?

The pizza roiled in Marcie's stomach, and it seemed

like hours before the rest of the family finished eating and they headed home to bed.

As unbelievable as it seemed to Marcie, Jan *was* dead. Randy hadn't been teasing in the mean way he sometimes did. He was a widower, his bride gone in the flicker of an eye.

Randy apparently couldn't bring himself to tell Jalina. As he often remarked, he had never been able to deliver bad news, to say it out loud. But Jalina started asking questions about where her mother was. He had to tell her something. He took the little girl aside that evening and told her only that her mother had fallen and was in the hospital. He seemed so calm that Jalina wasn't upset. She expected her mother to come home in a day or so.

3

Randy Roth was up early the next morning, Saturday, November 28. He had several phone calls to make. On his way home from their doomed climb, he had arranged for his dead wife's cremation, but there were other arrangements that he felt should be accomplished as soon as possible.

Who would have ever thought that all the safeguards they had built to hold off disaster would have to be put into play so quickly? As Randy had told Janis only two months before, it was extremely important that their mortgage be paid off if anything happened to either one of them. They had two little kids to think about—two kids who would need their only parent free of financial burdens—and Janis had agreed with him.

Randy ate breakfast and then placed a call to Darrel Lundquist, his insurance agent in Seattle. It was early on Saturday morning. In fact, Lundquist was still in bed when his phone rang. When he heard Randy's voice, Lundquist's first thought was that he wanted to cancel his policy. But it wasn't that. Randy said he wanted to file a claim.

"But there has to be a *death* before you can file a claim in this kind of policy," Lundquist explained.

"My wife died yesterday," Randy said flatly. Randy told Lundquist that Janis had been killed in a terrible accident. He wanted to began to process his insurance claim at once.

Lundquist woke up in a hurry and muttered condolences. Answering Randy's questions, the agent explained what Randy would need in order to collect on the $100,000 policy that had been written on Janis's life in September. The company would require a certified copy of Janis's death certificate, of course. "And we'll need to have her Social Security number."

Randy promised to get back to Lundquist as soon as possible with the necessary documents and information.

Janis had been dead only twenty hours.

Randy Roth didn't know his wife's Social Security number, but he figured her former employer at the pediatric clinic must have it on record. Shortly after 8:00 A.M. he placed a call to Shirley Lenz, who ran the doctor's office up in Seattle, and asked if she knew Janis's Social Security number.

Shirley explained that she didn't have access to the information that Randy wanted, that it was locked up in the doctor's files. She asked him to call back after

9:00 A.M. when she could talk to the doctor. "Doesn't Janis know it?" she asked belatedly, but Randy had already hung up.

When Randy called back after nine, Shirley Lenz read off Janis's Social Security number to him: 452 06 5537. But she had had an hour to wonder and worry about his request, and she asked him if anything was wrong.

"Yes," he told her. "We had an accident when we were hiking, and they had to fly Janis out in a helicopter."

"How *is* she?" Shirley asked, concerned.

"I don't know," he said.

"You don't *know*?" she persisted. "What hospital is she in?"

He grunted something she couldn't understand. How peculiar, she thought, and how frightening, but before she could question him further, Janis's husband had gone off the line. Shirley held the dead phone in her hand, staring at it.

Randy packed up his family's things, bundled the two children into the car, and headed toward Interstate 5 to Seattle. He had told Jalina that her mother was in the hospital. As they drove out of Washougal, Jalina craned her neck to stare out the back window, and asked, "Couldn't we go just *see* her?"

"She can't have visitors," Randy answered.

They could be home in three and a half hours if traffic wasn't heavy. Despite Sandy Roth's offer to take care of his children until he made funeral arrangements for Janis and recovered a little from the shock of his sudden loss, he insisted on taking Jalina and Greg with him. He told his stepmother he was fine.

The rest of the family was not fine. It was difficult— well nigh impossible—for Sandy and Marcie and the boys he left behind in Washougal to cope with the thought that Jan had been there with them, laughing

38

and smiling, at Thanksgiving dinner and now she was just gone.

Randy called no one in Janis's old world to tell them that she was dead. Not her mother. Not her sister. Not her best friend, Louise. Not Jalina's father, Joe Miranda.

Randy didn't even call his own best friend, Nick Emondi.

He could not stomach being the bearer of sad news. And there could be nothing sadder than the sudden end of his second marriage.

When he arrived in Seattle, Randy stopped by Louise Mitchell's house to pick up Janis's mail. Louise wasn't there, but her children were. He thanked them for keeping the mail. He did not tell them that Janis had fallen to her death the day before. Nor did he ask that they have Louise call him.

Nick Emondi called shortly after Randy got home. He was shocked to hear Randy say bluntly, "Janis is no longer with us."

When he finally realized what Randy was saying, Nick rushed over to Randy's to see if he could help out, but Randy seemed annoyed and sent him away, saying, "Everything is fine." Nick was back in his car before he recognized the smell in Randy's house. It was the aroma of cookies baking.

Randy called the mothers whose babies Janis had taken care of. He didn't tell them that she would never be able to look after their youngsters again; he just said they would need to find someone else to sit on Monday. One mother stopped by to pick up her playpen, and still, Randy never mentioned that Janis was dead.

Shock can do funny things to people. Randy Roth seemed to be in complete denial. He took care of business, and he took care of his children. He considered that Jalina was his, too; her mother was dead, and he was her father now. He baked cookies and tucked the children into bed. Sometime he would have to tell them that Janis had gone away forever. But not right away.

On that Saturday night one of the other receptionists at the clinic called Shirley Lenz to tell her she had just heard about the climbing accident on the radio. Janis wasn't recovering in a hospital; Janis was dead.

The two women could scarcely believe it. "Her husband didn't tell me," Shirley said. "He didn't even sound very upset."

The next day was Sunday, and Randy took Greg and Jalina to church. He saw his friends Ron and Nancy Aden there, friends whom Randy felt so close to that he had listed them as alternate beneficiaries on both his and Janis's life insurance policies.

Ron Aden grinned when he saw Randy and joked, "Where's your better-looking half?"

"She died."

"What?"

"She's dead," Randy repeated.

Dazed, Aden realized that Randy wasn't making an exceedingly tasteless joke. Janis *was* dead, and there seemed to be no comforting Randy. He was handling his loss in his own way, sitting there in the congregation dry-eyed as Ron directed the choir with wooden arms.

Randy was grieving stolidly, apparently unable to let himself cry any more. His friends concluded that he was forcing himself to stay strong for the children. They had never seen a human being exercise such control. The Adens were surprised to learn that Randy and Janis had listed them as alternate beneficiaries on their insurance policies. They had not known. It was academic anyway; thank God Randy was alive and well and able to care for the half-orphaned children.

Although Randy would have preferred not to have an autopsy performed on his wife, Skamania County

Coroner Bob Leick ordered that a postmortem exam be done. It was standard in violent deaths. Dr. Eugene Blizard of Saint Joseph's Hospital in Vancouver performed the autopsy. There were no surprises. Jan Roth's petite body bore scratches and terrible head injuries, the expected result when a human skull comes into contact with rock outcroppings at the speed generated during a 300-foot fall. It wouldn't have mattered if they had found her a moment after she landed in the dark thicket of evergreens. No medical procedure could have saved her.

After the postmortem, Janis's body was cremated according to her widower's orders. He requested that her cremains be boxed and sent to his home.

Ultimately Jalina had to be told that her mother was dead. The story of the tragedy was headlined in the *Seattle Post-Intelligencer* on Sunday, November 29, 1981: "Hiking Accident Takes Life of Young Mother." Shirley Lenz called Randy on Monday to ask him when Janis's funeral would be. And then she asked him, "Why didn't you tell me she was dead when you called on Saturday?"

"I've never been able to tell bad news," he said quietly.

Poor little Janis, she thought. Poor, poor little Janis. Shirley could close her eyes and picture Janis's blissful face when she had brought in the bouquet from Randy. And now it was all over. So soon.

Randy did not tell Louise Mitchell that her best friend was dead until the Monday after the accident. Louise was devastated—and appalled—to think that he had come by her house, picked up his mail, and never said a word. Confronted, he confessed again that he simply could not bear to deliver such awful news to anyone—especially to Louise; he knew how close she and Jan had been.

It was Louise who notified Billy Jean Ray that her daughter was dead. She called Billy Jean on Monday,

November 30, wondering how she was going to explain that Janis had been dead for more than two days already and only now was her mother being notified. "I only found out myself today," Louise explained. "And I was the only one who had your number."

Down in Skamania County, Ray Blaisdell had no way of knowing how strangely Randy Roth was reacting to being an instant widower. Still, Blaisdell tried to look at Janis Roth's death from all angles. Belatedly, he asked Roth to take a lie detector test. He pulled a fresh sheet of paper and printed a heading and a list:

Possible Reasons to Believe Death
Was Other Than Accidental

1. No witnesses
2. Married March 13, 1981—Accident November 27, 1981
3. $100,000 life insurance policy—claim already filed for. $7500 under name of Janis Miranda. (No double indemnity.)
4. Refused to take polygraph examination.
5. Conflicting statements. Told me he was behind wife when she fell—told Bill Wiley he was ahead of her.
6. Roth didn't tell vic.'s best friend of her death. (Louise Mitchell very upset.)
7. Ex-husband asked not to attend funeral.

The Skamania County undersheriff had located Joe Miranda, and Miranda told him he was planning to come up and get Jalina. Janis's ex felt that at least half of any insurance Janis had should go to her daughter. "All she had of value in her life," Joe said, "was Jalina."

Jalina Miranda remembered what her mother had told her the day before they left for Washougal, although it seemed like a bad dream now. Janis had gone into the bedroom, pulled the little drawer out from the wall, and shown Jalina where the envelope was taped. She had shown her all the bills and papers and a couple of checks that had not been cashed. With her mother's voice leading her in her mind, the little girl hurried to the bedroom and repeated the same sequence of events.

Jalina held the envelope in her hand. She wasn't sure what she was supposed to do with it; she was only eight years old, and her mother was dead. She was heading toward her room when Randy walked up and asked her what she had in her hand.

Jalina held out the envelope and explained that her mother had told her to find it and keep it if anything bad ever happened. Randy reached for it and looked at the contents.

"This is something else she's been hiding from me," he said quietly. "I think I should take this, Jalina."

Jalina wasn't sure what to do. She liked Randy. He had been very good to her ever since she had known him—almost a whole year—and for an eight-year-old, a whole year is a very long time. But she kept hearing her mother's voice telling her that the envelope was their secret and that she mustn't tell anyone.

Randy still held the envelope. He was smiling when he said, "I'll keep it, and I'll use it to buy you presents."

He wasn't asking her a question; he was telling her what they should do, and that seemed all right to her. He was like her daddy. And he took good care of her.

Randy Roth had become the only security Jalina had, and she felt that she had no choice but to believe everything he told her.

Billie Ray had never met her daughter's new husband. In shock, she prepared to fly to Seattle for Janis's memorial service, which Roth informed her would take place on Friday, December 4. She and her daughter, Sharon Waldrep, arrived in Seattle before dawn on the morning of the service, and they had reservations to fly out the next morning. They were not invited to stay at the Roth home and checked into a motel.

Somehow it seemed as if they could handle Janis's sudden death more easily if they just knew more about it, but Randy didn't volunteer any information about the accident and he answered their questions with the briefest responses. He seemed very calm and under control, but they didn't know the man at all. They had no idea what normal behavior might be for him. Billie Ray knew from Janis's letters that Randy still had flashbacks and nightmares from his marine service in Vietnam; she didn't want to ask him too many questions for fear of making everything worse.

On the Tuesday after Janis fell, December 1, Joe Miranda arrived in Seattle to pick up his daughter. Randy was adamant that he didn't want Joe in his home, nor did he want Jalina to go and live with her natural father.

Jalina didn't want to leave Randy, either; he was the only father she remembered. He had always been kind to her, and she had grown to love Greg like her own little brother. But her father and his new wife wanted her. Her real daddy loved her, although Randy didn't tell her that; he seemed furious as he threw a few of her things in a bag and delivered her to Joe Miranda.

With all he had on his mind, Randy never got around to buying the "presents" he had promised Jalina he would buy with the money that Jan had put aside for her daughter. Nor did he mention the money to Miranda. Randy didn't give Jalina any of her mothers' clothes, jewelry, or keepsakes. He didn't even give her a picture of Janis. He told her to pack what she wanted. She was only eight years old; she didn't know what to take. He sent her down to Texas with little more than the clothes on her back. He later explained that glibly enough: he thought she was only going for a Christmas visit and would be coming back to live with him.

But Jalina never came back. In the years ahead, Jalina Miranda never heard from her stepfather again, and she didn't get one penny of the money her dead mother had saved so carefully for her. If her mother had left her a letter, she never got that, either.

Randy told Billie Ray that Janis had just taken out an insurance policy but he wasn't sure if the face value was enough to cover her funeral. Either he was lying or his memory was clouded, because $107,500 would pay for the most lavish of funerals.

Janis's memorial service at the Silver Lake Chapel was not lavish. The funeral home in Camas had charged Randy only $541 to cremate her. The service in December was simple and tasteful. Randy explained that he had arranged to have a hand-carved wooden chest made to hold his dead wife's ashes, but it wasn't done in time. He broke down at the funeral and sobbed as if he would never get over losing her. Shirley Lenz, curious about Janis's husband, noted that. So did the Adens. They vowed to have Randy and Greg and Jalina over for dinner often in the next weeks and months.

But Jalina was gone, living somewhere down in Texas, and Joe Miranda wanted nothing to do with Randy Roth. Randy and Greg were alone again, "batching it" and trying to recover from the loss of the woman who had brought warmth and love into their home for such a short time.

Randy was so grateful to the Adens for their support that he took their family along when he and Greg flew to California for a vacation at Disneyland. He insisted on paying for everything. When they saw how much it meant to him to have them share the Disneyland trip, they were touched. Randy seemed to long for a family, and he had almost created one with Janis. The Adens felt sorry for him; he had lost Jan and then Jalina.

A hundred and fifty miles away, Skamania County detective Mike Grossie, Paramedic Duane Hathaway, and State Park Ranger Don Bauer climbed Beacon Rock to the approximate point where Janis Roth was reported to have fallen. It was a shortcut off the main trail, and it led up a small dirt and rock cutoff trail to a second cutoff trail that ran along a rock ridgeline. They could see that if someone went south along the rocky ridge, he or she would have an exposed rock cliff on either side. The climber could go no more than a hundred yards before coming to a sheer dropoff to the southwest. To the northeast, the trail cut up through some small trees and came out onto the main trail close to the summit of Beacon Rock.

Apparently, after getting to the top of the first cutoff trail, the victim had fallen to her death off the left-hand side of the trail. Near the place where they had been told that Janis had fallen, there were several protruding roots and brushy shrubs that she might have grabbed hold of. The mud was hard, just as it had been on November 27, and there was no standing water or ice on the trail. Bauer could walk easily at least twenty feet down the slope that led to the ravine without fear of plunging over.

Odd.

The three investigators had no difficulty keeping their balance on the shortcut, although they did have to crawl on their hands and knees to get to the top. Once they got there, they were able to stand up, although they noted that the slope of the rock made them all automatically bend forward as they turned to the right.

"It sure would be possible," Grossie speculated, "for someone to fall from this spot—if she was accidentally bumped or if her back was to the ravine."

Randy had said something about Janis taking a picture at this height, but he didn't have their camera when the deputies found him, nor had they found a camera on or near Janis. It might have been caught in the trees below, just as her gold necklace probably was.

The investigators now took photographs from both sides of the trail and then aimed their cameras over the edge, catching the trees, the fields, and even the mighty Columbia River far below in their lens.

The view was awesomely beautiful and, given the circumstances, ultimately chilling.

Down and down and down.

4

On January 24, 1982, Detective Mike Grossie traveled to Mountlake Terrace and talked with Randy Roth in the kitchen of the home he had shared with Janis Roth. Mike Grossie could hear a man's voice somewhere in the house, but Roth didn't offer to introduce whoever it was and Grossie didn't ask.

Nick Emondi had come over to entertain Greg at Randy's request. Curious, he shushed Greg and listened to Randy repeat his story of the tragic accident.

The more he had thought about it, Randy told Grossie, the more he blamed himself for letting Jan climb Beacon Rock wearing slippery leather-soled shoes. Sure, it had been at his wife's insistence that they climbed the rock that day after Thanksgiving, but

47

he should have known better than to let her talk him into it. If he had only refused to indulge her crazy romantic impulse to climb the mountain that day, he wouldn't have lost her forever.

Despite Randy's grieved expression, Grossie noted that he kept veering off the subject of Jan's accident, and he would not sit down and talk with Grossie; Randy was continually doing dishes, wiping down counters, and sweeping the kitchen floor as they talked. It was unsettling to talk to a man about his dead wife while he went about his chores. Grossie would remember that Roth had rarely, if ever, looked him in the eye.

Randy Roth's main concern was what he should do with his wife's ashes. Where to store them was his "biggest worry." Grossie had no opinion on that; he was a frustrated detective.

It was a most unsatisfactory interview.

After Grossie had gone, Nick Emondi walked into the kitchen and stared hard at Randy. He had heard everything that was said in the interview with the Skamania County detective.

"What's going on?"

Randy looked away. "Don't ask me to tell you something you'll have to lie about."

Long acquaintance had taught Emondi not to press his luck, and he asked nothing more.

While the officers of the Skamania County Sheriff's Office kept their death investigation file open on the tragic demise of Janis Miranda Roth, they were having difficulty finding evidence that would prove her fall was anything but accidental. They didn't have solid physical evidence, and they didn't have any eyewitnesses to Jan's actual fall from Beacon Rock. They only had witnesses after the fact.

It was quite possible that the case would have to be closed and stamped "Accidental Death."

* * *

The early months of 1982 were hard for Billie Jean Ray. She had lost not only her daughter but also her granddaughter; she hadn't seen Jalina since Jalina had left Texas. She wrote to her dead daughter's second husband, and Randy answered quickly: "I received your letter today and felt compelled to respond immediately that the facts might be properly presented. First of all, Joe never asked for any shot records at all; he wanted a death certificate, birth certificate, and a Social Security number. These items are necessary for him to collect monthly payments from Jan's Social Security for Jalina. I informed him that I was aware of how he was handling Jalina and would not help him. The sheriff had already informed me that Joe was trying to get in on insurance money so I was very abrupt. I absolutely will not cooperate with him while he is circling like a buzzard looking for easy money!" But if anyone had been circling like a buzzard, it had been Randy—not Joe.

Randy went on to prophesy that Jalina's life would not be happy with the Mirandas, which didn't ease Billie Jean's mind any, but he ended with a cheery report on the weather in Seattle. He said that he and Greg were staying really busy, "working and playing all day, and cutting wood," he ended, "so life can go on."

He promised to send Billie Ray a picture of Jan and some of Jan's things so that she could save them for Jalina.

He never did. He had so much on his mind.

Randy had cogent reasons to want to block Joe Miranda's application for Social Security survivor's benefits payments for Jalina. He himself had already applied for benefits for Jalina on December 14, a little over two weeks after her mother died, and twelve days after Joe Miranda had taken her back to Texas.

"Jalina is in my custody," Randy had told the Social Security interviewer. "She's with relatives in Texas for Christmas." Although Joe Miranda had given him his phone number in Texas, Randy said he had no way to reach him—no number, no address.

Randy was also applying on Greg's behalf. Although Jan hadn't given birth to Greg, Randy was gratified to learn that she had been Greg's stepmother just long enough for the little boy to qualify for Social Security payments as if she had been his own mother. After the Social Security representative processed the applications, Randy began receiving payments monthly for both Greg and Jalina.

When Jalina never returned from Texas, however, the Social Security Administration learned that she was not living with Randy Roth. He was required to reimburse the government for the benefit checks he had received and cashed for her.

"It was a question of interpretation," Randy explained. "I *was* attempting to get legal custody of Jalina. My intent was to contact the Social Security office and inform them [that she was not living with him]. In *my* mind, I had not relinquished custody of Jalina."

Randy had a great deal of paperwork to wade through. He furnished all the documents that Darrel Lundquist asked for to facilitate the payoff of the $100,000 Farmers VIP policy on Janis's life, and waited months for a decision on that. He had also remembered that he had an older policy with Allstate Insurance; anyone who had a Sears charge card could elect to have a family policy for $7,500 accidental death benefits. Randy had taken it out for himself and Greg, and when he married Janis, she became part of that. He had that policy for years before he met his second wife, but he suddenly remembered it and filed for those benefits, too.

It was ironic. When Jan was alive, they had struggled so hard to meet their financial obligations. Now that she was gone, Randy no longer had to worry about money.

He filed his 1981 tax return as a widower, listing

50

only his own income from Vitamilk. He didn't file for Jan; his late wife had done all her own paperwork for her day-care business, and he said later that he couldn't find it. When the IRS contacted him by mail about the fact that Janis Miranda Roth had not filed a return for 1981, he wrote back, explaining that she was deceased. He heard no more from them.

Even though his friends tried to make things easier for him and for Greg, Randy said he could scarcely bear to live in the home he had shared with Jan for only three months. "I had a lot of bad feelings about being in the house. . . . We bought the house together. It was the house that she wanted," he would say sadly. "It was her dream house. . . . I don't know that I would have been able to feel comfortable and live in that house."

Besides that, he was having trouble making the $871 monthly payments on the new house now that he didn't have Janis's baby-sitting income to add to his paycheck. He couldn't keep up with his utility bills or other pressing commitments, either. He didn't know if he would ever get the $100,000 due him on Jan's insurance. "The thought hadn't occurred to me that I could borrow money [on the insurance policy] to make house payments."

Randy received the $7,500 from the Allstate policy and gave $5,000 of it to a real estate agent to sell the house he could no longer bear to live in. "I felt bad and empty being in the house. . . . This was my first house, and it was her first house to buy."

Because he had no equity built up, it cost him money to sell the house. He sold it to the listing agent.

On March 23, 1982, Randy received the proceeds of Jan's $100,000 policy. Policy #1611546 with Farmer's New World Life Insurance Company paid $100,014.11. The $14.11 was a premium refund for money automatically withdrawn from Randy's bank account after Janis was already dead. With the money, Randy was finally able to move to another house, where he and Greg hoped to patch their lives back together. He had found a house in the Amber Hills district of Bothell, Washington.

Randy put $50,000 of Jan's insurance down on the house, which cost $89,950. His mortgage payments were far lower than what he and Jan had paid on the Mountlake Terrace house, and he had a solid equity besides.

In his loneliness, Randy had turned to Lily Vandiveer, his one-time baby-sitter, for comfort. The question of whether their affair was platonic or intimate is obscured by supposition and gossip. Lily's husband, Karl Vandiveer,* later said they had once been lovers, and he believed they had never stopped. He said he came home early on one occasion and found them stretched out in front of the fireplace in an intimate embrace. He confronted Randy. "I told him to stay away from my house [or] I was going to the [Skamania County] prosecuting attorney."

The relationship, which Lily insisted was only a matter of two old friends having lunch together from time to time, ended abruptly even though Karl Vandiveer never did report it to the Skamania County investigators. In truth, that threat had been a bluff. There was something about Randy Roth that stopped him. "Hell," Vandiveer said, "I was afraid of him."

Even without Lily's emotional support, Randy Roth's life, which had seemed so bleak, was looking up. He put many thousands of dollars and his own sweat into landscaping his new yard. He had the finest roses on the block, velvety grass, and lush evergreens. He might have spent $5,000; it might have been $10,000. He wasn't sure. He turned his Amber Hills home into a showplace.

Randy put the balance of the insurance payoff in the bank to use over the next few years. He had been pinched for money for so long, and suddenly he no longer was. He spent freely. He bought two motorcycles, one for himself and one for Nick Emondi. He loaned Nick and his wife $1,500. He bought two chain saws so that he and Nick could cut firewood for extra income.

Somewhat surprisingly, Randy and Greg didn't live in the new house in Amber Hills for very long—only two years. Randy's money from the insurance settlements hadn't lasted as long as he expected, and his large equity in the home didn't help him with his monthly bills as much as he thought it would.

In May of 1984 he sold the Amber Hills place for exactly what he had paid for it, despite all his landscaping improvements. He had a cash offer and took it. He bought a house at 3012 169th S.E. in Misty Meadows, a pleasant area less than two miles away.

The Misty Meadows home was only in the $70,000 –$75,000 bracket, but it was very nice. Randy kept some of his cash-out money for expenses, and he loaned Nick Emondi another $4,000, this time so Nick could buy a double-wide mobile home to put on some property Emondi had purchased.

Emondi, who now worked for a local fire department, remained ambivalent about Randy. Ever since Randy had asked, "Could you kill your wife?" on that Halloween night weeks before Janis died, Nick had tried to pull away from Randy. But that wasn't easy to do. No one left Randy; *he* had to be the one who decided a relationship was over, and quite frankly, Nick needed money badly and Randy had it to lend. They agreed that the Emondis would repay Randy in baby-sitting. Carrie would take care of Greg, and for each week of child care, Randy would reduce the amount of their debt by fifty dollars. In two and a half years they would be even. But then, suddenly, Randy moved Greg to Lily Vandiveer's home. Nick promised to make payments on the debt, but he wasn't making enough to repay the $200 a month Randy demanded.

Randy's newest home was painted brown and

cream, a pseudo-Norman split level with massive exposed beams. It was built on a cul-de-sac where Greg could play outside safely. The lot was pie-shaped. Randy planned to landscape this yard and make it the most beautiful on the block. There was a tall stand of fir trees out in back of all the homes on their block and, behind that, an easement where high-power lines hummed and throbbed.

Misty Meadows was a friendly neighborhood. There was an older couple right across the cul-de-sac who doted on Greg and were like foster grandparents. Best of all for Randy, another couple, Ben and Marta Goodwin, whom Randy had known since 1982 through Greg, moved from a rental a few blocks away and became his next-door neighbors. Their son Ryan was Greg's age, and they had an older boy named Travis and a daughter, Brittany. Randy hadn't seen his own brother, David, for a long time, and Ben became like a brother to him, just as Randy became Ben Goodwin's best friend.

Randy was an avid classic car buff, and he had always supplemented his salary by buying older cars, fixing them up until they were in cherry condition, and reselling them. He and Ben Goodwin both admired old Chevy pickups.

Ben, a handsome but laconic Vietnam vet half a dozen years older than Randy, recalls the first time he ever saw Randy Roth: "He was driving down the street in a 1973 Chevy pickup—just like mine, except it was gold—and I said to Marta, 'Now, that looks like my kind of guy.' I guess those old trucks made us friends first. His Chevy was just like mine, only it was a four-wheel drive, and he was pulling a trailer all full of stuff. He missed the turn, and then I saw him coming back, and he turned into our street, and that's the first time I ever saw him."

Ben and Marta Goodwin would become perhaps the best friends Randy Roth ever had in his life. Their closeness would last for almost a decade, and they would share traditions as if they were family and not just neighbors. Randy had no family any longer—not since Jan died—but with the Goodwins he did.

The Goodwins saw a side of Randy that no one else ever glimpsed. Although they never forgot the good times they shared, their closeness would cost them dearly.

Marta was a pretty, slightly plump woman in her late twenties, and Ben was a whipcord-tough six-footer in his mid-thirties when they met. Ben came from a huge family; he'd made his own way, and he had seen a great deal of action in Vietnam. Randy confided that he, too, had been in the thick of battle in Nam and hinted at darkly violent missions that had left him with nightmares.

"He was my best friend for eight years," Ben Goodwin recalls. "But we knew he hated women. He especially hated women who he said 'looked like whores.' He was always nice to Marta, respectful—as if she represented his ideal of what a woman should be."

Perhaps she did. Marta never saw Randy do anything wrong. He seemed to want her to see him as perfect. When she quit smoking, a habit Randy detested, he sent her flowers. But he never even came close to making a pass at her.

She was the perfect wife. The perfect mother.

Ben Goodwin's first meeting with Randy was anything but cordial. Ben Goodwin is a brusque, sometimes artless man. He loves his own kids and is concerned about all kids. Long before Randy and the Goodwins became next-door neighbors, when Ryan Goodwin was six and in the first grade, he asked if Greg Roth could come home with him and stay after school at their house every day.

"Where's his mom?" Ben asked.

"He doesn't have a mom," Ryan explained. "His mom fell off a cliff, and his dad has to work all day. See, here's his picture."

The child in the school picture was adorable, with cheeks like a little chipmunk, and small. He looked about four years old. The Goodwins stared at each other as they realized that six-year-old Greg went home to an empty house every day after school and spent hours alone. Ben marched over to Randy's house and punched him in the chest and demanded, "Look, you s.o.b., what do you mean leaving that little kid all by himself?"

That should not have been the propitious beginning to a friendship, but it was. They worked it out without an argument. Randy said he was a widower who had just moved into the neighborhood, and he didn't know anyone who could look after Greg. Marta felt sorry for him and agreed to look after Greg until Randy got home from work. Ben and Randy soon found they had a lot in common. Cars and rock and roll golden oldies, camping, and, of course, their service in Vietnam.

Randy was a good-looking man with a well-trimmed beard and mustache. He had dark brown eyes, and, although he was short, he had the massive biceps of a weight lifter. There wasn't anything he didn't know about the innards of a car. He was definitely a man's man.

As Randy got to know the Goodwins, he confided in them, sharing memories of his own bleak childhood. He explained that his mother was now very old and bedridden, too senile for him to visit, but he remembered how she had punished him when he was very small. "He said she made him take his pants off and kneel on the tile floor in the kitchen for hours until his father got home from work to punish him," Marta recalls. "He didn't talk much at all about his brother or sisters."

He did not talk at *all* about Janis. They hadn't the vaguest notion that Randy's marital history was complicated. They had heard only that he was a widower and the story Ryan repeated about Greg's mom falling off a cliff.

Ben finally mentioned that story to Randy, and Randy acknowledged that it was true that Janis had fallen, but it was too painful for him to discuss. The Goodwins believed Randy had only been married once. They didn't know that there had been a wife before Janis—Donna Sanchez Roth, who was Greg's natural mother. "He never volunteered *anything* about the women in his past," Marta remembers. "He'd answer questions, but he wouldn't tell you much."

Randy Roth came into the Goodwins' life "like a whirlwind." He was the most energetic man either of them had ever met, and he was a truly good neighbor. After Ben mentioned casually that they had to do something about cleaning out an eyesore area in their front yard, they woke one Sunday at seven to hear the roaring of a Rototiller. Randy tilled the yard and then shrugged off their thanks. When they wanted to cut down a tree that was growing too close to their back deck, Randy said, "You want it down? Let's take it down," and took a running leap off the deck, clung to the fir twenty feet off the ground, rocked it back and forth with ever-widening swings, and rode it to the ground when it snapped at the base.

"That was Randy. If something needed to be done, he did it right now."

He was a little guy, but powerful. In one day, he built a 200-square-foot outbuilding to use as a gym and weight room, amazing Ben Goodwin. He and his friend Nick sawed and split wood all day long to earn extra money, and Randy never tired. He could split a log into five sections at a time for firewood. He looked like a teenager, but Ben knew he had to be older because he'd served in Vietnam.

Ben had a bronze plaque honoring his marine service. On one of his few visits to Randy's house, he was a little surprised to see that Randy had an identical plaque on his wall with his own name emblazoned on it. Randy was totally gung ho about the marines. He had his picture on the wall in his dress blues and innumerable shoulder patches and framed memorabilia. While Ben would just as soon have forgotten Vietnam, Randy was obsessed with his service years, as hellish as they might have been.

"For the eight years I knew him," Ben says, "he wore marine camouflage fatigues, and he had his kid and my boys wearing them. On patriotic holidays he wore his uniform. I told him the only difference between us was I wanted to forget Vietnam and he kept reminding himself about it."

The Goodwins found their new neighbor fascinating. "He kept us active," Marta recalled. "With Randy around, we couldn't stay home and watch television. We had a good time. He would come over and drag us out to go motorcycle riding, river rafting, or out to dinner. He'd call up and say, 'Hey, I got a car for us to look at,' or 'Let's go look at the Christmas lights.' You couldn't say no to him. He could cheer anybody up. Every year he went out and chopped us a Christmas tree—never one for him, but he always got ours."

There was one television show that Randy never missed, however. Every Thursday night, religiously, Randy came over to the Goodwins' to watch "The Cosby Show." He always brought an apple pie and a gallon of vanilla ice cream for them all to eat while they watched.

"I asked him once," Marta says, "why he didn't bring lemon meringue or blueberry pie once in a while, and he just looked at me solemnly and said, 'Ben likes apple.'"

The macho ex-marine was an immaculate housekeeper and a good cook too. A perfectionist. He cooked for himself and Greg most of the time, although they were frequent guests at the Goodwins' table. Randy almost always contributed something. He made the dressing for the holiday turkeys, he baked date cookies, and one year when Ben cooked Thanksgiving dinner, Randy furnished the dessert: a rather bizarre-looking angel food cake with bright blue frosting. Everyone ate it so that his feelings wouldn't be hurt.

He was a paradox, though, and the longer the Goodwins knew Randy Roth, the sharper the dichotomy in his personality became. He would help in any way he could, but there was a quality about him—a "watching sense"; he was someone who stood off to one side and studied people. There was a calculating air about Randy, as if he was always taking someone's measure and thinking his own private thoughts. The Goodwins put it down to some residue of his experiences in Vietnam.

Ben and Marta knew he was strict with Greg and that he thought they spoiled Ryan, Travis, and Brittany. "We let the kids take turns unloading the dishwasher—you know, bottom, top, and silverware—and for some reason that bothered him. He said it wasn't efficient; they should each unload the whole thing for a week. It was a dumb thing, but it drove him nuts. Greg did all the chores by himself and without question."

Randy bought Greg the very latest and most expensive toys. He had a Nintendo and dozens of games to go with it as soon as they came on the market. Greg had new four-wheelers three times a year and expensive bicycles. It was hard for Ben Goodwin to explain to his sons why Greg had so many things; he couldn't hope to keep up, even though he had a good job at Safeway, while Randy never seemed to hold a steady job. In fact, Ben was puzzled at how Randy managed to afford all the toys, especially when he was cut back to half time at Vitamilk.

Randy hugged Greg and often told him he loved him. Greg always called Randy when he got home from school to talk to him. No one could deny that there was a strong bond between the little boy and the only constant parent in his life. Greg rarely spoke of his natural mother, who visited infrequently, and Janis had been in his life for less than a year. His father was always there.

And yet there was a dark side to Randy's parenting. Maybe it was the vicious circle that all social workers recognize: an abused child becomes an abusive parent.

"Greg could say thank you, but he was not allowed to say please," Marta Goodwin remembers. "Randy told Greg that 'please' was a 'begging word' and he must never beg for anything."

Greg was disciplined as harshly as any young marine in boot camp. When he forgot to put the garbage can out one scheduled pickup day, Randy dumped the whole can and spread the trash all over the cul-de-sac. In the pouring rain he made Greg gather the refuse up with his hands. "He was out there on his hands and knees, and he got it all picked up," Marta recalls. "All except for one little scrap of paper. When Randy saw that, he dumped it all out again, and Greg had to start all over."

If anything was out of place in Greg's room, Randy ransacked the closet, the drawers, stripped the bed—everything—and made Greg put every item back in place. Ryan Goodwin had seen that happen, but Marta and Ben never had. They thought Ryan was exaggerating until they saw the garbage can incident.

The worst example of Randy's discipline came when Greg's third grade teacher called him and said Greg hadn't turned in his homework. Randy grounded his son. Greg completed his homework all right, but he apparently was so frightened that it might not be perfect that he didn't turn it in. The third time his teacher called, Randy was livid, so angry he was frightened by his own rage. "He called me at work," Ben says. "He asked if Greg could stay at our house for a few days because he was afraid of what he might do to him. We said fine, and Greg came over with his sleeping bag and his little suitcase."

But Randy called at nine the first night and summoned Greg home. He had changed his mind. Randy told Ben he was fine, all cooled off. Ben questioned him carefully; he wasn't about to send Greg home if Randy was still out of control, and in his own rough way Ben warned Randy that he would have to answer to him if Greg was harmed.

"No, no, I'm fine. No problem," Randy said easily. He sounded perfectly calm.

But he wasn't. That night Greg forgot to flush the toilet, and Randy erupted. He held Greg's head in the toilet and flushed it again and again until the boy almost drowned, and then he kicked him in the stomach until Greg vomited.

Ryan Goodwin heard about it the next morning when he could see that Greg winced with pain and favored his stomach. Eight-year-old Ryan marched into the principal's office at school and told on Greg's father. Randy was reported to Children's Protective Service and put on probation; he didn't speak to Ryan Goodwin for months.

But he still came over to the Goodwins every Thursday night with pie and ice cream to watch "The Cosby Show," about the perfect American family where no one ever got angry and each episode ended happily.

There were so many things about their bachelor neighbor that the Goodwins didn't know, so many little lies and so much cruelty that lay just beneath his almost boyish veneer. Randy did not care for animals. When another neighbor's cat left footprints all over the hood of his newly waxed car, he didn't complain to the owner. Instead, he caught the cat and bound it to the drive shaft of its owner's car with duct tape.

When the car's engine started, the cat was quickly dismembered, its screams muffled by the sounds of the engine.

One of the young women who worked with Randy would never forget Randy's idea of a joke. She had found a little frog and had shown it to Randy. Later he called her into the shop and pointed to a damp spot that no longer resembled anything alive; he had placed the frog under a rotary sander. He laughed when she started to cry.

It might have been Randy's "family" relationship with the Goodwins that made him distance himself from Nick Emondi, or it might have been one of the surest destroyers of friendship: money. Nick and Carrie were unable to repay the money they had borrowed as quickly as Randy wanted, and he bombarded them with letters that had the thinnest edge of threat in them:

The first was scrawled on the back of a torn envelope, "Nick, I received a bankruptcy letter, and if you are treating *me* the same as all your creditors and have no intention of paying back the money, then we have got some serious talking to do. I can't believe you would destroy the most valuable thing I know—faith and trust of friendship. Call me so I know what is goin' on." The letter was signed, "Randy."

When Nick did not respond with payment, Randy wrote again: "Nick and Carrie, I would like you guys to consider—*seriously consider*—payments of $75 a month until the money is repaid. I am somewhat disappointed that you have given me to date only $50 toward the loan. I lent you the money against my better judgement for fear something like this would happen. However, I gave it to you in good faith and trusted you to repay a thousand dollars a year. I believed you, Nick, and that is the only reason I went against my instinct. . . . You have made no attempt to make good. Our friendship is very much cherished by me and I don't want to lose it over this."

Randy went on and on about his hurt and his disappointment that his faith in his old friend had been misplaced. He had always been the dominant man in their friendship, and Nick had walked softly around him. Now Nick had betrayed him where he lived. Money was very, very important to Randy. Even though Randy was the one who changed the terms of repayment, his resentment over Nick's failure to return his money ate at him.

On July 30, 1984, someone spray-painted obscene threats on Nick Emondi's home.

Randy finally recouped his money from Nick after Emondi's home was burglarized in January of 1985. Nick Emondi's insurance was enough to pay back his old friend.

PART TWO

The Second Donna

5

Marta and Ben Goodwin were surprised that
Randy seemed in no hurry to remarry. Greg needed a
mother, and Randy was certainly attractive to wom-
en. He never had a problem getting dates. To begin
with, he was a good-looking man and he could flash a
heart-melting smile. Beyond that, he had Greg, who
was cute enough to do commercials. It was hard for
pretty young women to say no to the adorable little
boy who approached them and said, "Would you go
out with my dad?" At the very least, the majority of
women Greg approached—always on Randy's orders
—agreed to meet Greg's father. And a lot of them
found the father as appealing as the son.

Randy dated, but he moved from one woman to
another, changing partners as often as he bought and
sold automobiles.

And then, as 1984 came to an end, he met Donna
Clift. She was his second Donna. His first wife, Donna
Sanchez, seemed relegated to his distant past. Randy
explained to Donna Clift that Greg's mother had not
been the mother Randy hoped she would be. And
Donna Clift respected him because he didn't bad-
mouth his first wife beyond that simple statement. He
had had a second wife too, he said softly, but he was
now a widower. She didn't press him for details.

Donna was twenty-one, a young divorcée (who had

taken back her parents' surname) with a three-year-old daughter. She had moved to the Seattle area on December 1, 1984, to be close to her father and stepmother, Harvey and Judy Clift. She was a very attractive young woman with long brown hair and a perfect figure.

Donna had taken a job as a clerk at the Plaid Pantry, one of a chain of twenty-four-hour fast-service markets. This one was in Bothell, close to Randy's Misty Meadows neighborhood. She had only worked there for a day or two before she noticed the darkly handsome man. They made eye contact and smiled a few times. She was five feet four inches tall, and he seemed no more than an inch and a half taller than she was, but he was very muscular and there was just something about him that she liked. "His eyes. When he stared at me with those dark, dark eyes, I was drawn right into them."

Donna didn't realize then that Randy had the large bright eyes that most nearsighted people do, lovely to look at but almost blind. He would not wear glasses, but his vision was corrected with contact lenses.

When Randy sent Greg up to the counter to buy something, Donna looked over at Randy and smiled. Randy and Greg asked her how long she had lived in Bothell, and she explained she was fresh from Arizona and didn't know anyone. Randy asked her if she would like to go out to dinner. He said he belonged to Parents Without Partners, but he hadn't met anyone who was right for him—and for Greg. He suggested that maybe Donna would like to go to a PWP dance.

Just as he had been for Janis Miranda, Randy Roth seemed the perfect man for Donna Clift, the suitor that a young mother alone hopes for but doesn't really expect to find. Donna soon responded to the double whammy of two lovable males, Randy and Greg, a seemingly inseparable duo.

* * *

Donna Clift had gotten pregnant right out of high school. "I wasn't prepared for it," she said. "It really devastated me." She married her baby's father, but they were too young. "It didn't work," she recalled. Now Donna was escaping Arizona and the ashes of a burned-out marriage. She was lonely, despite the open-armed welcome she had received from her father and her stepmother.

Brittany was three, a beguiling blond little girl. Greg Roth was seven, a sweet kid who deserved to have a mother. When Randy took Donna to see the house he had recently sold—the Amber Hills home—she was very impressed. It was huge and very expensive-looking. The Misty Meadows home next to Ben and Marta where he currently lived was very nice too, and perfectly kept—if a little Spartan. There no pictures on the wall, no homey touches. Rather, he had a weird medieval-looking weapon hanging on his bed, a chain with two balls. He had a club with nails poking out. Throwing Stars. Macho things.

But all the landscaping Randy had done was wonderful. He seemed to have a real affinity for growing things, and he pointed out bushes and trees that would bloom come spring.

"Randy never came across like he just wanted me to go to bed with him. It didn't seem important to him. He just seemed to like *me* for me."

Nevertheless, he proved to be a wonderful lover. He was sweet and passionate. He called Donna all the time. He sent her a dozen American Beauty roses three or four times a week. He bought her a solid gold necklace and *two* leather coats. "They were exactly my size, and they were *fitted* coats; I don't know how he knew just what to buy.

"I thought he was really handsome and well built. He had a beard and a mustache. I thought his son was really well mannered. I thought it was really neat that a single parent could be a man."

Donna Clift's parents met Randy and they liked him. Randy explained that he was working part-time at Vitamilk Dairy and that he also worked the graveyard shift as a chemist in Lynnwood.

"How can you leave Greg alone all night?" Donna asked, horrified.

"I just tuck him into bed and make sure he's asleep, and then I go to my night job. I have no choice."

Donna already loved Greg, and she hated the thought of his being alone every night. She worked the graveyard shift often herself. She knew Randy was out late at night because there were many nights when he came to her house and threw pebbles at her window at two or three in the morning. When she peered out the window, she could barely see him. He was like a dark ghost, dressed all in black. She could hear him call out softly, but he darted around the yard just out of her line of vision and then another pebble would drop next to her window. It didn't scare her—not really—but it gave Donna Clift a prickly sensation along the back of her neck.

"I told him not to do that because my dad would be mad."

Perhaps not. Donna Clift's father and teenage brother, Todd, found Randy energetic and fun to be with. Randy and Greg were welcomed into Donna's family almost from the beginning.

At Christmas 1984, Randy gave Donna's parents a studio portrait of himself and Greg. On the back, Randy wrote, "Dec–84, Randy (30 years) & Greg (7 years)—To Mom & Dad, Love, The Roths."

It was kind of sad, Randy trying to make himself and Greg sound like a whole big family when there were only the two of them.

Just as he had with the Goodwins, Randy drew Donna's family into his life-style of outdoor exercise, camping, rafting. He *was* fun to be with.

Randy told Donna about his days in the marines, haltingly—as if the memories were so full of pain that he could hardly stand to speak of them. He had been in a Special Forces unit, he explained, with only ten highly trained men. "He told me that one night they had to kill a whole village of women and children in Vietnam. He was so badly wounded himself that he had to be in a special hospital for ninety days."

Randy had scrapbooks filled with gruesome pictures, including photographs of bodies lying in ditches in Vietnam. It helped Donna to understand why he had such terrible nightmares. He was still reliving his marine days. He had stacks of military magazines like *Soldier of Fortune,* and he once gave her a book on Vietnam, suggesting that she read it: "If you want to see what I've been through, read this. The authors interviewed me, and this part in the book is about me. It *is* me."

The book explained a lot to Donna. Randy had been through hell.

And his life had continued to be marked by tragedy. Randy explained to a stunned Donna Clift how his second wife, Jan, had died. This was why he had been as lonesome as she was, maybe more so. Donna Sanchez had left him and Greg, and he had lost Jan in a tragic accident. Painfully, Randy described how he and Jan had been taking a shortcut down a mountain. "I was in front of her. I heard gravel . . ."

Donna held his hand as he said that Jan had slipped on pine needles and rocks, describing how he had grabbed her but couldn't hold on and had to watch helplessly as she fell to her death.

His memories of the tragedy made Donna cry. What a terrible thing for him to have gone through—and how awful for Greg too.

Randy never told Donna he loved her—not in so many words. She was infatuated with him, and she understood that a lot of men never said "I love you"—even if they did love a woman. Randy seemed to her a highly educated man; he used big words and spoke in a careful, almost emotionless manner. What he did say to Donna was, "I want to make an investment in you."

"Why are you doing all this for me?" she asked. "All these presents?"

And he answered again, "I want to make an investment in you."

Donna Clift took that as a sign of Randy Roth's love.

Although she had some reservations about Randy, Donna couldn't help falling in love. She felt Randy was too rough on Greg, his punishments too harsh in her view, but she thought she could talk Randy into taking it easier on his son if they were all living together. She was sure there was a sensitive, loving man under all that macho veneer.

On Valentine's Day, Randy took Donna out to dinner and dancing at the Top of the Hilton. It was an incredibly romantic evening. At just the right moment he produced a small velvet box. There was a ring inside, gold with a tiny diamond set in a swirl of black onyx. A gold wedding band would nest beside the diamond. She accepted the ring, believing that he truly did love her.

The flowers and the presents continued to arrive, and Randy urged Donna and her daughter to move in with him and Greg. In March 1985 she agreed. "My mom didn't like it at all. She's really my stepmother —but I call her 'Mom.' We're close. She was always telling me to go slow with Randy, but I was infatuated. I guess I shut my eyes to a lot of things I should have seen more clearly."

Shortly after Donna Clift moved in with Randy, she cleared out the floor of the bedroom closet so she could put her shoes away. At the bottom of a jumble of Randy's clothes and shoes she found a black box; at first she thought it was a videotape. She carried it to the light and saw that it was not an overdue movie rental. The name Janis L. Roth was written on the top of the black plastic box. Randy had not even gotten Jan's middle initial right.

Donna had inadvertently stumbled across her predecessor's ashes. The cremains of Janis Roth had been in the closet even as Donna shared the bed with Randy.

"At first I was really upset. Why would he still have them? And then I tried to think of reasons that Randy kept her ashes there. I'd had a friend who kept her husband's ashes near her, and I tried to tell myself that it could just be a loving thing to do. But not like that—not just shoved under everything in the closet. I went over to my mom's house. Randy knew where I'd be—I didn't know anyone else. He came over, and he was sweating bullets. He told me that he 'just forgot' about Jan's ashes. He said, 'I'll take care of them,' and he came home later and told me he had thrown them in Silver Lake. He showed me the box, and it was empty. Later I found he'd thrown the box away in the garbage."

There was another occasion that startled Donna Clift. She and Randy were still just living together when he brought home a stack of papers. He explained they were insurance applications, and Donna somehow got the impression it was something that was being offered as an employee benefit from Vitamilk Dairy. "I remember we were sitting on the bed discussing it," Donna says. "He explained that if anything happened to me, he would be left alone with Brittany and Greg, and we should think about insurance. We had never talked about it before; he just came home with the information. There was a $250,000 policy—I remember that—that would pay off if I drowned. If I lost an arm, it would be so much: if I lost a leg, it would be so much: and if I died, it was more, but I can't remember how much. I know I didn't sign anything. And I don't think we talked any more about that."

Randy and Donna were married at the Chapel of the Bells in Seattle on May 18. They had a "sweet lady minister," and Donna wore a burnt amber chiffon dress and a crown of baby's breath. She carried a bouquet of white roses and baby's breath. Her stepmother, Judy, was her matron of honor in a pale pink dress similar to Donna's. Randy and his best man, Donna's father, wore gray tuxedos, and Greg's was just like theirs, only in miniature. Brittany wore gray dotted swiss, a picture hat, and a wrist corsage of roses. The sun shone brilliantly, and it was a lovely wedding.

But it wasn't legal. Randy had pushed and pushed Donna to get married "now," and she had gone ahead with the ceremony even though she wasn't positive that she was legally divorced from her first husband. Actually, her divorce came through three days after her second wedding. "I went to my lawyer, and he did the paperwork so Randy and I *really* were legally married. Randy was so anxious that we were."

They left for their honeymoon in a 1974 two-toned Pinto, one of Randy's gifts to his bride. Donna had no idea it was identical to Janis Miranda's car, the one that was stolen, destroyed, and paid off by an insurance company a few months after Jan's marriage to Randy in 1981. How could Donna have known? She knew virtually nothing about Janis Miranda, only the way she had died.

The 1974 Pinto was perhaps only a macabre coincidence.

A second coincidence, another that Donna didn't know about then, was that she and Randy honeymooned in the very same spot where he had taken Janis: the Empress Hotel in Victoria, British Columbia.

"It might have even been in the same room,"

Donna said later. "I felt something wasn't right on our honeymoon night, but I didn't know what it was. Just an eerie feeling. I suddenly realized I didn't really know him at all."

Randy's sexual ardor faded shortly after he and Donna became husband and wife. "A couple of weeks after we got married, everything changed," Donna said. *"Everything* changed. Sex was great before we got married. It wasn't long before he didn't want sex at all. I kept wondering what I was doing wrong. He wouldn't even *kiss* me. . . . I was so young, so stupid."

Donna had married Randy because she loved him and because she was beguiled by his apparent absolute devotion to her. Like Janis Miranda before her, she brought few assets into the marriage. And she soon learned that Randy was in charge of all finances. He did not add her name to his checking account. "If I ever needed anything, I had to go to him."

But she seldom needed anything; Donna wasn't even allowed to shop for groceries. Randy took care of that. He bought the cars, the sports equipment, their clothes. She became completely dependent on his decisions.

The marriage limped into that summer of 1985, and Donna Clift Roth became more and more attached to little Greg; he bloomed under her love and attention—even if his father did not. Although Donna had thought Randy's discipline of his son was a little strict *before* their marriage, she was appalled at how Spartan, even cruel, it was after. "It was as if Greg was in the military," she said. "Randy beat him with his belt or he'd put him under a cold shower. Or he'd make Greg do like a thousand push-ups outside in the cold. One time he knocked Greg so hard in the head that he swelled up so fast. I flipped. I ran out of the house, and Randy was running after me, and I screamed, 'Leave me alone. Keep away from me.'"

That time Randy had hit Greg with a removable shower nozzle, and Donna had inadvertently walked in on the discipline session in the bathroom. She couldn't bear to see the little boy she had grown to love being treated so badly, and she tried to cover up for him. "I didn't know what to think. Greg wet the bed all the time, which wasn't surprising. I used to hide his sheets from Randy so he wouldn't punish Greg more."

It seemed that every day or so Donna would learn something that jarred her. The least of it was that there were no more gifts, no more flowers. The romance was seeping out of her marriage, but she couldn't bear to tell anyone. She felt like such a fool.

On the surface, when things were good, Randy could seem like the old Randy, the one she had fallen completely in love with. Greg loved his father, and Randy coached a Little League baseball team. Their home was neat, their yard was green and perfectly manicured, and Randy's roses bloomed without blight or bugs.

But when Randy was in a black mood, which was more and more often, Donna tiptoed around him. She would go to Marta Goodwin and ask for advice. "I knew something was wrong with our marriage," she explained, "and I'd say, 'Golly, I don't know what to do. I've tried everything.'"

But then things would get a little better, and Randy talked as if they would be together forever. He wanted to adopt Brittany. He was vehement about that, but Donna explained she could not allow that: "Brittany already had a father. Her father was her father."

By July, Randy was unemployed. He explained that he had been working on an on-call basis at Vitamilk and that he had simply told them he needed a regular income. In truth, there had been a severe misunderstanding about Randy's use of company gas in his own vehicles. Donna's father got Randy a job where he himself worked, at Cascade Prestige Ford in Bellevue, and they car-pooled together. Randy had to take a salary cut of almost four dollars an hour.

Donna Clift was barely twenty-one and in way over her head only a few months after her wedding. There were too many secrets, more each day. She knew nothing about Randy's family, and he volunteered little. "You will *never* meet my mother," he said flatly. "She's hooked on Valium." He added that his mother was totally obsessed with rock singer Rod Stewart.

Donna believed that Randy had one sister and thought her name was Lisa. She didn't know about any other siblings. She did meet Randy's father, Gordon, however. Randy looked like his dad, only about twenty years younger. She liked Gordon Roth. He lived in a tiny one-room cabin down across the river from Portland.

Perhaps the most chilling information Randy gave his bride about his family concerned his younger brother, David Marvin Roth. David, Randy said, was in prison. He had run into a girl from their home state, North Dakota, and given her a ride. "Randy said they got in a big old fight and David, who was twenty then, strangled that girl," Donna explained. "Then he put her body in the trunk of her car and filled it full of bullet holes. It was really weird how he told me. In one version he said he helped his brother hide the car for a while before he finally talked him into turning himself in. Then he said his brother stabbed her to death before he put her in the trunk."

Donna didn't know whether to believe him or not. It could all have been some of Randy's weird teasing.

All in all, Donna Clift's perfect bridegroom was turning into something she could never have imagined. She had seen only the mask he wanted her to see, and now she realized that there was horror behind the mask. What horror she didn't fully comprehend. His stories of violence were so troubling. She could deal with the Vietnam memories, but she wasn't sure if he was simply teasing her sadistically with the things he told her about his brother having murdered someone —or if he was telling the truth.

She had learned that he was cruel when he teased. "I had heard about the Green River Killer—the one they never caught who was supposed to have murdered all those girls—before I came up here from Arizona. The police had been looking for him since 1982, and it was still on the news all the time. Randy liked to scare me by teasing me about him."

The secrets multiplied. Randy would never tell Donna how old he was. "You don't need to know," he said flatly.

In the beginning his age had not mattered. He looked to be only a few years older than she was, and he was in excellent physical condition. But then, with all the ugly surprises that kept popping up, Donna became obsessed with finding out everything she could about this stranger she had married. She had begun to feel like the heroine of a Gothic novel. Like Jane Eyre or Rebecca. Did Randy have an insane wife or a psychotic relative hidden away someplace? Or was he planning to do something to *her?* He kept the shed out in back locked all the time. She wasn't allowed to look in there.

Marta and Ben Goodwin had known Randy for a long time, and they thought they knew him well, but Randy had never told them much of substance about his background. They had seen a woman and young children come to his house once on Christmas Eve, watched as she knocked futilely on his front door. When she finally gave up and drove away, Randy and Greg came over to their house to celebrate Christmas as usual. "He told us that was his sister—but he had no intention of letting her in," Marta recalled.

* * *

The more secretive Randy became, the more determined Donna was to find out the truth.

"I snooped through a lot of stuff. I found his birth certificate, his military papers, and an old expired driver's license. They all had different birth dates on them. His birth certificate looked as though it had been altered. . . . I did a lot of snooping. I broke into his file cabinet. He kept it outside under lock and key, and I found the key. I went through his papers trying to find out something about him."

She found out a great deal. Although he had warned her they had to be very cautious about spending money, she found a savings account passbook that showed a current balance of $99,000. "I figured it had to have been from when he sold his house," she said. "He told me he had no money, but he had a red Ford panel wagon, all race ready. I knew that was worth at least $20,000. I knew a lot about cars because of my dad; we used to go to the drag races together. Randy had other toys that [cost] a lot of money."

Randy also had a bank account in Arizona, something Donna had had no knowledge of until she found a statement in his papers.

She discovered that Randy had received two Social Security checks a month at one time. From what Donna could make out, he was getting almost a thousand dollars a month from Social Security. "It made me suspicious. He was working. Why would he be getting Social Security checks?" Donna discovered Social Security numbers for two children whose names she had never heard. She had no idea what that could mean.

In what Randy would have called a "reconnaissance mission," his new bride looked through files he had never meant her to see. She found to her surprise that Randy was embroiled in a lawsuit. She hadn't known that, either. He was suing the state of Washington for $1.8 million for negligence in the death of his late wife, Jan. According to the legal papers, Randy was maintaining that the trail had not been marked clearly. How odd, Donna thought. Randy had told her that they weren't even *on* the trail when Jan fell, that they were taking a shortcut off the trail.

Randy and Donna Roth had not even been married three months, and yet the marriage was disintegrating like a cheap condominium in a hurricane. His cruelty to Greg, his lies, and the secret life that Donna was uncovering in her desperate search for answers had well nigh destroyed the love she felt for him.

She also suspected he was being unfaithful to her. If he wasn't, he was living the life of a celibate monk; he certainly wasn't satisfying his sexual needs with her. The woman she sensed was her rival was a most unlikely candidate: Lily Vandiveer, his former baby-sitter, the same woman who had worried Jan so much. Lily was also the mother of one of Greg's best friends, Brad.*

"Lily always seemed to be around," Donna said later. "She used to live near Randy in Amber Hills. He was a widower and she had just gotten divorced, and she seemed to be terribly in love with Randy. He told me he wanted nothing to do with her—he just felt sorry for Brad. She called the house constantly. You know, it was 'Randy, my car needs fixing.' She was a lot older than I was, and older than Randy—*however* old he really was. Randy didn't drink—except maybe we'd have a Smith and Kerns with dinner—but I found beer in the back of his pickup truck. I knew he'd been over to Lily's. When he took Brad home, he wouldn't come back for hours."

Donna couldn't prove infidelity, though—with Lily or with anyone else. Actually, Randy's being unfaithful would have been easier to deal with than the sense of foreboding that walked with Donna always. Randy still liked to dress in dark clothes, and he often went running at night wearing a full black bodysuit.

Sometimes Donna noticed that his hands were scratched. But he was, after all, an automobile mechanic. It would be natural for his hands to be scratched and bruised.

Their marriage had already begun to wind down when Randy grabbed Donna's three-year-old daughter by the ear and pulled her upstairs. "I couldn't stop what he was doing to Greg, but I wouldn't let him touch my daughter. My mother really told him off too. The only other person who could make him back off was Ben Goodwin. Ben loved kids, and he would get right in Randy's face about how he treated Greg. I thought they would come to blows over it, but they never did."

And then one day Donna went outside and caught Randy coaxing Brittany to jump from the roof. "He said he was going to catch her. He was teaching her to trust him."

It was all too obvious that Randy didn't like little girls.

6

Randy Roth lived a clean life. He was an athlete, an outdoorsman, a jogger, a man who utterly detested smoking and frowned on alcohol. He was apparently not highly sexed, or—at best—he was only sporadically moved by desires of the flesh; both Jan Miranda Roth and Donna Clift Roth could have attested to that. He was, however, thrilled with grown-up toys—cars, beautiful homes, and money in the bank.

And power. Randy Roth exulted in having complete and utter control over people around him, especially over his wives.

Whatever Donna tried, it was never enough to please him. She did agree to change the beneficiary of her one existing life insurance policy, a policy with a payoff of only $3,000. "It was supposed to go to Brittany," she explained, "but I changed it to Randy's name."

It didn't seem that big a deal, not when she knew that Randy had almost $100,000 in the bank.

Donna, and often her parents, too, went on outdoor expeditions with Randy. Her dad and her brother liked him so much that she began to wonder if there was something the matter with *her*. But her stepmother, Judy, agreed with Donna. Randy had a mean streak in him. He certainly showed it with Greg, and despite his entreaties that he still wanted desperately to adopt three-year-old Brittany, he sometimes grabbed at her as if she were a rag doll, lifting her by her cheeks, by her ear. He made the mistake of grabbing Brittany's cheeks one day in front of Ben Goodwin. He never did it again, at least not in front of Ben.

Donna might have taken physical punishment herself, trying to patch up the marriage that had never really begun, but she loved her daughter with a visceral fierceness, and her love for Randy had begun to die.

Randy had bought still another set of ATVs (all-terrain vehicles), and he and Donna went alone to test his newest rig on a steep hill. She was not afraid of taking chances. Indeed, with the encouragement of Harvey Clift, who was a huge Bob Glidden fan, she had participated in Figure 8 stock car races. But riding with her new husband straight up a hill made Donna's stomach contract.

Just as they almost crested the hill, Randy suddenly jumped off. The ATV stalled, rolled over, and Donna tumbled over and over to the bottom of the slope. She looked up to see the ATV bouncing backward toward her as if in slow motion. There was nothing she could do; it landed on top of her, bruising and twisting the lower part of her right leg. She could not stand up, and she ultimately lost sensation in that part of her leg permanently.

Randy laughed at her before he finally came down the hill to help her up.

The Skykomish River courses along the route leading to Washington State's Stevens Pass, a deceptively treacherous waterway full of hidden currents, sudden froths of white water, and undertows that have pulled scores of waders and rafters to their deaths. Snohomish County sheriff's deputies specializing in search and rescue have pulled both living and decaying bodies from its heedless path, but yearly warnings to neophytes seem to do little good.

Randy couldn't swim. He had explained that to Donna, and when they went to the athletic club pool, he always stayed in the shallow end. She had never seen him in water any deeper than three feet. He always stayed in the shallow end with Greg. He was so muscular, always bench pressing in his weight room in the basement, that she wasn't surprised Randy didn't float. She *was* surprised that he was so enthusiastic about going rafting. They had rafted once with her parents, Harvey and Judy, at a Cascade Ford company picnic, but he hadn't seemed to enjoy it that much. Now he bought a cheap raft made of such thin material that it seemed better suited to a backyard pool than to a river.

Donna was a good swimmer. That wasn't why she didn't want to go rafting. It was more than that; she had grown afraid of her husband. Only when Randy suggested that they invite her parents to accompany them on a rafting trip on the Skykomish would Donna agree to go. But she wasn't happy about it.

It was a hot July day, but the Skykomish is always cold, chilled by the snowpack high in the Cascade Mountains. They took two rafts along, the larger raft for the elder couple and the cheap two-man raft for Donna and Randy. Donna's parents had a net bag with life jackets and extra paddles with them, but they left it in the car, taking only a paddle for each raft. Randy and Harvey both had great upper-body strength, and they would paddle while the women enjoyed the scenery along the river. Randy suggested that Brittany and Greg go with the Clifts and that they take the ice chest, too.

Judy Clift whispered to Harvey, "Do not let my daughter out of your sight." Harvey looked puzzled at Judy's insistence, but he nodded.

Keeping Donna and Randy in sight wasn't as easy as it sounded. Although the river was fairly calm that day, Judy and Harvey Clift's raft was caught up in the current and they sped ahead of Randy and Donna. The Skykomish has bends and turns so sharp that there is no way separate parties can travel downriver together or even hope to keep each other in sight. The roar of the water blocks out all but the loudest sounds.

When Judy and Harvey's raft had disappeared from view, Randy suddenly started having trouble steering. Alarmed, Donna turned to see that they were headed toward the huge sharp rocks that wait beneath the Skykomish. Instead of paddling away from the rocks, Randy seemed to be deliberately steering their tiny raft *toward* them. With no paddle, Donna had no control at all.

Far ahead, Judy insisted that Harvey Clift pull their raft over where they could grab on to an overhanging branch and wait for Randy and Donna to catch up. She stared back at the river.

"What are you doing?" Donna screamed, but Randy ignored her as he drew closer and closer to the jagged boulders that could easily pierce the thin raft.

Ahead, Judy Clift turned again to look for Donna and Randy. Five minutes had gone by. She could no longer see them, but she heard something. A bird's screech? Maybe just the slight change in the river's song as it widened, narrowed, and twisted past the land. Judy was worried; she had come to believe Donna when she said there was something strange about Randy Roth, possibly even something dangerous.

"I was afraid my daughter would not come off that river," Judy remembered with a shudder.

"Listen!" Judy shouted. "I hear something."

And she did. She heard Donna screaming in complete panic, *"Dad! I'm going to die! Save me! I'm going to die!"*

Judy also heard Randy's voice. He was shouting, *"Shut up! Shut up! Shut up!"*

Harvey Clift kept his raft motionless, waiting helplessly. When the small raft finally rounded the crook in the river, they saw that it was barely afloat, so filled with water that it rode low in the Skykomish River.

Randy seemed calm. Donna was nearly hysterical with fear. They got the two rafts to a spot where they could pull onto the bank of the river. Judy calmed Donna while her husband helped Randy put patches on two holes in the small raft. Nobody knew quite what to say. What Judy Clift suspected was unthinkable, unspeakable.

Donna Roth would not get back into the raft with Randy; she rode the rest of the way back to their cars in her parents' raft, and Randy paddled the flimsy raft alone.

She never lived with her husband again. She had seen something in his face, in the grim set of his jaw as

85

he steered their raft deliberately against the river rocks until water began to seep in through the holes the sharp edges tore. Donna Clift Roth could not prove that her suspicions were correct. Even her own father looked at her a little quizzically when she talked about her fear of Randy. All she really had to go on was the cold feeling in the bottom of her stomach, the stories that she could not prove were lies, the facts that did not mesh with other facts.

Her parents accepted her decision not to go home to Misty Meadows with her husband of three months. She moved into the Clifts' Bothell home with Brittany for a month, and then in September of 1985 she went to Arizona for another month—to think, to find a quiet place where she could sort out what was real, what was only fear, what might be imagination.

When Donna flew back to Seattle, Randy was there at the airport, smiling, at the gate. Everything would be fine, he said. He was still car-pooling with her father. It was all a misunderstanding. He told her that her father had even gone with him on another rafting trip and nothing bad had happened. Randy had come to pick her up and take her home, but she accepted only a ride to her parents' house.

"I couldn't go home with him, not ever. My mother believed me, too," Donna Clift recalled. "She told my dad, 'He's not what he appears to be.'"

When he realized that Donna was not coming back to him, Randy filed for divorce. "I would have," Donna recalled, "but I had no access to money."

It didn't matter who filed, she decided; she would be free of her terror-ridden marriage.

Oddly, Randy did not let his third wife go easily. Even though he had instigated the divorce, he pursued Donna. Rather, he stalked her. He hadn't seemed to want her when he had her, but he refused to let her go. He would come into the 7-Eleven where she had found a job and watch her. Often he wouldn't say anything at all, but she was aware of him as he gazed at her, his face inscrutable.

Donna found flowers and notes from Randy on her car. He seemed to know where she was all the time. It was ironic. In the beginning, less than a year ago, she had been flattered when he stared at her while she worked and thrilled by his notes and bouquets. Now she found the same behavior threatening. He seemed to be everywhere she looked, where she worked, where she ate lunch, in one of his many cars following her as she drove.

"Finally my mom went to him and told him to leave me alone, and he stopped stalking me—for a while. But then he had Greg call me."

Leaving Greg behind had been the hardest thing for Donna to do, and now Greg called her often, crying, and begging her to come back. If she hadn't been so frightened, she would have gone back—if only for Greg's sake.

One day in the fall of 1985 Randy came in once more to the store where Donna worked. He had tears in his eyes as he told her that he had just gotten terrible news. His mother had been killed in a car accident. But that wasn't the worst of it, he continued. "My sister got so distraught in the hospital that she shot herself. She's dead too."

"I believed him," Donna says ruefully. "It was kind of farfetched, but you never know. I told my mom and dad and they didn't believe it."

She almost went back to him, moved by sympathy for his pain and by her concern for Greg. But Judy Clift talked her out of it.

Randy Roth continued to stalk his third ex-wife. In his dark jogging suit or in his mechanic's clothes, he followed close behind her, keeping track of her. She thought she would never be free of him, this man whose attention had thrilled her only a year before.

"He kept it up until I started dating another man. Once that happened, Randy left me alone," she recalled. "I was with Jerry* for four years. Randy just went away, and it was almost as if I'd never known him at all. No, that isn't true—because I really loved Greg, and I missed him and worried about him."

Randy's divorce from Donna Clift was final on September 24, 1985.

PART THREE

1985

7

There is an odd synchronicity in the way parallel
lives veer to touch one another, change direction
and then come close again and again until they connect and hold for whatever it was that fate intended to happen. Sometimes synchronicity can be
heartwarming—when it leads lost lovers back together against all odds. Sometimes it can be starkly tragic.

Nineteen eighty-five was a watershed year in the
lives of a number of people who were, who had been,
or who would one day be part of Randy Roth's life.
Donna Clift was courted by, married to, and divorced
from him—all in 1985.

Although Randy had not discussed it with Donna
and she found out only through her "snooping,"
Randy had filed a suit against the state of Washington
and the Department of Parks and Recreation of the
state of Washington in November of 1984. On January 19, 1985, he signed a formal contract with
Lynnwood attorney Ginny Evans, who agreed to
represent him and Jalina Amelia Miranda on a con-
tingency basis. Randy maintained that it was negli-
gence on the part of the state and the Parks
Department in not providing adequate trail barriers
on Beacon Rock that had caused Janis Roth's death.
All through 1985 he huddled with his legal advisers in
pursuing his claim.

Breaking his financial losses down, Randy asked for the following:

Funeral expenses for the decedent:	$541.00
Cost of selling family home because Mr. Roth could not keep up payments without decedent's contributions:	$5,863.62
Loss of consortium for each claimant, $250,000.00:	$500,000.00
Lost earnings:	To be determined

It cost Randy only $500 out of pocket to file the tort claim against the state for $1,186,404.62. If he won, he would have to pay his attorney one-third of his settlement. He really had nothing to lose.

Randy didn't even know where Jalina was living. He had neither written to her nor sent her presents. He had forwarded none of her dead mother's belongings to her, and so she had very little to remember Janis Miranda Roth by. Still, he presented himself as a fighter on her behalf, anxious to see that Jalina got her due from the negligent state of Washington. He gave her address in Texas, but it was really only the last address he had for Janis's mother, Billie Ray.

Neither Randy's second wife nor his third wife had learned much about his history. Both women had met his father, but not his mother or any of his siblings. His mother was apparently dead, either from old age or by suicide; he had told many different stories about her and her demise. If he truly had a brother, David was reportedly in prison for murder. Randy had told both Jan and Donna again and again about his marine service in Vietnam, and both women had heard him scream at night from the grotesque nightmares that haunted him.

Donna Sanchez Roth, Randy's first wife, had apparently slipped completely out of his life, and no one knew where she was.

Anything that might have happened in Randy Roth's life before his marine years was caught somewhere in his memory, either blurred deliberately or repressed when he talked with his ex-wives. In actuality, Randy had never moved very far—at least for very long—from the area just north of Seattle. He had attended Meadowdale High School in Lynnwood, only a few miles from Bothell, Mountlake Terrace, and Mill Creek. Although he moved often, he did not venture beyond familiar territory.

Although there is no evidence that they ever knew each other, a young man named Tom Baumgartner attended Meadowdale High at the same time Randy did. They both graduated in the early 1970s, but they moved in different circles.

During the time Randy married and divorced three times, Tom Baumgartner married only once, and for life. In 1976 he married pretty blond Cynthia Loucks. They became parents of two cherished little boys: Tyson Jeret Baumgartner, born on December 15, 1979, and Rylie Thomas Baumgartner, August 18, 1981.

Tom was a hard worker, taking a job with United Parcel Service and working his way up to provide security for his growing family. He joined the Teamsters Union and with that membership came both medical coverage and death benefits for survivors. Short of an occasional trip to the pediatrician for the boys, neither he nor Cynthia expected to need Tom's teamster insurance. Tom also took out life insurance.

The Baumgartners' marriage ended in 1985 too, about the same time that Donna Clift and Randy Roth were divorced. But Cynthia and Tom Baumgartner did not choose to be apart. Not yet thirty, Tom had contracted Hodgkin's disease, a form

93

of cancer that affects the lymph nodes. Although the often fatal disease was being treated with some success in the mid-eighties, Tom's case was far advanced when he was diagnosed. He was dead in six months at the age of twenty-nine.

The widowed Cynthia Baumgartner and the newly divorced Randy Roth did not meet in 1985, although they shopped at the same stores, their sons were close to the same age, and they traveled the same roads. Had Randy encountered Cynthia, he undoubtedly would have hit on her; his technique for finding women to date was carefully honed to perfection. Randy seemed to prefer divorced or widowed women in their twenties or thirties, and he scarcely looked at women without children. He liked pretty women, obviously, small women, perhaps because he was so short himself, and he invariably approached shy, dependent women—as if he had antennae that could scope that out without ever speaking to them.

Randy Roth must have asked hundreds of women for a date, or rather he sent Greg to ask them, "Would you go out with my dad? He's right over there."

Many women—many, many women—said yes. The kid was so cute, and the father smiled so charmingly.

Cynthia Baumgartner began to put together the shattered fragments of her world. She struggled to cope with raising her boys alone, something she had never expected to have to do. Tom's insurance and Social Security survivors' benefits made it possible for her to stay home with Tyson and Rylie. Many years back, she had worked for Jimbo's Family Restaurant in Lynnwood and later as a legal secretary, but that was before the boys were born. Now she devoted a lot of time to volunteer work at her church. Although her heart was broken, she was comfortable financially and she prayed that time and the strength of her faith would help her overcome her grief. Cynthia had solid family support from her parents, Hazel and Merle Loucks, and from her older brother, Leon.

Cynthia Loucks Baumgartner didn't really think about marrying again; it was much too soon after Tom's death. However, her friends knew that it would take a very special man for Cynthia to fall in love again. Her own morals and her religious beliefs dictated that any candidate would have to be either single or widowed. She would not marry a divorced man.

Randy Roth had a life to rearrange too. His heart was not broken, and his divorce had cost him nothing. However, his "investment" in Donna had not paid off, whatever the payback he had planned on. Donna had once believed Randy's protestations that he was investing his emotions and his future in her. She no longer did.

Randy continued to spend his Thursday nights at Ben and Marta Goodwins', bringing always the apple pie and ice cream, and they all watched "The Cosby Show" together. Randy was still hurt because Ryan Goodwin had turned him in to Greg's principal and the Children's Protective Service had investigated him.

He seemed confused, totally unable to equate his treatment of Greg with the humiliating and painful punishment he told the Goodwins *he* had suffered as a little boy, a little boy kneeling on a hard floor for hours. And yet Randy's discipline of Greg was ultimately demeaning, and with Donna gone, Greg had no one to take his side once the doors were closed.

One night in the fall of 1985 Ben and Randy were in a tavern at Thrasher's Corner when a woman who knew Donna Clift well walked by and recognized Randy. She stopped suddenly, slapped his face, and spat, "You child-abusing son of a bitch!"

For once, Randy was shocked, taken completely by surprise by an enemy he had not recognized.

"Randy and I both got thrown out." Ben grinned. "He was really upset. I had to take him home, wake

Marta up, and we both tried to console him. He cried real tears. He said, *'Nobody* is more important in my life than Greg. Greg is my whole life.'"

And, indeed, he seemed to be. The Goodwins had seen that women came and went in Randy Roth's life, but Greg remained the one constant. "I think he really loved Greg," Marta Goodwin said. "He really felt bad when that girl criticized him for being a bad father, but he could not grasp that you didn't discipline children the way he did Greg."

Greg and Randy had shared their last Christmas with Donna and her family, but on Christmas 1985 the neighbors were back together around the Goodwins' tree. Randy would be thirty-one the day after Christmas, but he still looked about twenty-five in the photographs the Goodwins took that year. Their daughter, Brittany, was almost fourteen, and she clearly adored Randy. When Randy teased her about being too heavy, she dieted until she was thin and weak, and her parents were afraid she would become anorexic or bulimic.

Brittany Goodwin would have done anything for Randy.

In the autumn of 1985, Randy Mullinax, a King County Police detective, had never heard of the man who shared his first name. They were about the same age and Mullinax was also compact and muscular, but there all similarities ended. Randy the detective had a deep and resonant voice, and Randy the mechanic spoke in flat, almost expressionless tones. Mullinax was a friendly and easygoing man, sensitive—perhaps too much so for his own good—to the pain of the people whose lives brought them in contact with the King County Police Department's Major Crimes Unit.

Even though he was born east of the Cascade Mountains in Yakima, Washington, Mullinax grew up as a Seattle kid. His parents moved to the Boulevard

Park area in the south end, and Randy and his brothers all grew up there and graduated from Glacier High School, whose campus later became the King County Police Academy. Mullinax got married when he was twenty. He went to work for the County Water District just outside Burien, a small town south of Seattle, and stayed there for eight years. "I got tired of using my back and standing outside in the rain," Mullinax recalls. He went to college, fitting in classes when he could. "I just took a few electives in police science courses at first—but I got hooked. I changed my major."

Mullinax majored in police science at Highline Community College, mastering the intricacies of crime scene investigation, arrest, search and seizure, and constitutional law for police. By day he checked for broken water mains, and in the evening he learned how to triangulate a crime scene so perfectly that the location of a body could be absolutely pinpointed long after a victim was removed. He learned that blood droplets that have fallen from three feet look different from those that fell from one foot or six feet, and he learned how to tell if glass has been broken from inside force or outside force. He learned about tool marks and skid marks and tire tracks, about rigor mortis and lividity and the transmogrification of the human body after death. He even had one ex-homicide detective instructor who claimed he had always preferred to work a crime scene alone "so he could talk to the body and find out what happened."

Randy Mullinax was prepared to be a homicide detective, but first he had to pay his dues. He joined the King County Police in January of 1979, and he worked his way through the usual steps like any rookie, patrolling first the sparsely populated southeast part of the county, then working in a proactive unit on burglaries and larcenies. By the fall of 1985, Randy Mullinax was an integral part of the enhanced Green River Task Force. He had worked on the baffling disappearances and murders of almost four dozen girls and women, most of whom had vanished since July 15, 1982, from the strip that runs by Washington State's biggest airport: Seattle-Tacoma International. The first five victims had been found floating in the Green River south of Seattle, hence the name. Once a country river that curved past verdant strawberry fields, the Green River was far less isolated by 1982; Boeing buildings covered the good black earth on its east flank, shopping malls on the north, and roads leading up a steep hill to the west crossed Pacific Highway every quarter mile or so.

The media and a number of insensitive citizens almost always referred to the Green River victims as "prostitutes" or "hookers." The additional pain inflicted on their families by this attitude could not be measured. The missing girls were very young—many of them fourteen, fifteen, or sixteen—the oldest in their twenties. Mullinax had a soft spot for children, and as he carried on an increasingly frustrating investigation, he would describe his job as "trying to locate young ladies." He was not being sarcastic. The victims had become very real to him, and their almost certain fate pitiable. Victims' groups praised Randy Mullinax highly for his tenacity and especially for his caring attitude.

So, in the fall of 1985, Green River Task Force member Randy Mullinax spent his working days and much of his off-duty time following one dismal trail after another, almost all of them in the area south of Seattle. By the time Mullinax found the young ladies assigned to him, however, they had long since turned to bone, hair, and sometimes a bit of connective tissue. It got worse for the Green River Task Force in 1985. Green River victims were discovered as far away as Tualatin, Oregon, almost 200 miles from where they had last been seen alive.

One of them had had her skull bisected, allowing the Green River Killer to play games with the task force by leaving the rounded calvarium in Oregon and the lower mandible in south King County, Washington.

Randy Mullinax would spend three and a half years in the Green River boiler room investigation with pressure from the media, from the public, from the politicos, and, indeed, from within himself. And yet, in 1993 the Green River murders would still be unsolved.

Women all around western Washington walked in fear of the man who had killed so many of their sisters and then disappeared like a wraith. Donna Clift was only one of thousands who shivered at the thought, and Randy Roth had delighted in teasing her sadistically about the Green River Killer.

When he finally allowed Donna to walk away from him, Randy moved on to new conquests. Many women would move in and out of his life in the next five years; he collected them like butterflies, pinning some helplessly on his own display board, discarding others when they did not meet his criteria. He never anticipated that there might be other women down the road, women who would dog his trail, annoy him, perhaps even frighten him, this man who confessed to no fear—ever. Some might say the fact that a certain trio of women awaited Randy Roth was poetic justice. Perhaps it was only a sign of the times.

Gradually in the last three decades the judicial system had changed. Female cops were no longer relegated to glorified secretarial and baby-sitting details. They worked in uniform beside the men; some of them even commanded the men. Female prosecutors were not automatically second-in-command anymore.

Three women he had not met would one day effect not revenge but a kind of ironic denouement in Randy Roth's life story.

King County detective Sue Peters would be first. She would work as Randy Mullinax's partner in an investigation totally different from but just as complicated as the Green River cases. Peters grew up close by that river. All popular cops have nicknames, and she would be called Sue P., pronounced "Soupie" by the officers she worked with. Five feet three and strong but graceful, with a cap of thick brown hair, Peters is a natural athlete who always expected to be a P.E. teacher and who still plays softball in season.

As a child she spent her summers in Adams County, far east of the Cascade Mountains. Ritzville—a town that could have been lifted out of the Midwest with its tree-shaded neighborhoods, Main Street, and hot summer days—depends on wheat farming. It is also the Adams County seat, and Sue Peters hung around the jail where her grandmother, Marie Thiel, worked as a deputy. "I was fascinated with what went on there," Peters recalls. "I asked for all the Wanted posters to take home, and I pored over the accident pictures. Once in a while my grandmother would give me a Wanted poster, but she would never give me one of the black-and-white accident photos."

Peters graduated from Kent Meridian High School, south of Seattle, in 1976 and went to Washington State University, where she majored in physical education. She transferred to Central Washington University in Ellensburg and graduated in December 1981. She soon found that there was no great demand for P.E. teachers. Perhaps the fact that there were already too many P.E. teachers was not as disappointing as it might have been; Sue had always had two interests, each as natural to her as breathing. Although she had never really planned on a career in law enforcement, it had almost literally been bred into her. When Marie Thiel, now eighty-two, was a deputy, there was women's work and men's work. Women deputies worked with women prisoners and often served as jail matrons. They were not half of the lead detective team working a major homicide case. Sue Peters followed in her grandmother's footsteps and became a King County deputy sheriff, graduating from the police academy in May of 1982.

Sue Peters, three years behind Randy Mullinax on the county force, began with basically the same duties he had; she worked three years in uniform in a patrol car out of Precinct Three in Maple Valley, and then in plain clothes in a proactive squad. Proactive squads worked whatever the biggest problem in their district happened to be at any given time. In Maple Valley in the early eighties Peters worked under cover tracking down small-time drug dealers. The fact that she could easily look like a high school girl made her an asset. She also worked the Green River murder cases and in the Special Assault Unit investigating sex crimes.

Looking back to 1985, Peters recalls that she was mostly involved in working on a new house she had bought; other than that, it was not a particularly memorable year. "I didn't even find time to play ball that year."

In October of 1990 Sue Peters moved into the Major Crimes Unit of the King County Police Department. In the old days—the sixties, the seventies—crime in the county was minuscule compared to what the Seattle detectives handled. King County's Major Crimes detectives usually investigated five or fewer murders in a year while Seattle's Homicide Unit averaged forty-five to sixty. Seattle continued to have forty-five to sixty homicides a year, but by the eighties, King County's regular homicides had climbed to twenty to twenty-five a year.

"They didn't count the Green River murders; there were just too many of them," Mullinax says. "It was as if the Major Crimes Unit had its homicides and the Green River Task Force had theirs, even though we were all in the same department."

However they counted, the county homicide rate was rapidly rising to a point where it matched the city of Seattle's. In 1985 both Sue Peters and Randy Mullinax could expect to work their share of murder cases. They would not work as partners for six years. Neither had ever heard the name Randy Roth.

PART FOUR

Good Neighbors

8

Brittany Goodwin was fourteen in 1986, and she began to baby-sit for Greg. She was thrilled to be asked to help; she had had a crush on Randy since she was thirteen. Nobody thought too much of it. Teenage girls were always mooning over older men. If it wasn't a rock star, it was a teacher or the guy next door. Harmless.

The Goodwins trusted Randy, even though they could see that their teenage daughter adored him. Ben began to feel vaguely uneasy first. He thought Randy was encouraging Brittany's attention a little too much.

Marta thought her husband was imagining things. "We knew that Brittany was madly in love with Randy," she said, "so we went to him and said, 'Look, this kid is really developing a crush on you. We just wanted you to be aware. Don't show her quite as much attention. Hold back. We need your help on this.'"

Randy nodded understandingly. "I will. I will. I wouldn't ever touch Brittany."

But her parents worried when they saw that Brittany was still mooning over Randy, despite Randy's heartfelt promises to his best friends that he was doing nothing to encourage it. One evening Brittany came home with a teddy bear that said "I love you" and went straight to her room. It was a present from Randy.

"Marta trusted Randy," Ben recalls. "She still did at that point."

"When Ben would start to worry about it," Marta says, "I'd look at him and say, 'Honey, Randy is part of our family, and he knows that Brittany is underage. He knows that's illegal. There is no way that Randy would do anything against the law.' I *actually* said that."

"Damn it Marta," Ben would rage. "I'm her father, and I know something is going on. I don't know what it is or how much it is, but there's something."

"Randy must have taken it as a compliment that this pretty little young girl thought he was King Randy," Marta theorizes. "I guess he thought he could train her to be the type of woman he wanted . . . but still, we were in a state of denial. Our lives were so intertwined with Randy's. We really didn't think that there was anything sexual going on. He was our *friend*. Besides that, whenever Randy was with Brittany, Greg and Ryan were always along too."

When Brittany was depressed, Randy could always cheer her up.

Ben Goodwin was torn. Randy was just about the best friend he had ever had, but Brittany was such a pretty girl and she was so innocent. He watched over her the way every father watches his teenage daughter, and he was suspicious. He knew what a ladies' man Randy could be. Ben went out to coach baseball one Saturday. He noted that Randy was working on his car in his driveway and called out, "See ya later."

But Ben had to turn around and go home to get his wallet. As he drove in his driveway, he saw Randy sitting sideways in the driver's seat of his Blazer with the door open. Ben's fifteen-year-old daughter was standing between Randy's legs and leaning her head on his shoulder.

Randy saw Ben coming and tried to push Brittany away, but he wasn't quick enough. Ben jumped over the fence and grabbed his daughter and pushed her toward the house. "I poked Randy in the chest and said, 'If I *ever* see you touching my daughter again, I'll kill you.'"

Randy knew Ben meant every word, and he downplayed his attentions to Brittany. Shortly thereafter, Randy became very cool to Brittany, leaving her devastated and depressed. Marta and Ben still believed that the relationship between Randy and their teenage daughter had been platonic, although they thought Randy had not used good sense in showering so much attention on Brittany. They assumed her depression was just part of the normal mood swings every teenager goes through.

It was not. Years later, when she was an adult, Brittany Goodwin recalled her pain at being abandoned. She had saved one of the many poems she had written for Randy, and rereading it was bittersweet.

My Eternal Love

I loved you then, and now
    you're gone.
I love you now, and all is
    wrong.
I try to tell you that I
    care,
but you don't seem to be aware,
that you've become my Mr.
    Right.
I think about you every night.
Your love for me has faded away.
Now all I can do is pray
    that someday you'll realize
    what you are to me
And together we'll spend eternity.

It wasn't long before there was a new woman in Randy Roth's life. Just before Memorial Day, Mary Jo Phillips, the mother of five, was grocery shopping one evening at an Albertson's supermarket. She soon noticed that a good-looking man with a little boy seemed to be waiting in every aisle she turned into. Flustered, she began to nod and smile at them.

When Mary Jo left the store pushing her loaded grocery cart, the little boy, who looked to be about nine, followed her out of the store calling, "Hey, lady! Hey, lady, would you go out with my dad?"

She did not know that it was a well-worn and effective pickup line. The father, who said his name was Randy Roth, walked up and stood behind his son, Greg. She was charmed, but not enough to give her phone number to a complete stranger—child or not.

Finally Mary Jo Phillips agreed to write down Randy's phone number. She didn't really expect to call him, but she kept it, debating for almost three weeks if she should do something so crazy.

When she finally did call, she got an answering machine. But she began to smile when she heard the message. It was for her. "Mary Jo," Randy's voice pleaded. "Mary Jo, if this is you, please, *please* don't hang up. There's got to be a way for me to meet you!"

Of course, she left her number. Randy called as soon as he got home, and invited her out to dinner.

When they reached the restaurant, Randy asked her to hold still for a moment as she started to get out of his car. He held a camera in his hand. "Baby," he said, "I just want proof that I was with such a beautiful woman." Mary Jo was touched.

Randy didn't even blink when Mary Jo told him about her large family. Rather, he seemed enthusiastic about dating her. She was a beautiful woman, very petite, with long, curly light brown hair, and she usually dressed kind of "country," in a plaid shirt, blue jeans, and tennis shoes. Mary Jo was so young-looking, peppy, and active that it was hard to believe she had given birth to five children.

For their second date he picked her up on his

motorcycle and whisked her almost to the Canadian border a hundred miles north. Just for breakfast. Just the two of them. Riding behind him with her arms locked around his muscular torso, Mary Jo couldn't help but think she had found the 1986 version of a knight on a white horse.

Once again Randy became the consummate lover. It was spring, and their courtship was swift and romantic. Mary Jo was as bedazzled as his first three wives had been. There was, of course, the usual proliferation of flowers. Roses and carnations and pots of azaleas. Nosegays and sweetheart bouquets. "He became the man every woman dreams about," Mary Jo remembers.

Randy was totally indulgent with Mary Jo. He combed her hair, he rubbed her back. He even suggested that they try to coordinate their wardrobes so they would match and everywhere they went people would know they were together.

Randy's relationship with Ben and Marta was back on an even keel. He had apparently kept his promise to Ben not to hang around with Brittany, and they were back to their regular "Cosby Show" nights and their outings together. Marta watched in bemusement the first time she saw Mary Jo arrive at Randy's house in a big Chevy Suburban. She counted five kids as they piled out and played in the yard.

After that she saw Mary Jo and her family often. Randy came to Marta and announced, "Mary Jo will be moving in, and we're going to try and make a relationship."

"The children too?" Marta asked. "How are you going to adjust to living with five little children?"

"I know about kids," he said calmly. Besides, he explained, Mary Jo shared custody with the children's father, so they wouldn't be living at his house all the time.

Six weeks after Randy Roth and Mary Jo Phillips

met, he asked her and her children to move in with him. She sold most of her furniture, preparing for a new life. She had raised dozens of exotic birds, and she had to sell off most of those, too. Mary Jo's apartment was about two miles from Misty Meadows, and the Goodwins followed Randy and his trailer and helped him move Mary Jo's belongings into his house. Randy had always been tremendously strong and lifted the heavy pieces easily.

Mary Jo brought a few of her favorite birds and her player piano. The birds were easy to move; the piano was not. Randy and Ben had to rig a pulley setup to move it up Randy's back steps.

Brittany, with her heart barely healing after Randy broke off with her, had to watch him move yet another woman into his house. No one realized just how much she was hurting—or why.

Just as they had when Randy was married to Donna Clift, the two couples socialized a lot. Either Ben and Marta went out to dinner with Randy and Mary Jo, or the Goodwins barbecued in their backyard. They hoped that Randy's relationship with Mary Jo would last longer than his abortive marriage to Donna; only a year had gone by, and it was summer again, but the roster of players had changed. Randy kept recasting the part of his fiancée-wife. Marta worried sometimes about Greg; he had no stability, no mother he could expect to be there for very long.

It wasn't until Mary Jo moved in with Randy that she learned about Janis Miranda Roth's death. Randy told her that the authorities were still investigating her tragic fall. Once again the actual details of Jan's demise changed in his retelling. Randy told Mary Jo that he and Jan had been climbing Mount Rainier. While they were high up on the 14,000-foot snow-capped peak, he said, Jan's ropes loosened, "I was holding her while she tried to retie her ropes. But she slipped out of my arms . . . and fell to her death."

Mary Jo, like all his other women, was shocked and saddened. What a terrible thing it must have been for Randy to see. Randy confided that he and Jan had had a troubled relationship. Although he had loved her, they had fought a lot. "She didn't appreciate me." None of his women had, he confided—until Mary Jo came along. Donna Clift, the third Mrs. Roth, had been "immature," according to Randy.

Randy seemed defiant about the law enforcement authorities who were allegedly still tracking him. (They were not.) "If they intend to charge me with anything, they only have a limited time to do so."

There is, of course, no statute of limitations on murder. If the Skamania County investigators chose to, they could have charged Randy Roth in his second wife's death when he was eighty years old.

Randy told Mary Jo that he had collected insurance money in Jan's death but that he had spent it unwisely. He wasn't used to having money, and he realized that he should have retained a financial planner.

Mary Jo and her children lived with Randy for four months. Once she was in his domain, she found him less romantic and much more dominating. He made it clear to her that certain areas in his home were off limits to her. Perhaps his discovery that Donna Clift had "snooped" into his papers and belongings had made him cautious. He was adamant that Mary Jo keep out of his things. She thought his demands a little odd, but she went along with them. The house was big, and she had no need to go into Randy's forbidden zones. And she still loved him; it was hard to forget the tender and imaginative lover who had courted her so beautifully.

Randy was the boss. He handled everything. He didn't even let her do the grocery shopping. Nevertheless, Mary Jo and Randy made plans to get married. One day, as they parked at one of the huge Fred Meyer stores, he asked her to go to the jewelry department and have her third finger measured so he could shop for a wedding ring. She knew everything was going to be fine with them after they were married.

There *were* a few more things that got in the way of their perfect relationship, however. Mary Jo had owned a rather lucrative day-care center with her ex-husband. After her divorce was final, she explained to Randy that she had handled her own property settlement, including the day-care assets. Randy was furious when he learned that she had not consulted him. He was angry, too, when she gave back to Donna Clift some clothing she had left at the house.

Mary Jo realized that she was not to make any decisions on her own. But she still adored Randy.

Mary Jo had an almost pathological fear of water, yet she let Randy coax her into going on a raft with him—and without a life jacket. The way he put it, it was a test, a way to prove her love for him.

One night Randy explained to Mary Jo that he had adequate life insurance and that she needed some, too. After all, they now had six children to consider if anything happened to either one of them.

Her heart sank.

Mary Jo had one secret she had not told Randy, something she had agonized over. She didn't want to lose him now that her life had suddenly become so full of love. Taking a deep breath, she told Randy her secret: she was not eligible for insurance. Mary Jo Phillips had been treated for cancer. She was not actively ill, and she had every hope that she would never have a reoccurrence. But she was definitely uninsurable. She studied his face and she saw no expression at all. He seemed to take it all right, and he didn't seem concerned about her cancer, either. At least not right away.

But within days Randy began to change toward Mary Jo. Where he had been warm and loving—if controlling—he became icy cold and distant. He never mentioned marriage again.

Mary Jo had kept a journal of their relationship; it was so beautiful in the beginning that she loved writing down all the wonderful surprises he gave her and all the romantic things he said. Later she wrote in it as a way to help her understand what had happened.

When Randy found out that Mary Jo had kept a journal, he told her it was "incriminating" and ordered her to destroy it. She did not.

Finally Mary Jo had no choice but to move out. Randy clearly didn't want her anymore. She had a heck of a time getting Randy to give her piano back.

9

Although Randy Roth almost always had a job—at Reynolds, at Vitamilk Dairy, at Cascade Ford, at Chuck Olson Chevrolet, and later at Bill Pierre Ford in Lake City—his life-style, his lavish homes, and all the adult toys he owned required more than his salary. His W2s for the 1980s indicated income that could not even have begun to cover his expenses:

1980	$22,412.93
1981	$33,100.00
1982	$28,300.00
1983	$16,951.00
1984	$29,201.00
1985	$30,912.00
1986	$24,830.00
1987	$26,432.00

The low figure for 1983 marked the time when Vitamilk put him on an on-call status. But most of Randy's big money had come from insurance payoffs. Within a few months of Jan's death, he had received $107,514.11 from two policies, and each month since her death, he had cashed monthly Social Security benefits checks of $419 for Greg as Jan's "surviving child," collecting almost $35,000 by the beginning of 1988. None of this money was legally reportable income.

Even the money Randy had loaned to Nick Emondi came back to him after Nick had a burglary and collected on his homeowner's insurance.

Randy was disappointed, however, in the outcome of his suit against the state of Washington. He had hoped to collect almost a million dollars, but after giving depositions, submitting to all kinds of questions, and wasting his time with a couple of lawyers, the suit was dismissed in 1988, and he got nothing.

Anyone with an ounce of deductive reasoning could recognize a pattern in Randy Roth's financial affairs. If ever a man believed in insurance, it was Roth. Even when his budget was tight, he had always found money to pay insurance premiums. His thinking was certainly sensible. He was the single father of a little boy, a man who apparently had no idea where Greg's real mother, Donna Sanchez, was. And insurance had paid off for him when he needed it.

After Mary Jo moved out, Randy continued to date; his choices were invariably divorcées or widows with children, and he always met his dates "cute" by sending Greg over as his advance emissary. He still saw Lily Vandiveer, although she didn't seem to be "his type." Those who knew both of them said Lily would have done anything in the world for Randy. But neither Lily nor any of his dates mattered enough for him to move them into his home.

Randy asked Marta Goodwin once if she and Ben

would like to go to a dance with him and a new woman he was dating, and Marta threw up her hands and said, "Randy! I'm not going to get attached to any more of the women you meet. I just get so I really like these gals and then you get rid of them!"

Randy laughed.

In the late spring of 1988 Randy was coaching T-ball for boys Greg's age. He was always involved in his son's sports activities—Little League baseball or whatever was in season. Some of the other parents called him "Super Dad" because he got so involved in the kids' games; some thought he was too rough on the boys and that he always forgot that games were only games.

Dina Clark's* son was on Randy's T-ball team. Dina was an extremely attractive young woman, a divorcée who lived in Mill Creek with her four children. She had ended her marriage despite the fact that she was expecting another baby.

"We were roller-skating at my kids' school, and Randy Roth started flirting with me. I was *pregnant,* for heaven's sake, but it didn't seem to bother him at all."

Dina found Randy attractive enough, although he was awfully short. "I remember he was wearing cowboy boots, and even then he was only about five feet six."

He was funny, though, and nice, and he insisted that he wanted to call her. He wheedled her address and phone number out of her. Randy did go to Dina Clark's house. She wasn't home, but the baby-sitter was. Years later Dina recalled what her baby-sitter had reported: "She said he stood in the front entrance, and then the phone rang and my answering machine picked it up. It was my boyfriend calling. I guess when Randy heard that, he decided I wasn't available, and he just backed out the door. He never called me again."

* * *

115

Randy and the Goodwins still lived next door to one another, and as he always had, he occasionally came up with secrets that shocked them. Ben had known Randy five years when he casually mentioned that his brother was in prison for murder.

"For *murder*?" Ben gasped. Randy had told Donna Clift about David, but he had sworn her to silence about his brother, and she had never told the Goodwins. "*Your* brother?"

"Yep."

"I didn't even know you had a brother. Why don't you ever go visit him? What happened?"

"Well," Randy began slowly, "my uncle was driving in Montana, going down the road, and he picked up this hitchhiker. The hitchhiker killed our uncle. About two years later my brother David was driving down I-5 [near Seattle] and he got up to about 128th Street—you know just about where you hit the Everett exit—and he picked up some guy hitchhiking. They were driving along, and this guy starts bragging about some old guy he killed in Montana. And it was our uncle. So my brother killed him, and they convicted David on circumstantial evidence."

Ben didn't know what to think. It was a pretty farfetched story, but then, he'd heard Randy tell some pretty good ones before. That was just a part of Randy he had to accept—wild tales out of left field.

Randy and Brittany Goodwin were still friends. In fact, as she grew from an awkward fifteen-year-old to a high school senior, he seemed to take a proprietary interest in her. He frowned on her dates with boys her age. On at least one occasion he disabled her car by removing the distributor cap so she couldn't join a group of her friends. Finally convinced that Randy wasn't hitting on Brittany, Ben and Marta had relaxed their rules a little. Randy, Brittany, Greg, and Ryan were kind of a foursome.

Whether Brittany and Randy were involved sexually or not—something her parents no longer suspected —they were together a lot. He took her and the boys bowling, swimming, and sometimes to a movie, and she listened raptly to all of his stories. In the summer of 1988 he explained to her exactly how he could rob his own house if he wanted to, collect the insurance, and make sure no one would ever find out. She didn't know whether to believe him or not. Randy liked to shock people.

During that same period Randy discussed a similar insurance scam with Nick Emondi. There were ways to do it and never get caught, Randy insisted. Emondi didn't encourage such conversation. It reminded him too much of the rainy Halloween night when Randy had asked him, "Could you kill your wife . . . if you had to?"

In truth, Nick was afraid of Randy, of the way he seemed to turn his imagination and his plans into reality. Randy Roth, for all his short stature, shared a kind of mystique with Charles Manson. He was smart, but it was more than that; Randy's gaze was so intense that it burned into your brain. He was a puppeteer, too, manipulating just the right strings to make his friends do his bidding or to convince them that things were not what they appeared to be.

Nick had always been ambivalent about Randy; he admired his guts and energy, but he feared him, too. On one occasion when Randy invited Nick to join him for a snowmobile trip into the backcountry, Nick was hesitant about going. He admitted to his wife, Carrie, that he was frightened—he never knew what Randy might do. "If I don't come back," he said, "tell somebody who I went with."

In September of 1988, Ben Goodwin had to go to California on business for a week. Ben was a notoriously light sleeper, perhaps a legacy of Vietnam.

117

"Nobody drives into this cul-de-sac at night without my waking up," he said.

Marta was the sound sleeper, although she never slept very well when Ben was gone. Then she was usually alert to even the slightest sounds in the night. Their three dogs were kenneled out in the backyard, and they barked if a twig snapped, so that was some comfort. Randy had his German shepherd, Jackson, chained in his yard too. The master bedroom where Marta slept was in the rear of the house only eight feet or so from Randy's backyard and the shed where he kept his tools and his weight-lifting equipment.

During the week that Ben was gone, Marta Goodwin and several of the neighbors noticed that Randy backed his truck up to his garage every night between nine and ten—after it was full dark. He loaded it up and then drove off somewhere. No one thought much about it; Randy often spent weekend days at the local swap meet, and Marta just assumed he was planning to sell some of his possessions. Another neighbor saw Randy take several loads away from his house after dark.

On September 17, two days before Ben returned, Randy Roth was the victim of a burglary. He reported to the Snohomish County Sheriff's Office that a truck had backed up to his house and stolen his property: valuable mechanics' tools, sanders, saws, both of his Stihl chain saws, and his Craftsman tool chest. Not only his work tools but also his home appliances were gone—cameras, television sets, Nintendos and other games, a Kenwood stereo, other music equipment. It was the sort of crime that could put a man who was a truck mechanic by trade out of business. In addition, the burglars had ripped his red wall-to-wall carpeting so that it would all have to be replaced.

Snohomish County Sheriff's Deputy Dean Munday responded to the scene. The investigating officer noted a deep groove in the grass of the Roth backyard and figured that the burglar's truck had gone in that way. He saw the broken garage window, the carpet that was stretched and ripped as if something heavy had been dragged across it, scratches on a banister. It looked like a typical residential burglary. There were so many of them in Snohomish County that it was hard for the detectives to keep up with them.

Randy asked Marta the next morning if she had heard "all the commotion" at his place the night before. She had heard nothing at all. He explained that he'd been robbed, and she was shocked. "I was in the bedroom," she said, amazed. "I was watching television until late. I didn't hear a thing. The dogs didn't even bark. That's really scary, to think I was so close."

Randy explained that Jackson was "passed out" on his deck. He was pretty sure somebody had drugged his dog. "He was gone when I got home last night. He came home this morning, dragging his chain. He's just lying there. He won't even respond to me."

When Ben Goodwin got home, he went over to see Randy and found him and Greg working on their motorcycles in the shed. "My God, Marta told me you were robbed! Are you okay?"

Randy was very calm. "Oh, yeah."

"Well, what happened?"

Randy pointed toward his yard. "See that track right there? That's where the truck backed in. They broke that window there in the garage, came in and took everything."

"Randy," Ben began, "that groove in your lawn is where you and I felled that tree."

Randy half smiled. "If that's what the detectives say it is, then that's what it is."

Ben was nonplussed. He had a suspicion that he didn't want to have. He knew Randy was probably hurting for money; he had just been terminated from Cascade Ford "by mutual agreement." And Randy seemed so calm about losing so many of his things. He explained that he and his friend Max Butts* had gone out to dinner and a movie, but that he had gotten home well before midnight. It was too late; almost everything he owned of value was gone.

Sixteen-year-old Brittany Goodwin didn't have to be told the details of Randy Roth's robbery. She already knew. She went to her parents and said, "Don't tell me how Randy was robbed. *I'll* tell *you*. Somebody backed a truck into his yard, right? And then they broke out a window in his garage, right? And all of his tools and things are gone? And I'll bet they tore his carpet up, too, didn't they?"

Ben and Marta nodded slowly.

"Well, I'll tell you that there's a storage locker someplace around here that's just packed full of all the things that Randy had 'stolen.' He was so worried about money, and he told me exactly what he could do to get some, but I thought he was only teasing me."

When Nick Emondi heard of Randy's robbery, he wasn't surprised either. But he knew when to keep his mouth shut.

Brittany Goodwin didn't go to the police. She was afraid, and her parents were afraid for her. They were beginning to wonder if the man who had been their friend for so many years wasn't who they thought he was at all. They didn't know what Randy might do in reprisal if they turned him in. Randy had always said, "I don't get mad; I get even," but that threat had seemed to be part of his macho posturing. Now they warned Brittany not to tell. When they thought about it, they realized that bad things seemed to happen to people who crossed Randy. Now they half believed the wild stories that he had told them over the years. He still lived so close to them that they could have tossed a penny onto his back deck with no effort at all.

Two months later Randy told Ben Goodwin that he had totaled up all his losses for his homeowner's insurance carrier, the Pioneer Insurance Company of

Minnesota. By his reckoning he was out close to $60,000.

Sixty thousand dollars! Ben felt the hair prickle at the back of his neck. *He* knew Randy's tools as well as Randy himself did—he'd always been free to borrow whatever he needed. And now Ben recognized the tool chest that Randy was using. *It was the same one he had reported stolen.* Ben also noted that Randy seemed to have his tools back.

Ryan Goodwin was puzzled to see that the Roths' "replacement" television set was the same brand, same size, same everything, as the stolen one. More than that, he and Greg had pasted stickers on Greg's Nintendo game. The "new" Nintendo didn't have stickers on it, but it had telltale glue marks in exactly the same places where the stickers had been on the "stolen" game. Besides that, the glue beads were the same shapes as the stickers. Ryan didn't mention this to his parents for a long time. Randy had been so mad at him the last time he told on him.

Randy had new carpeting; the ugly worn red rug that he had hated so was gone.

"At least Randy's got rid of that red carpet," Ben said sarcastically to Marta. She frowned and looked away.

When Randy filed his claim with Pioneer on November 11, he asked Ben if he would describe his missing tools to Pioneer's insurance adjuster. Ben agreed, feeling queasy about it—suspecting what he suspected. He didn't want to get involved at all. He didn't want to lie, but he sure didn't want to get on Randy's bad side.

The adjuster handed Ben pages of lists of tools and Ben spent twenty minutes checking off the tools he remembered that Randy had owned. He answered all the questions asked of him, but he didn't volunteer any information. The Pioneer adjuster was ready to leave when Marta asked him a general question about insurance—she had just lost her grandmother, whose insurance policies made her estate a complicated disaster.

"*I* didn't even talk to him after that first twenty minutes," Ben recalls. "Nobody mentioned Randy's claim after that, but the adjuster was here for over an hour, mostly talking to Marta and her mother. When I went out in the yard later, Randy walked over and said, 'What the *hell* were you talking about for an hour and a half with that guy?'"

"It was only about twenty minutes."

"Bull*shit*—I timed you."

When Ben finally confronted Randy about the fact that he seemed to have "found" all his missing tools, Randy looked at him without a flicker of expression and said, "These aren't the same tools."

They were neighbors still, but they were never close friends again. "He never really spoke to me again," Ben recalls.

Brittany tore up all of the pictures of Randy they had pasted in their albums over the years, all the Thanksgivings, Christmases, picnics, all the outings he and Greg had shared with her family. All those years of being so close.

She still kept some secrets to herself. If her father knew what Randy had done to her, she was afraid he would kill Randy.

Randy didn't seem to notice that the Goodwins avoided him, or, if he did, he didn't care.

The friendship was over. On both sides.

The Pioneer Insurance Company never attempted to prove that Randy Roth had not even had a burglary; they did, however, take issue with the $58,000 plus that he claimed was his loss. Claims adjuster Shelly Bierman first got suspicious when a receipt of sale that Randy provided for a stolen radio turned out to be a credit slip for the *return* of the described radio. Further, Roth was unable to provide documentation for many, many items he had lost. The insurance company felt the claims made were highly inflated over what they felt the actual loss had been. Pioneer filed a declaratory judgment action against Randy, alleging that his insurance claim was fraudulent.

Pioneer eventually settled with him on October 9, 1990, by paying Randy $28,500 and agreeing to dismiss its court action against him. All parties concerned submitted a stipulation and order of dismissal of claims "with prejudice."

Nothing about his "burglary" had gone smoothly for Randy. It had taken two years to collect, and he had to pay an attorney $11,000 of his settlement.

PART FIVE

Cynthia

10

Cynthia Rae Loucks was born a precious gift to her parents, Merle and Hazel. They had prayed for fourteen years to have "a darling little girl" to raise with their son. Her older brother, Leon, was in his teens when Cynthia was born. She was such a tiny little thing; she weighed only three and a half pounds.

One of the delivery room nurses ran down the hall to Merle Loucks and asked him if he believed in infant baptism. "I'm sorry," she said softly, "but we don't think the baby is going to make it."

Merle and Hazel Loucks's church did not believe in baptizing children until they had reached the age where they could make their own commitment to Christ, but he bent his head in prayer, "Lord, don't leave her go now. You have brought her this far. We want her."

The baby lived. After three weeks in an incubator, Cynthia weighed five pounds, and her parents were allowed to bring her home. She brought such joy and happiness to them.

After a scary start, Cindy Loucks thrived. She was a beautiful blond little girl, and she grew up to be a beautiful blond woman. She was raised in the church, and she did not depart from its teachings. They all attended the Westgate Chapel in Edmonds, Washington regularly. Merle Loucks was a deacon.

When Cindy and Tom Baumgartner were married in a church wedding, it was a union blessed by both sets of parents. No one ever dreamed that Tom would be dead of Hodgkin's disease in 1985 before he was thirty. Almost before he and Cynthia could cope with the diagnosis, the lymph node cancer swept all through his system like wildfire and he was gone.

Cynthia Baumgartner had never expected to be a widow, certainly not at twenty-seven. She was, quite naturally, overwhelmed at the responsibility of raising two lively little boys without a father. Her family and Tom's family were there to help, but the enormity of her loss was almost incomprehensible.

After six months Cynthia had to do something to fill up her days. She volunteered at her current church—the Silver Lake Chapel. It was, coincidentally, the same church where Janis Miranda Roth's memorial service had been held four years earlier. There Cynthia met the young woman who was to become her best friend: Lori.

Lori Baker was a pretty young woman, about Cindy's age, with short dark hair and glasses. She was employed at the Silver Lake Chapel as an administrator, and the two women talked a lot when Cynthia did her volunteer work. They had many interests in common. Cynthia wanted to get married again—someday. But it would be a long time before she could imagine finding anyone to compare with Tom. A widow with two children is not every man's dream woman; most men didn't want the responsibility of raising another man's children. Beyond that, Cynthia had restricted the possibilities of whom she might get serious about by ruling out divorced men. She would have to find a Christian man who was single or widowed.

But in 1985 Cindy wasn't looking. She just wanted to make a stable home for her boys who were only four and six. It made sense for Lori to share the house Cynthia owned at 2419 139th Street S.E. in Bothell.

She had no mortgage to pay; Tom had seen to that. Both women felt more secure at night, and there was always someone to stay with Tyson and Rylie. A month after they met, the two women moved in together. Lori paid rent, and they shared cleaning and cooking and friendship. They bowled in a league together, and they were pretty good, collecting trophies. They pooled their money to pay the expenses. They opened a joint bank account for convenience, and they also shared a safe-deposit box at the Everett Mutual Bank: box number 2212.

Cynthia had a new will drawn up in December of 1985, and she named Lori the executor and her chosen guardian to raise Tyson and Rylie if something should happen to her. She stipulated that the house they all lived in was to go to Lori, too, so that the boys could be raised in their own home. There were things of Tom's that she wanted the boys to have when they were older—his pocket watch, wedding ring, other jewelry. The will, the jewelry, certificates of deposit, and other important papers went into the safe-deposit box in Everett. Cindy didn't tell Lori about the will; it just made her feel better to know it was taken care of, and she trusted Lori implicitly. She saw no need to mention it; she had every reason to believe she would live to be an old woman and that Tyson and Rylie would be grown men who could take care of themselves.

The two young women and Cindy's two boys lived together in harmony for over five years. Cindy was active in her church and in Little League. She wanted her boys to be around masculine influence, and they loved playing ball.

Merle Loucks had worried about his daughter ever since Tom died. She was such a young widow, naive and trusting and comparatively wealthy. "Men may court you for your money," he had warned her gently. "Just be careful." She had promised him that she would be. And for five years Cindy was very careful.

Tom Baumgartner's father, Jim, talked to Cindy about her remarrying. "You're too young to raise those boys by yourself," he told her. "You should try to find a nice guy to marry, to raise the boys and provide a father image."

"I'm looking," Cindy would say, smiling, "but I can't find any good guys out there. They're all just looking for the same thing—if you know what I mean."

Cindy Baumgartner and Lori Baker were like family, like sisters. Lori's mom, Dorothea Baker, taught piano, and Rylie had been one of her students for three years. His grandparents had bought him a piano. Dottie Baker found Cindy "very lovely, very pretty, very happy. Wherever she was, laughter just entered the room. She was just—*life.*"

Cindy took good care of herself so that she made the most of her natural beauty; she had her hair lightened regularly and her nails done professionally. She dressed in a very feminine way, and her person was as immaculate as her house was.

Cindy helped out at Little League wherever they needed her, whether it was as a coach or manning the concession stand. In 1990 she took over the stand. She made sure it was fully stocked and that different parents took turns selling hot dogs, cold drinks, popcorn, and potato chips.

Randy Roth was still a coach in the ten-to-twelve-year-old league. Some of the parents really liked his win-win-win attitude. Some called him "Super Dad" because they admired him, and some did it in a sarcastic way and were put off by the way he criticized kids for mistakes and shouted constantly. He took Little League so seriously; he was, in fact, the quintessential Little League parent who seemed to have his child in the game not for the *child* but to fulfill his own needs.

Practice started in March of 1990, six weeks before their first scheduled game. In the ensuing weeks, teams would be set up and players assigned to their positions.

Randy Roth met thirty-three-year-old Cindy Baumgartner the same way he had met almost every woman who would become important in his life—through his son. At first they just made small talk when Randy bought things for Greg at the concession stand. Later it was Randy's turn to help man the concession stand. He and Cindy got along so well that he arranged to work the stand with her every night for a week. The other parents grinned when they saw how attracted Randy was to Cindy.

He almost missed meeting her. In the spring of 1990 Cindy was thinking seriously of selling her home and moving to Arizona so that she could live closer to her parents' winter home. Meeting Randy Roth changed all of her plans.

Cindy liked him right away. He was handsome and he was fun. And, most important, he really seemed to care about his son and about all the kids who'd turned out for Little League. He was a widower, he explained, and Cindy must have smiled inwardly. No matter how much she cared about a man, she would never have married a divorced man.

Randy's approach to Cindy Baumgartner was humble. "I noticed you right from the beginning," he said. "But the way you look, the way you dress, I figured you probably had money. I didn't feel worthy to introduce myself."

Before Cindy could protest, he hurried on. "But then I saw you drove an Escort—and I drive an Escort too, and I figured anybody driving an Escort couldn't be rich, so I felt I *could* introduce myself."

When he asked her out the next week, she accepted readily. Lori Baker and her mother could see that Cindy was really interested in this man. "She told me that she had met Mr. Right, and she was excited," Dottie said. "Her idea of a husband was a man who had to be one that had never been married or who was a widower. He said he was a widower. He was just what she had been looking for."

Lori met Randy when he came to the house to pick Cindy up, and she saw that he was very attractive and very taken with Cindy. He showered Cindy with red roses and phone calls and notes. But Cindy's best friend and her family were concerned. "Cindy did have money," Dottie Baker recalled. "She did own her home, and her husband had left her well taken care of. This man was just coming into her life *way* too fast. Cindy was such a sharp girl—level-headed—and just thought about everything carefully. I wondered why she was rushing into this."

Cindy was amazed at how much she and Randy had in common. They both had their boys, of course, and the problems of raising them alone. Randy said he'd come originally from North Dakota, just as Merle Loucks had. They were both involved in baseball, neither of them smoke or drank, and they were family oriented. If Cindy Baumgartner had drawn up a blueprint for the kind of man she wanted for a husband, it would have been the Randy Roth she met in the summer of 1990. They dated, but most of their dates included the boys. Randy was always a perfect gentleman with her, affectionate but never aggressive about sex.

They went to the Strawberry Festival in Marysville, just north of Everett, and had a wonderful time. After that, Cindy invited Greg to spend the night at her house. The boys got along. They went skating, to the movies. It seemed the most normal thing in the world for Cynthia to start cooking supper for them all afterward. Somehow they just seemed to fit—as if they were two halves of a family seeking each other.

Haltingly Randy told Cindy about his wife who had died. "She actually died as I was holding her in my arms," he said. "She left me with a three-year-old boy, and I've been alone ever since, looking for someone like you."

Cindy saw they had the same beliefs, the same respect for marriage. Randy told her that he had been thinking about going to church, even though he had turned his back on religion after he lost Janis. "There has to be more to God, but I think I'm getting there."

Cindy explained to Randy that he had just met another of her personal prerequisites. For her to love a man, he had to be a strong Christian. "My church means more to me than any man. If you want to go to church with me, fine."

"I think that's what I've been looking for for so long." He smiled.

Cindy's parents, Tom's parents, and the Bakers all wanted Cindy to be happy. And yet they were worried that things were moving too fast. Cindy had been cautious all her life, and now she was absolutely enthralled with a man she had known only a few months.

The Goodwins saw that Randy had a new girlfriend, but it wasn't like the old days when he would have brought her right over to meet them. His latest girlfriend was a cute little blonde, they noted, and she often called out a friendly "Hi!" over the fence when she visited Randy's home in Misty Meadows. Cindy drove a little black Ford Escort, and they knew Randy had bought one just like it that spring. Randy made no move to introduce them. And there were certainly no more double dates or barbecues.

Randy kept Cindy to himself. By the time he started dating Cynthia Baumgartner in the summer of 1990, the Goodwins were almost completely estranged from him. They believed he had faked the burglary of his own home, and they suspected that he had lied to them about many things. Randy was angry because he thought that they had cooperated with the insurance company against him, a misconception on his part.

The friendship they had once enjoyed had been based—at least on Randy's part—on deceit. The Goodwins would eventually come to learn that he had broken the most sacred trust anyone could with a parent and then lied about it as blandly as he lied about everything else he did.

And so, as he began his intense courtship of Cynthia Baumgartner, his former best friends could only observe from a distance.

"We only met Cindy once over the fence. She was standing in Randy's yard, and he'd gone off to do something. They had just become engaged. She showed us her ring," Marta said. "Ben said something, and Cindy looked surprised and said, 'Well, what's the matter?' and Ben repeated, 'All I want to say is just be very careful. Just be very careful about what you're doing.'"

Cindy Baumgartner looked at Ben Goodwin as if she thought he was crazy. And then she turned and went to find Randy. She undoubtedly found his neighbors a little odd and could understand why Randy wanted nothing to do with them.

When the Goodwins learned that Cindy had two boys, they were worried. They couldn't imagine any mother allowing her sons to be treated the way Randy treated Greg. Did Cindy know about the garbage can incidents, the rages, the military discipline? They couldn't tell her. They could only hope that she would become disillusioned, as Mary Jo had—and as Donna had—and get out before she was in too deep.

But Cindy was in love. She was deeply impressed with Randy's warmth and kindness, with the devotion he showed his son, and with the way he had taken her boys under his wing.

Toward the end of July 1990, Randy asked Cindy if she would like to go to Reno with him for a classic car show and parade. At first she had a sinking feeling. Oh, no. Was he going to turn out to be like all the other guys she'd complained about to her father-in-law—out for only one thing? Probably. He had just taken longer to ask. Knowing that she might see her wonderful romance evaporate in a moment, Cindy explained to Randy that she would never travel overnight with a man she wasn't married to.

Randy's response was that it wouldn't be a problem. They were all getting along so well, and the boys were getting along so well, that he thought they should think about marriage. She wondered if he was proposing. Randy used so many words to say something where most men spoke in simple sentences, and he sometimes had such a roundabout way of speaking. While she let hope bubble up in her heart, Randy just kept talking about how well their families blended.

Finally Cindy blurted, "Are you asking me to marry you? If you are, the answer is yes!"

Randy grinned and then immediately called an 800 number for a list of wedding chapels in Reno.

They had been dating only a little over a month.

Making such a momentous decision in a heartbeat was completely unlike Cindy, but she felt it was the right one. Her parents were visiting in North Dakota. Even her former in-laws, the Baumgartners, were away on vacation. But this was *her* decision. She wanted to marry Randy, and she wanted to go to Reno with him. It seemed like such a romantic adventure and such a wonderful way to start a marriage.

There probably wasn't a debater in the world who could have talked Cindy Baumgartner out of her decision to become Mrs. Randy Roth. Lori Baker and her mother begged Cindy to at least wait until her parents got home. But it didn't do any good. Cindy believed in Randy and she loved him. She had, of course, no idea that she would be the *fourth* Mrs. Randy Roth. She believed that she had found a man who had suffered the loss of a spouse, just as she had, a man who had never been divorced, a man who adored her and who would care for her forever.

They drove to Reno and walked up and down the street hand in hand admiring the gleaming, perfectly restored cars from other places in time. It was August 1, 1990. Their wedding day.

When they drove home as husband and wife, Cindy tried to find a way to cushion the shock of this sudden marriage for her parents and her former in-laws. The Louckses and the Baumgartners were poleaxed. They could scarcely believe that Cindy had chosen to get married in a gaudy "marriage mill"—a commercial chapel in Reno instead of in a religious ceremony in a church. They barely knew the man she had married. They worried, but most of all, they wanted her to be happy.

Swallowing their disappointment and their concern, Jim and Marge Baumgartner went to Cindy's house to meet Randy and welcome him into the family. Jim moved to give Randy a hug. The older man felt awkward when Randy stood motionless and did not return the greeting. He showed no emotion at all. In fact, he said nothing. A little nonplussed, Jim Baumgartner tried again, inviting Randy and Cindy to come to his house anytime and to bring all three of the boys. Randy brushed off the invitation.

"After that visit, I asked him many times to come for dinner, but he would never come over," Jim said. "Cindy brought the boys, but she always came alone."

Well, maybe it was understandable, Jim decided. Maybe Randy didn't want to be haunted by the memories of Cindy's first husband. Maybe he was just insecure, afraid he wouldn't measure up to the kind of man Tom had been.

They had married in such haste that Randy and Cindy hadn't even decided where they were going to live. Either of their homes was big enough to hold the two of them and their three boys, but Cindy's was a little larger, a little more expensive. Either way, either house, they would have to do extensive remodeling to accommodate all of them. And then, of course, there was Lori, who would have to find another place to live. Cindy didn't want to rush her; Lori and she had weathered some bad times together, and they would be friends for the rest of their lives.

Finally they agreed that it would be best for Randy and Greg to move into Cindy's house. The newlyweds lived with Lori and the three boys until Lori found her own place. They got along well enough. Lori was glad to see Cindy so happy.

After a little painting and refurbishing, Randy put his house in Misty Meadows up for sale, asking $175,000. The figure was way too high for the real estate market in the Seattle area in 1990. Although Randy had added the workshop and landscaped the yard beautifully, he really couldn't expect to get $100,000 more for his house than he had paid for it only six years before. Maybe he just set a high figure so that Cindy wouldn't notice the discrepancy in value between his house and hers. Cindy was far better established financially than Randy was.

11

After Lori moved out, Cindy and Randy lived in her house for a while, but then they decided they wanted a place of their very own, a new house in which to start their new marriage. After church on Sundays, they looked at several places and found exactly what they wanted in Woodinville, a small town just south of the Snohomish County line. Woodinville, once isolated, was being swallowed up in the nineties in the huge urban sprawl on all sides of

Seattle. In another era, the house they chose would have been a farmhouse—it even *looked* like a farmhouse—but this house was brand new, a sunny yellow two-story with multi-paned bay windows, brick trim, and a three-car garage. It had a little front porch with a railing, and room for a swing and a rocking chair. The lot was huge and surrounded by trees—alders and, farther back, Douglas firs. There were a few ancient apple trees, the last vestiges of the farm the development had once been.

The house at 15423 232nd N.E, cost $275,000, a big jump up for both of them, but they loved it so, and it would be the perfect place to raise three rambunctious boys. Cindy's home sold almost immediately for $160,000. That sale closed simultaneously in October with the purchase of their new Woodinville house. So it was all Cindy's money that they paid down on the new house. The monthly payment would be $1,400—a hefty amount, but they felt they could manage; Tyson and Rylie's Social Security survivor's benefits of almost $1,500 could take care of it.

When Randy got his insurance settlement from Pioneer, he wrote a check for $11,000 into the house account, but Cindy wrote him one back for $10,000 right away. They were essentially living on Cindy's money. And, in truth, Randy retained control of his insurance payoff from Pioneer, which was only about $18,000 after his lawyer had taken his percentage. It was a big step down from the $60,000 he had sought originally.

Randy's house didn't sell at $175,000 or at $149,000. Eventually he dropped the price to $135,000 and it sold, but he stubbornly refused to throw in the shed he had built in the back. He demanded an extra thousand for the structure, or he threatened to have it moved. The buyer wouldn't budge. Apparently, Randy discovered how much it would cost him to move it, because he made a last visit to the Goodwins. Would they pay a thousand for it? Ben said he could use it, but he couldn't go that high. It was almost Christmas, and he needed the money for other things.

Marta bought the shed from Randy for $500 for Ben's Christmas present, and the two men who had been best friends but were no longer, moved the shed across the property line into the Goodwin's yard. They were like two strangers working together now; it seemed odd to Ben Goodwin to think that their camaraderie was completely gone.

Refusing to throw the shed into the house deal was a spiteful thing to do to the new buyers, but Randy was funny about money. It meant so much to him that he didn't seem to care what lengths he had to go to to get it.

After eight Christmases spent together, the Goodwins celebrated without Randy. It seemed kind of hollow. They kept asking themselves how things could have gone so wrong. They were happy for him that he had a new wife, and they liked Cindy—what they had seen of her—but they were afraid for her too. And they could not even say why or what it was they feared.

Randy had a number of debts—at least that was what he told his bride. Although he realized almost $50,000 after the sale of his Misty Meadows home, he didn't put any of the money toward the mortgage on the Woodinville house. Cindy's money had made the huge down payment, and Cindy's sons' Social Security survivor's benefits was making the monthly payment. Perhaps for the first time in his life, Randy was free to buy all the cars, trucks, motorcycles, and ATVs he wanted.

It didn't matter to Cindy. They were a family now, and her assets were Randy's, just as he had assured her that she now shared in everything he owned. He didn't want her to work outside their home. He would work as much overtime as he could at Bill Pierre Ford.

Lori Baker took her papers and valuables out of the safe-deposit box she had shared with Cindy, and

Randy's name was added. Lori noted that Tom's pocket watch and Cindy's important papers remained in the box.

When they moved to the yellow house in Woodinville in the autumn of 1990, Randy informed Cindy that he didn't want her taking the boxes of things that had been Tom's—clothes, sports equipment, memorabilia, things she was saving for the boys. She asked Jim Baumgartner if she could store Tom's stuff at his house, and of course he agreed. But he felt a chill. He thought it was peculiar that a man wouldn't let his stepsons have the comfort of their dead father's things. Naturally, Jim was afraid of losing contact with his beloved grandsons. But it was more than that. He hated to see Randy Roth calling all the shots. Cindy had been a feisty, happy young woman who made up her own mind. Now she seemed to follow every order her new husband gave her.

The Baumgartners had always gone to watch Tyson and Rylie play in their Little League games, and they continued to do so. Cindy and the boys were always glad to see their grandparents, but Randy scarcely acknowledged them. He spent his time shouting at Greg, Tyson, and Rylie when they made an error or struck out. He routinely refused the Baumgartners' invitations to go out to eat together afterward. It was clear he was deliberately snubbing them.

Cindy took her boys to see their paternal grandparents as often as she could. She always had some excuse why Randy hadn't been able to come with them—but Jim and Marge Baumgartner knew. He obviously wanted nothing to do with them.

During the fall of 1990, despite Randy's sometimes boorish behavior, Cindy Baumgartner Roth was a very happy young woman—happy in her marriage, happy with her new life. She was kept busy decorating the huge house in Woodinville and driving the boys to all of their myriad activities. She and the boys attended the Four Square Church in Everett or the Silver Lake Chapel, and sometimes she persuaded Randy to come with them.

Cindy chose mauve and blue for her basic color scheme in their new house. It went well with the gray carpet. They bought a lot of new furniture, choosing oak for the coffee tables, the wall units, and the display cabinet for Cindy's doll collection. Where Randy's homes had always been clean, but bare of any decorative details beyond marine gear and sports plaques and photographs, Cindy added many homey touches to the new house. She chose comfortable couches with mauve and blue throw pillows, hanging baskets of mauve or blue artificial flowers, blue candles, and framed prints in the same complementary colors. The decor was "country cottage," in keeping with the house, and Cindy delighted in finding new things that made it even prettier, like the straw wall hangings with lace and artificial flowers.

The master bedroom had a king-size bed with a ribbon-edged pale mauve spread with a tiny white flower pattern. The pillow shams and throw pillows matched. Behind the bed, they had a huge wall unit with a mirror and storage units for each of them.

In deference to the men in her life, Cindy was glad to let Randy decide what went into the upstairs recreation room. That would be the "guys' room." There went the console television, the VCR, the Nintendo, the drum set, the Exercycle, the baseball team pictures, the trophies, and of course Randy's Marine Corps memorabilia. On the wall he tacked a bright red Marine Corps banner bearing the legend "FMF, 3 ENGR BN SPT CO." It didn't match anything, but it made him happy, so what did it matter?

In every other house he had lived in, Randy had set about immediately to landscape the yards. Their Woodinville house had no landscaping and offered great possibilities. The yard was scrubby crabgrass, and there was a problem on one side with drainage, but one that could have been fixed with a French drain. There were no shrubs, flowers, or roses. There was only the partial fence of horizontal white boards and two giant rocks that sat on either side of the driveway. But Randy made no effort to work in the yard. He didn't plant grass, and he didn't plant a single rosebush. He complained that the yard was "a swamp," and he seemed to have no interest in changing that.

It was almost as if he didn't plan to be there long enough to bother.

Randy left Bill Pierre Ford for two months in November and December and took a job "in management" with Washington State. "My job requirements mandated that I work with the public—make inspections of vehicles . . . make adjustments."

The job had a rotating schedule. Sometimes he worked eight to four, sometimes noon to eight. "I was uncomfortable with the change of schedule," Randy recalled. "It was creating a hardship on my family. We were newly married, and we had adjustments. I indicated to my employer that I wasn't suited for an office job."

Randy recalled later that they were all "involved with family and the holidays" at the end of 1990. In his memory of the first six months of his marriage, *nothing* was more important than family. He was not about to leave Cindy and the boys alone at night in their semi-isolated country home. Their family time together was so important to him.

They were in their new house for Christmas of 1990, their first as a married couple. Actually, Randy and Cindy hadn't even known each other at Christmas of 1989. Many of Randy's friends were surprised to learn that he was married. The arrival of a Christmas card with a picture of the new family was the first clue for most of them that he *had* married again.

Cindy invited Lori and the Bakers over for Christmas, and they all celebrated together. Things seemed fine.

After Christmas Randy returned to his mechanic's job with Bill Pierre, and to more regular working hours.

Cindy Roth was not the kind of woman to spill private secrets of her married life, but the people who knew her well sensed a quiet unhappiness in her that seemed to begin after Christmas. While she had been blissful in the first few months after her marriage, she no longer was. She still went shopping with Lori Baker every Friday night, but her whole personality seemed muted, diminished. While the women shopped, Cindy's boys went with Greg and Randy and helped clean up the shop floor at Bill Pierre Ford.

Dottie Baker, too, noticed that Cindy seemed changed. When she gave Rylie his piano lesson at four every Wednesday afternoon, as she had for years, she was shocked to see that Cindy was no longer the bubbly, joyful woman she had known. In all the years Dottie had known Cindy, her house had always been spotless. Now, in the first gray winter months of 1991, the house was still neat, but there was dust on the new furniture, and the floors were not as spotless as they had always been. Cindy herself seemed drabber and less well groomed. She was letting her blond hair go, and the roots were her natural brown, and she hardly wore any makeup. Cindy had always worn earrings and other jewelry to match her outfits, but she no longer bothered.

Cindy didn't explain these changes to Dottie, but the truth was that Randy didn't approve of bleached hair, so reluctantly Cindy was letting it go back to its natural color. Also, Randy was outraged when he found out how much she paid to have her nails done. Cindy had always enjoyed having long, perfectly polished nails. She even had a tiny "diamond" applied to one—a custom manicure. After her marriage, she still went to have her nails done, but she paid half by check and half in cash, and the color of the polish had to meet with Randy's approval. She paid partly in cash when she had her hair cut, too. That way, Randy wouldn't know how much it had cost.

If it occurred to her that they were living in a magnificent house paid for with *her* money, that they derived a healthy part of their monthly income from *her* sons' Social Security benefits from their father, and that she had money saved on her own and had every right to spend a little of it on herself, she never mentioned it to anyone.

Cindy seemed chastened, afraid to speak up, always looking to Randy for approval before she spoke. Any woman who had ever been involved with Randy Roth could have warned Cindy that he was *the boss*. Whatever else mattered in any relationship he had, the most important thing the woman had to remember was that Randy ran things. He did not believe in women's liberation, and woe be unto any woman who argued about that.

Cindy was discovering that, just as all the others had. The romance vanished and the dictator emerged. Each time she bent a little to accommodate Randy's views, he pushed her a little further. And, because she believed in being the kind of wife who made her husband happy, she bent still further. She was not allowed to join a health club because she might "meet men there." Randy, however, *did* join a health club where dozens of attractive young women in their teens and twenties exercised with the men. Randy still left the house whenever he pleased without saying where he was going. He still spent long hours at Lily's house whenever he took her son home after he had visited with Greg.

Cindy was allowed to join the North Shore YWCA to take females-only aerobics classes and join walking groups; Randy deplored excess fat on women. Cindy had perhaps five extra pounds around the middle, and Randy never let her forget it. Her walking group met three times a week in the morning, and the women walked four or five miles. To the other members, basically strangers, Cindy seemed cheerful and friendly, and she quickly got into very good shape. She mentioned she was married and had children, but she didn't elaborate.

When Cindy signed up at the Y, she stressed to the business office that all mailings must be in her husband's name. "He has this thing about everything being in his name," she said half apologetically. He had been angry when she received catalogs addressed to Cindy Baumgartner. Even a flier addressed to Cindy Roth rather than Mrs. Randy Roth would upset him.

What a jerk, the girl at the desk thought. *Has to have his name even on some silly little fliers from the Y.* She didn't say anything to Cindy Roth.

Randy Roth recalls early 1991 as a hectic but happy time. "After the holidays, on New Year's, we loaded up the kids and went down to my dad's new place. . . .

"The next baseball season, 1991, was quite a trial for all of us. Three boys, three practices, three different game sites. She [Cindy] would go grocery shopping between dropping the boys off for practice. I would pick up Rylie and take him to piano lessons."

They all went to a couple of weeks of tryouts and then two days of drafting players. They were among the parents who were truly involved in Little League, and they had to cajole and argue to get help from less enthusiastic families. They still needed managers and coaches. Tyson and Rylie played their games at the main field complex, and the older boys, including Greg, played at the field on Highway 9 on the way to Everett. Regular Little League games ended in the middle of June, and All-Stars were picked by the coaches to go on to the championship competition. Greg was chosen as an All Star, and Randy was very proud.

Five of the mechanics from Bill Pierre Ford joined up to work as a pit crew for local car race competition, too. It was indeed a busy spring.

Maybe that was part of the reason Cindy Roth seemed less bubbly and energetic to her old friends and her family. Compared to her old routine, being married to a human dynamo like Randy must have been exhausting. Randy had a schedule that few men could have handled. He wanted things organized, neat, and he was frenetically busy all the time—sports, racing, work. He wanted his wife slim, trim, and obedient. He spent money—*her* money—freely, buying cars and other adult toys. He also bought ATVs, four-wheelers, for all three boys, with helmets and gloves to match.

One of the things Randy had been concerned about soon after his marriage to Cindy was life insurance. They were married on August 1, 1990, and in October of that year Randy approached Cindy about the situation. He was worried about their boys. He told her that he had had $100,000 worth of life insurance with Prudential since 1985. His beneficiary, he said, was his father, Gordon, whom he could count on to care for Greg and, if the worst should happen, for Tyson and Rylie, too. Cindy explained that she already had a $115,000 policy on her life with New York Life, all paid up.

Randy shook his head worriedly. How far would $215,000 go toward caring for and educating three boys? With the rate of inflation and considering the hefty payments on their $115,000 mortgage, Randy felt they were underinsured. The way he explained it, Cindy could see his point.

He told her that he hadn't been very happy with his own insurance agent's performance in the past, and she suggested they call her agent, Bruce Timm, who represented New York Life. She had been very happy with Timm's sensitivity and professionalism when Tom Baumgartner died. Since Tom had died within two years after his policy was issued, there was a fairly thorough investigation before her claim was paid. But it had been patently and tragically clear that Tom had died of rapidly progressing Hodgkin's disease— something the medical records supported—and Bruce Timm had helped Cindy through all the red tape as quickly as he could.

When the Clifts learned that Randy had remarried, Donna and her stepmother, Judy, had an ominous feeling. Although it had been four years since the rafting incident on the Skykomish River, Donna still panicked when she thought about it.

Judy Clift looked at Donna and murmured, "That poor woman. I have a terrible feeling that she'll be dead within a year."

"I wanted to look her name up in the phone book," Donna says. "I wanted to call her and tell her to run, to hide, or just to be careful, or think of some way to warn her. But what would I say? She probably would have thought I was jealous. Oh, how I wish I had."

If Donna Clift *had* called her, Cindy Roth probably would have been mortified. She didn't even know Donna existed. She had no idea that Randy had been divorced after he was widowed. Had she known, she never would have married him. He would have broken the very first rule she had about a potential mate.

But there were so many things she didn't know about Randy. As January and February of 1991 passed, the Gulf War seized the headlines, and there was a war of a different kind in the perfect home in Woodinville, Washington. Nobody knew how bad things were. Nobody knew how many terrible secrets Cindy Roth was learning. Her skin and her hair grew duller and drabber, and her housekeeping continued to falter. She had never been sick, but now she was often ill. She had always been happy and optimistic about life.

She no longer was.

On July 17, 1991, Cindy gave little clue to her real feelings in a letter to Tom's mother. She explained that Randy's uncle—who had just celebrated his fiftieth wedding anniversary—had been killed in a tragic accident. The whole family had been in a "dizzy state."

Randy's father had been working on the hot-tub behind the yellow house, but was having trouble getting it wired so the function switch worked properly, Cindy wrote. She thanked "Dad Baum" for buying all the wires, but insisted that that was far too generous a "house warming gift." Cindy wrote that she and Randy wanted to pay for at least part of the cost.

Cindy closed her letter as effervescently as she always did, "Thanks bunches and bunches. We love you. Give me a call when you get home. We'll work something out to get up to the cabin . . . August 1st or 4th, we're going to Reno for our anniversary."

The Baumgartners were vacationing in the latter half of July, and so were Cindy's parents, Merle and Hazel Loucks—just as they had been the year before when Cindy and Randy eloped to Reno. Now Cindy had suggested that she and Randy should return to the place they had been married. Perhaps she was hoping to rekindle the romantic love that had vanished from their marriage. She had not the faintest notion of how many other women had tried to do the same thing.

PART SIX

July 23, 1991

12

King County detective Sue Peters was on call for Major Crimes on the evening shift after the hottest day of the summer, July 23, 1991. The temperature had rocketed up to 99 degrees at four that afternoon, an almost unheard of heat wave. In western Washington, summer evenings were usually comfortably cool no matter what the day's heat had been, but at 7:30 P.M. it was still baking. Five minutes later Peters received a call from her sergeant, Spence Nelson, to respond to Idylwood Park on Lake Sammamish on a possible drowning. The victim was a female. That was all the information that was immediately available.

Peters went into service, and a marine unit came on the radio to report that no one involved was left on the scene. Peters drove to Precinct Three, arriving at a little after eight, and called Marine Officer Elaine Hood, who had been on the scene shortly after 911 was notified. Hood said that a woman had drowned in Lake Sammamish. Apparently she had been rafting or swimming with her husband. At any rate, she had been clinging to a raft when a powerboat raced by and its wake overturned the raft. She said, "The victim was blue. The husband refuses an autopsy."

It was the beginning. Sue Peters had no reason to think she was embarking on a particularly unusual case, beyond the fact that the raft had come in to shore with water in it and water-sodden items in the bottom. Hood reported that some of the witnesses had reported that the husband's demeanor was rather strange. Drownings on a hot summer day were tragically predictable around Seattle. Unused to hot, sunny days, northwesterners flocked to lakes and waterways during unusually warm weather, and a lot of them couldn't swim. They leapt into inner tubes, rafts, jerry-built boats or Styrofoam paddleboards without life preservers, and too often they slipped off and drowned in water still cold from mountain snow runoff.

Peters jotted down some notes. The victim's name —not yet released to the media—was Cynthia Roth, no age given. Her husband was known only as Mr. Roth. Driving his own vehicle, he had followed the Bellevue Medic One rig in which paramedics continued giving CPR to his wife. At Overlake Hospital in Bellevue, the victim had been pronounced dead at 1835 hours—6:35 P.M.—by Dr. David M. Roselle.

There were probably a hundred witnesses to the drowning; the park had been packed with people all day. There were lifeguards on duty, sunbathers, swimmers, and fifty to sixty boats zipping around the north end of Lake Sammamish when the drowning occurred. Sue Peters hoped that she could find enough of them to get the true story.

Peters started by placing a call to Overlake Hospital. She learned that Detective Larry Conrad of the Redmond Police Department and Mr. Roth had already left the hospital. It was seventeen minutes after eight. Roth had seemed in control, although the staff on duty had noted that he did nothing to comfort the two weeping children who sat in the quiet room only a few feet from him. The two little boys had been seen by a grief counselor, and it was hoped that they and their father would be able to cope with their terrible loss.

Larry Conrad was easy to locate. He was at Redmond Police headquarters finishing his paperwork.

Peters could sense immediately that Conrad was feeling hinky about the case. The Roths had apparently been out on the lake in an inflatable raft, he reported. The woman had gone swimming and developed a leg cramp, the raft had flipped as she clung to it, and she had lost consciousness before her husband could pull her into the raft and row for shore to find help. Officers at the beach had gotten the impression that the raft had been swamped by a speedboat, but in Mr. Roth's first statement to Conrad at the hospital, he said he didn't think the boater was at fault, estimating the speedboat was at least 50 yards away from them.

"Roth said his wife could swim better than he could," Conrad finished.

Sue Peters knew that people expressed grief in different ways, and she knew what shock could do. She hadn't met Mr. Roth yet—but she intended to. For the moment, she arranged to pick up any physical evidence, including the raft, as soon as possible.

Conrad told Peters that Roth was upset when Dr. Roselle explained that his wife's body would have to be held for the medical examiner's office.

But that was the law.

Detective Conrad had taken the first statement from Roth, whose full name was Randolph G. Roth. Roth said he had been waiting for someone "with some authority," and he seemed relieved to meet the Redmond detective. Conrad noted that Roth's vehicle was an Isuzu Trooper II and that the folded-up raft and the paddles were in the rear of the Trooper, and he had seen at least one plastic sack containing wet towels and/or garments. Roth had appeared calm, but both of the boys, who appeared to be about eight and ten, had cried inconsolably.

It wasn't the facts of the tragedy that bothered Conrad, however; it was the affect of the widower. Randy hadn't seemed grief-stricken. The two little boys were hysterical—but not the guy. At the hospital, the raft had been taken into evidence, and this had seemed to infuriate Roth. "He became very agitated and angry," Conrad told Sue Peters. "He said we had no right to take it."

Randy Roth had given a written statement to Conrad at a few minutes after seven, repeating the same basic facts of the tragedy. One minute Cindy had been alive and clinging to their raft, albeit with a cramp. The next, the raft had flipped over on top of her and by the time he had righted the raft and pulled her in, she was no longer breathing. "He wrote out a statement," Conrad told Sue Peters. "I'll get it over to you."

Early the next morning, Sue Peters called the King County Medical Examiner's Office and asked to have a copy of the autopsy report on the victim. And then she started going down the list of possible witnesses. In any shocking event, different witnesses perceived things differently. She wondered what she might hear from those who saw the "blue" woman lying on the beach at Idylwood Park the afternoon before.

The Redmond Police Department had written the case up as Accidental Death—Case 91-4177.

A possible accident? Or a possible homicide? All Sue Peters had to go on at this point was a detective who felt hinky about a widower's demeanor. It wasn't much, but it was enough to keep her from writing the case off as "Accidental" in the county files.

Sue Peters designated it as a "Death Investigation." The King County Police number was 91-225773. Peters would begin by contacting the people who had been at the beach on that tragic Tuesday afternoon, and trying to find the victim's relatives and friends. Peters asked the media relations officers to distribute green fliers on the east side of Lake Washington, particularly in the Lake Sammamish area and beyond. She was seeking anyone who might corroborate

Randy Roth's story. It shouldn't be difficult to find witnesses. The tragedy was the talk of the east side.

The *Journal American*, published in Bellevue, the largest city close to Lake Sammamish, ran the headline "Woman Drowns in Lake Sammamish" on July 24. The thrust of the story was that there were so many people in the park that no one realized Cynthia "Ross" had drowned until they saw the aid units arrive. One witness, Pam Chicoine, was quoted: "There were so many people down on the beach, I don't see how anyone could have seen it. It certainly makes you wonder how these three lifeguards will be able to see every accident."

The reporter acknowledged that the drowning had occurred far from the area protected by lifeguards and said that the lifeguards *had* jumped in when the woman was finally brought to shore. Still, there was just the merest suggestion that Cynthia Roth had drowned because the popular park lacked adequate safety precautions and was understaffed.

Redmond Police Sergeant George Potts told the paper that the dead woman and her husband had crossed from Idylwood Park to the east side of the lake in their two-person raft and were swimming when the victim got a cramp in her leg. The husband pulled her into his raft when he got it righted and paddled "for at least twenty minutes back to Idylwood to get help."

No one had stopped to help the couple, Potts said, but the man hadn't tried to flag a passing boat either: "He was intent on getting her back to shore for help as fast as he could. There's a lot of potential here for these kinds of things to happen, especially with a small raft low in the water—they can be easily overlooked by passing boats."

Mike McFadden, nineteen, was one of the guards on duty that afternoon. He told Sue Peters that he had seen the man paddling his raft near Idylwood Park; he was rowing very slowly, facing the beach. "That's not the most efficient method of rowing for maximum speed," the young guard commented. Indeed, the man had come dangerously close to the roped-off swimming area, and McFadden had blown his whistle and waved him off. The man in the raft did not, however, indicate at that point that he was in trouble. McFadden saw no other person in the raft. When the man beached his craft, McFadden noticed that he sat motionless in the raft for two or three minutes.

The first time the lifeguard knew anything was wrong was when one of the two boys who seemed to be with the man ran over to him. They were so polite and subdued that he was about to send them up to the guard shack for assistance, assuming one of them had a minor cut or some small problem.

"Then I saw the body and the hand laying on top of the raft," McFadden recalled. "I called code 88 [emergency alert] and ran to the boat."

The raft had had quite a bit of water in the bottom, perhaps four inches, and the woman's condition looked bad. She was not breathing, and her color was the blue-gray of death. McFadden shouted to the man he would come to know as Randy Roth to help him get her out of the raft and onto the beach so he could start CPR. Initially the man was so detached that McFadden assumed he was in shock. Roth didn't attempt to help resuscitate the woman; he stood off to the side and watched, his face expressionless.

The man muttered that a boat had come close to them and a wave had caused the raft to capsize, and his wife had swallowed water.

Once, when McFadden stepped aside to let another guard spell him on the CPR, he was surprised to see Roth calmly folding up his raft.

Other guards, including Kelli Crowell, immediately closed the beach to swimmers and joined McFadden as he worked over the woman. Crowell, twenty-eight, overheard Roth say that he had already bailed a lot of water out of the raft, leading her to believe that it had been full of water; possibly it had sprung a leak. She was under the impression that Roth had simply found the drowned woman floating in the water; she had no idea that they were together. The man was too removed emotionally. She didn't realize the two little boys were with him, either. He made no effort to comfort them.

Pam Chicoine had called 911 on her cellular phone, and the Bellevue paramedic team had left for the lake at once.

The victim's sons were terribly upset, with tears streaming down their faces.

Patti Schultz and her boyfriend, Michael Mann, were at Idylwood Park that afternoon. It was their day off. And had the woman's condition not been so hopeless, their presence might have changed tragedy into relief. They were both highly trained paramedics with the Seattle Fire Department. As they strolled on the beach, Patti's experienced eye picked up the frenzied activity near the shoreline. A crowd had gathered around someone on the ground, and she saw that the lifeguards were working over a woman in a one-piece bathing suit. Her skin color was mottled and cyanotic, and pinkish froth was coming from her mouth and nose. Both Patti and Mike joined in trying to resuscitate the victim.

When Patti bent to perform CPR she saw blood in the woman's mouth, as well as copious amounts of sticky sweet-tasting pink fluid, which she evacuated from the woman's stomach by forcibly turning her onto her side. Schultz also noticed discoloration around the victim's neck.

Emergency medical technicians from the Redmond Fire Department, under the direction of Captain Rudy Alvarez, arrived first. Paramedics from Medic I in Bellevue received the 911 call at 5:36 P.M. and were out of the firehouse a minute later, arriving at Idylwood Park at 5:49. Paramedic Mike Helboch recalled that he leapt from his van and raced to the woman lying on the sand. But his own heart sank at the sight of her. So did that of his partner, Chuck Heitz, Jr. Her skin had a bluish tint from the top of her head to her chest. He knew this meant she had been without oxygen for a significant amount of time.

"She had a very, very, very low chance of survival when I got there," he said.

While paramedics inserted an airway and tried to clear away more of the pink froth that blocked the passage of oxygen to Cynthia Roth's lungs, other onlookers were stunned to see her husband methodically gather his possessions from the raft—clothes, towels, thongs—and pack them into a number of plastic and paper bags. And then he calmly deflated the raft and folded it up. He seemed utterly dispassionate, almost more concerned that he would lose some of his belongings than that he would lose his wife. Indeed, most people, like Kelli Crowell, didn't realize that the man was even *with* the drowned woman. He seemed to be just another bystander.

For fourteen minutes, the Medic I team from Bellevue worked in vain over the body of Cynthia Roth. She had no heartbeat. No pulse. They gave her one milligram of epinephrine and used a vasoconstrictor three different times, with no reaction. They tried atropine with epinephrine. Nothing. They tried a bicarb injection. None of the chemical methods that sometimes got a patient breathing and her heart beating again worked.

Attaching the leads of the Life-Pak, the paramedics shocked Cynthia Roth's heart. The Life-Pak monitor leads showed asystolic heart activity—absent or incomplete contractions. The shock therapy didn't work either.

Finally they put a cervical collar in place and strapped her to a backboard. They knew in their gut that she was dead, but they continued to do CPR as they lifted her into the paramedic's rig for their speeding trip to Overlake Hospital. The woman was so young, and even in extremis they could tell she was beautiful.

When the Bellevue paramedics arrived, Kelli Crowell took charge of the two little boys, walking them to the guards shack where they couldn't see their mother. Even an adult couldn't have been expected to cope with such a heartrending loss. One minute the family had apparently been on a happy outing, and the next they were torn apart. The little boys, who told Crowell their names were Tyson and Rylie Baumgartner, were clearly in deep shock, their teeth chattering and their skin pallid beneath their sunburns.

It was past six. The boys had apparently been alone on the beach for hours with no supervision while their parents were on the lake in the raft. They had had nothing to eat except a sandwich offered by the father of some boys they knew. They had no idea how long they had waited for their mother and their dad to come back. It had been a long, long time, and they had begun to get really worried.

The Medic I rig was pulling out, and Patti Schultz saw the boys' father walk away from the scene, his raft slung over his shoulder. He was strolling. He still appeared to her to be in shock; there was no expression at all on his face. Tyson and Rylie hurried to be with him, then walked 20 feet or so behind him. He didn't seem to even notice them. Patti offered to help carry the plastic bags of wet towels, which were so heavy that the children couldn't lift them. Randy Roth told her they were all the things that had fallen out of the raft when it tipped over.

She had noticed that the widower had refused to let police drive him to the hospital where his wife had been taken, and Patti Schultz offered to ride to the hospital with the man and his sons; Mike Mann would follow in their car. The man, who she learned was named Randy, agreed. She had been afraid he would drive too fast or erratically as he trailed the van and its wailing siren to Overlake. But he did neither. His driving was fine; he stayed slightly under the speed limit of 55 miles per hour.

Randy explained that he knew CPR and that he had felt for his wife's pulse, but she had none. Schultz wondered why someone trained in CPR hadn't performed it rather than delaying any resuscitation efforts for the twenty minutes it took him to reach shore. Twenty minutes at a time like that could have been important.

"How long does it take a person to die without oxygen?" Roth asked suddenly. "How long can someone survive—you know, come back—without a heartbeat?"

Schultz didn't want to tell him that, realistically, the time was very short—about four to six minutes. She fudged. "With CPR, maybe thirty minutes."

"It's only four minutes," he said shortly.

If he knew the answer, why had he asked?

Sue Peters detected a chilling pattern emerging as she talked to the lifeguards and other witnesses who had been at Idylwood Park on July 23. Not one of them recalled that the man in the raft had *raced* back to shore to get help. Rather, he had seemed to paddle in an almost leisurely fashion, as if he was out for an enjoyable day at the lake.

One witness, Kristina Baker, a thirty-one-year-old housewife, had been at the park that day with her family and her neighbor's two children. She was sitting between the boat launch and the swimming area, watching the lake. About a half hour before the man and the blond woman launched the gray raft, a police boat had come by, directing all the rafts and inner tubes back toward shallow water and away from the dozens of speeding boats far out on Lake Sammamish. She was surprised to see the gray raft head out toward the deep water, and she watched, expecting the police boat to show up and make them go back.

She looked for the couple in the raft off and on, keeping one eye on the children she had brought to the lake. She saw the man and woman dive off the raft and splash around in the water, and she noticed arms waving in the air. She remembered thinking how foolish it was to swim in a lake so full of powerboats.

Kristina Baker's attention was then diverted for about two minutes. The next time she glanced out at the couple, she saw the man standing in the raft, then kneeling as he pulled the woman aboard. Nothing seemed amiss. Then she saw him sit down and row toward shore. Oddly, she could no longer see the woman. The raft made its way slowly to shore. Baker estimated it must have taken about twenty minutes before it pulled into the beach.

Dr. Donald Reay performed the autopsy on Cynthia Rae Roth the morning after she had drowned. Redmond investigators had classified her death as accidental, but Reay was not ready to be so definite. However, his assessment was not much help to King County Police investigators. If they were looking for definite evidence of foul play, they weren't going to find it in the autopsy report.

"The body is that of a normally developed white female five feet two inches in height, weighing 129 pounds," Reay dictated. "She appears to be in the mid-fourth decade of life. Her nutritional status shows mild obesity. Rigidity is 4+ in the upper and lower extremities. Lividity [the pooling of blood in the lowest portions of the body after the heart stops pumping] over the back—not fixed. Light brown to blond finely textured curly hair eight inches long. Brown eyes."

Even in death Cindy wore eye shadow. A nasal gastric tube used by the paramedics was in place. There was also an endotracheal tube in her mouth, left by those who had struggled to force oxygen into her lungs. A bit of beach sand still clung to her face.

Cindy Roth's fingernails were quite long and perfect, neither broken nor split, and painted pink. Three small clear jewels were set in the polish of her left forefinger. Her toenails were painted pink too.

There were old marks on her body—the striated stretch marks of pregnancy, and some minor scars on one shin. Reay bent to examine two fresh scratches on the left side of her neck. He described them as "two obliquely directed scratches measuring up to two inches [in length] and separated . . . by a half inch and each scratch measuring one-eighth inch [in width]."

"The pathological diagnosis is: (1) Asphyxia by freshwater drowning; (2) Visceral congestion; (3) Needle puncture wounds *of therapy."* (Another desperate measure taken by medical personnel—medications injected in a groin artery and in her forearm.)

Dr. Reay, whose expertise is highly respected, wrote, "This woman's death is due to asphyxia due to drowning. She was recovered from a lake where she was rafting. The death is classified as a *possible* accident."

Peters was perplexed. "Basically, the scenario didn't make sense to me," she recalls. She talked with Dr. Reay and with Bill Haglund, his chief investigator. But they could tell her nothing definitive. Even after they heard Randy Roth's explanation of the events of July 23, heard about his delay in getting help for his wife who had stopped breathing, they still had to say the postmortem had shown only signs to be expected in drowning. Beyond the two scratches, everything spelled death by drowning.

And that, of course, was how the rescuers at the beach had treated the emergency situation.

* * *

Having spent less than a year in the Major Crimes Unit, Sue Peters had yet to work a truly memorable homicide case. Most of the murder investigations in any department are routine—if murder can ever be considered routine. Motive, means, manner, and opportunity were usually obvious. Spouses and lovers killed each other out of jealousy or in a drunken rage. Gang members killed each other to look like big men. Victims were murdered during the commission of other, lesser crimes.

But this case was already different. Peters requested a computer check on Randy G. Roth, DOB 12/26/54, seeking any criminal history. Either he was the calmest man in the face of a major disaster she had ever encountered or things were not what they seemed.

Peters read the statement that Randy Roth had written out for Redmond detective Larry Conrad a half hour after his wife was pronounced dead. Roth's knowledge of grammar was rudimentary, and he rarely used commas or periods. His handwriting was unusual, the letters tilting in one direction and then in the other.

We arrived at the lake at approximately 2:30 P.M. Then started to inflate the raft and inner tubes for the kids—so it was sometime after 3 when we reached the beach. The two boys were going to float in the swim area as they had done with their Mom twice before. Cindy asked me to row to the east side of the lake where it would be more romantic. I said it looks like a long way. She replied With your strong arms, you can do it. We rowed to the other side and paddled around for awhile and started back. She asked if I would like to cool off with a swim and I said O.K. We swam for almost 10 minutes and she said the cold water is giving her a cramp in her leg. I said let's head back. We were on the side of the raft and she was holding onto the raft and I said Hang on, I'll go around and hold the other side so you can get in. As I was working my way around a wake from a passing boat about 50 to 100 yards away went by and the raft turned over on top of her. She coughed once and I hurried to right the raft which took about 30 seconds. She was already floating face-down and I couldn't get her into the raft from the water. I managed to climb in and pulled her aboard and proceeded to row for the beach side where help could be found. On beaching, a life guard was summoned by my son on shore and they started CPR. I think my son, Tyson, who was on shore—and they started CPR.

Randy G. Roth

Little things niggled at Sue Peters initially, but they soon seemed bigger. Why hadn't Randy tried to get help from one of the passing boats? Why had he rowed for twenty minutes or more to get his drowned wife in to shore? He had told Patti Schultz that he knew a person could go only four minutes without oxygen before it was too late. Why had he sent a child to get the lifeguard? For that matter, why hadn't he started shouting for help the minute he got within hearing distance?

Peters looked for logical reasons. Denial. Roth could have been so stunned that he had tried to pretend it was all a bad dream, that he had just kept rowing, rowing, rowing, hoping that at any moment Cindy would sit up and everything would be okay.

But the discrepancies warred with the easy explanations. Randy told one rescuer that Cindy had coughed, another that she had gulped. In one version, he was sitting in the raft while she swam; in another, he was swimming with her.

On Monday, July 29, Sue Peters placed a call to the Roth residence and left a message on the answering machine. Nine minutes later Randy called her. He explained that this was the day of his wife's memorial service. His voice was flat, but he obligingly gave Peters a short tape-recorded statement of what had happened on July 23. He was very matter-of-fact.

"When you interview someone about the death of a spouse—in an accident, particularly—they're going to be upset, *you're* going to be upset," Peters says. "If someone had called *me* about someone in my family only three or four days after a death, especially on the day of the memorial, I think I would have said, 'Call me later. I can't talk right now.' He didn't. He basically just went along with the program. . . . He answered my questions, gave a scenario of what had happened, and he gave long answers to short questions."

Randy gave Sue Peters information about Cynthia's parents, the Louckses' names, and their phone number. He said she also had a brother, Leon Loucks, in Lake Stevens and gave his phone number. He repeated the events on the lake without a vestige of emotion in his voice.

He explained that Cynthia had been cremated shortly after the postmortem examination. "It was what we both wanted," he said. The Louckses had been upset about that, but Randy had convinced them that he was sure Cindy wanted that, told them that he had called one of her best friends in another state who said that was what Cindy would want, and her bereaved parents had finally agreed.

Bracing herself for another sad call, Sue Peters called Merle Loucks. This was the second year in a row that Hazel and Merle Loucks had returned from their vacation in North Dakota to learn shocking news. Compared to this year's tragedy, last year's surprise wedding seemed minor now. Losing their precious daughter at the age of thirty-four in a shocking accident was almost more than they could bear. Merle Loucks said that he didn't know of any marital problems that Cindy might have had; he knew that

she and Randy had a trip planned to celebrate their
first anniversary, which would have been August 1,
only two days away. He thought they had tickets to
either Lake Tahoe or Reno, and Cindy had been
looking forward to their trip.

Peters asked if Cindy had been able to swim, and he
said that she was a *very* good swimmer. Merle Loucks
said that he would be able to talk with Peters in more
detail later on; he just needed a little more time to
adjust to Cindy's death.

Shortly after one o'clock on the day of Cindy's
memorial service, Sue Peters received a telephone call
from a young woman named Stacey L. Reese, who
explained that she and Randy Roth were co-workers
at Bill Pierre Ford. Stacey, a single mother with a
young child, was worried and upset. She felt that
Randy's behavior both before and after his wife's
death had not been that of a loving husband. In fact,
some things had shocked her.

With Stacey Reese's permission, Sue Peters taped
the phone call. Stacey said she had hired on to work in
the office at Bill Pierre's Ford dealership in February.
Starting in May, Randy had begun to spend an
inordinate amount of time coming to the office for
coffee or just to talk. She figured he must have come
into the office three or four times a day. He had
invited her to lunch at a local hamburger place and
had wasted no time in telling her that his marriage
was not happy. It was, in truth, not really a legal
marriage anyway—only a "verbal marriage." He told
her that Cindy was obsessive and nasty toward him
and that he did not expect to be with her much longer.
He didn't really see how he could go on in such a
stifling relationship.

At that point, Stacey didn't know whether to believe
him or not. He seemed very nice and very unhappy.
But, on the other hand, married men often played out
that kind of line.

Stacey had never dated Randy, nothing more than the quick hamburger lunches, sometimes with him alone and sometimes with other employees. He had told her and other Bill Pierre employees that his "contract with Cindy was up on August 1."

Juanita Gates, the senior cashier and office manager in charge of accounting at the auto dealership, had noticed that Randy was hanging around the office and had teased Stacey about it.

When Juanita asked Randy if he was married, he had answered, "Kind of. Why do you want to know?"

Juanita kidded back, "Well, if you invite Stacey and me to dinner, we need to know whether to bring candy or candles."

Stacey didn't know what to think. One time, she had gone to an auto race in which the company's mechanics had a car, and she had seen the woman she thought was Randy's "live-in." She had pointed the petite blonde out to Juanita and said, "That's the woman who lives with Randy Roth."

On Wednesday, July 24, Stacey had learned that Randy's wife had drowned—the newspaper story had said "wife." Stacey wanted to do something to help. At the very least, she felt she should call. She left a message on Randy's answering machine, and he soon called back. She asked him how he was doing, and he answered, "I'm fine. Why wouldn't I be? It was a horrible thing—but a relief, too."

But that wasn't all. Stacey told Peters she had received a second phone call from Randy Roth on July 26. He talked to her about his upcoming interviews with the police.

"They don't think you murdered Cynthia, do they?" Stacey asked him, somewhat nervously.

"It's all interpretation," he answered smoothly.

On Saturday, July 27, Randy had called Stacey to ask her if she would like to go to Sunday breakfast with him and his boys at the House of Pancakes. Since Cynthia's memorial service had not even been held yet, Stacey declined. Randy seemed a little more worried about what the police were thinking and told Stacey he was afraid the police might be coming to arrest him that very weekend.

Although she didn't say so out loud, that made Stacey Reese even less interested in going to breakfast with him. He was beginning to sound like a man who was coming on to her instead of a grieving widower. She was worried enough that she thought she should contact someone working on the case.

When Sue Peters hung up, she was troubled too. How could a man who had lost his wife only a day before talk about her that way? *A relief?* Cynthia's drowning had been a relief to him?

Marta and Ben Goodwin learned of the death of Randy's fourth wife by reading the funeral notices in the paper. They were stunned, but there was no mention of how she had died in their paper. They attended the memorial service. "Quite frankly," Marta said, "I wanted to know what had happened. Had she had cancer or something?" It was only near the end of the minister's eulogy that Marta felt icy chills as she heard his words: "Who could have known that on that beautiful sunny day Cindy would drown?"

Marta clutched Ben's hand. They didn't dare look at each other. They were both remembering the day Ben had said to Cindy Baumgartner, "Be careful. Just be careful."

After the service, they saw Randy standing at the end of a long hallway, leaning against the wall. He was smiling faintly.

Marta found Greg eating cake in the church basement. She gave him a hug, and he grinned at her. "My new mom and my dad went out on the lake and she drowned." He said it as if it was business as usual; he had become so used to the comings and goings of mother figures in his life that he was inured to the pain of loss.

He has lost so many new moms, Marta thought, that he doesn't even react to tragedy anymore. He just thinks this is the way things are.

13

On July 30 Randy Mullinax joined Sue Peters in the investigation of Cynthia Roth's death. The case was spreading out like a spiderweb. There were far too many strands for a lone detective to follow up. They would work partners on the investigation into what had seemed to be an accidental drowning, but no longer did. They had never worked together before; they would turn out to be naturals.

They went over the case together, memorizing details, highlighting incongruities. On August 1, they would interview Randy Roth in depth—August 1, Randy and Cynthia's first wedding anniversary.

In a matter of a few days Sue Peters had found out things about Randy G. Roth that she suspected he would never have wanted her to know. It wasn't just his blatant flirtation with Stacey Reese and his cold statement about Cindy's death. It wasn't that Randy had not even bothered to notify Cynthia's parents and brother of her death and had let them hear it on the eleven o'clock news. It was more than his almost complete lack of emotion. More than the long, long time he had taken before he called for help for Cynthia.

No, Randy seemed to have had a whole other life

that Cindy either did not know about or had found out about in the months before she drowned.

Cynthia Baumgartner Roth could no longer speak for herself, but her friends could, and Peters's phone had begun to ring almost from the moment the first newspaper stories of Cindy's drowning hit the stands. One friend told Sue that Randy had been alone with another of his wives when she died in an accident. She didn't know the details, but she thought Cindy had become aware of the tragic incident.

"Her kids were her top priority and it would be very unusual for her to leave them alone on the shore, playing in the lake without supervision," the woman added. "Very unusual."

Mary Jo Phillips, who had expected to be Mrs. Roth number four, called to tell Sue Peters about the man she had almost married. She said there had been a *first* wife who was Greg's real mother and who might be living in California. Apparently no one had seen or heard from her in years. That wife had come *before* the wife who "slipped off a rope on Mount Rainier," and then there had been Donna Clift, the wife who came after the mountain tragedy. Mary Jo believed that Randy had been investigated in his second wife's death and that he had collected a couple of hundred thousand dollars in insurance over that. Mary Jo and Randy had actually broken up, she said, because she was uninsurable. From the moment he found out she had been treated for cancer, his ardor cooled rapidly.

There was more. "Randy doesn't like women . . . [and] little girls. . . . Randy has a military background . . . he worked in Vietnam and he has gone through three months of brainwashing on . . . killing people and mutilating women and children."

Randy supposedly had a brother in prison for murder, and he himself had been investigated for a tool theft.

Randy Roth was perhaps, Sue Peters pondered, much more than a simple diesel mechanic with a flat personality and a monotonal voice. He had clearly touched many lives and left most of them diminished in one way or another. She and Randy Mullinax could not arrest a man for showing no emotion over his wife's drowning, but they might be able to arrest a man whose past was riddled with blatant lies, bizarre coincidences, and suspicious circumstances.

Sue Peters and Randy Mullinax weren't even positive that Randy Roth *was* Randy Roth. They half expected to find he had half a dozen aliases, that they had stumbled upon a kind of modern-day Bluebeard with a trail of dead wives.

Sue Peters could not find a death certificate for a Jan Roth in either King County or Pierce County. When she called the Office of Vital Statistics in the state capital in Olympia, she learned that there had indeed been a Janis Miranda Roth who had fallen to her death—not from Mount Rainier but from Beacon Rock in Skamania County. It had happened in November of 1981 while the victim was hiking with her husband, Randolph G. Roth. Peters learned that Jan Roth's date of birth was July 26, 1952, her birthplace was Texas, and she had lived at 6207 227th S.W., Mountlake Terrace. That would have made her twenty-nine when she died. According to Vital Records, Jan Roth had died of a depressed skull fracture. Like Cynthia Roth, her remains had been cremated immediately after autopsy.

That death, too, had been classified as an accident.

Either Randy Roth was a most unlucky man when it came to wives, or Peters and Mullinax had found the end of a thread that they could follow to an elusive and terrible truth.

Peters found that Mike Grossie was still with the Skamania County Sheriff's Office. Grossie remembered the case very well indeed. He had interviewed Randy Roth himself in his Mountlake Terrace home, but the widower had been unable to explain just how his wife might have fallen backwards off the trail.

173

Grossie said he and the rescue people had tried to duplicate the circumstances of Jan Roth's fall, but they had had no difficulty at all keeping their balance on the same trail up Beacon Rock. They had never figured out how she had fallen or if she had fallen from the spot her husband pointed out. Grossie promised to forward a copy of his investigation at once.

Peters and Mullinax could not help the excitement they felt. In a detective's world, this case was like finding a pebble, polishing and examining it a little, and discovering that it was a diamond. Certainly they were out to see that Cynthia Baumgartner Roth was avenged—if avenging was indicated—but they also suspected they were on the trail of a man who had gotten away with murder—quite literally—for a long, long time.

One of Sue Peters's callers had mentioned that Cindy's very best friend was a young woman named Lori Baker. In fact, the caller said, Cindy and Lori had lived together for more than five years after Tom Baumgartner died.

On July 31, Randy Mullinax and Sue Peters went to interview Lori Baker at the Silver Lake Chapel where she worked as a church administrator. Lori described her long friendship with Cindy Roth and her dismay —shared by Cindy's relatives—when Cindy decided to elope with Randy only a month after she began dating him. Cindy had always been a cautious woman, and it had been completely out of character for her to elope to Reno. Lori was as devastated by Cindy's sudden death as the rest of the people who had loved her. Like Leon, Cindy's brother, Lori had had to keep calling Randy to learn even the most minute details of the tragedy. Randy hadn't called any of them voluntarily.

Friends had heard a report about the tragedy on the radio, and she had hoped against hope that it wasn't true. She had finally reached Randy at ten o'clock on the night Cindy drowned.

"I called Randy and asked to talk to Cynthia. He said that 'wasn't possible.' I asked him why, and he told me."

Randy told his dead wife's best friend about the wave that had hit Cynthia in the face. "I really got a lot of water out of her," he explained, referring to his efforts to save Cynthia while they were still out on the lake.

The shock was so great that Lori had hardly been able to speak to this man who had been married to her best friend.

Lori explained to the detectives that she had paid Cindy $300 a month rent during the time she shared Cindy's home. They had also shared a safe-deposit box in Everett. After Cindy got married, Randy's name was added to the list of those who could have passkeys. Lori believed there should be a will on file for Cynthia Rae Baumgartner. Cindy was the type who would have seen that her boys were provided and cared for. Lori Baker also provided Mullinax and Peters with a list of Cindy Roth's friends, people who might be able to tell them about the woman she had been.

The two King County detectives headed up to the Snohomish County Courthouse. They read Thomas A. Baumgartner's will and saw how well he had provided for his wife, Cynthia, and for his sons, Tyson and Rylie.

Public records can be a treasure trove for detectives. Peters and Mullinax discovered the million-dollar suit that Randy had filed against the state of Washington in the "accidental death" of Jan Roth and saw that it had been dismissed. They reviewed records, now dusty, on the death of Janis Miranda Roth in November of 1981.

And so, when Randy Roth came into King County Police headquarters at a quarter to eight on the morning of August 1, 1991, the two detectives who greeted him already knew a great deal about him, far more than he realized.

It was the first time they had seen him in person. They noted that he was a good-looking man, quite short, but very well buffed, with bulging biceps, broad shoulders, and a trim waist. He appeared to have tremendous upper-body strength. He was clearly a man who took good care of his body and was proud of it. He was at least four or five inches taller than Cindy Roth had been and thirty pounds heavier. As always, he wore contact lens in his brown eyes to correct his extreme myopia.

Randy Mullinax asked the questions and Sue Peters took notes as Randy Roth talked about his background and once more repeated the events of nine days before.

"We obviously knew things about him that he didn't know we knew," Mullinax recalls.

Mullinax asked Roth "nuts and bolts, simple questions." But Roth seemed incapable of giving a short answer. "We could ask him one pretty basic question, and ten minutes later he would still be rambling on about it."

Roth had a ponderous way of speaking. If asked a question like "Did you and your family swim often?" he would answer, "That would be the type of activity in which we would participate for our recreational needs." He seemed incapable of a simple yes.

Perhaps he was stalling, filling the air with enough words to block out troublesome questions.

"He didn't realize the extent of what we knew," Peters says. "At that point we knew about Jan's death—we'd already researched all of that. That was one of our things—to ask him real casual questions. Randy [Mullinax] would ask him how many wives he had had and then ask him to talk a little about each wife. So it was just kind of out of the blue, 'How'd *she* die?' and he'd describe it."

It was cat and mouse, but the mouse didn't realize

how well prepared the cats were. "He'd lie," Sue Peters remembers, "and we would know it—but he didn't know we knew. There were at least four or five lies that could help us in a trial."

Randy Roth lied particularly about the amount of insurance he had taken out on his wives. He seemed to believe that there was no way for the investigators to check that out. Indeed, Sue Peters and Randy Mullinax did not know just how much insurance was involved—not at that point—but they had every intention of finding out. Some of the subject's evasions and exaggerations were immediately obvious; others would grow like Pinocchio's nose as the detectives continued their probe.

He repeated essentially the same story he had told the Redmond Police. He and Cindy had rowed to the far shore of Lake Sammamish, and she had suggested they go for a swim to cool off. She had had a cramp in her leg, and he had instructed her to hold on to the ropes on one side of the raft while he steadied it from the other so she could climb in. A boat had gone by, and its wake had flipped his raft. Cindy had been trapped underneath for 30 to 45 seconds, he estimated. He had heard her gulp just once. When he got the raft righted, she was unconscious and floating facedown.

Randy was just as calm talking about Cindy's death as he was about describing his occupation. "While they were working on her, there was no oxygen in the building. They couldn't get oxygen to her because it wasn't available. The paramedics took control and I just watched. They gave her a shock. I thought they were going to use cords to jump her or bump her to get her going. I talked to the Redmond police, and then they hauled her away to Overlake Hospital."

Both detectives noted that Randy talked of his dead wife as if she had been an inanimate object—as if he were talking about a car engine that didn't work any longer.

He recalled that he had deflated the raft with the help of one of the boys, and he thought a paramedic had helped too. (That would have been Patti Schultz.) He didn't know her name, but she went to the hospital with them.

"A doctor came in and said they couldn't revive her." He recalled talking to a social worker and a detective, who had taken his raft away.

"We left—and I asked the boys what they wanted to do. I decided to take them to Burger King, and then we went to rent videos to watch at home. The boys seemed to be pretty good, but the little one [Rylie] cried. I didn't want to really talk to them about what happened. I was looking for a distraction. That's why I rented the videos."

"Do you remember what you rented?" Mullinax asked.

"One was *Short Circuit 2* and the other was *Weekend at Bernie's*. I can't remember the third one."

The two detectives exchanged glances. *Weekend at Bernie's* was a black comedy about a wealthy man who dies at his beach home and whose corpse is carried from place to place, propped up, buried in the sand, thrown off a speeding boat, and posed to look as if it is alive. It seemed at the very least a most inappropriate selection for two little boys to watch for "distraction" after having just seen their mother's drowned body.

"We got home around eight-thirty or nine, and we all took showers and then watched TV."

"Did you notify anyone that Cynthia had died?"

Randy shook his head. "Cynthia's parents were on the way back from North Dakota, and I didn't think to call anybody. The next day I was just sitting around the house and Cynthia's girlfriend Lori and her brother called and left messages on the answering machine."

In the same flat voice, Randy Roth said he had called Leon Loucks back. "He said he'd heard it on the radio and wanted to know if it was true. I told him

178

Beacon Rock, rising almost 600 feet above the highway. The Thanksgiving Day celebration with Randy Roth's father and family in nearby Washougal, Washington, turned to tragedy the next day when Janis plunged to her death from near the rock's summit.

Janis Miranda Roth as a happy new bride who had found "a man who was going to take care of her."

Randy Roth gave all his women roses *before* they were married. These were given to Donna Clift prior to their marriage. She was so thrilled, she took this picture of them.

Donna Clift Roth and Randy after their wedding
ceremony at Chapel of the Bells.

Randy Roth at
thirty with his son,
Greg, age seven.
This photo was
given to "Mom &
Dad" (Donna
Clift's parents)
a few weeks after
Randy met
Donna. It was
signed "The
Roths."

Randy Roth with Brittany Goodwin behind him; Marta Goodwin; her son, Ryan; and Randy's son, Greg, on a skateboard outing in a church parking lot.

Randy with Brittany Goodwin at a Christmas Eve celebration. Marta and Ben Goodwin didn't know that thirty-year-old Randy had seduced their fifteen-year-old daughter.

Randy (middle) with Ben Goodwin on his left. Randy always had one good male friend. Ben was the only one who wasn't afraid of Randy.

Cynthia "Cindy" Baumgartner—who became Randy's fourth wife on August 1, 1990, in Reno, Nevada—posed next to one of Randy's prize rosebushes.

Cynthia Baumgartner Roth's last address. The Woodinville house belonged solely to Randy after she died.

The master bedroom in Cynthia and Randy's new house. He "hated her pink things."

Photos of Cynthia's two sons, Tyson and Rylie Baumgartner. The day after Cynthia's death, Randy removed all traces of her. These photos were found in a bathroom closet when police searched the house after Roth's arrest in October 1991.

The badges and patches that Randy kept to substantiate all the places he'd been while in the Marines. Beside them are the receipts for purchasing them.

A reenactment of how Randy Roth claimed Cynthia drowned. Even creating water rougher than during the alleged incident failed to tip the raft.

King County detectives Sue Peters and Randy Mullinax with the Roth files in the evidence room. *(Leslie Rule)*

King County senior deputy prosecutors Marilyn Brenneman (left) and Susan Storey conferring on their strategy in the Randy Roth trial. *(Leslie Rule)*

Randy being led by guards from the courtroom. While in jail he went on a diet, lost his muscular build, and became a shadow of his former self. *(Leslie Rule)*

it was and that the services were set for Monday
morning. I told him that we both had decided we
wanted to be cremated when we died."

Although the Loucks family had wanted to bury
their daughter, they went along with the cremation.
"Cynthia's dad took her ashes, I think."

"Did you and Cynthia have wills?" Mullinax asked
casually.

"No. We didn't have one together. I don't know if
she had one. She told me that she didn't, and her
friend Lori was there when she said that."

Mullinax and Peters kept perfectly straight faces.

Randy talked on. "We really didn't talk about
Cynthia's past—that was her private life. We just
talked about softball practice, the kids at school, how
she felt bad because the kids had more respect for me
than her and because they liked me better. *I* raised the
boys," he said with a trace of smugness.

Asked again about life insurance policies, Randy
acknowledged they had one—but only to pay off the
house if one of them died. Randy thought it was for
about $200,000. They owed nearly $120,000 on the
Woodinville house. He didn't really know about any
other policies that Cynthia might have had, but he
said they were each other's beneficiaries, and his
father was his alternate beneficiary.

Randy said he had called the life insurance company on Friday, July 26, on Monday, July 29, and again
on Tuesday, July 30, to find out what to do to put in
his claim. "It was Cynthia's idea, you see, to get life
insurance so our home would be paid for in case of an
accident."

It was a familiar tune, but Mullinax and Peters
didn't know *how* familiar yet. Randy hadn't let any
grass grow under his feet before he tried to collect on
Cindy's insurance. They listened as Randy explained
that their house had cost $275,000 and they had both
sold their previous homes to use as the down payment. "The mortgage is in both or our names . . . we

have combined finances, a joint checking account since our marriage. I also opened a savings account and put five hundred dollars in. Actually, we didn't talk about our finances much."

Randy told the detectives that he had realized a $50,000 profit from his house, which he had put down on the new house. He wasn't sure how much Cindy's profit from her house had been. But *they* were—it had been $160,000, the total down payment on the Woodinville house. Whatever he had done with his $50,000, he hadn't contributed toward buying the house.

"I plan on raising Cynthia's boys, but it won't be easy because that's two more." Randy sighed.

"You've been married before?" Mullinax asked casually.

"Yes, to Donna Roth in 1975. We were married for five years. Donna just didn't like being committed. She had a daughter from a previous marriage."

This would have been the first Donna—Donna Sanchez Roth, Greg's mother. Randy said he hadn't talked to her in several years, but that she did have visitation rights with Greg.

"Jan was my second wife. We were married for nine months. She died in a hiking accident in Skamania County in 1980 or so."

When they asked him about Jan's fatal plunge from Beacon Rock, Randy described it, stressing that there had been eyewitnesses. He implied that six or seven people had been standing right beside him when Jan fell. He himself had been walking "eight or ten feet behind her. She was dead at the scene."

There had, he admitted, been a police investigation and, he thought, an autopsy: "I felt like I was being watched for about three weeks."

"Did anyone see what happened?" Mullinax asked.

"Well, *yes.* They were right there," Randy answered.

* * *

"We *knew* there were no witnesses," Peters says. "So it was 'Okay, here we go. . . .'" Randy Roth was lying again.

Randy's third wife, he explained, was another Donna. He thought he had married her in 1985, but he wasn't sure of her maiden name. He had met her at Christmastime, married her in May, and she left in September. The second Donna, according to Randy, hung around with a wild crowd and was involved in "drug deals. She slapped her daughter around, and I asked her to leave, and we got a divorce. Very immature . . . very. I think she went to Utah or Colorado to live with her former husband."

Until he met Cynthia in 1990, Randy said, he just dated casually and had no thoughts of marrying again. He had had no insurance policies.

"You have male friends?" Mullinax asked.

"My best friend is Max Butts. I met him in 1985 or '86 at the Bellevue dealership where I worked. Cynthia was real social, but I just had a couple of friends."

Randy explained that he and Max, his three "sons," and Brad (Lily Vandiveer's son) all went motorcycling together.

Cynthia's friends had been a woman named Sally who lived in Colorado, the women from her aerobics class, Pam "the fingernail lady," and Lori Baker, who Randy said was probably his wife's closest friend.

Randy said that he grossed about $3,000 a month in his present job at Bill Pierre Ford and had cash assets of about $20,000 and $4,000 in the bank. He added to his income by buying and selling cars. Cynthia had her money "spread around," and he supposed she had perhaps $20,000 or $30,000. He had no idea how to "access" Cynthia's money.

Randy said his only debt was $1,000 on his Visa card. All of his motorcycles and ATVs were paid for. He said he had purchased the last three vehicles after his latest marriage for Cynthia and her sons.

Asked about his criminal history, Randy rambled into a story of a girlfriend he had in 1974 before he went into the service. When he returned, he met Donna Sanchez, broke up with the first girl, and that ex-girlfriend "set him up." Snohomish County Police had charged him with second-degree burglary. "I wasn't locked up and didn't get any jail time. I lost my voting rights."

Mullinax asked Randy about his family. He said his father, Gordon, lived in eastern Washington, and his mother's name was Liz. He had three sisters: Lisa, Debbie, and Darlene. His brother's name was David. He offered no additional details about his family.

Asked to recall the events leading up to the day that Cindy Roth drowned, now only nine days past, Randy did so in his odd stilted way. He seemed to make a real effort to sound intellectual, but his vocabulary was not unusually large and he crowded as many words into a sentence as possible. He never took the easy way to say anything.

Cindy had been ill, he remembered, the week before she drowned. She had suffered stomach and head flu. She had been either in bed or on the couch through the week, but she felt better by the weekend. She had been anxious for him to take a half day off so that the family could enjoy a picnic at Lake Sammamish.

And that was what he had done on Tuesday, July 23, hurrying to finish up an engine rebuild so he could spend the sunny day with Cindy and their three boys. Who could have believed that Cindy's plans for a wonderful family day could end in such heartbreak?

Sue Peters and Randy Mullinax had picked up quickly on the fact that whatever bad things had happened in Randy Roth's thirty-seven years, they had always been somebody else's fault: Donna Sanchez didn't want a commitment; Jan wanted to go hiking on Beacon Rock because it would be romantic; Donna Clift ran around with a wild crowd and took drugs; Cynthia wanted to go to the lake and row across because it would be romantic. "Whatever it was," Mullinax recalls, "he always tried to diminish his part in it. It was always the women's idea."

It sounded as if all the women in Randy Roth's life had manipulated *him*. He was the innocent single father of a little boy who had only tried repeatedly to build a happy family, only to have all of his "families" break up because the women involved spoiled things.

At the end of the two-hour interview, Mullinax asked Randy Roth if they might take his fingerprints. They needed major-case prints to prove that this man in front of them really was Randy Roth. Fingerprints would answer that question. They could run an AFIS (Automated Fingerprint Identification System) check and find out exactly who he was. Randy readily agreed to be printed, but he balked when they asked him if he would take a lie detector test. That didn't surprise them; they knew he had also refused a polygraph after Jan's death.

"I'd have to talk to my attorney about that," Roth said.

Randy Roth had retained George Cody, one of Seattle's most competent criminal defense attorneys. He was obviously ready to dig in his heels and make a stand.

The interview was over.

But the investigation had really just begun.

14

Randy Roth had told a number of women about his brother, "the murderer." He had not been so forthcoming during his interview with Mullinax and Peters. Sue Peters placed a call to Gary Singer of the Washington Probation and Parole Department. Singer entered the name in their computer system and found a David M. Roth, born on June 6, 1957. Singer said that David Roth was indeed serving time for first-degree murder; the conviction had come out of Snohomish County. David had a brother named Randy and sisters named Darlene, Debbie, and Lisa. David's mother's name was Lizabeth, and his father was Gordon. Either this was a series of amazing coincidences or Randy Roth and David Roth had to be brothers. This was one of Randy's stories that appeared to be true.

While Randy was a very short man, David was extremely tall, well over six feet, and his mug shot showed a face pockmarked with scars from teenage acne. The details of Randy Roth's younger brother's crime were similar—but not identical—to the version of that murder that Randy had described to his wives and girlfriends.

On August 13, 1977, David Roth, who was twenty and living in Lynnwood with his mother, had been stopped for a minor traffic violation in Gold Bar, a tiny hamlet in the western foothills of Stevens Pass.

While Officer Fred Vanderpool was searching Roth's 1963 Chevrolet, he found a .22 caliber Marlin rifle and a clip with fifty-nine live rounds in it. David was arrested on a concealed weapons charge. He seemed to be an amiable enough young man and he was booked into the Snohomish County Jail for only two days and then released.

On August 14 a couple waded into a thicket of blackberries near Mariner High School in the 200 block of 120th S.W. in Everett. Intent on filling their buckets with the abundant crop of sweet wild berries, they almost didn't see the still figure lying in the underbrush. It was a woman, fully clothed, and she lay facedown with her arms at her sides.

Snohomish County detectives found she had been strangled, and shot in the head seven times. She had been dead only about twenty-four hours when she was found. Her wounds would make it difficult to identify her. She was young, probably under twenty. Detectives checking missing persons reports and dental records found no matches.

David Roth's arrest on August 13 and the discovery of the girl's body the next day did not seem to be connected. However, David went to a friend's home after his release from jail and talked about how he had killed a girl. He said he had been driving near the Boeing Company's Everett plant when he saw the young woman hitchhiking. He said he picked her up and they bought some beer and then drove to the woods near Mariner High School to drink it. After they had consumed most of the beer, David told his friend he had tried to have sex with the girl, but she had resisted, and he had strangled her with an elastic cord. Then he took the rifle from the trunk of his car and shot her repeatedly in the head.

David Roth's friend went to the Snohomish County Sheriff's Office four days later and told them what he had heard. Because a records check had shown that

David was to appear in district court on August 22 for a pre-sentencing interview on a possession of marijuana charge, Snohomish detectives planned to arrest him there.

But David Roth did not appear. In fact, he remained a fugitive for more than a year. He was finally arrested on January 18, 1979, in Port Orchard, Washington, across Puget Sound from Seattle, and he confessed to the arresting detective during the ninety-minute ferry ride back to Seattle. Although he later recanted his confession and pleaded not guilty to first-degree murder, he was convicted in Snohomish County Superior Court in Everett in November of 1979.

The physical evidence against David Marvin Roth was solid. The bullets found during his arrest in Gold Bar were the same make and caliber as the seven slugs in the victim's body. More damning, the bullets' land and groove markings proved that they had been fired from David's rifle and no other. He was sentenced to life in prison.

In Washington State that meant he would become eligible for release in March 1997.

It was apparent that David Roth had not known the dead girl, and no one had ever come forward to identify her. She was still listed in Snohomish County files as Jane Doe, and her body was buried in a pauper's plot at Cypress Lane Cemetery in Everett.

Snohomish County investigators and court personnel recalled that Lizabeth Roth, an avowed devout Catholic, had attended David's murder trial holding her rosary and praying under her breath continually. Lizabeth and one of her daughters were chastised many times by the judge for disrupting the courtroom. Anonymous threats were made against the judge and court officers, who were issued bulletproof vests to wear during the trial. The trial had been so bizarre that Snohomish County authorities had doubled up on guards in the courtroom.

Lizabeth had fired David's court-appointed attorney, Mark Mestel (one of the area's best), after jury selection was complete. Since David had confessed to the murder of the unknown dead girl, Mestel wanted to plea-bargain for second-degree murder, but Lizabeth wouldn't hear of it.

A defense psychiatrist testified that David Roth had an "abnormally" close relationship with his mother.

The King County detectives wondered where she was now. Was she dead, as Randy had claimed? There were no records showing that Lizabeth Roth had been killed in an accident or that one of her daughters had committed suicide by her bedside. There was no male hitchhiker who had bragged about murdering an elderly Roth relative in Montana.

Sue Peters found that Lizabeth Roth was alive and well—and relatively young at only fifty-two; she was not the aged mother that Randy had described to the Goodwins, not the old woman who lived in a nursing home. Nor was she, apparently, the drug addict that he had told Donna Clift about.

One thing was certain: this was turning into the most convoluted, grotesque case that King County detectives had seen in years. Peters and Mullinax were on the run constantly. All the facets of Randy Roth's life were akin to the thousands of beads of mercury that burst from a broken thermometer—slippery, minute, and often impossible to grasp, and when one bead was grasped, it often separated into two or three or four more. The King County detectives wanted to be sure they had all the mercury back in a container.

On August 2, 1991, Randy Mullinax and Sue Peters located Cynthia Roth's will on file on the Snohomish County Courthouse. According to what they had learned so far, Randy Roth had had a Svengali-like control over all his wives. Certainly he would have wanted Cindy to change—in his favor—whatever will she might have had before she met him, but that had not happened. The detectives suspected he had not even known about Cynthia's 1985 will. By the time Randy asked her about a will, she might have already had reasons to be secretive about her financial assets.

Much to her surprise, Lori Jean Baker had been named executor of Cindy's will. She had promised that she would serve as Tyson's and Rylie's guardian, but she had thought that was just one of those things that young parents talked about in abstract terms, not believing it would ever come to pass. The will stipulated that if Lori could not or would not serve as the executor, then Cindy's father, Merle Loucks, would be the backup. Cindy had designated that her silver, china, and crystal was to go to her "beloved mother, Hazel Loucks, or, if my mother does not survive me, I bequeath my silver, china, and crystal to Lori Jean Baker."

Cindy had directed that a trust be set up with the Everett branch of the Seattle First National Bank for her two sons and any other children she might bear or adopt in the future. With Lori designated as guardian, she wanted her boys to have a live-in mom, as they had always had: "It is further my desire that the trust also operate to benefit the legal guardian of my children to provide minimum benefits to said guardian to assure the fact that said guardian be able to stay home with the children and not be forced to work outside of the home full time. It is my express desire that the guardian of the children be able to provide a satisfying, meaningful home life for my children without the duress of working out of the home. However, my primary desire is to provide for the children as the first priority of this trust."

Lori Baker was perfectly willing, *happy,* to take care of Cindy's boys. She loved them, and they had all been like family for many years. The will had been signed on December 12, 1985, and as far as Peters and Mullinax could determine, there had been no subsequent will to replace it, nor had any codicils been added to it.

Glancing over the will, Lori remembered something that she had forgotten in the days immediately after Cindy drowned. "Before they were married," she told Sue Peters, "Cindy asked Randy if he would sign a prenuptial agreement. He wouldn't do it. He said that would show mistrust on her part, and she backed down."

Lori remembered, too, that Cindy had been disturbed because one of Randy's former neighbors had advised her to be "very, very careful" of Randy. (That would have been Ben Goodwin.) She hadn't been deterred from her elopement, but she had wondered why anyone would say such a thing about Randy.

Lori furnished Sue Peters with the name of Cindy's insurance agent, Bruce Timm.

Timm was on vacation until August 6, but Mullinax and Peters were kept busy in the meantime tracking down Randy Roth's other insurance claims over the years and his criminal record. There was nothing big-time—the second-degree burglary charges, a robbery of a gas station where Randy had formerly worked, and an accident investigation. Randy had reportedly been the victim of a few burglaries—notably the $60,000 burglary of 1988. His former best friend, Nick Emondi, had also suffered at least two burglaries of insured items. So had one of Randy's relatives.

One of the vital questions that had to be answered —and soon—was just how easy it would have been for the wake from a passing speedboat to tip over Randy Roth's gray Supercaravelle Sevylor raft. On August 5, Sue Peters, Randy Mullinax, and Detectives Ross Nooney and Mike Hatch went to Idylwood Park.

Hatch had his own 17-foot speedboat, and two lifeguards—Greg Isaacson, seventeen, and Linda Baer, twenty, whose height and weight approximated the Roths'—sat in the inflated raft. The investigators located the area on the east side of the lake where Randy said he and Cindy had gone swimming.

With the lifeguards in the water holding on to Randy's raft in the positions that Randy had described, Hatch revved up his Mastercraft water-ski boat until the waters of Lake Sammamish churned into good-sized wakes. "I was trying to create as large a wake as I could," Hatch recalled. "My instructions were to try to flip the raft." Nooney videotaped each pass the speedboat made as it moved closer and closer to the raft. Although the swimmers were buffeted around and took sprays of water in their faces, the rubber raft didn't even come close to tipping over. It remained completely stable even when the boat passed within a few feet of it. In fact, the only way the lifeguards were able to flip it over was to put their full weight on the near side and then reach across and deliberately pull the far side over on top of them.

Linda Baer said later, "I don't believe that raft *could* flip if the boat was even twenty yards away. Even five to ten yards away the wake might have rolled over my head, but it wouldn't flip the raft. In my opinion, the raft was very stable."

Moreover, Linda said, when the raft was purposely tipped over and she was underneath it, there was a large air pocket between the raft and the water; she could breathe just fine. She was a lifeguard, but she was recuperating from an automobile accident, so she wasn't in top shape.

There would be other tests, but this first reenactment left the King County investigators wondering how a boat 50 yards away could have overturned this raft with its wake. And if the raft had tipped over, why had Randy Roth still had three bags of towels and clothes with him when he rowed in to shore? Had he taken time to dive for them when his wife wasn't breathing? Surely not. Also, he had said that Cindy was floating when he managed to flip the raft over. But drowning victims don't float—not at first.

The police were going to need experts in water safety to sort it all out, but for the moment nothing matched up with Randy Roth's version of Cindy Roth's death.

Randy Mullinax talked with New York Life Agent Bruce Timm on August 6. Timm said he had handled Tom Baumgartner's life insurance policy. His company had paid Cynthia $200,000 when Tom died. She had subsequently put down $10,000 to pay up a $100,000 policy on herself, one that would benefit her sons. "That policy is now worth about $115,000," he said.

Bruce Timm said he had gone to the Roths' Woodinville home in October of 1990. He remembered that "Cynthia looked happier than I had ever seen her." What took place during his discussion with Randy and Cindy would be remembered differently by Timm and by Randy Roth.

According to Randy, it was Timm who suggested how much insurance they needed, using a matrix that took into account their income, the mortgage, and the number of children. The amount needed for each of them, was, he recalled, either $250,000 more than they already had, on the low end, or $350,000, on the high side.

Bruce Timm recalls, however, that it was Randy who suggested the amount. Timm agreed that it was Cindy who called and asked him to come out to Woodinville to talk about insurance for herself and her new husband, Randy Roth. They had decided on the $250,000 policies, naming each other as beneficiary. Because they were both young, the monthly premiums were less than fifty dollars apiece a month.

Randy had suggested that his father should be the

adult beneficiary who would look after the boys if both he and Cindy should die. "My father is twenty-five years younger than Cindy's," he explained. Later Cynthia had called and asked Timm to put Randy on her $115,000 policy too—in place of Tyson and Rylie. "I want to make Randy my beneficiary," she insisted. Timm was shocked that she would take her sons' names off, and questioned her. "No, no, you don't understand," she said. "I *need* to do it. My husband has already changed his [policy] to *my* name."

Bruce Timm delivered the $250,000 policies on March 11, 1991.

Mullinax totaled up the insurance and found that Cynthia Roth, dead, had been worth $365,000. At this, his calculation was short; Mullinax didn't know that it was really $20,000 more than that. Her husband, Randy Roth, had insured her life for that amount with Allstate using his Sears card.

$385,000.

If Cindy died, Randy was her beneficiary. If Randy died, Cindy believed she would be his. And she was—at least on the larger policy. But Gordon Roth's name had never been removed as beneficiary for Randy's $100,000 policy. Although Randy assured Cindy that he had changed his policy from his father's name to hers, he never had. It was a mistake, he would say later—he had called his agent repeatedly asking for change-of-beneficiary forms, but all he ever succeeded in doing was changing his address from Misty Meadows to Woodinville.

Cynthia's sons stayed with Randy for the first day or so after their mother died, but by early August Tyson and Rylie Baumgartner were staying with Hazel and Merle Loucks in their Marysville home, a quiet little town north of Everett, or nearby with their uncle, Gary Baumgartner. Randy and Greg were living in the Woodinville house.

Mullinax and Peters wanted to wait as long as they could before they talked to the boys. Sometime soon they would *have* to; the little boys, who were now completely orphaned, were eyewitnesses to the events surrounding their mother's drowning.

In the meantime, Randy Mullinax and Sue Peters had more than enough to do. There were dozens, scores, of witnesses, friends, and acquaintances who wanted to talk about Cindy and Randy Roth. For some it was as if they had seen a freight train roaring down the tracks toward an unknowing victim and been helpless to stop it. Others had tenuous ties to Randy Roth and seemed to need to talk about him. Each of his wives had to have talked to *someone*, someone who might remember vital information, and people seemed to be coming out of the woodwork with tips, information, advice, psychic feelings, and remembrances of Cindy and/or Randy.

Donna Sanchez Roth did not come forward, however. She was still missing. She had apparently moved completely out of both Randy's and Greg's life. Peters and Mullinax wondered if she was even alive. Jan Roth was dead. But Randy Mullinax located Donna Clift at a dry cleaning shop where she worked. He found a shy woman, a frightened woman, who was nothing at all like the wild party girl Randy had described. Donna gave him a statement about the wonderfully romantic courtship of Randy Roth, which was immediately followed by an icy cold marriage. "I never went back to live with him after he tried to drown me."

Drown her? Mullinax's ears stood up.

Donna assured him that her mother and father could verify the terrifying incident on the Skykomish River back in 1985.

As, indeed, they did. Judy Clift said she was saddened but "not surprised" to hear that Randy's latest wife was dead—drowned.

So Donna Clift was alive, but where was Donna Sanchez Roth? Had she, too, taken out way too much insurance before she and Randy parted?

Sue Peters canvassed the homes on the east side of Lake Sammamish, hoping to find someone who had seen Randy and Cindy Roth at the far end of their "romantic" raft trip. After twelve contacts, she got only one hit, and that one was indefinite. One man thought he remembered seeing a gray raft 25 or 30 feet from shore with two people sitting in it, but he couldn't say if they had been men or women. He hadn't seen the raft tip over. He was sure of that.

Randy had called Lori Baker and told her that he was "too bummed out" to use the tickets that Cindy had bought for the trip to Reno. Then why had Randy and "a small boy" appeared on July 26 at Mill Creek Travel to pick up the Reno package? Debbie Erickson, the travel agent who had sold the tickets, recalled to Randy Mullinax that it was Cindy who had paid for the tickets on July 12. She had read about Cindy's drowning in the paper and had expected Cindy's widower to ask for a refund. But only three days after her death, Randy Roth had seemed in good spirits— and he never mentioned that he didn't need the tickets any longer. He only asked if the vouchers he received were the equivalent of a ticket.

Cindy Roth's friends remembered how excited she had been about her upcoming wedding anniversary and the second trip to Reno.

Evidently Randy intended to use his tickets. He could no longer celebrate his wedding anniversary, but that did not seem to deter him.

In the offices of Bill Pierre Ford, Juanita Gates heard Stacey Reese answer her phone a few days after Cindy's memorial service. Stacey talked for a few minutes and then hung up, setting the phone back in its cradle as carefully as if she held a snake. She turned to Juanita with a peculiar look on her face. "Oh my God! Oh, my God! You'll never believe it! That was Randy, and he wanted me to go to Reno with him."

Stacey had muttered a shocked no to Randy's invitation.

Detectives learned later that Randy had then called his old standby, Lily Vandiveer, and invited her to go to Reno with him, saying he already had the tickets.

But for once, Randy couldn't seem to get a date. The tickets went unused.

Sue Peters and Randy Mullinax were getting a feel for the kind of existence Cynthia Roth had lived during the last six months of her life. She had been a sweet, vulnerable, trusting woman who believed in God and in her fellow man She had waited five years for the right man to come along. And she had fallen in love with Randy Roth.

She had to have been a woman of pride; even her own family apparently hadn't known how bad things were. She had talked a little to Lori Baker—but not much—and Dottie Baker had known Cindy well enough to sense trouble.

Pam Neighbors was Cindy's manicurist—the "nail lady" Randy had referred to, and one of the very few people Cindy confided in. Pam had been aware of Cindy's entire relationship with Randy, from its beginning to its sudden ending. Pam told Sue Peters that she and Cindy had talked as she worked on Cindy's nails, and they had become good friends.

In the summer of 1990 Cindy had raved to Pam about the wonderful new man she had met. He met her criteria; he was a widower who really liked kids. Cindy had decided to date him. After the marriage, Pam met all three of Cindy's boys and assumed that Greg was the child of Randy's wife who had died. Pam remembered Cindy as "darling—a cute little girl. She was adorable, absolutely adorable. Bubbly and happy and she never said anything bad about anybody.

Angelic. You can't imagine. Any man in his right mind would have been thrilled to have somebody like her."

The manicurist recalled to Sue Peters that the Roths' marriage had started out wonderfully, that Randy had seemed completely oriented to being a family man. "They went camping. He was going to teach the boys to hunt. Archery. They did everything together. He was basically the kind of man that Cindy had wanted."

"Did Cindy ever mention life insurance to you?"

Pam shook her head.

"How did you find out about her death?"

"The hairdresser who originally referred her to me had read it in the paper. She called me and asked me if I knew, and I started checking around. I couldn't get an answer. I called the house, and all I got was a recorded message for two days. I finally got ahold of him about Wednesday or Thursday of the week after her death. And I just asked him . . . It was a short—short and emotionless—conversation. I asked him if it was true, and he said yes, and I said 'Well, what happened?' and he said, 'Well, she died in a drowning accident.' I didn't know what to say because he was so expressionless."

Pam had offered Randy any help she could give. "He just said, 'No, thanks. Bye.'"

Pam Neighbors, like most of Cindy's friends and relatives, was surprised to hear that Cindy had drowned. She had been a good swimmer, and very athletic.

It was to become a more and more familiar story. Incredible but familiar. Cindy had drowned accidentally; Randy bought the boys hamburgers, rented a movie about how funny a dead body can be, and immediately went on with his life.

On July 26 Randy had turned in three slightly used ATVs to Aurora Suzuki. He bought new Model LT-160 Suzukis for a total price of $5,389.70. He planned to raise all three boys, his own and Cindy's, and he wanted to start out their new life with the very best toys.

He sold another ATV to a private citizen, explaining that he no longer had a need for it. "My wife was in an accident," Randy said sadly. "She was in the hospital for a long time, but she didn't make it."

If all of Randy's financial juggling had worked out, he would probably never have had to work again. He believed that he was the beneficiary of Cynthia Baumgartner Roth's insurance policies. That was $385,000 going in. He expected the house would be in his name only. A $275,000 house with $160,000 equity was nothing to sneeze at. He already got $419 a month for Greg on Jan's Social Security account. If he could find a way to double-dip so that Greg could get money from Cynthia too, it would be at least that much more. Add to that the $1,500 that Tyson and Rylie got from their father's Social Security and it didn't take an accountant to see that Randy expected to have at least $2,500 a month coming in from survivors' benefits. If he handled the $385,000 in life insurance better than he had managed Janis's insurance payoff, Randy would have it made. He could spend all his time buying and selling cars, auto racing, and whizzing around on four-wheelers.

As Randy geared up for his new life with his three sons, he was totally unaware that Lori Baker had been appointed guardian for Tyson and Rylie and that they would not be coming home to live with him. The $1,500 a month in Social Security survivors' benefits that the two boys collected on their father's account would now go to their legal guardian.

Two weeks after Cindy died, Lori Baker called Randy about getting into their jointly held safe-deposit box. He insisted he knew of no box. With the help of a bank officer, Lori opened box number 2212. It was empty. A copy of Cindy's will should have been in the safe-deposit box in the Everett bank, but it wasn't there. Nor were Tom's wedding ring, his pocket watch, his other jewelry or the CDs Cindy had owned.

A check of bank records showed that the last person to enter the box was Randy G. Roth. He had signed the register two days after Cindy died. Since bank customers are offered privacy as they enter their safe-deposit boxes, no one could say what Randy might have taken away with him.

Tyson and Rylie continued to stay with their grandparents, but Lori hoped to have them with her as soon as possible. In the meantime, Randy assumed that the boys would be with him. He knew how to raise boys; he had said that often enough. The marines had taught him how to be a man, and he would teach Greg, Tyson, and Rylie.

15

Although Sue Peters and Randy Mullinax were working overtime, they still found it hard to keep up with all the interviews and investigative work that had to be done. They were building an incredibly complex circumstantial evidence case, but they needed more than that. On "Matlock" and "Perry Mason" circumstantial cases don't need to have all that much substance. And invariably, eyewitnesses burst into the courtroom at the crucial moment. In real life, cases without solid physical evidence were squeakers. Even eyewitnesses were not the strongest weapons available to the state's case; they could be wrong or tainted, or they could—and often did—misperceive what they had seen, or thought they had seen. It took prosecutors with real guts to go for a circumstantial case. It was much easier to get a conviction with blood and fiber matches, fingerprints, ballistics, and other convincing kinds of physical evidence to show to a jury. When the suspect was related to the victim, and especially when he lived in the same house with her, most of those prime areas of physical evidence were useless. Circumstantial cases needed three or four times as much backup in court.

The King County team knew where they wanted to go, and they believed they were right in homing in on Randy Roth. When he told his potential girlfriends that police were checking him out, he was telling the truth. The police certainly *were* checking him out. Daily and constantly.

The King County prosecutor's office, headed by Norm Maleng, had been following the Roth investigation avidly. The prosecutors wanted to confront the constant widower in court, but there were still too many unanswered questions. If Roth should be charged with murder and acquitted, double jeopardy would attach and he could never be tried again. If, as Sue Peters and Randy Mullinax suspected, the man was a modern-day Bluebeard who courted, seduced, married, and then killed women all within the space of a year's time, he had years ahead to cause untold tragedy. He was only thirty-seven.

Somebody had to stop him.

The investigation had been difficult from the beginning, and it wasn't getting any easier. "There are times when a case comes in and you say, 'I've got him,'" Randy Mullinax recalled. "I don't think that happened this time. It seemed every step we took opened a door to a lot more questions."

Indeed it did. Insurance questions. Burglary questions. And murder questions.

The King County detectives had had conferences with Lee Yates, a senior deputy prosecutor. In his decades with the prosecutor's office, Yates had prosecuted some of the most difficult homicide cases the county had ever come up against. Indeed, he had once taken a man to trial not once but *twice* for the strangulation murders of his wife and infant daughter. Lee Yates won, but he knew all too well the difficulties encountered in the investigation of an intrafamily murder. When Yates prosecuted race-car driver Eric Haga in 1973 and again in 1975, it was for a double murder that had occurred in the Haga family home. Fingerprints, hair, fibers, even the necktie and the satin ribbon from a teddy bear that were used as garottes, were no good as evidence. They all *belonged* in the home.

Randy Mullinax and Sue Peters went to see Senior Deputy Prosecuting Attorney Marilyn Brenneman. Brenneman's office was sometimes referred to as the "office of last resort"—the Special Operations Unit. Brenneman had been the first woman assigned to the unit, and the possibility that a female would enter such heady territory had obviously been unforeseen; her key wouldn't fit the rest room door. The unit usually dealt with police departments' intelligence divisions, working the most complex and unpredictable cases. Brenneman was in her element. She thrived on cases that challenged her, and she enjoyed walking the tightrope where one misstep could send her plunging down.

Although she had been the first woman assigned to the Special Operations Unit, she was not the last. By 1993 there were three women—Brenneman, Susan Storey, and Kate Flack—and one man, Duane Evans, working cases in Special Operations.

Marilyn Brenneman had paid her dues and could usually decide whether to take on a case or not. She listened as Sue Peters and Randy Mullinax outlined what they had discovered about Randy Roth and his many unfortunate wives. She was fascinated. She wanted it. There were so many hidden areas, and the case offered the possibility of bringing what appeared to be a truly wicked man into the courtroom. Whether the Roth case would be a boon to her career or an albatross around her neck remained to be seen.

On August 7, Detective Joe Lewis and Stan Chapin came on board to lend a hand. Lewis's first job would be to create a comprehensive summary of the investigation for Marilyn Brenneman. Always a hands-on prosecutor, Brenneman wanted to play catch-up in a hurry. The King County detectives had stacks of reports and scores of witness statements. Brenneman would commit them to memory until every detail of the Roth case would become second nature to her.

Joe Lewis would also try to locate Cindy and Randy Roth's bank accounts, CDs, and maybe the missing jewelry from her empty safe-deposit box. Chapin would attempt to determine the whereabouts of the first Mrs. Randy Roth, Donna Sanchez.

Cindy Roth's eagerly anticipated first anniversary had long since passed, but there were no celebrations, only tears. Randy Mullinax and Sue Peters had delayed talking with her orphaned sons as long as they could, but by August 8 it was time.

They arrived at the Merle Loucks residence in Marysville at two-thirty that Thursday afternoon.

They talked to Tyson first. At eleven, he was a slender, handsome boy, and very polite. He wanted to cooperate with the detectives; that was clear from the beginning of their interview. Asked how he felt about Randy, Tyson said he was "pretty nice" and that he had enjoyed playing baseball in Little League and going four-wheeling with Randy, whom he referred to as Dad.

"Do you remember the day you all went to the lake?" Mullinax began.

Tyson did. He recalled that his mom was in the bedroom getting ready to go. He thought the lake trip was his mom's idea, and he remembered that she and Randy had talked about it the day before—Monday. Randy had never been to Lake Sammamish, but he and his brother had gone with his mom a couple of times. He didn't know just who had wanted to take the raft. They had all been rafting in the Skykomish River the weekend before and had even taken Greg's friend Brad with them.

"You wore life jackets on the river?"

Tyson nodded. "All of us did."

They didn't take a picnic the day they went to Lake Sammamish. Their mom had fixed their lunch before Randy came home—peanut butter and jam sandwiches and milk. At first just Randy and their mom were going to Lake Sammamish, but then their mom had asked the boys if they wanted to go, and the boys said they did. Tyson and Rylie had asked if they could take their "little raft" but their mom had said no.

They loaded up their stuff when Randy came home and arrived at the lake, Tyson thought, about two that afternoon. They pumped up their inner tubes and the big raft. He and Rylie stayed in the swimming area, and Randy and their mom told them to keep their inner tubes in the shallow water. "They were going to the other side of the lake and check it out," Tyson said.

He remembered there were some bags in the raft with lotion, towels, clothes, and maybe a diet Pepsi. The boys swam in the shallow water until they got cold, and then they saw a friend and got out to sit in the sun to warm up.

"I saw Randy about halfway out in the lake, and he was coming back," Tyson said, adding that he couldn't see his mother in the raft anymore—only his dad.

When Randy docked the raft, he told Tyson and Rylie to "Get a lifeguard, but don't make a commotion." Their mother, Randy said, had had a cramp in her leg.

Tyson did as he was told, but he couldn't understand. His mother had been a *much* better swimmer than his father. Randy had told them what happened after they got back to the house with the movies he had rented for them. "He said he did CPR on Mom and yelled for help, but no one in the boats would stop to help them."

Peters and Mullinax had now heard yet another version of Cindy's drowning.

Asked what kind of father Randy was, Tyson said he was very strict. He spanked the boys about three times a week with a belt. He often made them do two hundred squat thrusts when they had done something he didn't like. Greg got punished just as often as he and Rylie did, and in the same manner. They usually got in trouble for fighting or for forgetting to put their clothes in the wash. Randy also got mad if they put the silverware in the wrong compartment in the dishwasher.

His mother and Randy had had "fights" about once a month, and once Randy had been angry because his mom had driven the red Trooper.

It was Tyson's feeling that Randy just wanted to forget about what had happened to their mom. On the Saturday after she died, Randy took them to the swap meet and they sold Randy's old couch, a red dresser, a stereo, and a television set. They also sold his mother's bike.

The day after his mom drowned, Tyson remembered, Randy began to get rid of her things. He emptied the refrigerator of all the food she liked, and "He put Mom's clothes in the corner, and he threw out all of her makeup."

Rylie Baumgartner was almost ten, a curly-haired stocky little boy with an outgoing personality. He, too, liked Randy and felt Randy had been good to him: "He takes us four-wheeling and to motorcycle shops."

The whole family went to a demolition derby on July Fourth.

Rylie also thought it had been his mom's idea to go to Lake Sammamish on that bad day. He and Tyson had stayed in the swimming area while his mom and dad took the raft out. Their parents hadn't told them how long they would be gone. It seemed to Rylie that they were gone about two hours. His mother was a good swimmer and had never had any problem before. He had seen Randy coming back alone; he was wearing his sunglasses and looking down as he rowed toward shore. Rylie and Tyson ran out to meet them, and Randy let the air out of the raft right away. Rylie didn't know what had happened to his mom until he heard Randy explaining it to a policeman at the hospital. Afterward, it was Randy's idea for them to go out to eat and rent some movies.

The next day, his "dad" started getting rid of his mom's makeup: "He packed it up and had us haul it to the garbage can. Then he made a big pile of Mom's clothes in his room on the floor."

Rylie also related that Randy's punishments were hard. If he did something "bad," he had to do exercises—bends and thrusts. But Rylie admitted that he guessed he usually deserved the punishments that he got.

Sue Peters and Randy Mullinax talked to Leon Loucks next. Older than Cindy by almost fifteen years, Leon was still baffled by what had happened. He thought that his sister was happy with Randy. He had found out about her death when another relative saw the story on the KIRO-TV eleven o'clock news. When he finally got Randy on the phone, Randy had been very calm and said the boys "were doing fine." His voice revealed no emotion, but Loucks didn't believe he was in shock. Randy was the same way at the funeral, he said. No emotion at all. He had given Leon still another story of how Cindy died. He said he hadn't tried to call for help because there was no one around, but he had tried to give Cindy CPR.

"My sister has been swimming since she was eight," Leon said. "She never had a cramp before."

The detectives talked to Merle and Hazel Loucks. The Louckses had been surprised the year before to learn that Cynthia was going to marry Randy Roth in Reno. She had been seeing him only about six weeks. "Randy took care of all the wedding arrangements."

Cynthia had handled all her own finances. The Louckses knew she had set up a trust fund for her boys and had made some investments. They hadn't known about her will, and Randy had told them he didn't think she had one.

Cynthia had told her parents that Randy was a Vietnam veteran and that he had bad dreams at night. Merle Loucks said that Randy had told him he had also served in the marines in the Philippines: "He told me he was trained to be tough and never show emotion."

The Louckses had noticed that Randy became increasingly nervous in the second week after their daughter's drowning. He was convinced that the police were coming to get him. He had been "scared" before his interview with Peters and Mullinax. He had shown up at their house after being out all night. "He told us he didn't want to go home because, if he went to jail, he would have to sit there all weekend."

Hazel Loucks had gotten a phone call from a woman who said Randy had invited her daughter to go to Reno with him: "She said she was afraid for her daughter." Mrs. Loucks didn't know who the woman was, but she knew he had also invited Lily Vandiveer to go with him: "I asked him, 'Why did you do this?' and he said, 'I also asked my mother, I asked Max, and I asked my younger sister to go, but I decided to stick around.'"

Like Janis Miranda, and like Donna Clift, Cynthia

had truly cared for Greg and had felt sorry for him because he didn't have his true mother with him. Hazel knew Cynthia had tried to give Greg a hug now and then, and he had appreciated it, but he always pulled away when Randy came into the room.

Randy hadn't had the sensitivity to explain to Greg what had happened to Cynthia. Mrs. Loucks said she heard he had handed Greg a newspaper article about the drowning. "Randy told Greg that if he never saw him [Randy] again, he was to call two telephone numbers Randy gave him."

When the Louckses asked to view their daughter's body, Randy warned them not to "because she looked swollen." But Merle Loucks had insisted. His daughter didn't look swollen at all. There was no outward sign of what had killed her.

"Randy didn't want her ashes—the cremains. He just left them at the church," Merle Loucks said. He didn't want any of the cards people sent, either. He didn't look at the flowers; there were no tears in his eyes. He just split from the church after the services."

Randy had told the elder Louckses still another story about the tragedy on the lake. "He said the 'raft just went over on us,' not only on her."

Sue Peters checked with the Lynnwood Police Department for any records they might have on Randy Roth. He had grown up there, graduated from high school there, and had two arrests in the Lynnwood files: August 25, 1973, robbery; February 14, 1975, robbery.

On August 14, Peters talked to a lawyer retained by the Pioneer Insurance Company in reference to a burglary claim Randy Roth had reported. She learned that Randy had asked for $60,000 and received a payoff of $28,500. The Pioneer Insurance Company had also filed a suit against Randy over the claim he had made after his home was burglarized in the fall of 1988. He had countersued, and both suits had been dismissed "with prejudice" on October 9, 1990.

Insurance claims popped up repeatedly in Sue Peters's and Randy Mullinax's retrospective on Randy Roth's life. They traced him back a decade, two decades. Randy's motorcycle was stolen; insurance paid off. Jan's car was stolen and then found stripped with no engine; insurance paid off. Nick Emondi, Randy's onetime good friend, had had two burglaries; insurance paid off. Jan died; insurance paid off. Randy had a burglary; insurance paid off.

And now Randy fully expected several insurance companies to pay him $385,000 in Cynthia's death.

Randy wasn't spending much time in the big yellow house in Woodinville. Perhaps there were too many haunting memories. Greg was living at Lily Vandiveer's house with Lily and Brad. Randy spent most of his evenings with Lily. Her mother was frantically worried. She called Sue Peters and warned her that she feared "Lily will be next."

But Lily Vandiveer would brook no criticism of Randy. She had stood by him before. She was not about to desert him now.

The headlines in Seattle area papers were discomfiting, both to Randy Roth and to the current women in his life. Bellevue's *Journal American* ran this headline on August 7, 1991: "Police: Drowning Might Be Homicide." It was no longer a secret that the King County Police Department's Major Crimes Unit was investigating Cynthia Roth's drowning. The article in the *Journal American* mentioned Janis Roth's accidental fall to her death a decade earlier. Randy Mullinax would say only, "We are very, very interested in this entire thing—and right now, we're particularly interested in anyone who may have been videotaping on the lake that day and may have videotaped anything about the incident, a couple in a gray raft—or even the rescue efforts."

Randy Roth, asked for a statement by reporter Cheryl Murfin, said he was shocked and confused that police had called him in for questioning: "I was emotionally and mentally shocked to have the police call me in for a statement and I was devastated to hear them tell me that the case was being investigated as anything more than an accident. I don't feel I have any concerns at this time. I volunteered the information [about the 1981 investigation] to the police. I didn't have anything to hide."

Two days later Randy called his own press conference. With his attorney, George Cody, beside him, they told reporters this would be Randy's last word to the press.

Looking stressed as his attorney repeated what had happened on July 23 on Lake Sammamish, Randy occasionally added further explanation. Cody said the Roths paddled their six-man rubber raft to the east side of the lake. They were swimming when Cynthia got a cramp in her leg. A powerboat 75 yards away had caused such a severe wake that it hit Cynthia full in the face and then flipped the sixty-pound raft over on top of her. Cynthia had been asphyxiated.

In answer to the investigators' questions about the length of time it had taken Randy to get help and about his failure to wave for help, Cody said that Randy *had* tried to wave for help. He had no explanation for why Randy had told police that he had *not* done so.

Cody pointed out that Roth had collected only a "moderate" life insurance payoff on Janis, but he refused to say how much. He also described as "small" the "$235,000" in insurance that Cynthia had and that his client stood to collect. The amount, of course, was too low by $150,000. But a quarter million dollars is hardly "small" to most people.

Randy said they had been forced to send Cynthia's children "out of town" because they were being "hounded" by the media.

Asked if he might ever marry again, Randy pondered that eventuality for the press: "It is impossible to deal with that idea at this time." He added that he and Cynthia would have celebrated their first wedding anniversary only a week before. He described Cynthia as "warm, outgoing, and personable."

Randy Roth looked directly into the cameras of Seattle's four major television stations—KING (NBC), KOMO (ABC), KIRO (CBS), and KSTW (Independent)—and viewers saw a handsome young man who seemed earnest and truthful. He had lost the woman he loved, and he was confused and miserable that his troubles were being exacerbated by a vindictive police investigative team.

Both Cody and Roth pleaded for friends and relatives of Cynthia's family to step forward to "defend" Randy's character. Randy proclaimed that he felt "in no way responsible" in the deaths of either his second wife or his fourth wife. George Cody, referring to Cynthia's drowning, said, "One would assume if there was any evidence of foul play, [witnesses] would have come forward then, or since then."

Background checks on Randy Roth with his former employers were producing interesting information. The jobs that he had left "by mutual agreement," according to him, had usually been terminated because he converted company gas or company products to his own use.

Just when the investigators had almost come to believe that Randy's first wife was probably dead too, Detective Stan Chapin found Donna Sanchez Roth. She had last been heard from in California, so Chapin checked the Department of Licenses in that state and found a listing for a Donna Sanchez in Brawley in

Imperial County, close by the Mexican border. Lieutenant Bob Kuhn of the Brawley Police Department remembered Donna Sanchez: "She was a police officer for a while. I think it was for the Imperial County Sheriff's Office."

Donna's first husband, Silas Sanchez, taught at Brawley High School. Apparently, Donna *had* gone back to her former husband. Records there showed that she had worked as a jailer from 1987 to July 7, 1991.

She *was* alive. At least she had been up until two weeks before Cynthia Roth drowned, and there was every reason to think she still was. When she left the Imperial County Sheriff's Office, Donna Carlson Sanchez Roth had left a forwarding address in Washington State. By working through a series of her relatives, Chapin finally located her at a teenage crisis counseling facility in Washington where she presently worked. He left a message for her there, asking her to call him.

Late in August, Donna called Stan Chapin. Unlike Randy's other wives, Donna Sanchez did not have a bad word to say about him. She had been married to him for exactly five years—from July 4, 1975, to July 4, 1980. He had been a "take charge" kind of man, but she hadn't minded; it had made her feel secure. Their parting had been amicable. He kept Greg, but she had visitation rights; she had custody of her daughter by her marriage to Sanchez.

When Sue Peters met with Donna Sanchez she saw a very pretty, small woman with a perfect figure. Donna number one looked remarkably like Mary Jo Phillips. She too had a kind of "country" sense about her, and she seemed remarkably naive for a woman who had worked as a jail guard for years. She was very quiet and very polite. If Peters thought Donna Sanchez might talk more freely when she was interviewed by a female detective, she was disappointed; Randy's first wife really did seem to hold no grudges or bad feelings toward him. She still believed that Randy had gone to Vietnam and participated in secret missions. "Those missions weren't even *documented*," she said, lowering her voice. "They were too secret."

The end of her marriage to Randy had come as a complete surprise to Donna Sanchez. "It was right out of the blue. We came home from church, and Randy just said, 'We're getting a divorce.'" Although she had not wanted the divorce and would have liked to keep her son with her, Donna said she had given up custody of Greg willingly. She had visited her son from time to time in Randy's homes, and she never had known what had gone wrong with their marriage. There were no recriminations. In fact, Donna asked if it would be okay for her to call Randy and see how he was.

Sue Peters shrugged, thinking, *Do what you've gotta do.* Whoever Randy Roth was, he had an almost hypnotic power over women—at least at first. And with this, his first wife, his spell lingered.

16

Senior Deputy Prosecutor Marilyn Brenneman has never been a woman to whom things came easily. Brains, yes, and an ebullient sense of humor, but she has fought hard for the respect she merited in her career. Were it not for the fact that she is basically a human dynamo, she might have given up years ago. She jokes that she would choose Meryl Streep to play her if Hollywood ever made a movie of her life. Streep could do it, but she would have to quadruple her energy level. There is a physical resemblance; Brenneman and Streep have the same kind of off-beat beauty. Her chestnut hair is too thick to control. It invariably falls over her left eye, and in trial she tosses her head impatiently to clear her field of vision.

Raised on one of the small coastal islands off Georgia—Saint Simons—Marilyn Brenneman went to school on the mainland in Brunswick. She embraced the law after she saw *To Kill a Mockingbird.* "I grew up in a family who didn't hold any of the political beliefs that everyone else in town did," Brenneman remembers. She is enthusiastic about everything and talks as fast as she thinks, although she has lost all traces of any southern accent. "I thought being an attorney would be the most wonderful career possible."

There was some delay about that, however. Always there was the subtle prejudice that women law students and attorneys find rising up like an invisible wall. "I wanted to be Atticus Finch, the lawyer in *Mockingbird,* but people suggested I should train to be a legal secretary."

Brenneman left home at seventeen, after she graduated from high school in Brunswick, and went to a business college in Florida. "I got married at eighteen and had my first child at nineteen." Married to an air force pilot, she put her lawyer plans on hold for a while. When her husband left the service, he took a job with the state of Florida, and Brenneman went to the University of North Florida to get her undergraduate degree.

When it was time for her to go to law school, she and her family had moved to Washington State and she was delighted to find that the University of Washington had an excellent law school. By her third year of law school, Marilyn Brenneman had two young boys, she was separated from her husband, and was working as a law clerk. She got good grades—but not the best grades. Who had time to go to the law library?

But she made it. "When I applied for the prosecutor's office in 1978, the man who interviewed me said, 'How are you going to handle this job with two children?'"

Knowing what she had gone through to get her law degree in the first place, Brenneman snapped, "Well, a lot better than I'd handle welfare!"

She got the job. Within a short time that question was no longer permissible in job interviews.

In 1991, as a prosecutor, remarried, and now the mother of four boys, Brenneman had not come to her position in the Special Operations Unit without a struggle. She never lost sight of her ambition to be a working part of the law, despite the first marriage, which didn't work, and the second marriage (to an attorney), which worked wonderfully, despite all the juggling of jobs and babies.

But she had made it.

In the spring of 1985, when Donna Clift was marrying her perfect man, Marilyn Brenneman's youngest child was a year old, her oldest was nineteen, and she was working days and nights to close down a teenage nightclub known as the Monastery. "I don't believe in coming in on a case in the end," she explains. "I try to *be* there."

Sitting in the dark on stakeout at two or three in the morning with surveillance officers, Brenneman was appalled to see that youngsters who looked to be only twelve or thirteen were going into the seamy club that sat hard by the I-5 freeway. Further intensive investigation uncovered child prostitution, drug sales, and pornography. Hampered by the brass in some law enforcement agencies who wanted to do it their way—which appeared to Brenneman to be agonizingly slow—but encouraged by outraged parents, she was instrumental in closing down the Monastery forever.

"When I think back," Brenneman muses, trying to

remember 1985, "my fall was relatively quiet in comparison. The Monastery case took months, and my cases that came after had to seem more routine."

By the spring of 1986, Marilyn Brenneman would find herself completely paralyzed from the neck down, a victim of Guillain-Barre disease. When her symptoms first began, she was frightened, wondering if she would ever be able to move again. She knew there were many diseases that she *might* have. "I went down fast, but once I was diagnosed and knew what I had, it wasn't too bad. I was lucky—I was only in the hospital, fully paralyzed, for a month."

Most sufferers of the malady eventually recover completely; some remain paralyzed. Brenneman was indeed one of the lucky ones. She had doctors who explained every facet of her illness to her and she was encouraged by their confidence in her. She did recover, and even her sense of humor came through intact. She never said "Why me?" She had seen too many people with permanent afflictions. Beyond that, Brenneman would always remember the bonus of love and support she got from the cops she had worked with, the other prosecutors, a huge circle of friends who rallied around her in a way she never could have imagined. Most of all, she had a family unit so strong that she could always count on them. Her teenage sons and her husband were rocks who never let her down; she never had to worry about what was going on at home and who was taking care of Adam, her youngest.

Although her personality, her sense of self, was stronger, perhaps, than that of the single mothers who had fallen in love with Randy Roth, Marilyn Brenneman had been where they were—alone with young children. Like Cynthia Roth, like millions of other mothers alone, she had had two little boys and been single, half hoping to find a full-time dad for them.

When she finished reading the case summary that

Joe Lewis had prepared for her, Marilyn Brenneman was anxious to find some way to get Randy Roth into court.

On August 19, Detectives Mullinax, Peters, and Lewis met with Marilyn Brenneman and Dr. Donald Reay to discuss the autopsy findings on Cynthia Roth. It still seemed impossible that she could have drowned so quickly, made only that one sound—a cough or a gulp, depending on which version Randy Roth gave—and then been gone. Reay was puzzled too. They had all questioned whether Cynthia might have been drugged, but the Washington State Toxicology Lab's report had come back with no sign at all of alcohol or drugs in Cindy Roth's system. The only item the drug screen produced was caffeine. Nobody drowns because of having too many cups of coffee.

Then *why?* Why would a healthy young woman, a strong swimmer, have simply taken one gulp of water and drowned? Reay explained that he was still convinced that Cynthia had succumbed to asphyxia by drowning. He had found absolutely no internal or external indication of trauma—nothing beyond the two slight scratches on the victim's neck. However, he said it would be relatively easy to drown someone without leaving any sign at all of forced drowning on the victim's body.

The answer to all their questions might lie in that last statement. Randy Roth had bragged to any number of people that he knew how to kill someone without leaving a mark on the body.

Was Randy Roth truly a deadly killer, trained by the marines to steal into Vietnamese villages and kill every man, woman, and child? Was the stuff of his nightmares based in fact? Every one of his women had described his restless nights, the way he had cried out during his bad dreams. They had all seen the odd weapons he kept near him always—the baseball bat studded with nails, for instance. It was difficult to separate Randy's fabrications from what had really happened. Some might call him an exaggerator, some a storyteller, and some an outright liar.

But one enormous lie had already been punctured. It was really only a matter of simple arithmetic. Ben Goodwin had always been suspicious about Randy and the Vietnam War, especially when he saw that Randy had the plaque for meritorious service exactly like the one he had seen on Ben's wall. He wasn't sure how old Randy really was, but he suspected he was younger than he claimed to be.

Randy Mullinax looked at Roth's birth date—the day after Christmas 1954. The gulf of Tonkin incident that really inflamed the situation in South Vietnam had occurred in August of 1964—when Randy Roth was only nine years old. Action in Vietnam was totally over by March of 1973. Randy graduated from high school three months *after* that. How could he have fought in Vietnam and gone to Meadowdale High School in Lynnwood, Washington, at the same time?

Detective Stan Chapin had checked with the National Archives and Records Center in St. Louis, Missouri, to see if a Randolph G. Roth had ever been in the Marine Corps. He handed Sue Peters a copy of Randy Roth's military records—a very thin folder. Roth had been in the marines all right, but that was in late 1973 and 1974. Randy Roth had never even *been* in Vietnam. It was obvious that all his knowledge of Vietnam had come from the books and magazines he collected so avidly. His only overseas duty had been on Okinawa, where he worked as a file clerk. He had never seen any kind of war action. He was mustered out of the service because his mother said it was a hardship to have him gone; he was needed at home. Randy Roth had certainly never been a member of any elite secret unit trained to kill in mysterious and bizarre ways. If he was having nightmares, they were being caused by something else.

* * *

Tyson and Rylie Baumgartner never returned to live with their stepfather. They had left with little more than the clothes on their backs a few days after their mother drowned, and almost everything they owned was still in the big new house in Woodinville. Knowing that she probably was not going to receive a hearty welcome, Lori Baker nonetheless called Randy and tried to make an appointment to get the boys' things. He wasn't cooperative. Lori and her brother, Harlan, went to the house, but Randy wouldn't let them in; he said he was sleeping.

It was Labor Day weekend, beginning Friday, August 30, when Lori, Harlan, and Dottie Baker, accompanied by Gary Baumgartner, went to rent a U-Haul trailer to pick up Cynthia's and the boys' belongings. Apparently everyone else had things to move that weekend, too, and all they were able to rent was a full-sized truck.

"I guess Randy thought we were going to take their furniture too," Lori recalled. "We weren't; that was just the only truck we could get."

Randy Roth was quietly furious. He had finally learned that he was not going to be Rylie and Tyson's guardian, and he was not happy about it. He let the Bakers into his home only grudgingly.

Dottie Baker had seen the house go downhill for a long time. During the long sad spring, Cynthia had kept it picked up, but it hadn't been as sparkling as Cynthia had always kept her home. Now, as they moved a few items aside, Dottie could see dust and dirt that had been building up for months. It looked as though Cynthia had simply given up, as if nothing had mattered to her anymore.

Randy had collected the things Cynthia had specified in her will, but he had jammed his dead wife's most valued possessions into black plastic garbage bags willy-nilly, with no concern at all for protecting them. Many of Cindy's and the boys' things were crushed and broken. Tyson and Rylie had pictures and posters that were ruined. Even Cindy's shoes had been jammed in and smashed.

When Tyson and Rylie asked if they could go into Greg's room to get some of their Nintendo games, Randy blocked their path. "You have no business in Greg's room. How do I know you won't try to take his things? You can only go in your room."

Their bicycles were gone, and so were their baseball cards and their BB guns. Randy wouldn't let them take the gloves and helmets that they had worn when they rode the four-wheelers. "They go with the four-wheelers," he said shortly.

Randy grew more and more agitated until his angry voice rang through the house. He pulled Lori Baker aside. "You have ruined my scenario," he raved. "The boys haven't had a father for seven years, and I planned to fill that spot. Now you will get the Social Security money and all the other benefits she [Cindy] had on the side and go off and you probably won't even have to work. How am *I* going to live?"

Appalled, Lori Baker just stared at him. His *scenario?* What about Cynthia's life? What about the scenario she had hoped for?

When Dottie Baker asked if they could take Rylie's piano, Randy came unglued, and they didn't push it, even though his grandparents had bought the piano for Rylie. They gathered up as many of the boys' clothes and possessions as they could and left hurriedly. They had seen that most of Cynthia's decorative touches had been ripped from the walls. *Why?*

It looked as if Randy had tried to erase every sign that Cynthia had ever lived there.

Randy put the house up for sale. He had apparently counted on the boys' Social Security survivors' benefits to pay off the mortgage, and now he knew he wouldn't be getting that money. Although he and Cynthia had paid $275,000 for the house in Woodinville and it was still in mint condition less than a year later, Randy set the price at only $225,000; he obviously wanted to be rid of it quickly.

DPA Brenneman had questions about the effect of speedboat wakes on the rubber raft belonging to the Roths. She asked that the lake experiment be repeated. On September 4, 1991, the investigative team again took the raft to Lake Sammamish. This time a detective, Laura Hoffenbacker, who was not a particularly strong swimmer, put herself in Cynthia Roth's place, and Sergeant J. K. Pewitt played Randy Roth. Once more, speedboats crisscrossed the lake, deliberately trying to overturn the raft. Sergeant Robert Cline provided his speedboat with Officers Mark Fern and S. L. Gallemore crewing, and they roared by the Sevylor raft, trying their best to tip it over.

They could not do it.

Randy Roth said he had gathered up the family's belongings that had fallen into the lake before he rowed for shore with his unconscious wife. Detective Joe Lewis carefully placed a plastic bag with clothes in it in the water. It floated. Next Lewis tried a beach towel. It sank in five seconds. Continuing to duplicate items Redmond detectives had seen in Randy Roth's vehicle on the night Cynthia drowned, Lewis took five pieces of clothing in a brown paper shopping bag, thong sandals, a department store plastic bag with two pieces of clothing, and a plastic bag with towels, and placed them in the raft. Then he deliberately overturned it. He counted off twenty-four seconds—ten to fifteen seconds less time than Randy had said the raft had been overturned—and then turned it upright. The bags of clothing and towels were strewn about in the lake and were already sinking. They were also separating and going off in many directions. The only way Lewis could retrieve them was by using a long grappling hook and by diving underwater to grab those sinking the most rapidly. Only the plastic bag and the brown bag were still floating; everything else was sinking toward the bottom. He never found the thongs.

Randy's version of Cynthia's drowning just didn't add up.

Possible Reasons to Believe Drowning Was Other Than Accidental

1. The raft wouldn't tip over, no matter how many speedboats chopped the water into strong waves.
2. When the raft was forcibly tipped, an air pocket remained underneath.
3. When the raft was forcibly tipped over a second time, the towels, clothes, thongs, and bags—which Randy had brought back sodden but intact—sank so quickly that one man could never have retrieved them all. And if his wife was drowning, why would he have even tried?
4. In his "desperate" attempt to right the raft, pull his unconscious wife from the water, retrieve all the items from the water, why had Randy not lost his prescription sunglasses? He was wearing them when he rowed back to shore. He was still wearing them in the quiet room of Overlake Hospital when he was told that his wife was beyond saving. He was so nearsighted that he couldn't see to drive—or to row—without them.

Randy was still in sporadic contact with Stacey Reese, even though he and Greg had moved out of the house he had shared with Cynthia and into Lily Vandiveer's residence.

Stacey told Randy Mullinax that Randy Roth had seemed definitely upbeat over the past few weeks. He apparently felt that the police were no longer fixing their suspicion on him. "My attorney told me that no news is good news," he had chortled to her. He said he had taken a polygraph test and that he had to pay for it, but he didn't tell her the results of the test. It sounded as though Randy's attorney wanted him to take a private lie detector test before he submitted to one administered by the police.

"Randy's going to sell his house," Stacey said. "He's going to move north."

How far north? Mullinax wondered. He didn't want to have to trail Randy Roth all the way up to Alaska if he and Sue Peters ever did get enough probable cause to arrest him. And that was a big if.

On September 19, Marilyn Brenneman, Randy Mullinax, Sue Peters, and Joe Lewis traveled to Skamania County. They met with Mike Grossie, who was now the undersheriff, and then followed the trail up the massive monolith. They climbed almost three-quarters of the way up the looming rock to the spot where Janis Roth had fallen to her death almost exactly a decade earlier. They found the shortcut between the two switchbacks, and Joe Lewis video-taped the terrain while Randy Mullinax described the area on tape. Up this high, the leaves had already begun to change. It was beautiful—but chilling—as the investigators gazed down. They were so high, they viewed the landscape and the river below as if they were looking down from a plane.

What must it have been like for a woman reportedly terrified of heights to feel herself sliding, sliding, and finally slipping over the edge? That was assuming that Janis *had* slipped, as Randy Roth had said. If she had been pushed, she would have been plummeting down, halfway there, before she realized what had happened.

Now a crew of detectives and a deputy prosecutor were re-creating that day after Thanksgiving 1981. It wasn't easy, tracking down the sheriff's men and women, the rescuers, and interviewing them ten years later. There is no statute of limitations on murder, but if Skamania County had not been able to find enough probable cause to bring charges right after Jan's death, there was no reason to think King County could do so a decade later. The one thing they had going for them in 1991—possibly—was a similar occurrence, a commonality, a *pattern*.

Randy had bragged to Stacey Reese that he wasn't worried, that nothing seemed to be happening in the investigation of Cynthia's death. But he was whistling in the wind. Randy Roth certainly had good reason to feel nervous as the summer of 1991 eased into autumn. At the request of DPA Marilyn Brenneman and the King County detectives, George Cody appeared with Roth at Sue Peters's office in the King County Courthouse. Randy was prepared to take a lie detector test. Polygrapher Norm Matzke advised Roth of his constitutional rights. He asked his preliminary baseline questions. Then he asked Randy Roth to briefly explain to him what had happened on July 23, the day Cynthia drowned.

George Cody objected. His client had, he said, already answered those kinds of questions. Suddenly the lie detector session was all over. "This is a witch hunt," Cody said. "We will not continue."

Cody and his client walked rapidly out of King County Police Headquarters.

Even so, Randy had no idea how closely Mullinax and Peters were walking behind him. He was a man who had never served more than fourteen days of jail time, who had collected on a number of insurance policies and never had to give a penny back, who had even let the U.S. government support his only child with survivor's benefits on a woman he had been married to less than a year.

Randy was ready to move on to the next chapter of his life. He had told some of his confidants that he planned to leave the area entirely. He had told others he simply planned to move one county north into Snohomish County. He had never left Greg behind before, but he had never been this spooked before. Now, Greg was armed with two phone numbers to be used in case of emergency, and Randy had settled his son in with Lily Vandiveer. If Roth rabbited, there was no telling if King County authorities could ever find him again.

17

It was October 1991. Unaware that Marilyn Brenneman had prepared a certification for determination of probable cause for his arrest, Randy Roth went to an office of the Social Security Administration on October 2.

Robbed, he felt, of Tyson's and Rylie's benefits, Randy had come up with another thought. Very quietly he made application to Social Security on Greg's behalf, asking for $768 a month in survivor's benefits. He knew from his experience with Janis that he had been married to Cynthia just long enough for Greg to qualify as her son. He explained to Candy Bryce, the Social Security Administration interviewer, that Greg's mother had drowned two months earlier. He did not mention that Greg was already collecting Social Security survivor's benefits after the death of another of his "mothers." Indeed, he said he had been married only twice—to Cynthia and to a

woman named Donna Clift. He completely omitted
any information on his other two wives, Janis Miranda and Donna Sanchez.

When Bryce asked if Cynthia Roth had any other
surviving children, Randy said no.

"Had Cynthia been married before?" Candy Bryce
asked.

"Yes," Randy answered smoothly. "Her first marriage ended in divorce."

Clearly Randy Roth did not expect to be arrested. If
he had, there were many things he would not have
done—not the least of which was to make the rather
unfortunate application for double Social Security
benefits for Greg. There were also things he might
have done. He might have moved or hidden items that
were not technically his own. But he was cocky. More
than two months had gone by and it seemed obvious
to him that the cops were chasing their own tails. They
didn't have anything on him. They had no way to
prove anything and they never would.

He was wrong.

On October 8, 1991, the Honorable Laura Inveen
issued search warrants directing law enforcement
personnel to search for and seize specified items of
evidence pertaining to the crimes of murder and theft,
from the defendant's residence at 15423 232nd Avenue N.E., Woodinville, King County, Washington.
Each item of evidence was supported by probable
cause and described with sufficient particularity to
satisfy the mandate of the Fourth Amendment to the
United States Constitution and Articles 1 and 7 of the
Washington Constitution.

The first search warrant was for items that could be
connected to the drowning of Cynthia Roth—
clothing, footwear (thongs), towels, documents, financial records or writings—and for tools and other
items that Randy Roth had claimed were stolen in his
1988 burglary report to Pioneer Insurance.

Everything was in place.

But first there was the matter of the arrest of Randolph G. Roth. It was ten minutes after nine on the ninth day of the tenth month of 1991. A Wednesday morning. Sue Peters, Joe Lewis, Randy Mullinax, and Sergeant Frank Kinney arrived at Bill Pierre Ford on Lake City Way. Sue Peters, who had begun this investigation on the baking hot evening of July 23, now officially arrested Randy Roth for the murder of his wife.

Randy was shocked. He stared straight ahead as Peters read him his rights under *Miranda.* He stated that he understood those rights, and he declined to make any statement. He also refused to provide the detectives with a handwriting exemplar, and he would not sign a voluntary consent to search of his home.

At that point Peters provided Roth with a copy of the search warrant. His jaw set, he said nothing. Just as he had been forced to give up his raft for police examination, he now was legally bound to let detectives search through his house.

Apparently he had not thought of that.

Roth, in his mechanic's coveralls, requested his street clothes, and Mullinax asked his supervisor to get his shoes, jacket, shirt, and pants out of his locker. Maybe Randy expected to be bailed out and wanted to have his street clothes ready. As the two detectives transported Randy Roth south on the freeway toward the King County Jail, they noticed a truck following them, the driver apparently talking to someone on a cellular phone. At length, Mullinax pulled over onto the shoulder and forced the truck to pass. He recognized Randy's best friend, Max Butts.

By a quarter to ten that morning, Roth had been booked into the King County Jail, and Peters and Mullinax drove to Woodinville to assist in the execution of the search warrant. They were understandably elated. They were perhaps halfway home. A police investigation rarely ends with the arrest; conscientious detectives are usually looking for evidence right up to—and during—a trial. Randy Roth was thirty-seven years old, and he had apparently been keeping secrets for most of his life. The two detectives had every reason to expect every room in his house to hold answers, clues, keys.

Maybe Cynthia had stumbled onto some of those answers, and maybe it had led to her death.

They were about to find out.

18

Even on real-life cop shows on television, patrolmen and detectives always seem to be bursting through front doors and yelling, "Freeze."

At the big yellow house there was no need to burst through the door; there was no hurry. Sergeant Frank Kinney, Joe Lewis, and Bill Bonair waited at the house for Sue Peters and Randy Mullinax to return from booking Randy Roth into jail. They looked at the scrubby yard that had never been landscaped and wondered why a man with the energy and obsessive need for order that Randy had had never bothered to at least throw out some grass seed. He had complained that the place was "a swamp," but that seemed an exaggeration. They could see where someone—possibly Randy—had dug a trench for drain tile and filled it in with gravel.

Someone—maybe Cindy—had placed planters with geraniums, nasturtiums, and marigolds on the front porch and in front of the triple garage. But Cindy had been dead for weeks, and no one had watered the flowers or picked off the dead leaves and blossoms; they were going to seed.

While Kinney, Bonair, and Lewis waited, they took pictures of the exterior of the empty house for the case file. When Mullinax and Peters arrived, they inserted a key in the front door and called out, "Search Warrant—King County Police."

No one answered.

Like most search warrants, this too was executed in a silent house with silent rooms. There was the thinnest layer of dust on the new oak tables, and a staleness in the air from windows and doors shut too long. There was no sound in what had once been Cynthia Roth's dream home. There were no living occupants. The only eyes left to follow the detectives as they worked were those of Cynthia's dolls, some of which still stood on pedestals in the tall oak display case at the bottom of the stairs.

Sue Peters and Randy Mullinax had come to "know" Cynthia Loucks Baumgartner Roth as well as—perhaps better than—they knew the living people in their own lives. They had talked to a hundred or more people about her. They had also come to know and sincerely like her parents, Merle and Hazel; her brother, Leon; her children, Tyson and Rylie; and her best friend, Lori Baker. They had talked to her husband.

But this was her *house.* Her essence remained in these rooms despite the fact that her widower had apparently tried to throw out all traces of her. The furniture she had chosen was still here. This was the house to which she had come full of hope, bubbling over with happiness, with a firm belief that she and her children would live here until she was old with the man she loved. Even though she was gone, the two detectives who had spent their every waking hour thinking about her for the past eleven weeks felt somehow that walking through her house was almost an invasion of her privacy. But they had to do it. There might be clues here that would explain what had led up to her death and let them see that her killer was convicted of her murder.

Dust motes floated in the sun that streamed through the multi-paned windows as Sue Peters searched the family room. Randy Roth apparently never threw any paperwork away. Peters collected stacks of it, including newspaper articles and miscellaneous papers which she found in a green plastic garbage bag. She found four books on the Vietnam War and photographed them. It wasn't hard to figure out where Randy got the material for his war stories. She knew he had told some of his other women that he was actually the subject of Vietnam books.

All lies.

At five feet three, the smallest member of the search team, Peters burrowed into a crawl space underneath the house. She saw several cases of Motorcraft motor oil from Bill Pierre Ford.

The other detectives were finding Bill Pierre items too. It looked as if Randy had brought home enough stuff to open his own garage. There were hundreds—thousands—of dollars' worth of auto parts. They had suspected that Randy might have taken unauthorized stock home from work, but nothing like this. The Bill Pierre and Ford items were not listed on the search warrant; the investigators would have to ask for an additional search warrant.

Frank Kinney found a VCR tape in the family room; someone had taped television coverage of Cynthia's drowning.

Joe Lewis bagged into evidence papers, tax records, real estate articles, an address book, bank records, telephone records, insurance, miscellaneous records, blank checks, keys, beach towels, women's thongs, and Cynthia Roth's financial and tax records.

Lewis also located scores of tools. They looked

remarkably similar to the tools that Randy had reported stolen in his claim to Pioneer Insurance after the burglary in 1988.

As the searchers moved from room to room, Randy Mullinax took photographs. His search area was the master bedroom. It was still furnished, but it seemed empty of life, as if Randy had left only the most basic items to make the house more salable. The only tender touch was a teddy bear on one shelf of the wall unit; the bear wore a sweatband.

Mullinax found Cynthia's wallet and checkbook. There was no identification in the wallet, but the check register appeared to have been written by Cynthia. The last check had been written to a Safeway store for groceries on July 23, 1991—the day of her death. There were several packages of condoms next to the bed and a small magazine featuring letters about sex under the bed. Randy had told many women he'd had a vasectomy. If he had been faithful to his new wife, he should not have had any need for condoms.

The next two bedrooms were completely bare except for some empty suitcases in the closets. The fourth bedroom held the peculiar weapons that Randy had always kept close by—clubs with nails driven into them. In the closet of that room, Mullinax found a black rubber diving suit. If Randy Roth couldn't swim very well, what was he doing with a wet suit?

The upstairs rec room contained photo albums with photographs of Janis, Jalina, Randy, Greg, Cynthia, and Lori Baker. There were more clippings about Vietnam. Next to the albums were a number of Marine Corps patches. They were brand new; the sales slips were close by. Mullinax perused the slogans on the patches: "Served and Proud of It," "POW-MIA— They Are Not Forgotten," "Republic of Vietnam Service," "3rd Recon BN: Swift—Silent—Deadly."

Randy also had patches from Korea, the Philippines, Camp Pendleton, Camp Delmar, Twentynine Palms, and Okinawa.

The man who had served in the marines for only a few months as a clerk had not gotten over his obsession. He had told the lies so many times to so many people that he might actually have believed he had served in Vietnam.

More likely, the stories and the patches were a part of his con technique. The older he got and the more remote the Vietnam conflict became, the better he might be able to carry off his swift-silent-deadly stories.

But not in jail. You can't con a con.

According to her sons, Randy had dumped Cynthia's makeup—blush, lipstick, mascara, and eyeliner—her perfume and nail polish, and most of her other beauty products into the garbage the day after she died. That was probably true; Mullinax found no cosmetics.

In the upstairs bathroom closet, he did find numerous family photographs, precious pictures that had obviously belonged to Cynthia Roth. There were framed pictures of Tyson and Rylie, from their earliest babyhood to more recent pictures. There was a picture of the Loucks family—Hazel, Merle, Leon, and a six-year-old Cindy—that looked as though it had been taken in the early sixties. There was a plaque from Little League that read, "Special Thanks Coach Cindy Baumgartner," and Mullinax found other plaques as well. Everything had been tossed carelessly in the bathroom closet. Those mementos should have gone to Lori or to the Louckses.

Cindy's pictures were there too, the country pictures of ducks and teddy bears, her country brooms decorated with lace and flowers, her woven baskets—so many of the little touches that she had placed around the house.

Randy had told Stacey Reese that he had gotten rid

of "all that fucking mauve." Well, he had. Most of it. He'd dumped it in the bathroom closet or thrown it in the garbage.

Mullinax searched a little outside utility shed and found two Stihl chain saws, one 20-inch and one 16-inch. Those were two of the items that Mullinax remembered Randy had reported stolen to Pioneer. Either he had replaced everything he had lost—or he had never lost it at all.

Randy Mullinax found another crawl space; this one was locked. Gaining access, he found more oil, more auto parts whose boxes read "Bill Pierre."

It was a wonder that they had enough equipment back at the Ford dealership to do business.

Bill Bonair leafed through a thin book, no more than forty pages long, and the hair on the back of his neck stood up. He had found it in Randy's "macho" rec room. It was a very old book on Japanese martial arts that described in detail how to kill someone with your bare hands and never leave a mark. Most of the illustrative diagrams showed techniques to be used around the head and neck.

The detectives were all getting hot and dirty as they swarmed over the yellow house, its outbuildings and crawl spaces. Clearly, Randy Roth had not expected to be arrested on that October day. Aside from the stuff he'd thrown away, sold at the swap meet, and dumped unceremoniously into the Bakers' U-Haul truck, Randy seemed to have hung on to *everything*.

Sue Peters moved into the triple garage. It was about 12:50 P.M. and she had been searching steadily for two hours. There was a little four-drawer brown file cabinet in the garage. It didn't look important. It seemed to be stuffed with more paperwork. Searching through it all was a little like preparing to do income tax, digging through receipts, checks, letters, and miscellaneous junk that should have been organized months before.

In the second drawer Sue Peters found a wadded-up clump of what looked to be sheets of typewriter paper. She was tempted to toss it. "I don't know why I bothered with it," she would say months later. "It looked like garbage. Do I want to bother with this? I dinked around with it, and I saw 'Randy hates Cindy . . .' and I said to myself, Holy Cow!"

If Cynthia Roth had been standing right behind Sue Peters and reached out to touch her lightly on the shoulder, Peters could not have had more of a sense that she had finally broken the code. Cindy hadn't been the kind of woman to complain to friends or to her family. Peters had learned by now that Cindy was proud and private and tried her best to make things work out.

But they had not. Staring down at the crumpled sheets in her hand, Sue Peters could almost hear Cindy's voice as she read her words:

> Randy does not 'love' Cindy,
> Randy Hates Cindy. . . .
> Randy Hates Cindy's Face Make-Up,
> Randy Hates Cindy's Blush
> Randy Hates Cindy's Lipstick;
> Randy Hates Cindy's Blonde Hair
> Randy Hates Cindy's Ugly toes—
>   they're the ugliest toes he's
>   ever seen.
> Randy Hates all of Cindy's
>   5 or 6 different perfumes.
> Randy hates Cindy's cold feet
> Randy hates Cindy's cold hands.
> Randy hates Cindy's fingernails.
> Randy hates Cindy's dolls in every
>   room.
> Randy hates Cindy's Pink Feminine
>   things in every room.
> Randy hates Cindy's Peach
>   feminine things in every room.

Randy hates Cindy's pictures.
  Randy hates Cindy's Furniture,
  Randy hates Cindy's drawers
    because they aren't real drawers.
  Randy hates the way Cindy
    drives because she'll wreck
    the cars and trucks.
  Randy hates the way Cindy
    cooks most of the time.
    Randy hates the way
Cindy buys groceries too
many times every week and
    spends too much money.
Randy hates the swamp that
Cindy made him move to.
Randy hates Cindy's hose,
  Randy hates Cindy's things,
  Randy hates Cindy's money,
  Randy hates Cindy's
    independent nature.
  Randy hates the way Cindy
    grinds her teeth.
  Randy hates the way Cindy
    picks up his papers all
      the time.
  Randy hates the way
Cindy uses all the hot
  water to fill the huge
    tub for a bath.
Randy hates that Cindy
  drinks coffee.
Randy hates that Cindy
  eats more than all of
  the boys.
Randy hates how
  Cindy decorates a house—
  Randy hates Cindy
    shopping,

Randy hates Cindy
leaving the house at
all.
Randy hates Cindy driving
the Trooper.
Randy hates Cindy's pants.
Randy hates that Cindy
likes to eat!! Because
she'll get fat.
Randy hates that Cindy
made a Cookie for
Valentine's Day & not a
cake.
Randy hates if Cindy
wants to help or volunteer
anywhere.
Randy hates Cindy having
Lori over to our house.
Randy hates coming home
from work instead
of shopping or doing
other things.
Randy hates not being able
to go shopping alone all
the time!
Randy hates telling
Cindy where he goes.
Randy hates Cindy's
monthly thing and
putting up with her
each month.

Sue Peters sat back on her heels. The document was written as if it were a desperate poem. The writing scrawled more with each line, and she could imagine the writer sobbing as she wrote. The words had been set down in black ink with a forceful hand.

Cynthia Roth—the bubbly, giving, friendly woman —had clearly been reduced to someone who had no self-confidence left, whose every move, thought, action, and behavior had irritated the man she had loved so much. Randy Roth had beaten her down until she had little left. Nothing she did had pleased him.

And yet Cindy had still held out that last hope—that their anniversary trip to Reno would somehow renew their marriage, and bring them back to the place in their hearts where they had been in the summer of 1990.

There was no date on the "poem." It had to have been written after Valentine's Day 1991; Cindy had not yet met Randy Roth on that holiday in 1990. Her friends had seen that Cindy had seemed quietly unhappy after her first Christmas with Randy. The insurance papers had been delivered in March.

Yes, Cindy had realized full well that Randy no longer loved her, but had she been afraid of him? Afraid for her life? Probably not. If she had been, she would not have climbed into that raft with him and headed so far, far away from the crowd on the beach at Idylwood Park. She would have not left her sons alone on the beach unless she expected to be back in a very short time.

As Sue Peters sealed the desolate poem into a plastic bag and labeled it, she thought of another little note she had found in her search, a note written in the same rounded cursive script. Cindy Roth had, like all the others, believed that Randy's nightmares were triggered by his horrible experiences in a faraway Asian war. And she had been trying to help him. Peters looked at the note: "Tuesday night, 7:30 p.m.— Tell Randy about Vietnam Vet meeting. Post Traumatic Stress Disorder?"

Peters looked at the little shrine that Randy had built for himself in the front hallway. There was a picture of him in marine dress blues—a very handsome, solemn young man gazing straight ahead—and a gold-framed display of two Marine Corps emblems. And, beneath that, the bronze plaque for valor awarded to "Sergeant R. G. Roth."

Bravery and valor? Hardly. Sue Peters knew that Randy hadn't earned the plaque, that he had copied one he had seen in Ben Goodwin's house. She plucked it off the wall, handed it to Joe Lewis, and said, "Put this in evidence."

It had been a very long day. She had arrested Randy at ten minutes to nine that morning, and it was now six-thirty in the evening. "Wait a minute," Peters said. She went upstairs and got the red scrapbook with the Vietnam articles in it and handed that to Joe Lewis too.

19

As late as it was, the King County search team contacted Rick Doss from the Bill Pierre Ford agency and asked him to come and take a look at the auto parts, motor oil, and other items that might have come from the dealership. Doss arrived and made an inventory list of possible stolen agency items.

The police secured the residence at twenty minutes after seven, and by eight, Sue Peters and Bonair were downtown placing all the items they had seized in the evidence room of the King County Courthouse.

Search warrants are precise in listing what detectives may remove. In the execution of the first warrant, the King County detectives had seen countless items that clearly belonged to the Bill Pierre Ford.

They immediately asked for a second warrant listing those items.

The second search warrant was issued. In lay terms, that meant that the King County detectives had the right to go back into the big yellow house and seize the motor parts, oil, gaskets, almost anything with "Bill Pierre" stamped on it.

Before they locked up the Woodinville house on October 9, Kinney, Lewis, Bonair, Mullinax, and Peters had carried and dragged the items that looked as if they had come from Randy's employer into two of the three garages. They photographed the stuff, but they couldn't really know how much it was worth, where it had come from, or if Randy was authorized to have it in his possession. The manager at the dealership that employed Randy Roth had no record that Randy had ever paid for the still-boxed products in the Woodinville home.

Armed with their second search warrant, detectives listed *ninety-five* items as they removed everything from coil springs to motor oil, gear boxes to steering fluid, brake parts to radiators, and almost everything else a man might need to rebuild cars at home. It looked as though Randy had never left work without taking something unauthorized along with him.

Max Butts arrived while the detectives spent their second day logging evidence. He picked up the Roths' dog and the motorcycles that were parked behind the house.

Sue Peters released the ninety-five items that belonged to Bill Pierre Ford to Dick Tutino of that agency.

The news of Randy Roth's arrest hit the papers on October 10, 1991. The next day, the specific charge of first-degree murder was announced. His bail was set at $1 million. Marilyn Brenneman's probable cause document ran eighteen pages and contained information that fascinated both the press and the public. For the first time, they learned about the many, many women in Randy's past—some dead, others only disenchanted. The "accident" on Lake Sammamish no longer seemed to be the result of a bitter twist of fate.

George Cody hastened to remind the media that the case against his client was purely circumstantial. Randy Roth, he said, was fully prepared to defend himself against the charge. Cody maintained that suspicions had been directed toward Roth solely because tragedy had struck him twice, that the King County prosecutors had no "smoking gun surprises" in the documents filed by Marilyn Brenneman. He called the evidence against Roth "a circumstantial web" that in no way changed his own determination to enter a plea of not guilty. He was ready to proceed to trial.

Lizabeth Roth, who had always been a shadowy, almost mythic figure in Randy's discussions of his background, called Sue Peters. Mrs. Roth explained that she was Randy's mother, and that she had been watching reports of his arrest on television and felt the situation was "unreal."

"Randy was heartbroken when Cynthia died," she said urgently. "When I hugged him at the service, he almost broke into tears."

Lizabeth Roth explained that her family was extremely religious and that they were not killers.

"Well . . ." Peters said cautiously—but there was no way to be tactful about her next question. "What about your son, David Roth? He's in prison for murder, isn't he?"

"He got a bum rap," Lizabeth Roth said indignantly. "It was a setup. He confessed by force, and the FBI is looking into it."

Randy Roth's troubles piled up. Chris Jarvis, chronicling Roth's daily troubles for the *Journal American*, reported that Roth was also under investigation for theft from Bill Pierre Ford, his employer. Randy had the murder charge and the $1 million bail hanging over his head in King County Superior Court, and Seattle District Court records showed that police had reason to believe he was also suspected of stealing more than $1,000 worth of auto parts from Bill Pierre. (The actual total was $2,254.)

Pioneer Insurance refiled charges of insurance fraud connected with the 1988 burglary of Randy's house. Randy Mullinax and Sue Peters had found too many of the things he had claimed losses for: the two Stihl saws, the Craftsman tool chest, a stereo set. For most people, it is a good idea to save receipts. For Randy, it had meant disaster. It was easy for investigators to match the dates on the receipts with the items squirreled away in and under the Woodinville house. Whatever had disappeared in 1988 had miraculously found its way back into Randy's possession.

Bill Pierre Ford fired Randy. That was the least of his troubles.

On Saturday, October 12, Randy Mullinax received a phone call from one of Lily Vandiveer's relatives. She had reason to believe that Randy had called Lily from the King County Jail. "Randy gave her a long list of things he wanted her to remove from his house right away," the woman said.

Mullinax immediately placed the empty yellow house under surveillance all weekend, but nobody appeared. It might have been too late. The same informant called him back to say that she thought Lily and a man named "Max" might already have taken things from the house that Randy didn't want anyone to know about. "I think they took them to store someplace in Snohomish County," she said. "I heard, too, that Randy gave Lily $25,000 before he went to jail."

Max Butts had had an appointment with Mullinax at ten o'clock on Saturday morning, but he hadn't shown up. On Monday the detective went to the body shop where Max worked. Butts pulled in driving Randy Roth's Ford pickup. He didn't seem particularly happy to see Mullinax.

Randy Mullinax noted that Randy Roth's toolboxes from Bill Pierre Ford were in the back of the pickup. Butts didn't want to talk to Mullinax at all, saying he had been advised by Randy's attorney not to.

"Is George Cody *your* attorney?" Mullinax asked.

"No."

"Well, I think it's very important that you talk to me about any involvement you may have had in picking up some of Randy's belongings from his house over the weekend."

Mullinax studied Butts. He saw the man was torn between loyalty to his best friend and saving his own neck.

His neck won.

Max Butts admitted that Randy had called and given him a list of things that he wanted out of his house: "He was afraid stuff that belonged to him might be taken away while he was in jail. He wanted his personal papers and other things stored for him. I took them to my house."

Mullinax called the office and spoke to Sue Peters. She had just received a call from Rick Doss at Bill Pierre. Max Butts *had* picked up Randy's toolbox, but he had also returned some large items that belonged to the Ford dealership. He had explained to the mechanic who helped him unload the equipment that Roth had "borrowed" it and Max was now returning it for him.

The items were a Walker one-and-a-half-ton bumper jack, a Weaver Acra-speed wheel balancer, and a Hunter strobe wheel balancer kit. Mullinax had seen all three of the items when he participated in the first search. The jack was in the crawl space, and the wheel balancers were under the front porch. Rick Doss said that Randy had never had permission to take either the jack or the balancers. Occasionally mechanics could borrow the heavier equipment overnight, but it was always due back the next morning.

Randy had never asked.

For a man who claimed to be as clever and competent as Randy Roth always had, his frantic return of stolen items was a little silly. He was charged with first-degree murder, and he was worrying about theft charges. But then, the theft charges were backed by physical evidence, while the murder charges really were circumstantial, just as George Cody said.

Could Marilyn Brenneman convince a jury *beyond a reasonable doubt* that Randy Roth had deliberately drowned Cynthia Roth? Could she find legal precedent that would let her bring the accidental death of Janis Roth into her courtroom? Winning or losing might all come down to that.

Sue Peters and Randy Mullinax had sensed from the very beginning that Randy Roth frightened the people whose lives touched his, that there had always been about him a subtle threat of danger. He was the man in black who prowled alone at night, the man with the nail-studded clubs hanging from his bed, the self-proclaimed expert in karate, and, the man who had carried out such vicious killings in Vietnam that he screamed out in the darkness of his dreams. And, of course, two of his four wives were dead, and violently dead.

Once Randy Roth had been arrested and was languishing in jail with a million dollars in bail keeping him there, witnesses began to speak more freely. Their fear of Randy might very well have been subliminal. He had spent most of his life perfecting his own brand of mind control.

Lori Baker had never been afraid of Randy; she had been afraid for Cynthia, but more afraid that Cindy would be hurt emotionally than physically. Marilyn Brenneman and Randy Mullinax went to Lori's home to talk with her. They showed her the four-page "poem" that Sue Peters had found in Cindy's little storage chest in the garage. If anyone could recognize Cindy's writing, it would be Lori.

Lori read through the words that showed how sad and diminished Cindy had been in her last spring. She nodded. Yes, she said, it was Cindy's writing. "She told me about writing this—all the things that Randy hated about her. I didn't know that she had saved it."

Lori would be an important witness in the case against Randy Roth, and she talked with Marilyn Brenneman about the close friendship she had had with Cindy Baumgartner. Combining their households had seemed like a good idea back in 1985, and it had been. Cindy hadn't needed Lori's $300 a month rent, but Lori had insisted. They maintained a bank account together to pay the household expenses. Lori had agreed to be the boys' guardian, but she had not expected to be the executor of Cindy's will.

"I remember when she told me that a man had asked for her phone number while she was working at the concession stand for Little League," Lori said. "That man turned out to be Randy Roth."

Lori recalled when Randy and his son Greg had come to dinner at the house she shared with Cindy. Lori had not had a chance to say much to Randy during the very short time that he and Cindy had dated; Cindy and Randy had eyes only for each other. Lori found Randy Roth pleasant enough, but his courtship was rapid and constant. She remembered that Randy kept asking Cindy to take overnight trips with him. "That was something that Cindy would never have done unless she was married to a man," Lori explained.

Cindy had been troubled that Randy was not a churchgoer. But she had been sure that she would be able to get him to attend church after they were married.

Things had not gone well after the marriage. Even though she told no one but Lori, Cindy had confided shortly after the honeymoon that her sex life with Randy was not very good. Randy had not proved to be the ardent lover she had waited for. After so many years of celibacy, it had been a disappointment. Cindy had expected that this would be a complete marriage, with both spiritual and physical love. Cindy had felt disloyal even in voicing her disillusionment about her almost nonexistent sex life. Randy had been such an impetuous suitor that she had expected him to be a warm and exciting lover. And he had not been.

"Within weeks of their wedding," Lori said sadly, "Cindy was having second thoughts."

Cindy Roth had been independent for almost six years, and she had come to value her freedom to come and go, but she told Lori that Randy wanted her to stay in the house all the time. His insistence that she was not to do *anything* on her own had quickly made Cindy feel suffocated. She was frustrated and annoyed once when she found her car wouldn't start. Lori came over to help and found that someone had deliberately disconnected a wire under the hood. "I hooked it back up," Lori said, "and she could at least do her errands."

Randy had operated under a double standard; he could join a health gym, but he didn't even want his wife to join an aerobics class if there were men in it.

Lori recalled that Cindy had been highly suspicious of Lily Vandiveer. When Randy took Lily's son, Brad, home, he would often be gone for hours. Cindy didn't trust Lily and Randy. She had begun to drive Brad home earlier in the day so that Randy had no excuse to make the trip. She hadn't been able to understand why the older woman seemed to have such a large place in Randy's life.

By the spring of 1991, Cindy had begun to mention to Lori that she had thought of leaving Randy. But Lori knew she never would have: "Her religious beliefs were too strong. She wouldn't have considered divorce."

"Do you know if Randy ever asked *her* for a divorce?" Marilyn Brenneman asked.

Lori shook her head. "I don't think so. Cindy would have told me."

Now that they knew they would be going to trial, Marilyn Brenneman needed to learn as much as she could about Randy Roth—every relationship, every detail—even those that seemed innocuous enough on the surface. Randy Mullinax was curious that Max Butts would run so many errands for Roth. What was he to Randy Roth?

Lori had met Max several times; he was always trailing in Randy's wake. "Cindy noticed it too," Lori recalled. "She said it seemed like everywhere they went, Max showed up." He had told Lori that he didn't think Randy would marry Cindy. When he came to her house looking for Randy on the weekend the pair had eloped to Reno, Max had seemed terribly upset to hear that news.

Mullinax had seen that Roth always had had a younger male friend who was totally impressed with him, someone to run and fetch for him. Once it had been Nick Emondi; now it was Max Butts.

Emondi was ready to tell the detectives anything they needed to know; he had broken away from Randy, while Butts was still clinging to his hero.

Lori Baker said that Greg had been very fond of Cindy, although he was careful not to show how much he liked her when his father was around. Cindy hadn't known why—except that Randy was so much into marine-style macho behavior. Real men didn't show their feelings, and that went for boys too.

There was one thing that Lori had never known about: Cindy had never told her about the way Randy disciplined the boys—Greg and her own two sons. After Tyson and Rylie moved in with Lori, however, she realized with dawning horror just how bad things had been.

"He made them do squat thrusts as discipline," she told Brenneman and Mullinax. "They told me once that they were doing them in the driveway on a cold night and he turned the hose on them because they weren't doing them fast enough."

Tyson had told Lori that Randy picked him up bodily once and threw him across the room so hard that Tyson's head made a dent in the wallboard. All three of the boys had to help Randy clean the shop at Bill Pierre Ford on Friday nights. They didn't mind that, but inevitably they never worked fast enough to suit him. To hurry them along, Randy had turned the high-pressure cold water hose on them. "They had to finish cleaning and ride home with wet clothes," Lori said. What might have been a lark in the summer was miserable in the winter.

Cindy had saved Greg from serious injury at least once, the boys had told Lori. His father had been about to throw him headlong into the stone fireplace when Cindy intervened.

Marilyn Brenneman and Randy Mullinax talked alone to Tyson Baumgartner, and they got a more fully rounded picture of what life had really been like in the picture-perfect yellow house in the country.

Cindy's older son said Randy had insisted that he and Rylie watch videos of *Platoon* and *Hamburger Hill*. Both Vietnam War movies were full of gruesome battle scenes. When the boys tried to turn away from the bloody action, Randy insisted they watch it all.

"Randy told us that he had to do a lot of the things we saw—when he was in Vietnam," Tyson said.

On some nights, when Randy was angry with Tyson or Rylie, he took out his rage on their mother. He would drive off in a spray of gravel and not come home until the early hours of the morning, or he would grab Cindy's arm so hard that she had bruises shaped like finger marks the next day.

Tyson remembered the "shop nights" at the car dealership all too well. Randy and Max, who invariably accompanied them, would laugh at the sight of the boys when they were caught in the needle-sharp spray of the high-pressure hose. The boys had just about frozen working in January or February in soaking wet clothes.

Asked if he remembered his stepfather ever bringing home "supplies" from the car dealership, Tyson nodded. He had seen Randy bring home oil and air filters and the jack that Randy Mullinax had found under the house during the search-warrant sweep. "He said he needed the jack to work on the Escort. He put the oil on shelves in the garage."

Tyson said that he had even seen Randy bringing home entire engines. One was still wrapped in plastic in a crate. He didn't know what had become of those big items. He had asked Randy once if he bought the things he brought home, and Randy had said sarcastically, "No, I did *not* buy them."

Cindy Roth's little boys were slowly coming out of their nightmare months with a stepfather who had never served in Vietnam but who behaved like a cruel marine drill sergeant. They had tried very hard to get along with him because their mother wanted them all to be a family. Sometimes Randy had done fun things with them—but mostly they had walked softly and jumped to do his bidding.

So had their mother.

20

Nineteen eighty-five had been a turning-point year for Cindy Baumgartner, Randy Roth, Sue Peters, Randy Mullinax, and Marilyn Brenneman—and for Deputy Prosecuting Attorney Susan Storey, who was chosen to be the other half of the King County prosecuting team. Because of what happened in that single year, none of them would ever be quite the same again. But, of course, not one of them had realized it. Watershed moments are only recognizable in retrospect.

When Donna Clift left Randy Roth in 1985, he became a single man and, in his own mind, a widower again. Cindy really was a widow. The two of them seemed meant, through some grim synchronicity, to meet and to marry, but for all the wrong reasons. Donna Clift would berate herself forever after for not calling Cindy to warn her. Ben Goodwin would wish he had been more convincing when he *did* warn her.

But nothing helped, and Cindy was dead. And now the most compelling murder case in King County in decades was going to trial. And it would indeed be a squeaker.

In the fall of 1985 Susan Storey was starting her last year of law school at the University of Puget Sound and working for a Tacoma law firm. Tacoma was a big city compared to Lewiston, Idaho, where she was born. She didn't stay very long in the town on the Washington-Idaho state line; Storey's childhood was peripatetic. She lived in Spokane, Seattle, and New Providence, New Jersey. She went to high school in Seattle and undergraduate school at the University of Washington, where she was an outstanding member of the crew team.

In 1985, Susan Storey had served a summer internship with the King County Prosecuting Attorney's Office in Seattle, and they had offered her a job when she graduated from law school in the spring. "I jumped at the job," Storey remembers. "I knew I wanted to practice criminal law."

Fledgling prosecutors don't get to handle much heavy-duty criminal law in the beginning, but Storey knew that. After Susan Storey graduated cum laude from UPS, she moved to Seattle and started at the King County Prosecutor's Office in October of 1986. Her first assignment was in a district court in Renton, a Seattle suburb. Next she worked in King County Juvenile Court. "I didn't come downtown until right about the end of 1988."

Dark-haired, with clear blue eyes, Storey shares Sue Peters's love for softball and served for a time as assistant commissioner of the Emerald City Softball Association.

In her first five years with the King County Prosecutor's Office, Storey moved steadily up to handle headline cases, including the Hung Tran Asian Gang case, in which the accused attempted to be tried as a juvenile after terrorizing and robbing families in his neighborhood. Forensic anthropologists used X-ray technology to determine Tran's age. He was not a juvenile.

Another memorable case for Storey was the trial of the Queen Anne Ax Murderer. Numerous homes in the historic Queen Anne Hill district of Seattle were broken into at night. At first, the pattern seemed bizarre, even kinky: the intruder would rearrange the furniture, write on the walls, or leave an ax inside the house. And then things turned deadly. A sixty-year-old woman was murdered with an ax as she slept. Detectives arrested James Cushing, who had no permanent address and rambled the streets of Seattle. He had become fixated on the Queen Anne neighborhood. Susan Storey won a conviction despite Cushing's insanity defense.

Marilyn Brenneman and Sue Storey had long since discovered, as had all female prosecutors, that the distaff members of the prosecutor's office bear an extra burden in the courtroom. Like all effective prosecutors, they had schooled themselves to remain dispassionate about the defendant, no matter what abhorrent crimes he or she might stand accused of. But it hadn't been that long since the lead prosecutor was always male, although he might be assisted by a female DPA. In the courtroom, the woman prosecutor still had to remember to walk softer. To speak softer.

"You never hear a male attorney being described as 'strident,'" Brenneman says, smiling. "Or 'bitchy' or worst of all, put them together and you have 'strident bitch!' Males don't have to think about keeping their voices modulated. *We* speak softly and calmly because we're aware that women can be fair game. Eventually this will go away too."

Petite female prosecutors could sometimes talk a bit louder and be a little more sarcastic, but Brenneman and Storey are tall women, and noticeable in the confines of the courtroom. Sometimes their height helps; sometimes it's a drawback. Brenneman, at five feet nine, is heartened to see one of Seattle's more massive defense attorneys in the opposite corner. She laughs, remembering when she was about as pregnant as a woman can get with her last child. Facing off with Tony Savage, one of Seattle's largest and most sought-out criminal defense attorneys, Brenneman quipped to the judge, "If this trial isn't over soon, I'm going to be bigger than Tony!"

She made it with a few days to spare.

Susan Storey, flushed with victory after a homicide trial, was chastened by a juror who murmured, "I know he was guilty, but did you have to be so mean to him in cross-examination?"

Although it was not deliberate, there was a certain poetic justice now in the fact that out of the prime detective-prosecutor team that stood against a man accused of seducing and killing women, three of the four members were female: Sue Peters, Marilyn Brenneman, and Susan Storey. Randy Mullinax was the lone male. Randy Roth had demeaned and abused females most of his life. He hated little girls. He was the embodiment of the kind of man who preferred his women to stay in their place, barefoot—but not pregnant.

Now he would face two smart, strong, and savvy women in the courtroom while a third, Sue Peters, would be sitting at the prosecution table as a friend of the court.

Mullinax and Susan Storey took aerial photos of Lake Sammamish and Idylwood Park. The game plan would be to re-create for the jury the events, the ambience, and the scene at the park on the day Cynthia Roth's life ended. It would not be a simple task to take that blistering hot summer day at the lake into a small windowless courtroom, to fill the jurors' senses with the sounds, sights, smells, and emotions of that awful day.

But they were going to do it. Cynthia Baumgartner Roth could no longer speak for herself; she could not say what had happened on the far side of the lake as her little boys scanned the water for some sight of their mother. But there were ways to reconstruct; Sue Peters and Randy Mullinax had steadily built a wall of probability, human memories and impressions, documents, expert opinion, similar transactions, and motivations. That wall would always have one stone missing—Cynthia herself—but it was strong enough to hold without her.

21

Contrary to a layman's view, even when a suspect has been arrested and charged, the investigation is not over. The detectives who had tracked and trapped Randy Roth worked harder, if possible, after he was arrested than they had before. He was a man whose whole life had been deliberately secretive as he carried out his schemes. Sue Peters and Randy Mullinax continued to burrow into the quagmire that was Roth's past, conferring constantly with Marilyn Brenneman and Susan Storey about the man they would come up against in court. Randy Roth had never, apparently, simply *lived* his life; he had played wicked games with everyone around him, delighting in keeping them off balance, in deluding and deceiving. Roth was a paradox. He seemed to have lied even when telling the truth might have been easier. He was not a master at Tae Kwon Do or a marine hero or a tender lover or a caring father or a score of other things he claimed to be.

He was, they were convinced, a cold and calculating con man and a killer who could walk away from his murders without a scintilla of remorse. He didn't know the meaning of the word. But he was smart—not educated smart but street smart.

Before Roth went to trial in the spring of 1992, the quartet who would face off with him had to find his Achilles' heel. They suspected that his weakness lay in the very behavior that had given him power: his lies. Given enough time, a lie invariably comes home to roost, and Randy Roth had an endless flock of lies circling him.

By sheer coincidence, Randy Roth was charged with first-degree murder exactly one year to the day after the Pioneer Insurance Company had paid him $28,500 on his burglary claim and dismissed its court action against him—with prejudice. Sue Peters and Randy Mullinax had found two solid witnesses who told them that they knew about the "burglary" before it ever happened. Both witnesses were afraid of Roth, however. Pioneer Insurance agreed not to make any move to vacate its 1990 court action until Roth was behind bars. The witnesses who could help prove Randy had faked his burglary feared retribution. Pioneer's lawyers promised the King County detectives they would not contact the witnesses until it was safe to do so. On October 9, 1991, with Randy Roth safely in jail, Pioneer filed its motion to reopen the case against him.

One of the frightened witnesses was Nick Emondi. He signed an affidavit that his onetime best friend, Randy Roth, had told him in the summer of 1988 that he was thinking of robbing his own house.

The second witness was Brittany Goodwin. She had given a statement to Peters and Mullinax a month after Cynthia drowned, but she would not sign it until she knew Randy was behind bars.

Brittany was the daughter of the man who had been Randy's best friend for almost eight years. Both Ben and Marta Goodwin had loved and trusted Randy, and they had been disillusioned. But even at the end of their friendship, they had not realized how deeply he had betrayed them or for how long.

Brittany had been in grade school when the Goodwins met Randy, but she blossomed into a very pretty, if shy, teenager. From the time Brittany was thirteen, she had a crush on Randy. She didn't know how old he was and he would never tell her. "Let's just say I'm in a box that's over seventeen and under thirty-five," he would tease.

While it is more normal than not for teenage girls to have crushes on older men, it is *not* normal for adult men to encourage that immature adulation. At first, Randy had only seemed so handsome and so much fun. Brittany was full-breasted early and could have passed for seventeen or eighteen when she was four or five years younger, but she was really only a child when Randy began to flirt with her. There was no way she was equipped to deal with his exploitation. "He'd always help me clean up after he came over for dinner," she said. "He would pinch me on the bottom, or rub against me when he was putting the dishes away. That was the way it started."

Brittany was "kind of jealous" when Randy married Donna Clift, and then when Mary Jo moved in.

Brittany Goodwin had never been out with a boy. She was a sitting duck for a man like Randy Roth. He defined who she was, how she would act, how she would look, even how much she would weigh. And he did it so subtly that even her parents berated themselves when they grew suspicious.

"The thing was," Brittany recalls with bitterness, "Is that the boys were always with us. Greg and my brother Ryan would go along when Randy took me anywhere. That made it look innocent, and Randy planned it that way."

Although Brittany's weight was within normal limits, Randy always complained that she was too fat. She was not fat; she was large-breasted, but her waist and hips were slim. More than most teenagers, Brittany felt insecure and imperfect.

Slyly, Randy became a sinister Pygmalion to the

fourteen-year-old girl who lived next door. "He wanted me to be thinner," she said. "He told me that every five pounds I lost, he would give me a reward—like take me skiing or inner-tubing, or he would buy me a new bathing suit. I tried, but I couldn't lose enough to suit him. I decided that if I threw up everything I ate, I would get thin, so I stuck a pencil down my throat and I just threw up all the time. I was really getting emotionally screwed up trying to be what Randy wanted me to be."

Randy kept an eye on everything Brittany ate. "He could go all day and not eat anything but an apple. He couldn't understand why I needed to eat. That was when all my problems with food and my body image started. With Randy."

While her parents believed Randy was taking an avuncular interest in Brittany, he was actually grooming her to be his lover. "He wanted me to be 'more worldly.' He wanted me to eat different foods, meet more people, and act grown-up," Brittany said. "He wanted me to be *thirty*, but I wasn't fifteen yet."

Brittany turned fifteen on February 7, 1987. On Valentine's Day while Marta and Ben Goodwin were out of town, Randy took Brittany and the boys out to dinner and then seduced his best friend's daughter. He promised Brittany that he would marry her when she was eighteen.

"He liked to talk about what my folks would say if they knew we were in love," she remembers. "He would say that maybe we could tell them we were getting married when I was seventeen and a half. He told me that I would never have to work—that he would spoil me."

Perhaps because he knew that Brittany was completely in his power, Randy showed her more of his life than he had other women. He took her—along with Greg and Ryan—to visit his father in Vancouver, Washington. While the Goodwins trusted him, he sent the boys away so that he and Brittany could be alone. "I think Greg knew about us," Brittany said, "but Randy told him he better not say anything. If Greg told, Randy would go to prison, and if he ever got out, he'd come back and get him for telling. Greg never told."

Randy also took Brittany to see his mother. Lizabeth Roth was in the hospital in Bremerton, Washington, recovering from gall bladder surgery. Randy didn't say much to his mother, and Brittany didn't know what to say either. He took her to see his sisters, too. Brittany was surprised at the way Randy's mother and sisters looked; they all wore thick, thick blue eye shadow and dressed in a way that seemed kind of trashy to her.

Randy's physical affair with Brittany was more convenient for him when she began to baby-sit for Greg. It was almost impossible for her to control Greg. If she told him to go in his room, she would look toward the street five minutes later and see that Greg had crawled out his window and was outside playing.

But Randy could make Greg mind. "We were all afraid of him," Brittany remembers. "We all had to do what Randy said. If I didn't push in my chair after dinner, we all had to do push-ups or bends and thrusts. It seemed kind of funny to me—that Randy made love to me and then treated me like a child."

If Brittany ever argued with him, Randy would refuse to have sex with her. And at the same time, he made her feel even less desirable than he usually did.

Greg got most of the punishment, though. He was pushed into a freezing shower if he lied, or he had to stand with both hands on his bed, his pants around his ankles, while Randy beat him with his belt.

Randy took Brittany to Parents Without Partners dances, she said. "I don't know how he explained me. I guess I looked old enough. There were a lot of young women there, and I was jealous. If I didn't learn a dance step on the first try, Randy got mad. If I chewed gum, he'd tell me not to act like a teenager—but I *was* a teenager."

Randy kept Brittany completely off balance all the time. He bought her a "promise ring," and she believed he meant it when he said he would marry her. He would leave a single rose on her car windshield or at the end of her driveway where she would see it and know it was from him.

When she baby-sat, Randy would pretend to drive away, then park his truck down the street and sneak back to spend the night with her. But she knew he was seeing other women too. She found notes from them, and condoms. He only laughed when she questioned him.

Randy particularly enjoyed touching Brittany when her father was so close it was dangerous. If Randy and Ben were working on a car, Randy would wait until Ben's back was turned and then he would blow Brittany a kiss or rub his hand over her breast. When the families went camping together, as they had for years, Brittany slept in a little tent a few feet from her parents' trailer. "Randy liked that. He liked to sneak in and have sex with me so close to where they were sleeping."

Brittany learned soon enough that Randy didn't necessarily keep his promises. She became less afraid of him but more depressed. Mary Jo or Lily would drive up to Randy's house after eleven and stay until four or five in the morning. She says, "My bedroom window was on that side, and I stood there all night, watching his dark house, trying to look in his bedroom window, until I saw them leave."

Randy seemed to take pleasure in tormenting Brittany. He flirted openly with other women when she was with him: "There was one woman who came to a wrestling match that Ryan and Greg were in. She had on those black mesh stockings, and Randy was all over her, saying, 'Can I come over to your house and count the holes in your stockings?' He knew that made me feel bad, but he always acted like that anyway."

She met Lily's daughter, Dawn,* at school, and Dawn stared at Brittany, astounded. "You *like* Randy? Don't you know he was in trouble for killing his wife?"

Brittany asked him about it, and he explained that Janis had died in a terrible accident. "He said they were on a trail and her foot slipped on a rock and she fell off. He cried when he told me about it.

"I only saw him cry twice. That time—and one time he was really worried about money. He told me that he might lose his house because he just didn't have enough money. He thought maybe he could turn it into a duplex and rent out the top half. He really cried hard because he needed money."

Randy Roth's tears came easily when he viewed his dismal financial situation, but he became annoyed with Brittany for crying when one of her favorite aunts died of cancer: "I was sitting on the lawn crying, and he told me to 'Quit crying, just quit crying. Death isn't important. Get on with your life.'"

For Randy, death was not important; money was.

Randy Roth seemed obsessed with youth. He wanted Brittany to see him as young. He liked to race "young guys" in his hot cars. "And he was so worried about going bald," Brittany recalled. "He'd put this hair formula on his head so his hair would grow back. But it never did."

During the first year of their physical affair, Randy Roth could have told Brittany Goodwin he had hung the moon and she would have believed it. During the second, she tried tentatively to break away from the man who wanted to run her whole life, but who wanted *his* freedom to do anything. Breaking away wasn't easy; he was always there, right next door. As always, the Roths and the Goodwins had Sunday breakfast together every week. As always, Randy sneaked pinches and pats behind her parents' back to validate some dark control he had over her—and them.

Brittany was bound to Randy by her own insecurity, her passion for the first and only lover she had ever known, and by a vague fear that he could hurt her if she went too far away.

When she was sixteen and about to start her junior year in high school, she yearned for more than a clandestine affair. She didn't want to be thirty; she wanted to be sixteen. She didn't want to sneak around and hide from her parents anymore, and she knew Randy lied to her far more than he ever told the truth.

Although Randy's constant criticism of her appearance would damage Brittany's self-image for many years to come, she stopped being so afraid of him when she turned sixteen. "I got just a little bit more independent—and not so scared."

On the first day of eleventh grade, Brittany walked to her car. It was a red Ford Fiesta. Randy had the same model, only his Fiesta was burgundy. She unlocked her car, but as she slid behind the steering wheel, she saw that someone had pulled all the wires loose from behind the dashboard and left them dangling like strands of spaghetti. Frightened, she turned the key and pushed the accelerator.

Nothing happened. Randy hadn't wanted her to go to the first day of school where she might meet boys her own age. And now she couldn't get there on time.

Even though Randy Roth had held Brittany Goodwin in an invisible cage for two years, it was he who broke up with her. She does not recall the scene with her father in the driveway, but she does remember a phone conversation that might have triggered the beginning of the end. "I was upset and I called Randy. My dad was just walking in Randy's door and he heard Randy's side of the conversation. Randy hung up quickly, and so did I. But I think my father knew it was me on the other end of the line."

Even after the affair ended, Randy remained close to Brittany. "He always told me 'Semper Fi,' and he always signed his notes the same way, 'Always Faithful.' He wasn't—ever—but he let me know he would never really let me go."

Long before the summer of 1988, Randy had told Brittany, in detail, how he planned to burglarize his own house. "If we ever split up," he warned, "what I've told you has to stay between us—or I'll come and get you. . . ."

She believed him. Even when Brittany was in love with another man, Randy would put his arm around her and flirt with her in front of her new love. He enjoyed that. Creating jealousy was one of Randy's most effective ways of tormenting people and keeping them in line.

Even after Randy married Cindy Baumgartner, he stopped at his old house, which was still on the market, and called Brittany over. He looked at her in the same penetrating way and asked for her new address in Everett. "I'd like to see you again," he said quietly. "I'd like to stop by your house and see you. . . . Semper Fi."

When Cindy drowned, Brittany knew she had to come forward and tell authorities what she knew. Once Randy was safely in jail, she signed the statement she had given about her ex-lover's "burglary."

"I'm not afraid of him anymore," an adult Brittany said. "But I hate him. He had no right to do what he did to me, and it's going to take a long, long time for me to deal with it without hurting."

22

By the time Randy Roth's trial date fast approached in early 1992, Detective Randy Mullinax had interviewed seventy people; Detective Sue Peters had made 498 entries of phone calls, interviews, and actions taken in the case and produced results similar to the old Russian diminishing peasant puzzle, where each doll holds a smaller doll inside—a case within a case within a case within a case. Their investigation had gone from accidental death to possible foul play to similar "transactions" in the past to murder charges, and the two detectives had uncovered side issues of insurance fraud, robbery, child abuse, and all manner of con games. To muddy up their investigative waters, Randy Roth had proved to be a man who stepped from one phase of his life into the next as if moving through an invisible curtain. Each phase meant a new woman and often a new job, new friends, a new house. The only real constant in his life was his son Greg, whom he alternately pampered and disciplined with harshness that bordered on cruelty.

If anyone knew just who Randy Roth was, Sue Peters and Randy Mullinax did. And yet they wondered if it was possible for any human being to really know what forces drove him.

He *was* really Randolph G. Roth and nobody else; they had tracked him from his birth on December 26,

1954. He was a skilled mechanic. He had been married four times, divorced twice, widowed twice.

And he hated women. If he did not harm them physically, he left each woman who cared for him worse off in some way.

The question was, as it always was, *why?*

Gordon and Lizabeth Roth had come from Bismarck, North Dakota, to the Seattle area sometime in the late 1950's. Randy would have been five or six then. His brother David was born in Richardton, North Dakota, a crossroads with 600 citizens, three years later. No one could really say what the Roth siblings' childhoods had been like. Randy had told Ben and Marta Goodwin that he had been forced to kneel for hours on a hard floor. Were those memories *true?* Or were they simply part of the elaborate life story he had manufactured out of whole cloth? Randy's tales of childhood punishment would never be corroborated, but something had gone terribly wrong; both of Gordon and Lizabeth Roth's sons had been arrested for the murder of a woman. One had long since been convicted and the other was now awaiting trial.

The King County detective team could find little evidence of family solidarity among the Roths. Randy had shut the door against one sister and her babies on Christmas Eve. He had told so many lies about his mother that his friends really didn't know if she was dead or alive.

The Roths had apparently been staunch Catholics, but that hadn't prevented Gordon, a plumber, from leaving Lizabeth in 1971. Randy would have been about sixteen then. Gordon was ordered to pay his ex-wife $375 a month in child support. It wasn't enough; Lizabeth qualified for welfare. Randy, still in high school, worked at various jobs—in a feed store, at a gas station—to help support the family. His one dream had surely been to escape, to become like his movie hero, Billy Jack. He feigned expertise in karate and carried a knife.

Randy joined the Marine Corps Reserves when he was a senior in high school.

Lizabeth Roth always blamed her ex-husband for quashing their children's ability to express their feelings. If they had grown up cold and lacking normal family bonds, it was not her fault—it was Gordon's.

It was hard to know what was true. When twenty-one-year-old David Roth was preparing for his trial in the strangulation-gunshot murder of the unknown female hitchhiker in Snohomish County in 1979, he had told a court-appointed psychiatrist that he counted on his mother, but that his father had beaten him.

"Whenever he wanted to do something to me or the other kids, my mom would stand up to him," David testified.

Then why had he strangled a girl he apparently didn't even know and shot her seven times for good measure?

Randy seemed to have bonded more with his father. His surviving wives and girlfriends recalled that the father and son even resembled each other physically —short, muscular, and powerful. Both were take-charge men.

At Meadowdale High School, Randy Roth moved somewhere in the middle stratum. He was an average student who hung out with guys who worked on their cars and raced down Old Highway 99. He wasn't a stoner; in fact, he was violently opposed to smoking, drinking, drugs, and anything else that would harm the body. Even in high school he was proud of his body and was pleased when the coach picked him out to demonstrate difficult gymnastics in P.E. class. He was short but muscular. He wasn't involved in extra-curricular activities. He couldn't be—he was helping to support his mother and sisters. He wasn't a nerd either; he was really more of a nonentity, one of the mass of mostly forgettable students who move through three years of high school without leaving much of an impression on anyone. The impression he did leave was mostly negative. He was known as a troublemaker, the "bad dude," the unpredictable bully. His girlfriends knew better than to talk to or even look sideways at another boy, and his male friends were only those who toadied to him.

If he lied—and he often did—they pretended to believe every word. When he bragged that he had beaten up the infamous Ted Bundy "to protect my sister," they nodded eagerly.

Randy Roth's high school yearbook picture shows a young man whose face is almost overwhelmed by his thick thatch of dark hair, sideburns, a mustache, goatee and beard. He had the large, dark, slightly unfocused eyes of a myopic who wouldn't wear glasses.

In 1983 Randy attended his class's ten-year reunion. He bragged of his accomplishments in the intervening decade. He spoke of his dangerous duty in Vietnam, the secret missions carried out by the elite marine squad he belonged to, and he said he was presently involved in the operation of a huge cattle ranch. (Gordon Roth had a few horses and a few cows down in Washougal.) Randy told his former classmates he also taught martial arts classes—Tae Kwon Do, karate, and other obscure Eastern methods of self-defense. He could, he said quietly, kill a man with his bare hands and never leave a mark.

Yes, he had been in the marines—Peters and Mullinax had substantiated that—but he was only a file clerk. He spent most of his eleven months in the service at Camp Pendleton, and his mother had ended any chance he had to move up in the Marine Corps by summoning him home to take care of her two years before his enlistment was up. Would that have made Randy hate her? Perhaps.

Randy had girlfriends in high school; he usually had

one steady girl for a year or more. They were all impressed with his strength—at least at first. His need to control females was evident even then. And even then Randy hated to see women cry. He hated any display of emotion.

Sue Peters eventually located all of the girls the teenage Randy had dated regularly. One was Dulcie Griffin,* who had known Randy since she was about thirteen. They had become "serious" when she was fifteen or sixteen. Dulcie recalled that Randy had an uncanny ability to use people even then. "I'm surprised that I'm alive," she commented cryptically.

"Why?" Peters asked.

Dulcie recalled a harrowing ride she had taken with Randy and one of his friends, Mike Conrad. Randy could only afford old beaters then, but he drove them as if he was racing in the Indianapolis 500. They were all laughing as Randy swerved around corners on some old road out in the country. One of the back doors flew open when he took a corner on two wheels. Dulcie started to clamber over into the backseat to shut the door and was halfway there when Randy took another corner at high speed.

"I flew out and just rolled over and over until I ended up against a curb."

She was bleeding and hurting, and she started to cry. Mike ran over to see if she was all right. Randy was right behind him—but he wasn't concerned; he looked furious. He was angry because Dulcie was sobbing, and he grabbed her roughly by the arm and hissed, "Don't you cry. Don't you dare cry! If you make any noise, I'll hit you!"

She knew he meant it, and she had managed to control her sniffling as Mike led her back to the car. "Randy didn't care at all if I was hurt," she recalled. "He just didn't want me to make a fuss."

At the time, Gordon Roth was dating Dulcie's mother, and both mother and daughter noticed how similar father and son were—hardheaded and "pushy."

Dulcie thought Randy was a little weird at times. One time as she and her mother drove up to their house Dulcie saw a man's feet disappearing through their kitchen window. It was Randy. When she confronted him about sneaking into their house, he just said he wanted to see if he could get in. All the doors had been locked.

Dulcie and Randy broke up over a silly fight. They had gone east of the Cascade Mountains to visit some of her family, and as a joke, she refused to answer him when he said something to her. He tried a few more times, and Dulcie, hiding a grin, pretended to ignore him.

She didn't know that she could have done nothing more devastating to her romance. Randy Roth, the macho man even then, could never allow a female to ignore him or make a fool of him. When Dulcie finally turned to Randy, he would not speak to her. Not then. Not for days. When he finally did, it was only to break up with her. "I don't want to go out with you anymore," he said coldly. "I'm too much like my father."

She didn't see him again until their high school reunion. At that time, he was long divorced from Donna Sanchez, and Dulcie heard him say to one of the guys, "I fired her. She wasn't working out."

For the last part of his senior year at Meadowdale, Randy worked for the Tire Mart service station in Lynnwood. His friend Jesse Akers was on duty one August night in 1973 when a short robber in a ski mask showed up with a knife. The masked robber threw Akers down, tied him up, and left him in the back room, before leaving with $240 in cash and some eight-track tapes.

Akers wasn't hurt, but he sure was puzzled. He had

recognized Randy right away, and he figured it was some kind of a joke. He'd been about to say, "Hi Randy," when he sensed danger and he kept his mouth shut.

"I knew it was Randy," Akers said later. "He has the most recognizable sort of bowlegged walk I've ever seen."

Randy was not arrested. He went into the marines the next month.

Randy's next girlfriend was a girl who had helped his mother write the letter that got him out of the marines. He was disappointed with his military career; he had expected to be in battle somewhere, not pushing a pencil. He wasn't in long enough to make sergeant—despite the plaque he had made up. "Sergeant R. G. Roth" was as fictitious as "Billy Jack Roth."

Lynn Brotman* and Randy got engaged when he left the marines. Her parents had a vacant house they were selling, and they let Randy live there. Their romance went fine until Lynn found a purse in the house that belonged to someone named Donna Sanchez.

Lynn broke their engagement, and three months later someone broke into her parents' house. Television sets, tools, a stereo, and Lynn's stepfather's Purple Heart medal were missing. They suspected Randy right away, and police found the missing items—except for the Purple Heart—in a house where Randy Roth was living.

Randy confessed to the burglary, but he blamed it on Lynn's stepfather because he felt the older man was responsible for his broken engagement: "He was the only person I could think of who would have goods that I could use to sell, and I would not feel so bad about having taken them."

When Randy broke into her family's home, Lynn was mad enough to tell the police that it was he who had robbed the Tire Mart too. He had needed the money to pay for her abortion, she said.

Randy Roth, then twenty years old, pleaded guilty to second-degree burglary for the break-in. The old armed-robbery charge at the Tire Mart was dropped. Randy received a fourteen-year sentence, with all but two weeks suspended. Although he had bragged to Mullinax and Peters that he never served a day in jail, he had. He served those two weeks.

He got out of jail on June 10, 1975, and he married Donna Sanchez on July 4.

Randy's probation officer found him something of a wise-ass, but he wrote in his report that he thought the jail time had been unpleasant enough to let Roth see what could happen to someone who continued a life of crime.

It did. And it didn't. Randy Roth learned fast. The crimes he was suspected of in the future were much more subtle, more sophisticated. He apparently never stopped stealing from someone, somewhere. Sue Peters and Randy Mullinax kept checking back further and further with his former employers, and they found incident after incident where Roth had stolen equipment, gas, time, milk—whatever he could get away with.

But those were only stopgap thefts. Randy Roth— the poor boy who had been humiliated when his mother lived on welfare, when she pulled him out of the Marine Corps so he could come home and work at some other dead-end job to support her—had bigger plans.

He had learned that he could make more money with roses and sweet talk and promises he never intended to keep than he ever could with a knife and a mask. If he chose the right women, he could make them love him.

That realization gave him a sense of power greater than he had ever had in his life.

PART SEVEN

Trial

23

The road to Randy Roth's trial was not without detours. The original trial date was December 1, 1991, but the defense team asked for a delay, and it was granted. This was not at all unusual in such a high profile case.

One hundred fifty witness subpoenas were served. Just serving those documents would cost the King County Prosecutor's Office almost $2,400.

Pretrial motions began with the New Year. Defense attorneys George Cody and John Muenster argued in January 1992 that the state did not have sufficient evidence to support a first-degree murder charge against Randy Roth and asked Superior Court Judge Frank Sullivan to dismiss the charge because the only thing DPAs Marilyn Brenneman and Susan Storey could prove was that Cynthia Roth was dead and that her husband Randy had been nearby at the time— and that he stood to profit financially from her death.

"In the course of human experience," Cody argued, "many people drown." That didn't make them all homicide victims. Cody used the original autopsy findings that the drowning was probably accidental to bolster his arguments. It had been weeks before Dr. Reay had told the prosecutors that it was indeed possible to drown someone without leaving marks on the body.

Marilyn Brenneman countered with myriad other facts that Cody had not mentioned, albeit all circumstantial: Randy Roth was losing interest in his wife, he had denied knowledge of her safe-deposit box even though he had cleaned it out two days after Cindy died, and the state contended that the Sevylor raft could never have flipped over the way Randy had described.

"There is physical evidence as well," Brenneman said quietly. "It just doesn't happen to be on the body of Cynthia Roth."

Sullivan declined to dismiss the charges. The state had won the first battle of a very complicated war.

The search warrants then came under the defense's scrutiny. If Cody and Muenster could have them declared invalid, everything Sue Peters, Randy Mullinax, Frank Kinney, Bill Bonair, and Joe Lewis had found would be thrown out. The theft charges (from Bill Pierre) would be dropped. In the worst case, the pathetic poem Cynthia had left behind would be gone.

Judge Sullivan upheld the search warrants and all the evidence gathered.

The pretrial days were like walking through mine fields for both the defense and the prosecution. Naturally the prosecutors wanted to show the jury Randy Roth's whole life, all the patterns of behavior that he had traced and retraced. And just as naturally the defense attorneys would just as soon stick to the here and now.

The mines were exploding on George Cody and John Muenster. On Monday, January 27, Judge Sullivan ruled that the jurors would be allowed to know that the Pioneer Insurance Company believed that Randy had staged a burglary at his own house to collect insurance. Marilyn Brenneman stressed that alleged insurance fraud was vital to the state's case:

"This is the most distinctive pattern of insurance fraud I have seen in my years at the prosecutor's office in the fraud division."

The few reporters who covered the pretrial hearing waited impatiently to hear *the* motion. Would Judge Sullivan allow Brenneman and Susan Storey to bring out the story of Janis Miranda Roth's fatal plunge from Beacon Rock in 1981? Randy had never been convicted—he had not even been arrested in that death. The two DPAs had done meticulous research and found precedent-setting cases in the Washington courts that could permit Sullivan to allow the mysterious death of Janis Roth into this proceeding. But would Sullivan agree with them?

He would. Judge Sullivan ruled that the fact that both Mrs. Roth number two and Mrs. Roth number four had been heavily insured when they died and that Randy Roth had either collected or tried to collect that insurance made the first death relevant to the case involving the second. Yes, he acknowledged that evidence relating to Janis Roth's death would be prejudicial to Roth, but its importance to the state's case outweighed the potential for damage.

John Muenster and George Cody took their argument about the rulings to the Washington State Court of Appeals. They argued that once the jurors heard about Janis Roth's death and the insurance fraud, any subsequent conviction could easily be thrown out on appeal. Because of what they considered Sullivan's "obvious and probable error," the defense attorneys alleged that the trial—scheduled to begin at the end of February—"will be a useless but extremely expensive exercise. . . . Mr. Roth wants his first trial to be a fair trial, not the second one."

On February 15, State Court of Appeals Commissioner Ellen Hudgins declined to send the defense's motion on for review by a three-member panel of appellate judges. George Cody argued that the state had no proof that Cynthia Roth had not simply drowned by accident. But Hudgins countered, "The problem I have with your argument is that no one could ever be prosecuted for a murder as long as he or she used a means that was more commonly an accident."

When a jury of Randy Roth's peers was selected, they would hear about his life, his insurance dealings, his wives, and how they lived—and died. It was a major, perhaps crippling, decision for the defense.

It would take a long, long trial to determine how crippling. As Marilyn Brenneman had said in her argument, Cynthia Roth had fallen into Randy Roth's trap "of wooing, wedding, and shedding his wives."

Could she and Susan Storey make that pattern come alive in a courtroom?

24

Jury selection began on February 24, 1992. Prospective jurors were warned that the trial would take at least five weeks and possibly as long as eight. An unusually large pool of jury candidates was provided. After more than a week, a jury was finally seated. Seven women and five men would decide whether Randy Roth was a killer or merely a very, very unlucky man. Was he a Bluebeard or simply a man who had, by the age of thirty-seven, suffered more personal tragedy than most people do in two lifetimes?

The crowds came when the trial officially began the first week in March, and there would never be a day when there was an extra spot available on one of the five long benches in Judge Frank Sullivan's courtroom. The first row was kept empty for use as a temporary perch from time to time for the attorneys' investigators; in dicey trials, where no one can be sure what the defendant may or not do, the front row also serves as a narrow safety zone.

The next two benches were reserved for family. The Louckses were there, and the Baumgartners, parents, aunts, cousins, friends. They filled the hard oak benches, gaining strength from one another.

The media clung tenaciously to the fourth bench, occasionally overflowing onto the fifth. All the newspaper and television reporters, the book writers—save one reporter who sat alone and aloof—saved seats for one another by spreading out yellow legal pads, raincoats, and briefcases. On the press bench there was always room for one more, even though it meant writing with an elbow in the solar plexus.

All together, there were only forty-eight legitimate seats. By crunching people together, sixty seats could be created. Bailiff Lori Merrick explained to spectators in the back row that those spots were reserved for the media too. They were welcome to sit there, but would have to defer to the press: "If they ask nicely, you're going to have to give up your seat."

"What if they don't ask nicely?" countered one stubborn court watcher.

"Then you can slap them," Merrick quipped. "But you'll still have to give up your seat."

Single cameramen took turns manning the television camera on the left side of the courtroom; the film would go into a pool for all the networks and independent stations. It seemed that everybody in western

Washington had heard the name Randy Roth. And everyone who read a paper or watched television was curious about him.

Randy Roth sat, shoulders hunched, at the defense table. In his news conference the previous summer, he had come across as a handsome young man, strong and thickly muscled in the chest and shoulders. Now, as the defendant in a murder trial, Randy looked entirely changed, as if he suffered from some fatal wasting disease. It was more than the prison pallor that colors all men locked away in jail for months. Randy had metamorphosed into a thin, fragile-looking man with thick glasses whose balding pate shone through his graying hair.

His suit fit him tightly, creasing across his narrow back. It seemed to those who had seen him before that it was a new suit, purchased perhaps to convince a jury that Randy had *always* been a weak little man, a man incapable of holding a healthy young woman underwater until she drowned, not strong enough to push a young woman off a mountain trail.

Any good defense lawyer thinks long and hard about how he will present his client. Ladies of the night show up in court in prim dresses buttoned to the neck, motorcycle gang members appear clean-shaven in three-piece suits that cover their earthy tattoos, and chronic imbibers of alcohol take the witness stand as sober as the pope. This is fair, and it is understood in the legal profession. Put the defendant's best foot forward.

Or, in this trial, make the defendant look as close to Casper Milquetoast as possible. How Randy must have hated wearing his glasses and letting his biceps become flaccid. He, who had aimed to become a latter-day Billy Jack, a martial arts instructor and a marine hero, looked like a mild little middle-aged clerk.

Harmless.

* * *

Susan Storey rose to give the state's opening statement. Skillfully, she wove in the myriad facets of Randy Roth's life—his romances, his marriages, his widowhood, his fascination with insurance. "He married for greed," Storey said flatly. "Not for love or companionship. And he murdered for money. It wasn't hate, it wasn't fear—or even passion."

The prosecution team had discerned the distinct blueprint in Randy Roth's behavior. He had been much like the producer of a play, and he presented it over and over—changing only the cast. Susan Storey told the jurors of the "short and intense—whirlwind" courtships, where honeymoons were followed by the purchase of large insurance policies. She described Roth's demeanor after the death of two wives as "cold and unemotional . . . and on both occasions he made different and contradictory statements about what had occurred."

It was important to present the design, the repetition, the identical—or nearly identical—game plan that Randy Roth had used over and over and over again. If Storey—or George Cody, for that matter—took only one of the marriages or one of the insurance transactions and presented it as an entity in itself, it might very well have been explainable in perfectly innocent terms. But, taken all together, the configuration of Randy Roth's behavior never changed.

Pointing to a chart propped up in the witness chair, Susan Storey gave specific examples of the defendant's consuming avarice and how he had gone about filling his pockets and his bank account. Storey's pointer tapped the chart: (1) the phony theft of Janis Roth's car; (2) Janis Miranda Roth's "accidental" fall and the $115,000 payoff; (3) Randy's fraudulent application for Jalina Miranda's Social Security benefits; (4) the phony burglary of Nick Emondi's home; (5) Randy's marriage to Donna Clift and the rafting "accident"; (6) Randy's whirlwind courtship of Mary Jo Phillips, which ended when he learned Mary Jo was uninsurable; (7) the phony burglary of Randy's home; (8) Randy's whirlwind courtship of Cynthia Baumgartner, the huge insurance policies, and Cynthia's death by drowning; and (9) Randy's fraudulent application for Greg's (second) Social Security benefits.

"This man stole to feed his hunger for money nine different times." Storey said.

Susan Storey explained to the jurors that Randy Roth's onetime best friend, Nick Emondi, had finally told detectives that his burglary had never been a burglary at all—at least not in the true sense of the term. When Nick had been unable to repay his loan, Randy had suggested that Nick set fire to his home. He could then collect insurance and pay Randy back. Emondi, employed by the local fire department, did not think that was such a good idea. Next, Susan Storey told the jury, Randy came up with another plan. He would be glad to take some of the Emondis' property away—say, a television set, the stereo, and other items that could easily be liquidated. Then Nick could report a burglary to his insurance agent. Randy would keep what he had taken away *and* share in the insurance payoff.

And that was exactly what had happened. While Carrie Emondi was working the graveyard shift on her job one night, Randy came to their mobile home and removed their television, their AM-FM cassette recorder, and other things he wanted. He also partook of the insurance proceeds.

Nick Emondi's debt was marked paid.

By the time Randy met Donna Clift a few months later, he had to have been a man who believed smugly in the denseness of insurance companies. Storey told the jury they would hear from Donna Clift; she was one of two wives who had survived. Donna Clift remembered that Randy had wanted her to sign up for heavy-duty insurance policies, but she never had.

Donna knew that "Randy knew how to operate a

raft," Storey pointed out to the jury. "But on this day, he was intentionally trying to sink it."

And why would Randy have tried to drown his new bride—the one with no life insurance? Well, Storey explained, Donna Clift *did* have life insurance. She just didn't know about it. Randy had managed to insure Donna for more than $20,000, and she had been completely unaware of it—until Storey herself informed her about it.

At the defense table, Randy Roth continued to stare down at his yellow tablet. For all the reaction he showed, Susan Storey might well have been talking about someone else entirely. Even as secrets that he must have thought were long since hidden emerged, he remained stolid and calm.

He always had.

As Susan Storey talked, a huge blow-up of Beacon Rock sat on an easel behind her, and she ticked off the cold facts of Roth's increasing fortunes. It was essential for Storey and Marilyn Brenneman to *show* the jury what had happened in the defendant's life over the past dozen years. They could not take the jurors by the hand and walk them up the steep trail to the top of Beacon Rock or float them all out in a raft on Lake Sammamish, but they could, with the judicious use of audiovisual aids, re-create much of the horror.

Susan Storey replaced the bleak rock with a picture of the raft that Cynthia Roth had clung to in the last moments of her life.

There was no mystery about why Randy had deliberately drowned Cynthia Roth, Storey said. The motive was quite plain—$385,000 in insurance.

"Help was only a shout or a wave away," she said of the moments after Cynthia became unconscious in Lake Sammamish. But Randy calmly and quietly rowed to shore.

"Sixty or seventy yards from shore, no wave. . . .

"Twenty-five yards from shore. Still, he didn't yell or wave for help. . . .

279

"Fifty or sixty feet, he was in no particular hurry . . . He did not yell or wave for help. . . ."

And when Randy finally reached the lakeshore, he stayed quietly inside the raft, Susan Storey told the jury. He didn't appear alarmed. He didn't make a move to get help for his drowned wife until the boys ran over and saw that their mother's flesh was blue and mottled.

This man—at whom the jury now stole quick peeks—seemed so "completely uninterested" in whether his wife would survive or die that people on the shore thought he was a stranger to Cynthia.

"He made vastly different statements. . . . She'd been swimming while he was rowing. . . . They were both swimming. . . . Cynthia was under the water for ten minutes . . . she was facedown for thirty-five to forty seconds. . . .

"The boat was very close. . . . The boat was fifty to one hundred yards away. . . . The boat was east of the raft. . . . The boat was west of the raft. . . . He didn't attempt CPR. . . . He *did* try two breaths. . . . He gave her fifteen to twenty minutes of CPR."

The elements of the case that Susan Storey revealed were shocking. She described the new widower as a man so unmoved by his wife's death that he rented three comedy videos on the way home from the hospital.

If Storey's litany of years of sociopathic behavior was true, Randy Roth was a monster.

For the Roth jury, the details of Randolph G. Roth's convoluted life must have been dizzying. The gallery remained transfixed, their startle reaction heightened when someone's beeper sounded, seeming as loud as an alarm bell.

"Turn it off," Judge Sullivan growled.

Susan Storey continued without missing a beat. The defendant, was, she said, a man who at 7:30 or 7:35 P.M. on July 23, 1991, left the quiet room in the hospital where his wife had just been declared dead, where a grief counselor noted that he had shown "not the slightest evidence or distress or grief or emotion of any kind," and stopped to have dinner with the victims' sons, then picked up the videotapes. Once home, Randy Roth had placed a phone call. "He did not call relatives," Storey said. "He didn't call friends, or people from church. He called this guy to see if his red Corvette was still for sale."

Two days after Cynthia drowned, Randy Roth had told Stacey Reese that he was wondering if maybe Cynthia hadn't *wanted* to die. His biggest problem seemed to be that it would take him "fucking forever to get the mauve colors out of his house."

Randy Roth had wasted no time, Storey continued, in applying for Greg's Social Security benefits, "lying twice." He claimed that Greg was Cynthia's only child, and he did not mention that Greg was already receiving Janis's benefits.

Three weeks after Cynthia drowned, Randy rejoined Parents Without Partners, filed to collect his $385,000 in insurance proceeds, and began to sell off his assets—"everything of value—his car, his four-by-four, his John Deere front loader, two new four-wheelers. He put his house up for sale."

And why, Storey asked, did he do this? Because he had told his co-workers that he was preparing to be arrested.

She had given the jury only a summary of what they would hear in this trial. "Now you understand the number of witnesses," Susan Storey finished. There had been so many frauds, frauds pointing to Randy Roth's greed and, ultimately, explaining why Cynthia Baumgartner Roth had to die to appease that greed.

Defense attorney George Cody told the jurors about an entirely different man, a man whose traits seemed to fit the quiet, somber man who scribbled notes on a yellow legal pad in front of him. Randy rarely looked up even as his own attorney spoke.

Cody saw his client as a prudent, careful man, a caring father who wanted to be sure that his children were provided for if either he or his wife should die. Randy Roth was, Cody said, a man who had suffered a "terrible accident," the kind that could happen to anyone. (*Two* terrible accidents in point of fact, although Cody did not choose to touch on that.) The case against Randy Roth was purely circumstantial, Cody said. He disputed Storey's argument that Randy had not tried to save Cynthia from drowning when he pulled her out of the water. Indeed, his attorney said Randy had tried desperately to breathe air into her lungs from his own—but he could not do it because her gag reflex had been too strong.

George Cody outlined for the jury a luckless shadow of a man who had lost almost everything he ever loved, who, but for the grace of God, might have changed places with any man and woman in the hushed courtroom.

If Cody was right, a terrible miscarriage of justice loomed. There was nothing predictable about this trial. It *was* in large part made up of a voluminous amount of circumstantial evidence. However, that didn't mean that the prosecution could not get a conviction.

Nor did it mean that Marilyn Brenneman and Susan Storey *would* get a conviction. A fingerprint in blood is the best physical evidence in the world. A drowning in the middle of a huge lake is one of the most difficult deaths to define absolutely.

The battle lines were drawn. The windowless courtroom was hot, almost as hot as the beach had been seven and a half months earlier. Nobody moved.

Outside in the hallway, television and radio field reporters watched the trial action on small monitors they had propped up on the long oak benches. Witnesses waited there too, forbidden to enter Sullivan's courtroom before they testified. Electrical cables snaked across the worn marble floor. There were deadlines to meet—for the five o'clock news, and, if not then, for the eleven o'clock news.

Nothing was a sure thing. Nothing except that this was the biggest, most sensational trial to hit King County in a decade.

25

If there was a single trait that marked Randolph G. Roth's whole existence, it had always been secrecy. No one, *ever,* had been allowed to look into all the segments of his life. He was the man who loved to prowl in dark clothing in the stillness late at night, the man who hinted at unspeakable acts he had been called on the perform in an unfathomable war half a world away, a man who hid his own family origins, and chose women he could hold under his thumb the way he'd held the hapless frog under his sander. Randy Roth had never looked back. In his view, the dead were gone—simply gone and no longer of consequence. Yesterday did not matter. Now *he* was forced to look at the panorama that was his life, to see those whose lives he had touched—and often corroded— and it was all in a public forum.

Worse, it was literally live and on tape.

Bill Wiley, leader of the search team in Skamania

County, testified about the desperate search for Janis Roth ten years earlier. Her body had been found 50 to 100 feet beyond where they expected to find her. "While anything is possible . . . it is at the far extreme and beyond anything in my experience," Wiley said, demonstrating on the giant photo of Beacon Rock where Randy said she had gone off and the spot where she had landed. She would almost have had to fall sideways to make Randy's version believable.

Sheriff Ray Blaisdell, who had been the Skamania County undersheriff in 1981, rescuers, and hikers on the Beacon Rock trail all testified. It had taken gargantuan efforts to locate the cast of characters who swarmed over Beacon Rock on that cold day in November so long ago. Most of them remembered Randy Roth as a man who seemed unnaturally calm in the face of tragedy, although Blaisdell said he had seen Randy cry twice after word came from the ground below that Janis Roth was dead. "At the time, he didn't say anything," Blaisdell said, but "he did show some emotion, and I did see some tears."

Marcie Thompson, a grown woman now, remembered that she had learned of Jan's death a few hours later in a pizza parlor when Randy slid the cremation receipt across the table to her as casually as if it were a menu. (Marcie had also told detectives that Randy subsequently tried to seduce her when she visited his Seattle home.) "I knew her as Jan," Marcie said, "so 'Janis' didn't ring a bell. I said, 'I don't know this person,' and he said, 'Yes, you do. Think about it.'"

Jalina Miranda, who had matured into a beautiful young woman, looked at the man who had once been her stepfather as she remembered finding the envelope her mother had told her about. "'If anything happens to me, I want you to come get this.' He took it right out of my hands," Jalina said. "He promised to use the money to buy me toys and presents."

"Did he?" Marilyn Brenneman asked.

"No. I never talked to him again."

Jalina said that her mother had been dead almost a week before she knew it. "I kept saying, 'Where's my mommy?'"

On cross-examination, John Muenster elicited from Jalina that Randy had been kind to her. It was true that her stepfather had always avoided giving her a direct answer, but he had taken her on his knee and explained about the terrible fall and about her mother being in the hospital. He had rocked her and held her tenderly while she cried.

And then Randy had answered the phone one day, and turned to her, saying, "Jalina, that was the hospital. Your mother just died."

Billie Jean Ray, Janis's mother, also admitted under defense questioning that Roth had seemed grief-stricken at her daughter's memorial service.

It was an uphill battle for the defense, however. For every witness who recalled observing some small crack in Randy Roth's austere facade, there were ten—or twenty—who described a man with the emotional makeup of a robot.

Darrel Lundquist told the jury that he had been awakened by his insurance client, Randy Roth, the day after Janis fell to her death. Randy had been anxious to collect on his policy. Shirley Lenz related how Randy had needed Janis's Social Security number that same morning because "Janis was sick."

Lily Vandiveer's ex-husband testified that Randy had had an affair with Lily after and during Randy's marriage to Janis, and that he found Randy and Lily in an intimate embrace on the floor in front of the fireplace in his own home. "I told him if he didn't stay away from my house, I was going to the prosecuting attorney."

But Vandiveer admitted he had never told the Skamania County authorities. "I was afraid of him," he said.

And so was Nick Emondi. But Nick was between a rock and a hard place. He had felt sorry for sad little Janis Roth. He suspected that Randy was seeing another woman. He had heard the Halloween conversation about "Could you kill your wife?" And then he had learned that "Janis is no longer with us."

Now Nick admitted on the witness stand that he had staged a burglary in his own home so that he could repay Randy money he had owed him. He had helped take his property to Randy's house and Randy had helped him fill out the insurance forms. They divided the $2,800 settlement, and Randy kept most of the "stolen" items. Nevertheless, the Emondis had eventually been forced to declare bankruptcy when Randy backed out of his promise to buy their home.

Nick had heard Randy describe how he would burglarize his own home—*before* the fact. He had been Randy's confidant; he had heard about all the women who didn't work out because they were "immature" and about Mary Jo's sudden fall from grace when Randy found out she'd had cancer.

Yes, he and Randy had been close friends. But Nick admitted he was afraid of Randy Roth, that he always had been.

George Cody questioned Nick Emondi persistently about the Halloween night conversation. Were not, he suggested, the two men discussing the Bible at the time? Weren't they talking about the Book of Revelation, the biblical end of the world?

That argument never went anywhere; the prosecutors objected to Cody's questions about the Bible.

Randy Roth, his panoply of invincibility shattered, was handcuffed and marched to and from court several times a day, tall court officers on either side of him. His expression never changed. His dark eyes glittered behind thick glasses, but he seemed to see no one. He could well have been shocked to find himself in the midst of a reunion that he would never have chosen to attend.

The women continued to appear, women Randy had long since dismissed from his life.

Brittany Goodwin, who had idolized him when she was a teenager, been seduced and betrayed, and who now recounted Randy's precise plan to rob his own home.

He didn't look up.

Mary Jo Phillips told of her magical courtship, of how Randy "became the man every woman dreams about." All his tender concern had shattered and fallen away when he learned that she was uninsurable.

Randy didn't look up.

Donna Clift recalled Randy's headlong pursuit of her, the lavish gifts he had given her, her perfect wedding . . . and then her bewilderment, which had turned to terror on the Skykomish River. Clift was clearly still angry at being so betrayed, and she testified not to the jury but directly to Randy Roth. She willed him with hard eyes to face her.

He didn't look up.

When Judy Clift testified that she had been afraid that her daughter would never come off the Skykomish River alive, defense attorney John Muenster asked Judge Sullivan to declare a mistrial. "Mr. Roth is on trial for something that happened in 1991," Muenster argued. "Yet he has been run through the wringer for things that allegedly happened as long as ten years ago. None of these people saw fit to report any of it until now."

Judge Sullivan refused the request, and the trial continued, gaining momentum with each day.

The Goodwins—the family that Randy had adopted as his own—testified for the prosecution. Ben and Marta and Ryan. Of all the people who had passed through Randy's life, they had perhaps cared for him the most. But they could not condone what they believed was a staged burglary—for profit. They all recalled the tools, the televisions, stereos, the Nintendos that were gone—and then were suddenly back again.

Marta had heard no sounds during that night in September 1988. Ben Goodwin knew the "tire marks" in Randy's backyard were actually the depression left by the great weight of a felled tree. Ben looked at the jury and repeated Randy's flat words, "He said, 'That's where the detective said the tires were, so that's where the tires were.'"

The burglary of 1988 had certainly come back to haunt Randy. One wondered if he berated himself now. He had asked for over $58,000, received $28,500 after a two-year legal fight, and had to give away all but $17,000 of that. Obviously the continuing testimony from so many sources about Roth's duplicity in the allegedly faked burglary was hurting him. Ben Goodwin identified several items that he recognized as having belonged to Randy both before and after the burglary.

Pioneer Insurance claims adjuster Shelly Bierman had become suspicious all on her own when she discovered that Roth had included a return slip from Sears for a Kenwood stereo radio that he claimed was stolen. Once that claim was questioned, all manner of inaccuracies had begun to emerge.

It was more than a week into trial, and still no witnesses had spoken of Cynthia Baumgartner Roth. Even so, there was the sensation of her presence there. Two rows were packed full of her family, their faces marked by grief and a kind of bleak acceptance of what they could not change. They were not vengeful people. Merle Loucks had said he did not support the death penalty—not even for the man he was convinced had deliberately drowned his beloved daughter.

* * *

And then suddenly there was another family there. Randy Roth's family—his mother, Lizabeth, and two of his sisters. The press bench murmured with speculation about who these rather bizarre-appearing women were. Indeed, they seemed at first to be strangers, more of the impatient would-be courtroom spectators who were angry at not finding a seat. There were many of those, held back by the court officers because there was not a single inch of extra space. One more body inside and the fire ordinances would be broken.

No, these women declared loudly. They were members of the defendant's family and had the right to be present. Lizabeth Roth was not what anyone had expected, at least not from her son's descriptions of her. Randy was now thirty-eight, and his mother looked no more than ten years older. Her hair was dyed a dark metallic auburn, teased and back-combed until it had become a huge helmet around her head, sprayed until it appeared brittle enough to break off if someone touched it. Her eyelids were heavily smudged with shadow and lined with kohl, her make-up resembled a thick mask, and her clothing fit her lush figure snugly. She wore a miniskirt and high-heeled pumps. A scent of heavy cologne moved with her. This was no aged mother who had been confined to a nursing home; this was Randy Roth's *real* mother.

The antipathy between mother and son was palpable. He scarcely acknowledged her presence. As Randy was led from the courtroom during a morning break, his eyes swept over his mother, who sat at the end of the second row. It was impossible to read his expression.

Randy's sisters were dark-haired too, slender and pretty. Like their mother, they had lined their eyes and teased their hair. They resembled a family of Gypsy women, exotic and flamboyant. They were outraged when they arrived so late that all the seats in the courtroom were taken. To the observer, it seemed that the Roth women had deliberately delayed their entrance so that they could cause a commotion and demand justice—at least in the seating arrangements —for their family. The victim's family slid over and made room for Mrs. Roth, and she settled down with much sighing and shifting. One of Randy's sisters sat on the arm at the end of the press row and pushed with her backside until she forcibly won a seat next to a startled reporter.

Through it all, their son and brother kept his back to them; it was as if he didn't know them at all, and certainly would not accept them as a cheering section come to show their support.

In the women's rest room where all factions of all trials meet on neutral ground, Randy Roth's sisters combed their hair and freshened their makeup beside reporters and cousins of the dead Cynthia. Randy's sisters spoke of their plans for Easter dresses.

When the Louckses and the Baumgartners had left to go back into the trial, Lisa Roth turned to a reporter and confided, "Everybody feels so sorry for *them,* but, you know, their troubles are over. Cindy's dead. It's Randy who has to suffer for the rest of his life."

The courtroom was stifling hot, and it would remain so. The King County financial office would brook no hanky-panky with its budget. The rules said that air-conditioning would not be turned on in courtrooms before April 15. It did not matter that the winter of 1991–92 had been almost balmy and that Judge Frank Sullivan's courtroom felt like August although it was March. Not only was air-conditioning officially forbidden for weeks, but the maintenance staff was cranking up the heat each morning to "take the chill off." The prize seat in the courtroom was just outside the jurors' room—the last seat in the last row. That room did have air-conditioning, and occasionally a corrections officer would prop the door open a few inches so that breathable air filtered out into the courtroom.

It was miserable, but no one left. The story of the last year of Cynthia Baumgartner Roth's life was about to be told. Her sweet blond visage smiled back from a photograph mounted on the easel at the front of the courtroom.

She had posed next to a bush of Randy's prize red roses.

26

Until now the jury had heard testimony that certainly suggested that Randy Roth was not a very nice man, that he was neither honest nor sincerely caring about anyone. According to the state's witnesses, he had lied and cheated. And perhaps he had deliberately killed his second wife. But he had never been charged in the death of Janis Miranda Roth. A prudent juror might very well think, "If they had enough evidence to show that he was guilty, if he really did it, why didn't they charge him with murder?"

He *had* been charged with the murder of Cynthia Baumgartner Roth, and the observers in the gallery tensed as they realized the testimony would henceforth deal with Randy Roth's relationship with his fourth wife, and with her inexplicable death.

It was now the third week of March 1992, and one after another prosecution witnesses related that something was desperately wrong with Cynthia and

Randy's marriage. One of Cynthia's best friends, Mary Barns, told the jury that she and Cynthia had gone to Idylwood Park on July 9; they had sat on the same beach where paramedics had worked over Cindy's body two weeks later. Cindy had confided to Mary that her marriage to Randy was deteriorating. Cindy had been concerned that Randy changed jobs so frequently; the stability she thought she had seen didn't exist. Mary added, "She said to me, more than once, 'We won't get a divorce.' It sounded like something she was trying to convince herself of because she was having doubts."

Sandra Thompson, who did Cindy's hair, said that things were not good in Cindy's marriage: "She did not want her husband to know what she was spending on her hair."

It had been the same with her nails. Randy had made Cindy explain every penny she spent.

Randy's co-workers at Bill Pierre Ford had never had a real understanding of his relationship with Cindy. It wasn't that Randy had been the only worker who complained about a spouse; it was that his remarks about Cindy had been exceptionally vicious. In truth, he never really acknowledged that he had married her. He called their relationship a "contract."

One witness recalled hearing Randy say, "Our contract's up in August, and then the bitch is gone."

Under Cody's vigorous cross-examination, the witness admitted that she did not care for Randy Roth, but she would not take back what she had heard.

Randy had complained vociferously about Cynthia at work—about everything from her cookies, "which wouldn't even soften if you dipped them in milk," to her temperament. He had gone out of his way to portray himself as a man who was trapped in a miserable relationship.

On March 18, Stacey Reese, who had quite possibly been Randy's first choice for the fifth Mrs. Roth, was a devastating witness to the defense. She too had heard about Randy's "contract" with Cynthia. She told the court, "He said it was a contract. He said they would see how it went for a year and that it would be up on August 1. And one of them would have to go."

One of them had, of course, gone.

On July 22, the day before the drowning, Randy had taken Stacey to a Lake City drive-in restaurant for lunch and told her of his doubts about his "contract." He said he was unhappy and that his and Cindy's "relationship" was almost up. He was packing his stuff, and it was "time to go."

Stacey testified to the four phone calls she had received from Randy in the four days after Cynthia drowned. She said she had become increasingly alarmed by his demeanor. The drowning had been "horrible," he said, but in a way a "relief." While Stacey listened, dumbfounded by Randy's attitude, he went on to comment about how he had always hated Cindy's pink and mauve color scheme. "He wanted to get it the fuck out of the house," Stacey said. She had been uncomfortable with his invitation in an earlier call to have breakfast with him, but she told the jurors she was profoundly shocked when he invited her to accompany him to Reno. It was clear that Stacey would have been a substitute for his dead wife—the wife who had purchased the tickets to Reno with such hope. Randy had said he didn't want the tickets to go to waste.

Mark Dalton, a vehicle maintenance instructor for Metro Transit (Seattle's bus system), took the stand to say that Randy Roth had been hired along with six other bus-fleet mechanics about a month before his wife had drowned. The first day of orientation for that job was June 17. Randy showed up, but he did not appear the next day or any day thereafter.

He had left a message on a Metro employee's voice mail system. "He said his wife had been in an accident in Idaho and he wouldn't be in," Dalton recalled. "He said it looked like she was in critical condition and might not make it."

In late June, Cynthia had not been in an accident in Idaho or anywhere else. Roth had chosen not to continue with Metro for his own reasons.

Carolyn Davidson, supervisor for Metro's vehicle-maintenance division, testified she had sent Randy Roth a registered letter on July 8, explaining that Metro could not hold his job open indefinitely. Tactfully, Ms. Davidson offered her sympathy about his wife's accident—she had no way of knowing if the woman was alive or dead—but she informed Roth that he would be fired if he didn't report for work by July 23.

Randy signed for the registered letter, but he did not go back to Metro. And of course by July 23, Randy Roth *was* a widower.

No one on the prosecution team could fathom why he had lied to Metro. Privately, Marilyn Brenneman and Susan Storey wondered if Randy had already been playing with the idea of Cindy's death weeks before she drowned.

The Sevylor raft that Randy had given up to the police so grudgingly on the night of July 23, 1991, was brought into the courtroom, inflated, and propped up against the far wall as dozens of witnesses who had been at Lake Sammamish on that date testified to memories that would never fade.

Kristina Baker, the woman who had seen the raft head out into the middle of the lake and watched its progress sporadically while keeping an eye on her children, described the tableau. She had seen two people jump into the water, and, minutes later, she had seen one of them swim away from the raft while the other trailed behind. A moment later she saw arms waving and splashes in the lake before the pair disappeared behind the raft, out of her view. She had seen a powerboat towing a water-skier slow down or stop near the raft, and she thought one of the swimmers had waved. She had turned away briefly to check on her children, and when she looked back she saw the one person dragging the other onto the raft. "It was a struggle to get the person back on the raft," she said. "You could see it wasn't an easy job."

Baker had idly watched the raft come slowly toward shore. It had taken twenty minutes. Baker saw only one figure now, but she didn't sense any danger. As it drew closer, she could see it was a man who was rowing so slowly.

Alicia Tracy had been at Idylwood Park that afternoon, and she had run to help Mike McFadden, the lifeguard. She had seen that the woman in the bottom of the raft had a blue cast to her skin and she had turned away. She saw the man she came to know as Randy Roth standing back from the raft, but she didn't connect him to the drowning. "At that point," she said, "he was just another man pulling his boat out of the water."

Needing to do *something* while the lifeguards worked frantically over the woman, Alicia had offered to help the man deflate his raft. She didn't realize who he was until a police officer had asked if anyone knew who the drowned woman was. At that point, he spoke up. "He said, 'Well, I know her. She's my wife,'" Tracy told the jury.

The officer had then asked Randy to stop deflating his raft. "He told him, 'I don't think we should be doing that—we might need it for evidence,'" Alicia said.

Randy Roth had ignored the policeman and gone right on folding up his raft.

With each witness who took the stand, the scene at the lake was painted in more grotesque strokes. The widower had made no effort at all to hurry to save his wife. He had been far more concerned about "making a scene" than he had been about Cynthia's survival. Again and again Randy Roth was described as "void of emotion," "so calm," "so normal," "had no expression."

An eleven-year-old girl had watched Tyson and Rylie Baumgartner run up to the raft where their mother lay motionless in the bottom. She said, "I saw the two boys run over to the raft and ask, 'What's happened to Mom?'"

And she testified that the man had said simply, "Go get a lifeguard, but don't make a scene."

If the testimony was shocking to strangers and press in the gallery, it was unbearable for Cynthia's family. Marge Baumgartner, Tom's mother, left the courtroom in tears when the girl on the stand described how Patti Schultz had knelt down and hugged Marge's grandsons to comfort them, and how their "father" had simply walked away from them.

"They had to hurry [to catch up]," the witness added.

Randy Roth had behaved like an insensitive automaton according to witnesses. Indeed, his behavior had been *so* cold that it might serve as an argument for the defense. If a man had deliberately planned to drown his wife, would he not have at least *pretended* to be grief-stricken? If he was truly in shock over the tragedy, might he not have acted exactly as he did— woodenly, as if he were slogging through quicksand, unable to cope with the fact that his beloved wife was gone? So stunned that he was unaware that the children needed comfort?

Or was Randy Roth a man so devoid of normal human empathy that he did not even know how to mimic it?

With each succeeding witness, the latter seemed to be more likely.

Roth had given his attorneys a great obstacle to

overcome. Considered among the very top criminal defense attorneys in Seattle, George Cody and John Muenster did their best. They argued that only a fool would have chosen to commit a murder on a crowded lake on the hottest day of the summer. Of *course* he had proceeded toward shore slowly, they maintained, to avoid attracting a crowd that might interfere with rescue efforts.

Randy's own family appeared to be thorns in his side. His glance swept over them almost contemptuously as he left the courtroom in handcuffs several times a day. One afternoon he moved into the corridor to see that his mother was giving a television interview. "Keep your damn mouth shut," he muttered out of the side of his mouth. "Don't talk to them."

She ignored him. In the glow of television lights, Lizabeth Roth criticized what passed for justice in King County, Washington. She made all three network channels that night.

Redmond detective Larry Conrad was the eighty-eighth witness for the prosecution. At last, here was a witness who recalled that Randy Roth had shown emotion on the day his wife drowned—but under rather odd circumstances. Conrad said he had just told Randy he needed to confiscate his raft. "He became somewhat agitated and angry," Conrad added. "He said he felt I had no right to take it. It was the first emotion he displayed."

John Muenster objected. Conrad had not mentioned Randy's agitation in his notes or in his reports, had he?

He had not, Conrad agreed.

Although Randy Roth was the center of everything that went on in the lengthy trial, the subject of each witness's appraisal, he showed no reaction and he said nothing. Would he? Would his attorneys put the defendant on the witness stand? That is always a risky ploy because it opens up the defendant to the prosecuting team's questions. Certainly everyone in the courtroom wanted to hear Roth speak, wanted to know how his mind worked and if there was some explanation for his unemotional response to Cynthia's death.

Sue Peters and Randy Mullinax devoutly hoped Randy would get up on the stand. *They* knew that he was a most verbose man, and they wanted the jurors to know him as they did.

The defense team gave no hint as to whether Roth would testify.

D'Vorah Kost, the grief counselor at Overlake Hospital, explained to the jury that she had asked Tyson and Rylie Baumgartner if there was anyone who might help them feel better. They said they wanted to be with their uncle, Leon Loucks. But at that point Loucks had no idea that his sister was dead; Randy had not even called him.

Leon Loucks testified about the way he learned that his only sister had drowned. On the evening of July 23, another relative had called him to say that a woman with the same name as Cynthia had drowned; she had just seen it on television. At first, Leon hoped that it wasn't true. It *couldn't* be true, he thought, or he would have been notified. "We questioned the fact that no one contacted us."

Cynthia's brother called Overlake Hospital and was told only that a message would be passed to Randy Roth to call Leon as soon as possible. Dreading what he might hear, Leon Loucks waited by the phone.

No one called.

At 11:30 P.M., Loucks finally reached his sister's home in Woodinville. A very calm Randy told him that it was true; Cynthia was dead. "Why didn't you call me or someone in the family?" Leon asked.

Randy said, "I wanted to do it in person, not by telephone."

But then, Randy Roth had never liked to be the bearer of bad news. He didn't like to talk about death or think about death. Word always filtered down sooner or later.

27

Randy Roth had long claimed expertise in a number of areas, bluffing that he was a karate and Tae Kwon Do champion, that he had been trained by the marines to silently stalk and destroy. There was some areas where he *was* proficient, but he did not brag about them—especially not in the months after Cynthia drowned.

Randy was a very good swimmer. In August of 1984, he had taken a scuba diving course from Donald Johnson, a certified scuba diver and instructor. The diving course met the standards of the Professional Association of Diving Instructors (PADI) standards and followed its procedures. Before a student is even admitted to a PADI course, he or she has to demonstrate proficiency in the water by swimming 200 yards using several strokes; swimming 40 feet underwater; treading water for five minutes, four minutes with hands and feet, the next thirty seconds with feet only, and the last thirty seconds giving a distress signal with the hands. The would-be student must also be able to sustain a survival float for five minutes.

Ill at the time of trial, Johnson's recall was admitted by affidavit. Randy's scuba instructor had stressed again and again the importance of using the buddy system, "meaning you stick to your buddy like glue," and the use of hand signals in times of trouble. "Waving the arm and hand overhead is a distress signal," he said.

But not one witness had seen Randy Roth wave or signal for help while his wife was drowning.

Beyond being a strong swimmer, Randy had also taken an eight-hour CPR course in 1990. Myron Redenn, a Snohomish County Red Cross official, outlined in court what Roth had learned in that course: "I emphasize that they should start giving emergency care *immediately*. It could mean the difference between life and death."

All students in the Red Cross course had been taught that the brain begins to die if a person stops breathing for four to six minutes. Apparently Randy Roth had committed that part of the instructions to memory; he had repeated it to Seattle Fire Department paramedic Patti Schultz as she rode with him to Overlake Hospital.

At any rate, he was not the weak swimmer he had told Donna Clift he was, the neophyte even Tyson and Rylie believed he was, a man who could not maneuver in the water unless he held on to a raft or an inner tube or stayed in the safe, shallow end of the pool.

The courtroom lights were dimmed, and the jurors' eyes left the raft propped up against the far wall and watched it on the screen in front of them. They scrutinized the first King County Police reenactment of the effect of boat wakes on the raft. Again and again, Mike Hatch's powerboat zipped by the Sevylor. The swimming "actors" were clearly never in danger.

Why, then, had the raft tipped over on July 23? Why had Cynthia, a strong swimmer, drowned so easily?

Dr. Donald Van Rossen, an expert witness, was next. Van Rossen is an aquatics safety expert and former professor at the University of Oregon. People *do* drown and laymen don't always understand why. Perhaps Van Rossen could explain what happens when humans, who are basically land creatures, enter a foreign atmosphere.

Van Rossen told the jurors that the American Red Cross recognizes two types of drowning—active and passive. Given Randy Roth's version of his wife's death, where he discovered Cynthia floating facedown when he righted his overturned raft, Van Rossen would have termed her death a passive drowning. The passive drowner "simply slips under the water immediately," he said. There are not the facial expressions of terror, the thrown-up hands, and the thrashing legs of an active drowner.

However, the Oregon expert went on, for Cynthia Roth to have drowned passively, she would have to have been suffering from some preexisting physical condition—alcohol, drugs, a heart attack, perhaps, a seizure, a stroke, or a blow to the head that could have made it impossible for her to save herself as she floated in terrible pain or, worse, unconscious.

A leg cramp? Van Rossen shook his head and said, "It's a worrisome thing, but it shouldn't lead to drowning." He had studied the autopsy report on Cynthia Roth. She had no preexisting conditions. She had suffered neither a stroke nor a heart attack. The only substance in her blood was caffeine.

Active drowning, Van Rossen explained, is quite another thing.

Susan Storey questioned Van Rossen about how a person drowns actively. He explained that the victim realizes she is in trouble and panics, trying to keep her head above water by kicking or clawing at the water's surface. "In their [attempt] to survive," he said, "they are struggling to keep their head above water, and there is a time clock that starts when panic sets in. The clock starts when the face is in the water."

Within twenty to sixty seconds after the active drowner's movements are no longer productive, the person drowns. However, the heartbeat may continue for some time. Rescue breathing, given at once, can help, but only someone wearing scuba gear could have given Cynthia two quick breaths in the water. Active CPR requires a hard surface beneath the subject.

Cynthia Roth's family sat stoically in the front rows of the courtroom, almost certainly visualizing the death of a young woman so dear to them.

Van Rossen said that active drowners are almost always poor swimmers.

"If a strong swimmer was 'in arm's length' from a raft," Storey asked, "is that person going to experience active drowning?"

"No."

There was no reason why Cynthia could not have held on to the raft or floated while she massaged the cramp from her leg.

Van Rossen turned more toward the jury. The defense's objections would not allow him to give his own assessment of how Cynthia had died, but he remarked that it was possible for one person to hold another person underwater.

"How does an individual react when . . . held underwater by another person?"

"I think their first reaction would be surprise," Van Rossen said. "Then panic sets in."

Van Rossen had conducted an experiment with two strong swimmers at the University of Oregon, and he had brought a videotape of that exercise to demonstrate his point to the jury. University student Matt Jaeger had been told to deliberately hold Allison Wade underwater. She had been given a panic signal that she was to use when she needed to come up. Jaeger testified that he had found it "pretty easy" to hold

Allison under the surface with his hand on her shoulder. Her panic signal was to duck and swim away. Actually, Allison had expected she could make her way to the surface because she was such a strong swimmer. She worked out five times a week for the swim team, she was a lifeguard, and she played water polo. She had built up her lung power so that she could stay twelve feet underwater for an extended period of time.

But she couldn't get away from Matt. Allison testified that Matt's hand kept pressing her shoulder down, and at one point he missed her panic signal and she felt true panic. Everything that was happening to her was *beneath* the surface; each time she tried to claw her way upward, she was forced back down. Their experiment continued for an hour.

She was relieved when it was over, and it was only an experiment, she said.

There was a question that Susan Storey wanted very much to ask Dr. Van Rossen: "Do you believe that Cynthia Roth was murdered?"

Judge Sullivan would not permit it. He ruled it would be "an invasion of the jury's province." Only the jury could decide that.

An inanimate object—the Sevylor raft—was the subject of the next expert's testimony. Thomas Ebro of Miami was an aquatic safety consultant and an accident investigator. Admittedly, Sevylor and its parent company, Zodiac, were his clients. Ebro had gone to Lake Sammamish in January 1992 and once more carried out a reenactment of boat wakes against the Sevylor.

Did he have an opinion?

He did.

"The statements by Randy Roth did not comport or correlate [with] the reality of what really happened."

Ebro explained that inflatable boats such as the Sevylor are very stable; they are chosen for use by

303

lifeguards and rescue teams because of their safety and stability, he said, "even in the surf with helicopter rotors above. I could not accept [that] this craft could be overturned by a motorboat wake at this distance."

The Sevylor raft was eleven feet long and five feet wide; it was designed to hold 1,100 pounds, and it had a double-chambered hull. Collapsed or inflated, its weight was about thirty-nine pounds. Even if one chamber was punctured, it would still float.

But would it overturn? Ebro was positive it would not. The Sevylor "exceeded" the criteria required for high wave conditions. "It rides like a leaf," he explained. "The waves pass *beneath* it."

The trial had been going on for weeks, and Judge Frank Sullivan's courtroom was like an oven. Randy Roth had yet to betray his feelings. He sometimes wore a gray and brown sweater, sometimes a suit and tie, and he seemed thinner and more sallow each week. At certain angles, his face looked almost skeletal. His eyes bored into photographers' lens, as if daring them to take his picture. Of course they all took the dare. If anything, he was even more Manson-like than he had been when court procedures began in February. Outside, it was April but it might as well have been December or August. Many of the witnesses who had testified were now in the gallery, listening to testimony, and the court benches were packed even tighter.

It was time for the black humor that always seizes the press section when testimony is too painful, the tragedy before them too real. Someone passed a mimeographed sheet down the row.

ROTH'S
ADVENTURE TOURS

The Thrill of a Lifetime
Rafting . . . Swimming . . . Hiking . . . Camping

A Rose for Her Grave

If you are a single woman
Between the ages of twenty and forty
And you like EXCITEMENT
ROTH'S ADVENTURE TOURS
Is your ticket to SPINE-TINGLING FUN

Spend the day hiking on a remote mountain crag,
Shooting the rapids,
Or just lazily boating on Lake Sammamish

The Evening Ends With Pizza and Videos.
We Guarantee it Will Be a Day You Will
NEVER Forget.

Beneath a cartoon of a raft, the caption read, Randall [sic] Roth, Proprietor: Personal Insurance Required.

28

The prosecution was nearing the end of its seemingly endless witness roster.

Candy Bryce, who had taken an application from Randy for Social Security benefits for Greg as Cindy's orphaned child, recalled that Randy Roth had filed in early October. He claimed that Greg was eligible for $768 a month. He said he had been married twice—to Cynthia Baumgartner and to Donna Clift. He said that Cynthia had no other surviving children—only Greg.

"Did you ask about Cynthia's prior marriage?" Marilyn Brenneman asked Bryce.

"Yes. He indicated it ended in divorce."

The Baumgartners, sitting in the second row, gasped. Tom had died; he would never have left Cynthia any other way.

Bryce said that she had realized that Roth's claim was fraudulent when she read about his arrest a week or so later. She did a computer search and discovered that Greg was already collecting Social Security on Janis Roth's account.

Marilyn Brenneman and Susan Storey had come to some of the people who had loved Cynthia the most, those who would undoubtedly still have been a part of her life if Randy Roth had not come along.

Lori Baker recalled how she and Cynthia had met at the Silver Lake Chapel and how Cynthia's sons had become like her own. At first she had been glad for Cynthia when Randy courted her. But everything had moved too fast when there seemed no need for such impetuosity. Nobody had disapproved of Randy; they just didn't know him.

"When did you hear that Cynthia had drowned?"

"Someone called and told me it was on the news. I called Randy and asked to talk to Cindy. Randy said, 'You can't do that.'

"I said, 'Why?'

"He said, 'She drowned.' "

Lori said there was a family meeting in Woodinville the next day. Randy handed her the Bellevue paper, remarking, "That's pretty accurate."

About a week after Cindy's death, Lori discussed the safe-deposit box with Randy, saying, "We'll need to go together."

"He said, 'We don't have one.'

"I said, 'Yes, we do.' "

By the time Lori gained access to that box, it was empty, and all the keepsakes meant for Cindy's sons were gone. She then answered the prosecutor's questions about Tyson and Rylie coming to live with her. "At the time he gave a press conference, he [Roth] lied about where the boys were," Lori answered quietly. "I had already taken custody of the boys through the will."

It was early in August 1991 when Lori had learned she would become the boys' guardian and the executor of her best friend's estate. She told the jury how difficult it had been to get the boys' belongings back from Randy. Randy had Cindy's clothing ready, and things like the china and silver, but not the boys' prized baseball cards, especially their Ken Griffey, Jr., card. They had not been allowed to take their bikes. He had never offered her or the boys Cindy's wall hangings, bowling trophies, or family pictures.

"He wouldn't let us take all their things," Lori said. "He'd thrown what he would let them have into big garbage bags. He said, 'Take it—I have no use for it.' It was not a happy meeting."

"Randy was a little upset?" Marilyn Brenneman asked.

"Yes."

"When you told the boys—" Brenneman began to ask, but George Cody objected.

"Overruled."

"When you told the boys they would be living with you, what was their attitude?"

"Relieved."

Roth's defense team cross-examined Lori Baker, implying that she had been interested only in gaining Cynthia's estate.

April 3 was a tense day. The courtroom was full of the curious who had heard that Tyson and Rylie Baumgartner would testify, and relatives and friends who were there to support them if they did. Suddenly the fire alarm sounded. Judge Frank Sullivan's courtroom is on the seventh floor of the aged King County

Courthouse, and survival-minded spectators were preparing to leave when a voice thundered over the public address system: "Everyone on the twelfth and ninth floor evacuate the building at once. The rest of you remain at your work stations."

If there were flames, they did not threaten the seventh floor. The trial ground on.

Cynthia Roth's two sons had to testify—there was no way around it. They were the only living witnesses, other than the defendant, who had been privy to what went on inside the bright yellow walls of the new house in Woodinville. Lori Baker had promised them that they would leave the courthouse behind when they were done, and fly to Disneyland. She hoped that the good memories could wipe out the bad.

Tyson Baumgartner, now twelve, took the stand first. He was a slender boy with brown hair parted on the side. He wore a bright blue shirt and tie, slacks, and Weejuns. Brenneman, the mother of four sons herself, girded herself for the questions she had to ask. Easy ones first.

"Your favorite subject?"

"Science."

"You like sports?"

"I *love* baseball."

Marilyn Brenneman asked Tyson Baumgartner to re-create, if he could, the day his mother drowned. Tyson remembered it all. He identified the towels they had taken to the beach, and he remembered that his mom had taken her suntan oil. Greg hadn't gone with them to Idylwood Park; he was at a friend's house.

Tyson said that "we all pumped up the raft. It took a half hour. And Mom and Randy said, 'We're going out on the lake. We'll be back in a little while.' "

"What time was it?"

"About one or two. We saw Joe from my baseball team. We ate chips and drank pop with him. . . . It seemed like a long time before they came back. I didn't see Mom until they got up on shore. . . . Randy was rowing really slow . . . he had his sunglasses on. I saw him first when he was twenty or thirty feet away. We got her [Mom's] stuff and went over and started waving. He just kept rowing. We ran over and Mom was laying in the bottom of the raft. . . . Randy said to go get a lifeguard without making a disturbance."

At Overlake Hospital a lady had offered counseling to Randy, but Tyson remembered Randy said he didn't need any. When the detective wanted the raft, Randy was kind of "huffy," but he gave it to the man. Tyson testified that they had wrung the water out of the towels in the hospital parking lot and then put them back in the plastic bags. He described precisely each towel, each pair of thongs, and the bags.

"On the way home, Rylie cried," Tyson recalled, "and Randy said, 'You don't really need to cry. It's over now. Where do you want to eat?' "

"I said, 'I don't really care.' We went to Burger King, but we couldn't eat."

When they were finally home, they watched the movies Randy picked out. "I thought some of it was funny." There had been a couple of messages on the answering machine, and Tyson remembered that Randy had called someone or someone had called him. He wasn't sure.

The next day, Cynthia's older son remembered, Randy had rushed to get rid of their mother's belongings, especially her makeup. "He said she had too much of it. He made us help. . . . He sold her bike at the swap meet a week later."

The boys stayed about a week with Randy, Tyson thought, and then went to their grandparents'. He remembered going back to Randy's to get their things. "He wasn't real nice to us," Tyson said. "He wouldn't let us take our Nintendo games. He said how could he trust us not to take Greg's things? He wouldn't let us take our BB gun or our rubber boots."

Tyson said he and Rylie had hoped they could live somewhere else.

"Did you want to continue to live with Randy?"

"I didn't really want to."

Rylie Baumgartner was the next witness to take the stand. He was clearly the extrovert of the two brothers. He wore a bright fuchsia shirt and a flowered tie. If anything, Rylie's memory was even more detailed than Tyson's. They had all pumped up the raft with a hand pump that didn't work very well, he said. Then they had left their bags in the raft "'cause they could have got stolen while we were swimming."

It had been a long, long time before they saw the raft come back.

"Three hours?"

"I thought one and a half to two hours. We went and looked out from the dock. I saw the same tank top Randy had on, the same dark hair, dark glasses. I said, 'That's him,' but we could not see our mom. I came to the conclusion she was lying down suntanning. . . . Randy was rowing very casually."

"Did you see your mother?"

"She was laying down, definitely unconscious, blue in the face, blue all over. Her eyes were closed, and her mouth was open." The little boy's face was white as he recalled his horror.

Rylie remembered Randy's first concern was that they all be quiet about what had happened. "Now, don't make a scene," he said. "Very calmly go over and get a lifeguard to help us."

He also recalled that "A lady saw us crying and we said it was our mom and the lady lifeguard took us up by the shed to help us get away from the crowd . . . we went to the hospital to a waiting room. We cried harder when we heard our mother died."

Although both of the boys had been in shock, their minds had registered clear images and statements. Rylie remembered that Randy had said to the detective, "I'm not wearing these glasses to hide anything from you."

As they drove away from the hospital, leaving their

mother behind, Rylie had been unable to contain his tears and Randy had seemed annoyed. "He told me there was no need to cry. 'Just quit crying.' The tears still fell down my face, but I tried to be quiet so he wouldn't hear me."

Randy had rented some movies. "He recommended a few movies—we didn't care. He picked out all comedies." Rylie described *Weekend at Bernie's* as a movie about a corpse that "two guys" kept moving around a beach. "He said, 'You'll like it. It's funny. I've seen it.'"

"Was Randy crying?" Marilyn Brenneman asked. "Was he upset?"

"Not a bit," Rylie answered. "I didn't see that much of a difference."

The boys had spent the evening trying to concentrate on the videos Randy had rented. The next day, when Randy started to clear their house of Cynthia's things, Rylie suggested they give his mother's makeup and twenty boxes of her special kind of fingernail polish to her relatives.

"He said, 'No, it's useless.'"

Rylie, who was a stocky, tough-looking boy, admitted he was afraid of Randy.

"Why?"

"The way he treated me—" Rylie shot a glance down at Randy, who stared at him from the defense table.

"How did he treat you?"

"Me and Tyson. Our punishment got worse. Under the hose in the wintertime. I couldn't breathe. We had to do exercises on the rocks and gravel outside. We had to do bends and thrusts—up to a hundred and fifty of them—on the driveway. If we weren't fast enough, he turned the hose on us. He was in the marines."

Rylie said he had been very excited to learn that he and Tyson were going back to live with Lori Baker.

* * *

At the lunch break, the court officers escorted Randy back to jail. He craned his head toward the elevator doors where his former stepsons were waiting. "Sissies," he sneered. "They're little wimps. And now they'll be worse."

On Friday, April 3, 1992, the prosecution rested. George Cody and John Muenster would now present the defense. They called a number of witnesses who testified that they thought Randy Roth had been in shock when Janis Roth fell off Beacon Rock. He had been pale and sweaty and muttering words like "wife," "fall," and "off the mountain."

On cross-examination, however, one such witness admitted that he might not be able to recall everything that Randy had said on that November day in 1981. It had been a long time.

A fellow mechanic who had gone to work at Metro at the same time as Randy had related that Randy had refused that job when he learned that Metro employees changed shifts every three months. The income was stable and the benefits would be much better than with the Ford dealer where he worked, but Randy had learned he would begin with the graveyard shift. He and Cindy had discussed his working 11:00 P.M. to 7:00 A.M. "He decided he would hold off working for Metro."

The witness said that Randy hadn't wanted to leave his family alone all night. He had returned to work at the Bill Pierre agency.

The witness was surprised to hear from the prosecution that Randy had gotten out of the job by saying his wife had been critically injured in an accident in Idaho.

Muenster and Cody were starting slowly; they seemed to be explaining small blemishes on the surface of an edifice that had suffered fatal internal damage. Perhaps they would attend to that as they progressed through their case.

Jeff Rembaugh, one of Greg Roth's two Little League coaches, described Randy as a strong volunteer who contributed much to the sport and to the kids who played: "We called him Super Dad basically —helping on the field, and coaching."

Rembaugh's wife, Patricia, recalled how impressed the other parents had been when love bloomed between Randy and Cynthia in the summer of 1990: "They were sitting there in the stands holding hands, and they were very much into each other."

Another mother, Linda Christy, concurred: "They'd stare into each other's eyes, and it was real apparent there was a lot of emotion."

On cross-examination, the Rembaughs and Christy admitted that they had no contact with the Roths since their elopement on August 1, 1990.

The defense presented their own raft-flipping video. Coy Jones, aquatics director of the Renton School District told jurors that his reenactment had proved the raft could flip over quite easily. Using two powerboats, his team had managed to flip the raft "four times in twenty passes." Prosecutors insisted the boats had made at least thirty-six passes. In fact, Susan Storey insisted the four capsizings were intentional—performed in the same way prosecution swimmers had turned the raft over by throwing themselves well up on the pontoons and grabbing the oarlocks.

Cynthia had weighed 129 pounds and stood five feet two; Jones's woman had weighed 153 pounds and was five feet six. Moreover, her wet suit had added 10 to 15 pounds. Under Storey's vigorous cross-examination, Sharine Wrigley acknowledged that she had practiced tipping the raft over in a warm pool before going out on Lake Sammamish and that her goal had *been* to tip it over.

Were the jurors satiated with boats, rafts, wakes, and waves? Perhaps. The word was that Randy Roth was going to testify. The inscrutable little man with the set jaw and dark eyes might let them see who he really was.

Neither Muenster nor Cody would say if he was or wasn't going to get up on the stand.

He was.

On Thursday, April 9, Randolph G. Roth stepped up to the witness stand. At his request, he was not filmed by the TV pool camera. He wore a tight-fitting navy blue pin-striped suit. He looked at no one but George Cody, and his speech was almost totally void of inflection and was stilted as he routinely spoke in the passive voice often used in military or police reports.

He did, of course, recall November 27, 1981, the day that his second wife had fallen to her death. The climb up Beacon Rock had been Jan's idea—a "romantic" idea.

They had taken the same shortcut to the summit they had used during the summer. "There's a slight step up that you take, and she took that step—she was perhaps three feet in front of me at this particular section—she stepped down with her left foot and the earth broke and her traction broke away and she fell at almost a forty-five-degree angle. . . . It actually looked like a cartwheel. The first contact she had with the ground was almost on her head and her shoulder, and at that point she did another roll.

"As she was falling, she was falling away from me and it was downhill. At that point she rolled to her side and disappeared over the edge . . . she hollered when she went over."

Roth testified that he had to run down the trail to find a vantage point from which he could see where Jan had landed. When rescuers finally found her, he had had trouble accepting her death; he wanted to see her body.

"She didn't look as badly damaged as one of the individuals had communicated to me. Her hair was matted down on the sides from being bloody, but other than that her face wasn't damaged."

There were apparently great blank spots in Randy Roth's memory. He didn't remember calling Janis's insurance agent the day after she died, taking the envelope of money from Jalina, or any staged burglary at Nick Emondi's house.

As for the Skykomish River raft trip that had frightened Donna Clift, that had been a misunderstanding: "Donna was uncomfortable with rowing. She wouldn't row, and I couldn't use both oars at the same time. Consequently, the raft zigzagged down the river. I couldn't steer and row at the same time."

The main outer chamber was punctured, Roth said, when he and Donna got onto the rocks and the dead trees. "Donna was upset and frightened. She thought there was something I could do. I tried to reassure her that we were all right. She was screaming. I asked her to 'Keep up! Keep up!' "

No, of course he had not shouted "Shut up! Shut up!"

Yes, Randy Roth had kept Jan's ashes, even four years after she died. Yes, Donna had questions about what to do with the cremains. "She thought they should be in an urn or in a mausoleum. They were in a very expensive wood box made by a cabinetmaker on Highway 99 to cover the plastic-coated cardboard box from the services. . . . I was still in an emotional state and couldn't bear to part with Jan's remains. . . . She [Donna] gave me an ultimatum: It was either her—or Jan's ashes. . . . I was confused and uncomfortable with the situation and didn't know how to deal with it. Instead of getting rid of the box, I took it to the attic."

Somewhat Freudianly, Randy said that the ash episode had not broken up his marriage, but "There always seemed to be some gray cloud hanging over us after she found the remains of Janis."

Donna Clift had been a problem for him, he testified, as she hung around people who drank and used marijuana. (Baffled, Donna Clift, in the gallery, shook her head.) "The real problem was an accumulation of circumstances," Randy said. "She wouldn't quit socializing with others I didn't know. She would not quit smoking. . . . I thought she might be buying marijuana." Nothing, of course, could have been further from the truth.

Randy also lied about Mary Jo Phillips. His romance with her had ended, Randy said, because she had not told him everything. It was not until she moved in with him that he had discovered she had three more children than he knew about, and over a hundred tropical birds. "I was a little shocked at this point."

Randy testified that Mary Jo also had two former boyfriends who had shown up. One had tried to run them off the road. Mary Jo's ex-love had confronted Randy. "He didn't think I had any rights to have access to his former girlfriend."

The other boyfriend had come to Randy's home. If that wasn't bad enough, Randy complained, the next shock was a woman from the IRS who said Mary Jo owed $10,000 in back taxes. Worst of all, Mary Jo had thrown Janis's remains away in a garbage can. "She felt I should be able to recover and go on with my life." There was no way he could get the cremains back. "I was upset."

In cross-examining him about these untruths, Marilyn Brenneman suggested that Randy's break with Mary Jo Phillips had really come about because he learned she'd had cancer and was uninsurable.

"I never discussed insurance of any sort with Mary Jo," he responded. "The first time I heard of cancer in relation to Mary Jo was when I was going over the paperwork for this trial."

It was a very long day of questions and answers. Randy disputed almost everything that Brenneman asked him. If not that, he answered, "I don't recall."

On this day, April 14, he could not recall more than a hundred occasions of interest.

As for his 1988 burglary, Randy had been meticulous in trying to re-accumulate what he had lost. He *had* replaced many of the tools he'd lost. He had to; he was a mechanic. He had borrowed tools and purchased used tools. Almost lovingly he listed dozens of tools.

The jurors shifted, yawned, and one woman in the front row had a coughing fit. In his droning voice, Randy continued to describe saws and clamps and rachets and vises and on and on. Oddly, his belongings seemed to evoke more feeling than the women who had passed in and out of his life.

Lizabeth Roth no longer sat in the courtroom. In a phone interview from her home, she castigated the prosecution for placing so much emphasis on her son's demeanor. "Randy and his brother were brought up by their father, who didn't allow them to show emotion," she said. "He was reprimanded for it. That's just the way he was brought up. The prosecutors are presenting him as coldhearted and cruel, but he's not."

Roth's mother claimed that she had stayed away from most of the trial "because it's just too heartbreaking for him to see us there. He'd rather just face it alone."

There was indeed a great deal of heartbreak in that courtroom; the victim's family had maintained—always—a heroic kind of control, and they continued to do so as they stared at the man accused of deliberately drowning Cynthia Baumgartner Roth. He never glanced at them.

Watching him, listening to him speak, was akin to observing a specimen from some other culture or even some other planet. Randy Roth seemed to have no sense whatsoever of his audience, choosing to appear to be a man in complete control and of superior intelligence. What came across was a chilling lack of empathy that permeated the courtroom. If ever emotion was called for, it was on those days when Randy told his own story, but he offered instead a rationale so suspect that both the media and the jury looked up again and again as if they could not believe they had heard him correctly.

He had an explanation for every question the prosecution brought up. If he realized how specious some of his rhetoric sounded, no one in the courtroom could tell. He was a robot, a brilliantly programmed robot, who seemingly had forgotten not one single word of testimony. And now he was setting everything right, arranging, adjusting, explicating, and making clear those things that had damaged him.

The "Idaho accident" was only a misperception on the part of the Metro staff. Cindy had bashed up the Escort in the church parking lot. The message he had really left with Metro was this: "My wife had an accident in our car and we need to take it in for an estimate."

Roth denied signing for a certified letter from Metro—even though that letter was in evidence.

July 1991 had been a bad month. His uncle was killed on July 11 when a tractor fell over on him, "and, oh yeah, a close friend died of heart complications on the fourteenth of July, and then Cindy was sick." Randy said she'd gotten wet on their previous raft trip and had come down with the flu. After a week's confinement to the house, "She expressed a desire to get out of the house—maybe go to the water."

In Randy Roth's vernacular, no one ever "said" or "told" anything to him; they always "communicated to me" or "expressed a desire."

Clearly his alleged lunches and phone calls with Stacey Reese were dangerous to Randy, and he plodded ahead to defuse them. It was Stacey who had taken an interest in him, he claimed. She had been eating lunch in a friend's car and asked him, "What's this Reno trip?"

Randy went on to say, "I told her we were celebrating our one-year anniversary by going to Reno." Stacey had asked Randy about his previous marriages, and he had told her that was "kind of personal."

"I just want to know about you," Randy quoted her.

"So I told her about Janis. I spent maybe twenty-five or twenty minutes with her. . . . I had little contact. She worked all the way in the front. We liked the coffee up there. She and Juanita joked over Cindy saying she was my wife—because I guess I didn't appear to be the type of person who would be married."

Tediously, Randy explained his work hours and his requirement to punch out on a time clock at Bill Pierre. There was no way, he insisted, that he could have taken Stacey Reese to lunch the day before Cynthia drowned; he had worked on a vehicle from 11:00 A.M. to 2:00 P.M. according to this time card. He could not have eaten lunch with Stacey, and he certainly had not complained about his marriage to her.

After five weeks of trial, Randy Roth finally gave his version of Cynthia's drowning, of the trip to the lake that had ended so tragically. Would it be his last retelling?

Cynthia, he said, had suggested a family trip on Monday night, but Randy could not get home early enough because of a turbocharger he was working on. He recalled that it was on an Escort. (He remembered cars the way most men remember women.) He had continued working on the car until "12:26" on Tuesday. He described just what he had done to the Escort's engine.

He had left work then and gone home. His wife had the boys pack up their things while he showered "to get the oil and grease off."

Randy described the plastic shopping bags, "one with snaps," and the paper bags the boys had. "I figure we left at two."

Randy testified that he had never been to Idylwood Park before. "We parked on the upper parking lot. . . . It was almost a hundred degrees, no shade. We took turns pumping. . . . Cynthia sent the boys to the swim area. We put Rylie's paper sack into a plastic sack. . . . We paddled out across the lake. . . . It was about three or three-thirty. We had no watches."

To Cody's question, Randy shook his head. No, he had had no time frame communication.

"Cynthia had organized the trip that day . . . we proceeded to row out into the lake. There's some small grassy areas and some houses on the east side. . . . There are two sets of oarlocks. They would have been in the front. Cynthia was sitting on the floor, with the bag between us. There was no reason to hurry to the other side. I'd told the boys they could have a ride when we got back."

Randy Roth described the exceptionally heavy traffic in the sandbar area; there were fewer boats out in the open water. A dozen jet skiers. "The water was real choppy, like Puget Sound. Real rough . . . agitated."

They got to the east side of the lake, even though it was much farther than Randy had estimated. There was an open area, and they rowed along looking for a nice place to land. They stopped in shallow water and got out, holding on to the raft so it wouldn't blow away. Randy had gotten his prescription sunglasses out of one of the sacks. He explained that he was very nearsighted "20/400 in my left eye—20/425 in my right." (A person with 20/200 uncorrected vision is legally blind.)

Suddenly Randy's voice dropped. "One of Cindy's thongs slipped off, and she swam to get it. We got in the raft and started across the very shallow water. We just stepped right into the raft. . . . There was boat activity north and south of us often. . . . We intersected all the traffic. . . . We were going west. We were on the Idylwood side. It was still fairly hot, and she asked if I wanted to get in and cool off. She put my glasses in a sack . . . she dove off and so did I. The raft was blowing around quite a bit. We stayed close. We were in the water at least five minutes. *She's* a better swimmer. She did the crawl stroke with her head out of the water. I did the breaststroke. She said she had a cramp in her foot from the cold water."

At this point Randy estimated they had 20 to 30 feet to swim back to the raft and his wife was ahead of him. "Her initial contact with the raft, she held on to the rear oarlock and the rope, which didn't keep her face out of the water. She tried to pull herself onto it. It kept bobbing up on the other side. We had never tried to get in the raft in the water. She said she couldn't use her leg to kick, and I started swimming toward the front so I could go around. . . . I got just to the bow. My back was toward her. A boat came by from behind us . . . the raft flipped over and cracked the water. I heard her cough. I heard the roar of the boat going away . . . it had been right beside us—50 to 100 yards away."

Randy Roth testified that he swam to the side of the raft and lifted it a couple of inches. "I swam to the bow and flipped it. I saw her on her face. The two plastic bags were floating. I didn't have a strong enough kick to bring her to the boat. I brought the boat to her. I held her nose and blew into her mouth. It was like blowing into a long birthday balloon where I couldn't get enough air into it. . . . I couldn't get her over the side. I let go of her and swam to the end of the raft and paddled to her. . . . I was able to get her hands and pull her over the back. I wanted to row. I needed the sack with my glasses—the one with the strings was floating deep. . . . I was headed for the lifeguard towers. In my mind, I was not more than a few minutes from the lifeguard. My arms were too weak. . . ."

The courtroom was hushed. Randy Roth said he only turned around to be sure he was rowing straight. He had told himself, "Just a few minutes . . . just a few minutes . . . to the lifeguard."

What had he told Cindy's sons?

"Run as fast as you can, but don't create a panic."

He had said that so everyone wouldn't run like they did in *Jaws* and get in the way. Above all, he had wanted to avoid a *"Jaws* effect."

If he had seemed detached, Randy explained that he was focused entirely on the efforts to save Cynthia. "I felt sick to my stomach, so I pulled all the stuff out of the raft and deflated it so I'd be ready to go."

For just an instant it seemed as though the witness might actually be crying. It was as close as he would ever come during his marathon testimony. People had been asking him questions.

How long had Cynthia been unconscious?

He thought "perhaps five minutes." He was exhausted, wanted to be with her, he couldn't find the boys.

"Someone said they had a pulse!" But it had been only a CPR pulse, Randy testified. They could not get an airway in, and they had elevated Cindy with towels.

"I knew I had gotten her to shore as quick as I could, and these people were working on her, and I thought they'd be able to bring her back on the way to the hospital. I kept saying, 'I have two boys here.'"

Randy said he threw his gear in the back of his

vehicle, and the boys got in the back. He drove, and the woman got in. She gave directions to the hospital. "I can't remember how fast I drove. All I had in my mind was Cindy in the aid car on the way to the hospital. The boys were really quiet. None of the three of us realized she wasn't going to be helped."

There had been many versions of what had happened after Cynthia was pronounced dead at Overlake Hospital. Now Randy gave his. He testified that he had been "preoccupied" by his conversations with Lieutenant Conrad. He had hated the thought of Cynthia's body being autopsied, but had to agree. Conrad had drawn a diagram of the lake and marked it "North" and "South," and Randy remembered having the boys wring out the towels. They had left about 8:30 P.M. He asked the boys where they wanted to eat. "They said Burger King.

"Both boys were real quiet—especially Tyson. None of us could eat. We went to a video place, and I told them they could rent two or three videos—pick a couple of comedy shows. . . . We went straight home and cleaned up. The message machine was blinking."

He had tried to call Leon, Randy testified, but the line was busy. He called the other number left on his machine. It was a man calling on an ad wanting to trade a crew cab for a Corvette. Randy spoke briefly and hung up. Between nine and ten the boys put stuff in the washer, they all took showers, and Randy made popcorn. The medical examiner's office had called wanting Cynthia's Social Security number. They had all fallen asleep on the couch and then gone to bed.

The phone had awakened Randy the next morning. He had tried his best, he explained, to keep the boys busy and preoccupied. "I had to go to the swap meet and clean out the garage, and get them larger four-wheelers."

He had not told Greg about the tragedy for a few days, as he was staying at a friend's house. The phraseology he used when he did was hauntingly familiar: "Greg couldn't really believe it. I told him that she wasn't with us anymore."

When had he talked to Cynthia's family? Cody asked.

Randy could not recall specifically when he had talked to Leon or Lori or Cynthia's parents. They had all come over. "I wanted to let them handle everything. They'd known her a lot longer than I had. They decided on the Silver Lake Chapel."

The service had been on Monday, July 29, and Randy had returned to work on Tuesday. People at work had been "very kind."

He could not recall seeing Stacey. She had called the house and left a message on the machine. How was he? How were the boys? She had left her number, and he had called and told her he was trying to distract the boys.

Yes, he had offered her the tickets to Nevada. They were prepaid and he couldn't use them. She couldn't take the time off work.

Tyson and Rylie had gone to visit relatives, and Randy testified that he had been stunned when Lori Baker called to tell him that they had located the will and that "the boys won't be coming home again."

The media had started to dog him, and he had given a press conference just to get them off his back. And then Lori had come over a day or two later with a truck. He didn't have boxes for Cynthia's things. He used sacks. Yes, he *had* protected Greg's bedroom. "I wanted to afford them all their areas of privacy and security."

Randy presented himself to the jurors—although he never looked at them—as a man bereft and robbed of the family he loved. "I guess I felt abandoned and somewhat betrayed because they took the boys away without my input."

It was impossible to discern what the jurors were thinking; some sat with their chins in their hands, some with crossed legs, but all of them were motionless and expressionless as they studied the man on the witness stand.

Randy went on to say he suspected greed on Lori's part, because the boys got about $700 apiece each month from Social Security. Randy said he earned only $2,200 to $2,800 a month and he could no longer afford the Woodinville house; he had already planned to buy a smaller home for himself and all the boys. As for the Social Security application he had made on Greg's behalf as Cynthia's surviving son, he said that Social Security representatives had practically "offered" it to him. He had never asked. *They* wanted Greg's birth certificate and other documentation. *They* sent Randy an application.

He could not "recall" ever telling them that Cindy had divorced Tom Baumgartner instead of being widowed; that must have been a clerical error. He could not recall the one check that had been sent for Greg on Cindy's account. He had been "told" it was in the bank.

Finally, George Cody had no more questions—and Randy Roth had no more explanations.

Marilyn Brenneman rose to cross-examine Randy Roth. She approached him pleasantly enough. He apparently never sensed that her questions might be troublesome, even perilous, for him. Still, he shifted in his chair to face her.

Brenneman was prepared to dismember the framework of Randy Roth's testimony section by section. She began by discussing the money that Cynthia had had in the bank.

"That money was accessed by Cindy," he answered smoothly.

"The money went to your benefit?"

"Ultimately, yes."

Marilyn Brenneman was fascinated that, until his court testimony, there had been no mention of

Cindy's holding on to the oarlocks of the raft, not in Randy's statements of July 23, July 29, or August 11, and not in his press conference on August 9.

He admitted that he had spoken in "generalities" before about the drowning. "This is my first opportunity to address that."

"You have prepared yourself?"

"In a manner of speaking."

It was obvious what Brenneman was getting at; the defense reenactment video clearly showed the female swimmer holding on to the oarlocks as she tipped the raft over onto herself.

Marilyn Brenneman moved a little closer, hitting Roth with one question after another that exposed big and little lies about his past. Cody tried to stop her with a hastily called sidebar. The defense could see what was coming the moment she asked Randy what he had done after high school.

"You have investments in cattle and land?"

"None at this point in time."

"Did you?"

"At one point—with my father."

"How far back?"

"At least ten years."

Bit by bit Roth had to give ground. He had not been a motorcycle racer, a martial arts instructor, the owner of a successful home repair business, or a three-year college student. He didn't own vast acreage on the Columbia River, and he did not plan to purchase an exercise gym.

He had never been in Vietnam.

All the things he had listed as his accomplishments in the program from his tenth anniversary reunion at Meadowdale High School were not quite true. "Maybe somebody changed the information," he finished weakly.

"What martial arts did you teach?"

"A street version—mostly exercise, no particular style."

"Tae Kwon Do? Kung fu?"

"Basically . . . basically specific reactions to situations a person might encounter on the street . . . primarily exercise and meditation."

She asked him if he had been influenced by Bruce Lee.

"I believe . . . I was involved in a style he created."

"What was it called?"

"I don't remember."

Brenneman moved through Roth's divorce from Donna Sanchez, his alleged refusal to let Greg talk to his mother on the phone, his control over Nick and Carrie Emondi.

"How?" Roth countered. "We lived twenty miles apart."

"You had control. . . . You're a very tough person whom Nick would not cross. You showed him a weapon."

"Nick's larger than I am. . . . I had a baseball bat sawed in half with nails pounded in and painted black." Randy rocked in the witness chair ever so slightly.

"Did you invite Mr. Emondi to go with you to move your mother?"

"No. She did move three or four years ago."

"She was being held against her will?"

"No."

"You took a gun?"

"I didn't have a gun to take with me."

"Never had access to guns?"

No, he had only had his homemade weapons, and Greg had his BB gun. Still, the tall prosecutor was making the defendant nervous. He didn't know where she was going to go next.

She moved through his marriages again, and he parried each thrust. The fault had never been his. It had been in the wives, in the women who left him. He spoke of them in his curious, ponderous manner. When he talked of dancing with Janis, he didn't say they had had fun by going dancing. He said, "That was one of the sources of recreation we utilized."

And when Janis died, crushed far below the perch where they had hiked, he spoke of "damage," as if her face had been only a fender on a car.

Brenneman asked about Randy's Pioneer Insurance claims. His recovery, he said, "was very small after the attorney's fees."

Although it took a most observant person to spot it, Randy Roth tensed ever so slightly when Brenneman asked him about his lunches with Stacey Reese. No. He had only a half hour for lunch; the office staff had an hour. He didn't know Stacey well enough to take her to lunch. He had just "run into her at Dick's Drive-in."

Randy insisted he always punched in and out on his job.

"Always?"

"Always."

"Were you close with Cynthia?" Brenneman asked suddenly.

"That's part of the reason we got married."

"Any problems?"

"All relationships have problems."

"The people at Bill Pierre can't remember one *positive* thing you ever said about Cynthia."

"It's always easier to remember the negatives more than the positives."

"Did you call her a bitch?"

"I never called any woman that."

"How *did* you feel about Cynthia?"

"We enjoyed each other. I wanted to spend the rest of my life with her."

Randy speculated that their only differences might have been over the way she handled the boys. He dealt directly with their activities, he explained, while she observed.

Brenneman kept asking him for more explication, and he obliged each time, digging himself in a little deeper. He felt that Cynthia might have been envious because he spent so much money on the boys' athletic equipment. "We spent twenty-three dollars for three athletic supporters and cups."

She asked him why he had signed up as a single person at Nautilus Northwest, a gym. He didn't answer, but admitted Cynthia had "expressed her unhappiness" over that.

"You told people at work that she was restricting your freedom?"

"No."

"You disabled her car so she couldn't leave the house?"

"*She* thought so. It was a clutch. . . . I fixed it."

Item by item, Marilyn Brenneman read off the "Randy hates—" poem that Sue Peters had found during the October 1991 search. Again and again he denied that those complaints were true. The witness's face grew, if anything, blanker, and his body language became even more guarded. He didn't recognize Cindy's handwriting on the document. He spoke of his wife always in the present tense, as if she still lived.

"Did you convey any of these feelings to Stacey Reese?"

"She asked about the marriage. I assumed because she'd talked to Cindy on the phone."

"You told her it was 'shit'?"

"That's not part of my vocabulary. That was Stacey's term, not mine."

Randy acknowledged he had met Stacey for lunch one time.

"You *never* let anyone at Bill Pierre think you were not married?" Brenneman asked incredulously.

He had told Juanita Gates he was "sort of married."

"You never said you had a one-year contract and it was about up?"

"No."

Randy insisted his marriage had been very stable, with only small disagreements. Stacey's testimony was inaccurate. He had had nothing in common with Stacey except they were both single parents. No, of course he had never tried to discourage her from dating other men. He knew nothing about her personal life.

"You never said, 'Before you go out with John, think about what he wants you to give up'?" Brenneman pushed.

"I was concerned for her well-being and safety, knowing the type of person John was."

The prosecutor switched gears again, bringing out the myriad problems that witnesses had seen in Randy's fourth marriage—the time he spent with Max Butts and the long absences when he took Brad home to his mother, Lily Vandiveer.

No, he insisted. No problems. Everything had been fine.

"You remember telling Stacey Reese you didn't want the relationship to go on?"

"No."

"That Cindy was obsessive and nasty toward you, that you only had a verbal marriage?"

"No." And no and no and no.

"Did you contact Stacey Reese the Thursday following Cindy's death?"

"Yes, in response to an answering machine message."

"Did you say, 'I'm fine. Why wouldn't I be? It was a horrible thing, but a *relief*'?"

Looking directly into Marilyn Brenneman's eyes, Randy Roth replied easily that Stacey had misunderstood. "It would have been a rhyme word—like I didn't know how I would deal with my *grief.*"

Randy's four phone calls to another woman in the week after his wife drowned had come back to haunt him, but he deftly deflected Stacey's memory.

Yes, he had told Stacey that the police might be developing a theory that he might be guilty of harming Cindy.

"Did you tell Stacey you were afraid they were going to come that weekend and arrest you?"

"I wouldn't have said *afraid*—maybe *concerned* about the effect on the boys."

"Did you invite Stacey to Reno?"

"No. I asked her if she had use for the tickets."

"You told Stacey you had life insurance, but just enough to pay off your home. You told her, 'It will take me fucking forever to get the pink and mauve out of my home'?"

"I don't use that word. All I did was respond to her question. Without a woman in the house, I felt uncomfortable having that much femininity in the environment around the boys."

Slowly and methodically Marilyn Brenneman was showing the dark nether side of all of Randy's previous testimony. She elicited responses that showed he had begun the very morning after Cindy's drowning to eradicate everything that reminded him or her sons of her existence. Makeup thrown away, her treasures thrown into closets, her dolls "centralized."

He explained away, again, the pesky insurance policies. Mortgage insurance, really.

The message to Metro was another "rhyme" misunderstanding. "I didn't say 'Idaho.' I would have said, '*I don't know* when I can come to work.'"

Roth was inflexible about the details of Cynthia's drowning. Anyone who remembered it differently was mistaken. He was not a good swimmer. He had not saved the life of a high school girlfriend, no matter that that ex-girlfriend had testified that he had. "It would have been impossible for me. I don't have a strong enough kick."

Despite his weakness in the water, he had done everything within his limited ability, to save Cynthia. Some things he could not remember, of course.

"You couldn't have helped Cynthia in the water?" Brenneman moved a little closer to the witness stand.

"It was not a matter of being able to help or not

being able to help. It was a question of her not being able to respond to the air breaths," he answered.

"Actually, Mr. Roth, isn't it a question of whether or not you were a strong enough swimmer to be able to pull Cynthia Roth under until she drowned?"

"That wouldn't have been a part of anything that happened." He stared back at Brenneman, his jaw tight, his eyes opaque.

The two of them had been sparring for days, but it seemed more like weeks. Perhaps—outside—true summer had come again. Finally, on Thursday, April 16, Marilyn Brenneman was down to her last questions.

"Isn't it a fact, Mr. Roth, that money—insurance proceeds—is why you murdered your wife Janis?"

"That's not true at all."

"That's why you murdered Cynthia, your fourth wife. Isn't that a fact?"

"That is not a fact."

"In fact, money has been at the root of every insurance fraud scheme that you've committed, that's been testified to in front of this jury. Isn't that a fact?"

"That's totally incorrect. My life-style has never been indicative of having or controlling any large amounts of money."

"Controlling people and controlling money is what your life-style *is* all about . . . from what we've heard here. Isn't that a fact?"

"No," Randy Roth murmured.

It was over. Roth stepped down from the witness stand and walked over to his attorneys. Very few members of the gallery and none of the jury could see the expression on his face as he looked at George Cody. He smiled, the faintest of grins that looked like nothing so much as a child who had just recited before a PTA audience and had done well. It lasted only an instant before his usual mask dropped down.

Jack Hopkins, court reporter for the *Seattle Post-Intelligencer* and a veteran of more criminal trials than almost any writer in the area, summed up Roth's testimony best:

> "Randy Roth, suspected of pushing one wife to her death off Beacon Rock and charged with drowning another in Lake Sammamish, spent close to 22 hours on the witness stand.
>
> "He never unbuttoned his sport coat.
>
> "He never crossed his legs.
>
> "He never slumped down in his chair.
>
> "He never looked at the jurors.
>
> "He never raised his voice in anger or shed a tear in grief.
>
> "For the better part of six days, he talked on and on about the past 10 years of his life, trying to convince a King County Superior Court jury the deaths of his wives were tragic accidents."

The only thing that marked Randy Roth as wary were his hands. He had held them in an almost unnatural position in front of him, and they were clenched. He was so thin his skin seemed transparent, his bones showing through. He looked to weigh no more than 125 or 130 pounds, the very image of a man who would have been too weak to save his wife from drowning and without enough stamina to row far enough fast enough to get her help.

But was he?

29

Jury selection had begun in February, and it was now the week of April 20. Time at long last for final arguments. The jury had heard well over a hundred witnesses—some who were expert, some emotional, some angry, some forgetful, some precise—and each section of testimony contributed to an almost unfathomable jigsaw puzzle, according to the prosecution. The prosecution maintained that Randy Roth was a cold-blooded killer of at least two of the women who had loved him. The defense found him only a tragic figure, besieged by loss upon loss, a victim of highly circumstantial evidence, and no more than that.

Marilyn Brenneman would present the state's final arguments, and she would do so at considerable disadvantage. Over the weekend she had been enticed away from preparing those arguments by a rollicking party to celebrate her son Adam's eighth birthday. The weather was wonderful and so was the sight of Brenneman's yardful of sons. There was a water balloon fight going on, and she chased after one of her offspring with a fully loaded balloon. As she confidently took aim and threw, she stepped in a hole and severely sprained her left ankle. The balloon missed and hit a rosebush.

A clean break would have hurt less. Brenneman would present her final argument on crutches with her ankle tightly bound up in an Ace bandage. Wearing a bright red jacket with a soft white blouse, the deputy prosecutor began a process that would take hours. From time to time, she winced slightly as she moved in front of the jury to the easel and back to a stool. For the most part, she was so involved in her intricately constructed argument that she didn't feel the pain.

Randy Roth was charged with three counts, and the jury was to debate each count separately. Count 1 was murder in the first degree. In order to convict on that count, the jury must believe that Brenneman and Susan Storey had proved beyond a reasonable doubt that Randy Roth had intentionally and with premeditation caused the death of his fourth wife, Cynthia Baumgartner Roth, and that this death had occurred in King County, Washington. The second count was theft in the first degree. To convict, the jury must believe that between September 17, 1988, and October 2, 1991, Randy Roth had gained by color or aid of deception over $1,500 from the Pioneer Insurance Company, and that that crime had occurred in King County, Washington. The third charge was theft in the second degree. To bring in a conviction the jurors needed to believe that between September 17, 1991, and October 15, 1991, Randy had wrongfully obtained by color or aid of deception over $250 from the Social Security Administration in King County, Washington.

Marilyn Brenneman was calm and deliberate, and her voice was soft. From time to time she glanced at Randy Roth as she unreeled the seemingly endless connected and similar circumstances of his alleged crimes. The jurors were fascinated; the gallery was transfixed, and even Judge Sullivan and his staff listened to Brenneman as if they had never heard all these coincidences and similar patterns before.

Direct evidence was what the jurors had heard from witnesses—those people who had seen and heard vital parts of the case with their own senses. Circumstantial evidence was what a reasonable person using common sense would deduce. For instance, Brenneman said, "If a car comes off the west end of the I-90 Bridge, common sense would tell us that it must have gone on the east side."

Almost nothing in human experience can be proved absolutely. Yes, a car could have been dropped on that one-way bridge by a giant helicopter or hoisted hydraulically from a submarine halfway across Lake Washington—but not likely. And nobody could do a U-turn on the I-90 floating bridge.

Marilyn Brenneman submitted to the jury in this seven:h week of trial that "the defendant, Randy Roth, cold-bloodedly courted, married, insured, and murdered Cynthia Baumgartner Roth. That he murdered her out of greed, and that was his reason. . . . The picture before you is now clear. And it is that the defendant did indeed murder his wife . . . and he did it cold-bloodedly, making it appear to have been an accident. He did it for $385,000 in insurance proceeds, her separate property, assets, and Social Security benefits."

Scarcely glancing at her notes, Brenneman reviewed the witnesses' testimony, the direct evidence, the circumstantial evidence. She reminded the jury that not only had the victims suffered at Roth's greedy hands but so had their children and their families. This is true of all murder cases, she said, but especially of the one they now were about to consider.

"The defendant is a cold-blooded and premeditated killer who stalks his prey, not with the traditional weapons," Brenneman said, "but with a smile, flowers, and marriage proposals."

Defense attorney George Cody argued that reasonable doubt existed and that the state's tactic of linking Janis Miranda Roth's death with Cynthia Baumgartner Roth's death was unfair. "What is going on here, in large measure, is the state is saying that you should more readily accept than you would under other circumstances that Randy Roth killed Cynthia Roth because Janis Roth died in 1981. What they are saying is you should accept more easily that Randy Roth killed Janis Roth because Cynthia Roth died ten years later. I don't believe you can bounce those two things back and forth in your mind like a Ping-Pong game."

Brenneman presented the whole puzzle, pieces neatly in place, some after almost eleven years. Cody worked to present individual segments from those years.

They were both very, very good at what they did.

Randy had caught Cynthia off guard, the limping prosecutor maintained. "He was stalking Cynthia Roth and he was using those weapons that he had used before, pretending to be enamored of her, pretending to love her. How many of us could say that we would have known any different than Cynthia Roth? To be loved is a natural human desire. To be loved intensely and immediately is overwhelming, and it is wonderful when it is *real.* But this was not real. . . . He covers his real intentions behind a false front of love, and he victimizes not only those who believe those false claims but the innocent relatives and children his victims always leave behind."

George Cody acknowledged that Randy and Janis Roth had had some differences in their brief marriage, but said that did not prove he had killed her. "If it did," he said, "there would be a motive for some kind of mayhem for virtually everybody who has been married at any time."

True.

Cody insisted that Randy's lack of obvious emotion at the time of Janis's death—and, inferentially, Cynthia's—only served to confirm his innocence. "If Randy Roth was at the top of Beacon Rock, alone with Janis, and he decided to kill her, you must ask yourself why he would tell a series of stories that the state says are inconsistent and raise suspicions about the death of his wife. . . . It would be relatively simple to come up with a specific version . . . and tell it and not do anything else."

Marilyn Brenneman had the burden of proof. George Cody had only to raise reasonable doubt and Randy Roth could walk away.

Concerning Randy Roth's apparent lack of grief and emotion at Idylwood Park, Cody walked a precipice as dangerous as any on Beacon Rock. His reasoning was somewhat intricate and threatened to boomerang.

"On the day of Cynthia Roth's death," Cody said, "we are talking about somebody going through a unique situation, going through, for the second time, the same occurrence—not the second *murder,* but the second *death.* I don't know how anybody would react in that circumstance, whether they would say all the right things and make all the right moves."

For veteran court watchers, listening to and observing both Cody and Brenneman was an ambivalent experience. Each was at once folksy and intellectual, colloquial and dead-on serious. At one point George Cody actually stood behind Randy's chair and placed his hand paternally on the defendant's left shoulder. And, as if he'd rehearsed the scene, Randy Roth lifted his eyes for the very first time in the seven-week trial and looked directly into the jurors' eyes.

Cody told an anecdote about a dog sent to the pound because he had blueberry pie stains on his face and an empty pie pan under his paw. *Circumstantial.*

Brenneman told an anecdote, much beloved by attorneys, about a defense attorney who promised that the missing—and presumed dead—"victim" would walk into the courtroom; everyone looked toward the door, save the defendant.

And beneath it all, the decision to come would be ultimately serious. If Randy Roth *was* guilty but the jury did not find him so, who knew how many female and child victims lay ahead of him. He was only thirty-eight years old. If he was innocent and the jury did not find him so, he faced life behind bars. There were no smoking guns, no fingerprints in blood, no hair and fiber matches, no confessions, no living eyewitnesses. This was not an easy case.

Not at all.

As Marilyn Brenneman rose to offer her short rebuttal, the last act of this long trial, she looked steadily and frequently at Randy Roth. She pointed out that the state had offered the jurors everything— the entire puzzle with no pieces missing. The defense had offered individual pieces—pieces that could not tell them if they were looking at sky or water or clouds. Or reality.

Randy Roth's patterns were far too predictable and repetitive to be coincidental. "The parallels are just too similar, and that is because they were . . . presented by a man with a plan. And the plan said if you have gotten away with murder once with a successful story, get as close to that story as possible if you want to get away with murder twice.

"If you fool me once, shame on you." Brenneman's voice dropped. "If you fool me twice, shame on me. That's the situation we are now in. . . . If he fools us today, shame on us."

The jury filed out of Judge Sullivan's courtroom in the afternoon of April 22, 1992. They returned on the afternoon of April 23 with a verdict. They had deliberated for eight and a half hours, a little more than an hour for each week of the trial. The verdict:

Guilty of first-degree murder.

Guilty of first-degree theft.

Guilty of second-degree theft.

Randy Roth stayed true to form. Beyond a quick glance downward, he showed no emotion. His attorneys told reporters they would file an appeal.

On Friday, June 19, 1992, Judge Sullivan gave Randolph G. Roth an exceptional sentence. The state had asked for a fifty-five-year sentence. Sullivan moderated that only a little; he sentenced Randy to fifty years in prison, as he agreed with Marilyn Brenneman and Susan Storey that Roth had shown extreme greed and coldheartedness in killing his fourth wife for insurance and in leaving her two children orphans. With credit for good behavior, Roth could conceivably be released after serving thirty-four years.

George Cody and John Muenster repeated their intent to appeal the conviction, just as they had predicted they would before the trial began. Their main objection was—and remained—the inclusion of Roth's prior behavior in his trial for a murder that had occurred in 1991.

Officials in Skamania County had been prepared to prosecute Roth in the alleged murder of Janis Roth had he not received a sentence in the fifty-year range. Such a trial, however, would have drained the county's budget. With the June 19 sentencing, Skamania County announced it would not reopen the case on Janis.

It will be years, if ever, before Randy Roth's name ceases to appear in some legal proceeding somewhere. There will be the sometimes endless appeal process. Lori Baker is suing on behalf of Tyson and Rylie Baumgartner to ask that Gordon Roth be removed as trustee from Cynthia's policies and that the money be designated only for Cynthia's sons.

In the meantime, the slender, ethereal Randy metamorphosed once again. Preparing for prison, he put on weight and restored the massive muscles that he had been so proud of. He grew a beard to go with his luxuriant mustache.

The man who had sat quietly throughout the seven-week trial never really existed. He was a character in a play that didn't succeed. The macho Randy Roth entered the Washington State Prison at Walla Walla in the fall of 1992.

Barring a successful appeal, he will be seventy-two years old when he is released.

Campbell's Revenge

"Don't the stories *you write frighten you?" It is another predictable question that I have heard two hundred times. Usually my answer is that I am rarely afraid, even though I have written about some of the most heinous criminals of the last three decades. But sometimes I must admit that a case cuts too close to the bone and triggers fears that all women have. We fear first for our children and only second for ourselves.*

Charles Rodman Campbell is a killer straight out of a nightmare. There should have been some way to keep him locked up forever. But he slipped through the loopholes of our justice system, and he was allowed freedom to stalk his unknowing victims. If ever there was a case that pitted innocence against pure evil, it is this one. He was out of his cage, and he was aware of every facet of her life, and yet his potential prey felt only a chill premonition of danger. He was a man consumed with rage and the need for revenge. Because of a neglectful bureaucracy, Campbell was allowed to take not one life—but three.

Clearview, Washington, is little more than a crossroads, a tiny neighborhood in Snohomish County, twelve miles south of Everett, the county seat. Travelers headed for Stevens Pass, one of the northern routes over the Cascade Mountains, pass through Clearview and scarcely realize it.

After it was over, Clearview residents cried, "This sort of thing doesn't happen here—not in Clearview." *Why* do people say that? Is everyone who lives outside a major metropolitan area convinced that he or she lives in a safe zone, under a kind of glass bubble where violent crimes never break through? Possibly—if the nightly news is any barometer. The cold fact is that tragedies and terror happen everywhere, no matter how sylvan the landscape, how slow the pace of life is, or how loving and protective the friends and neighbors. Psychopaths move among all of us, their motivation usually hidden behind a winning, clear-eyed smile and sincere promises. Many of them are handsome or beautiful, successful—at least for a time—and persuasive. And sometimes all of us trust too much, too soon.

He was not like the smoothly handsome predators. He frightened most women just by the way he looked. He was so big—almost six feet five—and his bushy mustache and tangled Afro hair were reddish brown and seemed to bristle with electricity. But it was his

345

eyes that caught them in a steady, mind-altering stare. They were like the entrance to a tunnel, the dark orbs fixed above an expanse of white beneath. *Sampaku,* the Japanese call them: "eyes of death." Like Rasputin's—the mad monk who mesmerized Russian nobility, another huge man who seemed impervious to his enemies—Charles Rodman Campbell's eyes had a life of their own. They were often glazed and a little crazy. To the cons in the Monroe, Washington, Reformatory, he was a "bad-ass," and to his guards, he was trouble. To his victims, he was the devil himself.

Renae Ahlers Wicklund was a beautiful woman— dark-haired and big-eyed, with the high cheekbones and symmetrical features of a model. Her career was beauty—the art of bringing beauty to other women. She was kind, responsible, and gutsy. She must have been gutsy to endure what she did.

After she graduated from high school, where she was a drum majorette for the band, in Jamestown, North Dakota, Renae Ahlers moved to California and then to Washington State. When Renae met her future husband, Jack Wicklund, she was working in a beauty parlor in Seattle. She was nineteen, and Jack was fourteen years older, divorced with two children from a previous marriage.

In 1972 they fell in love and got married. Renae was expecting her first baby when they moved into their own home, a neat one-story rambler set far back in a stand of fir trees near rural Clearview. Lots were acre-sized, and being neighborly required some effort. Running across the street to have coffee meant almost a quarter-mile jog. But Renae and Barbara and Don Hendrickson grew close right away. Don was forty-three and Barbara forty-one. They had lived there for ten years, and they became almost substitute parents; their children—Peggy, Susan, and Dan—were family, too.

Jack Wicklund spent much of his time on the road, and as Renae neared term in her pregnancy, she was more grateful than ever for the Hendricksons. When she went into labor, Jack was out of town, and it was Peggy Hendrickson who drove Renae to the hospital on that day in 1973 when Renae gave birth to a baby girl she named Shannah. Shannah looked just like her mother—she had the same huge brown eyes and chestnut hair. Renae adored her, and everywhere Renae went, her baby went along.

It is impossible to know if Shannah remembered the first bad time. Probably not. She was only a year and a half old when it happened. It is likely, though, that the toddler sensed her mother's frantic terror, that the feeling surfaced in bad dreams through the next eight years. The first time, Shannah lived only because her mother did what any mother would have done to save her child: Renae Wicklund gave in to a rapist to keep him from harming Shannah.

December 11, 1974, was an unseasonably warm and sunny day for western Washington, where December usually means rain, rain, and more rain. Taking advantage of the weather, twenty-three-year-old Renae Wicklund decided to wash her windows. Knowing that darkness comes near four on a winter afternoon in the Northwest, Renae hurried to gather rags, vinegar, and water to accomplish the task. It was about 1:30 P.M. when she carried Shannah out and plopped her down on the grass in the sunshine, talking and singing to the baby while she worked on the windows.

On that Wednesday afternoon, Renae Wicklund suddenly became aware of someone walking toward them along the long driveway that led through the trees to her house. She saw a tall figure out of the corner of her eye and turned to stare directly at a youngish man with a copper cast to his hair. When she did that, he turned and walked back out to the main road. She thought he had probably been lost and realized when he saw her that he had the wrong house.

Leaving Shannah on the grass, she stepped into the house to grab some more rags. Moments later she returned and stood at the front door. The man was coming back, and this time he was moving fast.

As she would testify later in court, "He was running. Toward the house. Up our driveway. I thought that he was after Shannah, so I ran outside to grab her. And before we could get inside the house, he was pushing the door."

Renae, dressed lightly because of the balmy December day, tried to hold the front door shut with her body, but the man was much too strong, and she had Shannah in her arms. When he burst through the door, she saw that he had a knife in his right hand. Keeping her voice determinedly calm, she asked if there was something she could do for him—thinking that if she pretended she hadn't seen the knife, it still might not be too late.

It was too late. "Yeah," the intruder said. "Get your clothes off right now or I'll kill the kid, and I mean it."

He was holding the knife terribly close to Shannah. Renae Wicklund didn't have to decide what she would do. She put Shannah down at the stranger's order and slowly removed her boots, her purple corduroy shorts, her black sweater and vest, then sat down in a chair, waiting for what she feared would come next.

But he didn't want intercourse; he wanted oral sex. While her baby daughter screamed, she complied until her attacker was satisfied.

She prayed he wouldn't hurt them and was relieved to hear him mutter "Thanks" and saw that he was leaving. Sickened, she ran to the bathroom and washed out her mouth. Then she flung her clothes back on, grabbed Shannah, and ran across the street to the Hendricksons'. Barbara Hendrickson took one look at Renae's face and pulled her inside.

"Renae said there was a man outside and she was afraid he was going to come back," Barbara told deputies later. "And she looked out the window, and I promptly locked the door and got out my shotgun."

Both Renae and Shannah were very, very upset. The women barricaded themselves inside the Hendricksons' home with a loaded shotgun and called the Snohomish County Sheriff's Office. A deputy arrived at 2:25 P.M.

Renae Wicklund was able to give a good description of the man who had sexually assaulted her and threatened to kill her baby. She said he was very tall, with frizzy reddish hair, and that he'd worn blue jeans and a red and black plaid shirt. She thought he was in his early twenties. She had detected a faint odor of alcohol on his breath.

With her description, Snohomish County detectives narrowed in on Charles Rodman Campbell, twenty, as a possible suspect. He was tremendously tall, and his hair stuck out around his head like a dandelion gone to seed. He had been in trouble since he was old enough to leave his own yard.

Charles Campbell was born October 21, 1954, in Hawaii. His parents soon moved to Snohomish County. Campbell's early problems were not his fault. He was always *different*—and in so many ways. Because of his Hawaiian descent, the kids at his school teased him. Perhaps more damaging, Charles Campbell's sister was crippled, and some of the thoughtless kids not only tormented her but teased him about it, too, shouting cruel epithets at him. He fought to protect her, and out of sheer rage. Charles Campbell's parents tired of the responsibility of children early on and had long since defected, leaving the boy's grandparents to deal with him and his sister. They didn't know where to begin, and they were not particularly interested in raising another generation of children anyway.

Charles Campbell was an angry child from the very

beginning, large and clumsy for his age with a chip on his shoulder. He was always fighting or running away. Detectives at the Edmonds, Washington, police department had dealt with him since before he hit junior high school. Even then they doubted that he would stay out of prison long. He had always seen the world as out to get him.

His first arrest came when he was sixteen years old after he stole a car. According to different sources, he stayed in school either through the ninth grade or the tenth—or the eleventh. Whichever, he was not a diligent student. He was too preoccupied, apparently, with drugs and alcohol.

Chuck Campbell married when he was nineteen, eloping with a twenty-two-year-old woman. His new in-laws were not impressed with him. The couple did not celebrate even a first wedding anniversary, divorcing after ten months. One month before their divorce, his wife gave birth to a child. He was ordered to pay $75 a month in child support, but his visitation rights were revoked after a judge decreed that he "poses a serious threat to the welfare of the child and the petitioner in that he has physically abused the child and petitioner in the past and neglected them." Since Campbell went to prison shortly thereafter, his ex-wife and child were assured that he would not visit.

That was why Snohomish County police were familiar with Charles Campbell. Once you saw a man six-and-a-half-feet tall with wild reddish hair and a kind of rage that almost vibrated, you didn't forget him—especially if you were a cop. They had a mug shot of him in their files. This photograph was included in a "lay-down," which they showed to Renae Wicklund two weeks after she was attacked.

Trembling but resolute, Renae Wicklund picked Campbell's picture immediately. "That's him."

Finding Charles Campbell would prove far more

difficult than identifying him. It would be more than a year before Campbell was arrested and placed in a police lineup. On March 1, 1976, Renae Wicklund looked at the line of men through one-way glass and instantly picked Campbell from the lineup. He was the man who had forced her to perform fellatio sixteen months earlier.

Campbell argued that he could not possibly have been in Clearview on December 11, 1974. He claimed that he had been living and working as a cook at a pizza restaurant in Renton, Washington, almost 30 miles away during the period in question. He insisted he had punched in to work at 3:30 P.M. on December 11 and stayed in the kitchen throughout his shift.

A closer look into Campbell's background, however, brought forth information that stamped him as more than the average hardworking pizza cook. He was wanted for a drug violation in Snohomish County in late December 1974, and he had been working in Renton under the alias Dan Leslie Kile to avoid apprehension. He had quit his job at the pizza parlor very suddenly on December 14, 1974, the day Renton police began their investigation into the apparent theft of $1,200 from the restaurant's cash register.

Campbell admitted that he could not say exactly what he had done earlier in the day that the Wicklunds were attacked, but said it was his pattern to drink in the morning—"just enough to get a buzz on"—and that he had probably done so on that Wednesday. He said he didn't even know where Clearview was for certain and that he had never had any reason to go there—despite the fact he had lived in Snohomish County for fifteen years until he moved into his mother's home in Renton a month before the sex attack.

Charles Campbell's juvenile record showed arrests for auto theft, burglary, and resisting arrest, and that he had spent time at a juvenile detention center. In

1973 he had been charged with defrauding an inn-keeper, and the 1974 drug charges had stemmed from his alleged possession of sixty tablets of amphetamines. And that was just in Snohomish County. Far across the Cascade Mountains, in Okanogan County, Campbell had been arrested in the fall of 1974—before the attack on Renae Wicklund—for violation of the federal firearms act, resisting arrest, criminal trespass, burglary, two counts of grand larceny, carrying a concealed weapon, and second-degree assault. Those charges were still extant.

All in all, Charles Campbell was not someone any woman would want to see running up her driveway.

Renae Wicklund was vastly relieved when Campbell was arrested after she identified him in March 1976. He was charged with one count of first-degree assault with intent to kill and one count of sodomy. By reporting what had happened to her, she had become one of the small percentage of women who have the courage to turn a sex criminal in to the police. Law enforcement authorities agree that statistics on sex crimes are almost impossible to chart accurately, that perhaps only one out of ten victims makes a police report. Women who have been raped and sexually molested are afraid and embarrassed. They are naturally hesitant to get on the witness stand and tell strangers in a courtroom the intimate details of an aberrant sexual attack.

But Renae Wicklund reported Campbell, and she got up in court and told it all. Her neighbor, Barbara Hendrickson, went on the stand, too. There was no way they could refuse to testify and face their consciences knowing that a monstrous criminal might go free to harm other women. Still, the ordeal was agonizing.

Under our justice system, the suspect has the right to face his accusers, and Renae had to testify about the sexual appetites of her attacker as Charles Campbell stared at her, this huge man with the piercing dark eyes.

Renae Wicklund's testimony was bolstered by testimony from a young woman who had once lived with Campbell. The woman said she lived near the Wicklunds' home and that Campbell had visited her often—including the week of the rape. Campbell's former lover said that he carried a knife and that he had told her, "You never know when you're going to need it."

The seven-woman, five-man jury found Charles Campbell guilty of both the assault and the sodomy. They also found that he had committed those crimes while in possession of a deadly weapon. At his sentencing, his prior record was introduced, and the consensus was that he was not fit to be on the streets for a very long time. Campbell had already pleaded guilty to second-degree burglary in the Okanogan County cases and had received up to fifteen years in prison with a five-year minimum. In Snohomish County, Judge Phillip Sheridan sentenced Campbell to another thirty years in prison with a seven-and-a-half-year minimum for the attack on the Wicklunds.

Charles Campbell's trial in the attack on Renae and Shannah lasted only three days. It didn't even rate a headline in the Everett papers.

The headlines would come later.

Renae Wicklund went home to pick up the pieces of her life, scarred as all sexual attack victims are by a pervasive fear that never quite goes away. Her marriage to Jack Wicklund broke up, partially from the lingering emotional trauma of the sex attack and partially for personal reasons. She and Shannah remained in the modest little white house in the woods, and Renae worked hard to support them. She worked as a beautician and also as an accountant for beauty parlors. She was a very intelligent woman and a single mother who wanted to be sure Shannah had everything she needed. Her own mother, Hilda, had always worked, and Renae's life was solidly grounded in the work ethic.

Renae remained on friendly terms with Jack after he moved out. She also stayed close to her in-laws, who lived in a little town in Kitsap County across Puget Sound. Jack's parents had always liked Renae. She joined their family get-togethers happily; her own mother and her sister Lorene were more than a thousand miles away in North Dakota. Renae was a great cook and brought food to every Wicklund holiday gathering, and she was a wonderful mother to Shannah, their granddaughter. Even though Renae was divorced from their son, she made sure that Jack's parents saw Shannah often.

Once they got used to Jack's being gone, Renae Wicklund and Shannah seemed to do all right. Don and Barbara helped out with chores Renae couldn't manage, and both the Hendricksons adored Shannah.

Jack Wicklund was the one who now became a target for violence. In December 1977 he was almost killed in a bizarre attack. Wicklund was found in his West Seattle home, tied to a chair and severely burned over most of his body. He was rushed to a hospital, but it was a long time before doctors would cautiously say he might live and even longer before Wicklund could give a statement. All he remembered was that a stranger had walked into his home carrying a package and wished him Merry Christmas. He insisted he had never seen the man before. The stranger then tied Jack to a chair, poured gasoline over him, and struck a match.

Miraculously, Jack Wicklund didn't die, but he was horribly scarred and lived with constant, unyielding pain. He was forced to wear a kind of rubber suit to minimize the formation of scar tissue.

In April 1978 Jack Wicklund left his parents' home

in Hansville, Washington, after a visit. They were worried about his burns, and it had been awful for them to see their son in his strange rubber suit, but he was alive. A few hours after Jack left to go home, a Kitsap County coroner's deputy came to his parents' home and broke the news that Jack had been killed in a one-car accident on the Hansville Road. His car had left the road and crashed into a tree, killing him instantly. There were no witnesses. The ensuing investigation into Jack Wicklund's death never produced any definite answers as to why the crash had occurred. After surviving what should have been a fatal torching, Wicklund had met his fate on a lonely road. The curve where the car had left the road was known to be dangerous, but Wicklund had traversed the county road countless times before, and he knew the curve was there; he should have been prepared for it. Perhaps he had been temporarily blinded by oncoming headlights. If so, the other car hadn't stopped. Perhaps he had been run off the road.

Seattle police have never solved the murder attempt on Wicklund. Perhaps he was suicidal and it took him two tries to succeed in destroying himself. Perhaps he was involved in something unsavory or dangerous— or both. Or perhaps Jack Wicklund was only a very unlucky man.

The shock of the deliberate torching of her ex-husband and then his accidental death coming so hard on the heels of the murder attempt only served to heighten Renae Wicklund's constant anxiety. The attack by Charles Campbell had made her think that the world was a terribly dangerous place where tragedy waited just ahead. She could not help but wonder if the incidents were somehow connected, if they were more than just random misfortunes. She told friends and co-workers that she lived and walked in terror that something awful was going to happen again. And who could blame her?

Still, Renae Wicklund put on the facade of a cheerful, outgoing woman who was confident that she could take care of fatherless Shannah. Maybe trouble came in threes; people always said that. If that was true, then her three were all used up: the sexual attack, the burning, Jack's fatal car crash.

Renae Wicklund didn't know much about the workings of the justice system. She knew that Charles Campbell had been sent to the Monroe Reformatory —Washington's mid-level penal institution. Security was not as tight there as it was in the state penitentiary at Walla Walla, but it was much stronger than at Green Hill Academy, the boys' training school in Chehalis. Renae didn't care where Campbell was as long as he was locked up. All together, he had forty-five years hanging over him. That seemed like a safety net. Renae assumed that Campbell would be over sixty-five when he finally got out. By then Shannah would be middle-aged and Renae would be an old woman. They would probably have moved far away, too, maybe even back to North Dakota.

To a layman, forty-five years does sound like a long, long time. However, Charles Campbell's two sentences would run concurrently, not consecutively. Although it wasn't likely, it was within the realm of possibility that he could serve only the seven-and-a-half-year minimum and be released in 1983 or 1984. He would, of course, have to have some time off for good behavior to do that.

Renae had no idea that forty-five years didn't really *mean* forty-five years.

She and Shannah stayed in their old neighborhood, and Renae worked to keep the house and yard up. Shannah grew through the toddler stage and became a pretty little girl with straight shiny brown bangs, a pageboy haircut, and big brown eyes. Tall for her age, she was quiet and a little shy. She went to the Shepherd of the Hill Lutheran Church Sunday school and they teased her fondly about being their "little missionary" because she was always bringing a new friend along with her.

Renae had played the flute as a girl, and Shannah had ambitions to master it, too. She invited Don and Barb over for "a recital," and they clapped as if she were a child prodigy. She took dancing lessons, and Don Hendrickson took pictures of her in her costumes. Her grandpa Wicklund helped her learn how to ride a two-wheel bike.

The neighborhood in Clearview was a good place for a little girl to grow up, even though it might have been easier for Renae to live in a city apartment where she didn't have to cope with leaking roofs and broken plumbing and keeping a yard clear of weeds. She really counted on her neighbors. She and Shannah shopped at the Clearview market, and everybody knew both of them. Barbara Hendrickson's grandchildren grew up along with Shannah, and they often played together.

Renae proved to be a really clever businesswoman. She operated her accounting business for beauty parlors out of her own home, and her clients were pleased with her know-how and efficiency. She was expert in helping students get grants and loans to help them through beauty school. In early 1982 Renae was only thirty-one, but she was shouldering her responsibilities with great maturity.

If she thought about the man who had broken into her home eight years earlier—and those close to her say she did—the scary memories crept up full-blown only when the moon was hidden behind scudding clouds and the wind sighed in the tall trees around her little house. He was part of a nightmare she couldn't quite forget, but his image was gone when the sun rose again.

Renae bought a large dog, an Afghan hound, more to keep her company than for protection. Afghans are not particularly territorial or effective as watchdogs.

But it would bark if anyone came around her property.

Less than 25 miles away, Charles Campbell was locked up in the Monroe Reformatory. He had earned the nickname "One Punch" because his fist was so powerful. He was a bully, and weaker inmates toadied to him, fearful of that fist. Guards were aware of Campbell's drug trafficking—*inside* prison—and his infraction record grew thicker and thicker.

Renae was serene in her belief that her attacker was locked up in prison and still had years and years to go on his sentence. Nevertheless, she was super-cautious, because she knew what could happen. Charles Campbell wasn't the only man who attacked women. Renae had strong locks on the doors and windows, and she warned Shannah never, never to go with strangers.

It snowed in early January 1982, and Don Hendrickson noticed footprints one morning outside the side windows of his home. Later that day, Renae told Barbara that she too had found footprints beneath her windows. Since her house stood so far back from the road, the large prints in the snow upset her.

Hilda Ahlers had been visiting Renae over Christmas, as she almost always did. Renae had never told her mother about the man who had attacked her seven years earlier.

"Renae was so strong," her mother said. "I never knew. She didn't want me to worry." But with the clarity of hindsight, Hilda would come to see that something was wrong that winter. "I remember one night when Renae's dog—who normally never barked at all—went wild and began barking fiercely. I thought there was something horrid outside, but I was afraid to look."

Not long after that, the Afghan nipped a neighbor's child, and Renae decided to give it away.

Looking back, Hilda Ahlers remembered more. "Another time, I saw Renae looking out the window at the road with the strangest look on her face. I said, 'What do you see out there?' and Renae just answered, 'Oh, nothing.' She didn't seem frightened; she was just watching so quietly."

Renae didn't know that Charles Campbell had been out of prison that weekend in January. Incredibly, and despite a stack of infractions, he had somehow earned time off for good behavior. He had served less than six years in prison, and he was already going out on furloughs.

Neither Renae nor the Hendricksons were aware of that. No one had bothered to tell them. Nor did anyone tell them when Campbell was transferred a month later to a work-release facility located less than ten miles from Clearview.

Renae missed the Easter service at church on April 11, 1982. She had a terribly sore throat. Don Hendrickson finally coaxed her into seeing a doctor. "I'll go with you; I'll hold your hand," he kidded. And he *did* hold her hand while an emergency room doctor examined her. She had strep throat, and she had to stay in bed for days, taking penicillin and trying to swallow the soft foods that Barb Hendrickson brought over to her.

April 14 was a Wednesday—just as it had been a Wednesday when Charles Campbell attacked Renae and Shannah in 1974. It was sunny but blustery, and the bright periods alternated with overhanging clouds. Daffodils, dogwood and fruit trees were in bloom, and spring had almost arrived. Except for the fact that Renae was sick, everything was normal. Barbara ran over in the morning to see how she was and found her a little better. She promised she would be back in the afternoon. Renae watched television and tried to read a little.

"Barb went out to the end of our driveway to get our mail that afternoon," Don remembers. "She met

Shannah coming home from school and told her to tell Renae that she'd be over soon to make Jell-O. I remember it was 4:20 when Barb asked to borrow my watch; she wanted to use it to check Renae's pulse."

Barbara Hendrickson then headed toward Renae's house. There were no loud sounds from the Wicklund home, nothing to alarm any of the neighbors. She was gone for quite a while, but Don didn't think anything of it. She and Renae and Shannah often visited for hours.

It seemed to get dark earlier than usual that evening. A gale-force wind battered the Hendrickson house. Don glanced at the spot on his wrist where his watch usually was and then got up from his chair and checked a clock. He discovered that it was almost six. His wife had been gone for an hour and a half.

Don put on a jacket and walked down his driveway, across the street, and up Renae's long driveway. He usually went in through the sliding glass doors to the kitchen area. The glass doors were partly open and he paused. *That's odd*, he thought, and then he slid the doors open more and stepped into the house.

"The house was *so* quiet," he said later. "It was unlike anything I'd ever heard before—or since. Totally still. And then, as I got further into the house, I heard something—water running from a faucet somewhere."

It was the faucet in the kitchen sink. He turned the spigot off and listened for some other sound. There should have been three of them in the house—Barb, Renae, and Shannah—and they always made enough noise for six. He listened again, but he heard nothing. Don looked around the kitchen and shuddered involuntarily when he saw that a chair had been knocked over near the dinette set. That wasn't right. Renae always kept everything so neat. The silence kept Don from calling out to his wife or Renae or Shannah.

Donald Hendrickson found them in a few moments of horror that he will never forget.

He had left the kitchen and moved slowly toward the short hallway that led to the bedrooms. He found Barbara first. His wife of thirty-four years lay motionless in the hallway, her throat slashed, the arteries severed. Even as he knelt beside her, he knew she was gone. A halo of blood soaked the carpet beneath her head and stained her beautiful prematurely silver hair. It was a scene that Don Hendrickson would never, ever be able to erase from his memory.

His wife's throat had been slit from one side to the other with a razor-sharp knife, allowing the blood to course out of her jugular vein and carotid arteries. She could have lived only moments before she bled to death.

Numb with shock, Don got up from Barbara's side and continued to make his way down the hall. He didn't want to, but he had to see what was behind the other doors. Shannah's bedroom was empty. He moved to Renae's bedroom next, pausing at the door before he made himself turn and look inside.

They were both there on the floor. Renae was nude—her body hideously bruised and her throat slashed with macabre efficiency. Shannah lay across the room from her mother. She had been almost decapitated by a knife's merciless edge. Nine years old, with her throat cut. All of them dead.

Automatically Don Hendrickson picked up the phone with nerveless fingers and dialed 911. Then he walked outside to try to make his mind function. "I heard a car engine start up," he said. "It was Renae's next-door neighbor and her daughters, and I ran out and shouted at them, 'Shannah and Renae are dead!' But they just looked at me, and then they got out of their car and ran back into their house. I think they were afraid of me because I was acting so wild."

Snohomish County deputies arrived shortly. They took one look at the carnage inside the Wicklund home and radioed in for the homicide detectives. What they encountered on April 14 would mean days of working almost around the clock. The public had no idea at first how ghastly the triple murder was. The Clearview story hit the media as a very short, deliberately succinct news bulletin. The detectives released almost no information: "Three people were found dead on April 14 in south Snohomish County. . . ."

Lieutenant Glenn Mann and Sergeant Joe Belinc would head the probe. If anyone could sort out the real story behind what had happened in the little rambler in Clearview, these men could. In addition, they would have twenty-nine investigators working on the Wicklund-Hendrickson case before it was finished. Belinc had been the driving force behind the apprehension of Washington's infamous Bellevue Sniper in the early 1970s. Now he had another headline case to work.

Someone had gotten into the Wicklund home, someone strong enough to overpower two women; the youngster could not have been much of an adversary. It appeared that Barbara Hendrickson had broken free and was, perhaps, running for help when she was struck down in the hall. It was even possible that Renae Wicklund and Shannah were already dead when Barbara Hendrickson entered the home. She might have called out to them, or she might have felt the same dread that her husband felt an hour later, might have heard the same thundering silence and been afraid—only to encounter the person with the knife and realize at the last moment that she had walked into horror.

The Snohomish County investigators spent hours at the scene, looking for bits of physical evidence that the killer might have left behind. The bodies were photographed where they lay before they were released to the Snohomish County coroner's deputies. Saddened and shocked neighbors stood at the edge of the crime-scene search area, along with cameramen from the news media who shot footage of the body bags being loaded into a station wagon—hearse for removal to await autopsy. It did not seem possible to them that Renae and Shannah and Barbara were dead. This couldn't have happened, not so suddenly and so quietly on an April day. One neighbor murmured how frightened she was, wondering if some madman was on the loose, waiting somewhere in the thick trees to strike again.

The investigators began a door-to-door canvass. They found no one who had heard or seen anything—but they did hear again and again that this was not the first time that Renae Wicklund had been the victim of a madman. Everyone knew that Renae had been attacked eight years before, and those close to her recalled that she had lived in a state of quiet terror ever since. She had feared that he might come back one day and wreak revenge upon her for testifying against him. No amount of reassurance that she had probably been a random victim, that he had probably forgotten all about her, could convince her.

She had seemed to know that she was doomed, that he—or someone—would destroy the safe walls she'd tried to build around herself and Shannah. And yet everyone described Renae as a wonderful person, a good friend, an intelligent hard worker. The extent of her friends' and neighbors' grief demonstrated just what a good person she had been. And so had Barbara Hendrickson. Once, Barbara had loaded a shotgun to protect Renae and Shannah. This time, she hadn't had the opportunity to seize a weapon to fight back. The slash wounds across each victim's throat stamped the killings as executions—cold-blooded, effective, designed to kill as if that was the murderer's only mission. He had wanted them dead. It seemed that simple. The child? She couldn't have harmed the killer, but she was old enough and smart enough to describe him, and so she had to die too. It seemed impossible that anyone could have had a grudge against a nine-year-old girl.

The detectives questioned Don Hendrickson, asking who he thought might have had reason to kill his wife and neighbors. He finally said, "The only person I could imagine that might have done this is the man who raped Renae."

At the time, he could not even remember Charles Campbell's name. Campbell was history, or he was supposed to be. But when the detectives checked on Campbell's whereabouts, they were shocked to find out that he had been living and working a short distance from Clearview, *without supervision*, almost every day.

The word from the Department of Corrections was not only startling; it was appalling. Records showed that in October 1981—less than six years after his conviction for raping Renae Wicklund—Charles Campbell had been moved to a minimum-security facility known as Monroe House. He worked there as a cook, and he was still confined, but eligible for furloughs. On February 24, six weeks before the triple murders in Clearview, Campbell moved even closer to complete freedom: he was released from the prison itself and assigned to an Everett work-release residence two blocks from the Snohomish County Courthouse. This meant that he would work outside during the day, sleep in the facility at night, and had to follow strict rules. In his case, particularly, he was to abstain from alcohol and drug use.

Even though Campbell was literally free for much of each day and within a dozen miles of the Clearview home where the 1974 attack had occurred, even though he was housed two blocks from the Snohomish County Courthouse, there was no notification to the sheriff's office. Some might say it was like dumping a fox in the chicken house without letting the farmer know.

On the night of the murders—April 14—Charles Campbell returned to the work-release residence obviously under the influence of alcohol. His blood alcohol reading was .29—almost three times higher than Washington's legal level for intoxication. Tests also detected the presence of morphine, codeine, quinine, methadone, and cocaine!

Because he had broken the cardinal rule of the halfway house, Campbell was taken back to the Monroe Reformatory. Of course, by then, Renae Wicklund, Shannah Wicklund, and Barbara Hendrickson were dead. They had neither been consulted nor informed about Campbell's early release in February. What happened to them was shocking, but the most shocking part of the horror was that it was preventable. There were so many ways the inexorable path to violent murder could have been blocked.

Back in the Monroe Reformatory, Charles Campbell was charged with three counts of aggravated first-degree murder on April 19, 1982. With the news that Charles Campbell had been charged with the three murders, citizens of Snohomish County—and, indeed, citizens all over the state—began to react with disbelief and anger. The owner of Rick's Clearview Foods, Rick Arriza, placed a petition in his small grocery store, where the victims had shopped, asking for signatures from residents demanding the death penalty for Campbell if he was convicted. People came from all around the state to sign it.

Along with the anger, there was fear. The number of women reporting rapes and other sexual assaults dropped dramatically. Women were afraid to report rapes. If they couldn't be sure that the men who had attacked them would be put away for a long time, if they had to fear violent reprisal, then they decided that it was safer just to forget what had happened—and try to live with it.

Sheriff Bobby Dodge, Lieutenant Mann, Sergeant Belinc, and their crews of detectives worked under great constraint. They had a job to do which required an orderly progression to bring a solid case against

Campbell. They would not—could not—talk to reporters, and they took the flak stoically. Snohomish County sheriff Bobby Dodge did appear on television decrying the system that had allowed a man like Campbell, with all the crimes he'd been convicted of, back into the same community where the crime against the Wicklunds had occurred—and without any notification to law enforcement authorities.

On May 1, 1982, Charles Campbell, now twenty-seven, appeared before Judge Dennis Britt and entered a plea of innocent. He was ordered to undergo psychiatric testing. Possibly a defense attorney would use the results later to enter a plea of innocent by reason of insanity. The hugely tall Campbell wore handcuffs and leg irons, and spectators were searched with metal detectors before they were allowed into the courtroom. Campbell wanted to go to Western State Hospital for testing, but the roster of sex criminals who had escaped from that mental hospital to do more damage to innocent citizens was too long already. Judge Britt ordered that Campbell would meet with psychiatrists in his jail isolation cell.

The first reports on Campbell's six years at the Monroe Reformatory indicated that he had a good record there. Parole board members were aware that Campbell had made a suicide attempt in custody in 1976, and he had been watched closely by the board, but they refused to comment on the prisoner's psychiatric records. Campbell's attorneys said he had acknowledged that he had a problem with alcohol and drugs and that he thought himself a "borderline case" who "snapped" when he was drinking and blacked out.

In a case that grew steadily more bizarre, the *Seattle Times* reported that one of the witnesses interviewed by homicide detectives was a drug and alcohol counselor who had participated in a program in the Monroe Reformatory until about 1980. According to records of her former employer, the young female counselor had resigned because she had broken one of the first rules of counseling by becoming romantically involved with her "patient." The patient was Charles Campbell. The woman refused to comment, but a relative admitted that Campbell had been a visitor in their home in early 1982 while he was on a furlough from prison.

Campbell's alleged close personal relationship with the woman was borne out by a notation in the Monroe House files on January 28, 1982. Campbell had returned from a furlough and said he was in a car that had hit a pole northwest of Monroe. The car, a 1974 Volkswagen, was found, abandoned, by a Washington State trooper. It was totaled, and the pole was heavily damaged. The trooper checked with the Department of Motor Vehicles for the car's registration and found that it belonged to the woman who had been a counselor at the prison. She later told her insurance agency that it had been wrecked, but no charges were ever brought because troopers could not determine who had been driving the Volkswagen.

Campbell may have had charm for one woman, but another, his ex-wife, seemed unimpressed by his charisma. She reported to a detective in the town where she lived that Campbell—whom she, too, believed was still in prison at the time—had come to her home on Christmas Day 1981 and raped her. She said he had returned twice to rape her again. She had finally gone to the police on March 16 and attempted to make a formal complaint of rape against Campbell but the police had advised her the case seemed too weak to bring to court.

This was the man who Renae Wicklund believed was safely behind prison walls. He had only been 12 miles away, working days in a landscaping firm, apparently maintaining some kind of romantic relationship with his former drug counselor and allegedly assaulting his ex-wife. There was another factor. He

had come to the attention of work-release authorities
on March 18 for "having possession of or consuming
beer at Everett Work Release." A female officer found
a partially filled can of beer on his bed and noted that
the room smelled of alcohol.

This report enraged Campbell. He hated having the
female officers at the facility write him up, and he
showed his resentment openly. He argued with them
about even the slightest order they gave him. He said
he had much more freedom in his social outings when
he had furloughs from the reformatory. He felt he
should have complete freedom to do what he wanted
while he was in work release.

A hearing had been held about his "poor attitude
and behavior" toward two women officers, but he was
allowed to remain in work release. He was given a
second chance primarily because of his good record
while in prison.

But *was* his record that good in prison?

A look at Charles Rodman Campbell's "good behavior" was startling. For some reason, when Campbell came up before the parole board seeking work
release, the paperwork that came with him cited only
three minor infractions during his first year at Monroe
and referred to him as a "model prisoner" thereafter.
The infractions mentioned were not that bad: mutilating a curtain; possessing "pruno" (an alcoholic bever-
age that cons distill from yeast and any fruit or
vegetable matter they can get their hands on: potatoes,
apples, oranges); and refusing to allow a guard to
search him for a club he had hidden under his jacket.
He said he carried the club to ward off attacks by
bullies in the yard.

After these minor incidents—more indicative of
the behavior of a bad boy than a dangerous con—the
superintendent of the state reformatory indicated to
the parole board that Campbell's record was spotless.

Not quite.

After Campbell had won his furloughs and his work-release assignment, *after* Renae and Shannah Wicklund and Barbara Hendrickson had their throats slit, and *after* Campbell was charged with those crimes, the head of the guards' union at the reformatory said that Campbell had used drugs as recently as the year prior to his work release.

It was obvious that someone had been covering up for Charles Campbell. Shortly after Campbell was transferred to the work-release program, the Washington State parole board discovered that the Monroe Reformatory had failed to forward copies of prison infractions to them. Hundreds of prisoners had been released without having their behavior in prison evaluated. And Charles Campbell was one of those prisoners who had slipped through the fissures in the justice system.

KIRO-TV in Seattle managed to obtain additional infraction reports on Campbell, incidents that occurred between December 31, 1977, and June 13, 1978; these infractions were never revealed to the parole board beyond a cursory notation in a counselor's report, which mentioned that Campbell had threatened a nurse and gotten into a beef with another inmate. According to the records, the huge bushy-haired con had lunged at the nurse on New Year's Eve 1977, when she refused to give him his medication because he was an hour late reporting to the hospital. "When I refused to give him the medication late," the nurse had said, "he jumped to his feet with his fists clenched and moved toward me in a threatening manner, as though he intended to hit me."

A staff member had stepped between Campbell and the female nurse, and a guard had dragged Campbell away while he shouted obscenities at her. On May 8, 1978, Campbell had kicked another inmate in the groin and ignored a guard's order to move on in a stand-off that lasted until additional guards arrived. Later that month, Campbell had cut into the chow line and angered other prisoners. He refused to move on and broke a tray in half in his hands. The situation was fraught with tension in the mess hall full of convicts. On May 24, Campbell was discovered high on drugs. He fought guards like a tiger until they got his jacket off and found an envelope in it containing three empty yellow capsules.

A month later Campbell again balked at a body search and tossed an envelope to another con. Guards recovered it and found a syringe and needle inside. He was punished with the removal of privileges for these infractions, but even his guards were afraid of him. They asked administrators to transfer Campbell from Monroe to the state penitentiary at Walla Walla. Nothing came of this request.

None of this information was available to the parole board when it came time for Campbell's parole hearing.

When the news of Charles Campbell's actual prison behavior reached the media, Washington State legislators immediately scheduled an investigation. One state senator put it bluntly: "Somebody obviously held back information that caused the death of three people." Prison administrators argued that the parole board had asked *not* to see all the minor infractions, and that they had held back the reports for that reason.

Charles Campbell apparently scared the hell out of a lot of people, guards and fellow prisoners alike. He was so big, so muscular, and so quick to erupt into rage. Guards who had reservations about Campbell's suitability for parole didn't want their names published, but said off the record that they thought he should have been sent back to prison.

Even more frightened of seeing his name in print was an ex-convict who had served time with Campbell; the label "snitch" is a sure way to commit suicide in or out of prison for an ex-con. But the anonymous man recalled that Charles Campbell had ruled his fellow inmates with terror, forcing the weaker cons to obtain drugs for him and to submit to sodomy. Prison "prestige" belonged to the physically strong.

It is quite likely that no one will ever know what really happened on April 14, 1982. The victims are dead, and the murderer chose not to speak of his crimes.

Charles Campbell went on trial in November 1982. If he was convicted of aggravated murder in the first degree, he could be sentenced to death. To accomplish that, the state had to prove that Campbell's crimes fit within the parameters of the statute as follows:

- He was serving a prison term in a state facility or program at the time of the murders.
- The victims had previously testified against him in a court of law.
- Campbell allegedly committed the murders to conceal his identity.
- There was more than one victim and the murders were part of a common scheme or plan.
- The murders were committed along with other crimes, including first-degree rape, first-degree robbery, and first-degree burglary.

They were all true. Renae Wicklund had been raped as her stalker wreaked his revenge. Her jewelry was stolen. Allegedly Charles Campbell attempted to sell the missing jewelry hours after the slayings. The burglary charges would indicate that the defendant made illegal entry into the home—by force or subterfuge.

Charles Campbell asked for a change of venue to

another state, claiming that he could not receive a fair trial in the state of Washington because of the media coverage. His request was denied.

On November 26, 1982, the day after Thanksgiving, the jury retired to debate the question of Campbell's guilt or innocence. They returned after only four hours. They had found the defendant guilty. Guilty on three counts of aggravated first-degree murder.

In the penalty phase of his trial, Charles Campbell was sentenced to death. At first he refused to cooperate with his attorneys' efforts to have his life spared. They appealed, but he said it was against his wishes.

He would spend years on death row in the Washington State penitentiary in Walla Walla, a fearsome figure who spat at Governor Booth Gardner when he had the temerity to peer through the bulletproof-glass window in Campbell's cell. For a man who one day soon might beg Gardner to stay his execution at the last minute, it was an incredibly stupid show of temper.

Campbell was visited regularly by his mistress, the ex-alcohol counselor and her child—Charles Campbell's son. They seemed a strangely mismated couple.

As the years passed and his attorneys continued to appeal his death sentence, Campbell was disdainful of their efforts on his behalf. All the while, he was drawing nearer and nearer to the hangman's noose. In March of 1989 he came within two days of being executed when his attorneys won a stay from the U.S. Ninth Circuit Court of Appeals. The three-judge panel agreed to listen to Campbell's attorneys' appeal, which contended he had been denied his right to a fair trial because he was not present when his jury was selected. (*He* had refused to come to court.)

The second issue was that having to choose the means of one's death was cruel and unusual punishment. (When Washington State added death by lethal injection to its roster of execution methods, Charles Campbell had balked. He would not choose, he insisted. In essence, the state was forcing him to commit suicide by saying which method of execution he preferred.) "That's against my religion," he said smugly.

The Ninth Circuit Court panel heard arguments in Campbell's case in June 1989, but the judges did not hand down their decision for two and a half years. In April 1992 they rejected Campbell's arguments—but later granted his request to have the same issues reheard by an eleven-judge panel. In addition, Charles Campbell and his team of attorneys filed another federal petition, his third. He lost the latter, but the second is still pending.

In the decade since his conviction, Charles Campbell has apparently come to believe that he too is mortal and that there is a fairly good possibility that the state of Washington *is* going to kill him. By the time Charles Campbell began to cooperate in the endless series of appeals, it may have been too late.

When Westly Allan Dodd, a murderous pedophile, was executed on Washington State's gallows on January 5, 1993, the state broke its thirty-five-year pattern of not carrying out the death penalty. Charles Campbell is expected to be executed before 1993 is over. Whether the execution will be by hanging or lethal injection is the only question left.

Few tears will be shed.

Renae and Shannah Wicklund are buried side by side in Jamestown, North Dakota, far from Clearview, Washington. Hilda Ahlers came to Clearview to settle their affairs, and grocer Rick Arriza drove her to the Clearview Elementary School to pick up Shannah's belongings. There wasn't much, because nine years is not enough time to gather much— beyond love. "I took her up to the school," Arizza recalled. "We picked up Shannah's things—glue, storybooks, an umbrella, notebooks. She just started crying."

Hilda Ahlers rarely sleepwalks anymore, but she did for years, reliving the moment she first learned of Renae's and Shannah's deaths.

"There was a light tap on my door at three A.M.," she recalls. "And I said, 'Who is it?' and this small voice said, 'It's me,' and I knew it was Lorene. I was so frightened when I opened the door, wondering which one of my grandchildren I'd lost. But Lorene was standing there holding her littlest one, and her husband, Jerry, was standing beside her with their other two children.

"I remember saying to myself, Thank God, they're all there, and then I looked behind them and I saw our pastor, and I knew it had to be Renae.

"'Airplane accident?' I asked.

"'No.'

"'Car accident?'

"'No . . . murdered.'

"My mind flew to Shannah. Who was looking after Shannah? And then I heard Lorene say, 'Shannah too.'"

The Hit Person: Equal Opportunity Murder

The case described in "The Hit Person: Equal Opportunity Murder" *is unique, I believe, because neither the victim nor the killer was what we have come to expect. But murder, like tornadoes, earthquakes, and hurricanes, is not predictable. The pattern is forever being broken, rearranged, and mutated.*

"The Hit Person" is also a case where, even now, questions remain unanswered. The reader will have to decide if justice was accomplished, partially accomplished—or never served at all.

If one was at all inclined to believe in fate or karma or destiny—whatever word works—the story of Wanda Emelina Norewicz Touchstone would serve to validate that belief. She had come halfway around the world to start a new life. She was an immigrant, but a modern-day immigrant—vitally attractive and brilliant. The life Wanda had foreseen in America never came to pass, and she was both bitterly disappointed and frightened by the reality of her situation. Still, on August 11, 1980, Wanda was beginning to believe that she had the power to turn things around. She was only thirty-four, and she had finally begun to feel *free*.

August 11 was a warm and sunny Monday in Seattle. There is no indication at all that Wanda had reason to be apprehensive as she set out from her bachelor apartment near the University of Washington. More likely, she had every reason to believe that the pleasant weekend just past signaled that her years of worry were over. She had some errands to do, and she ticked them off in her mind as she drove along the wide tree-shaded streets of the U. District.

In truth, she had only a half hour to live.

Wanda Touchstone was born in Lodz, Poland, on Valentine's Day, 1946. She missed World War II by months and was too young to notice the havoc that war had brought to her homeland. She heard the stories, of course, as she grew up and saw the skeletons

377

of bombed-out buildings, but the war wasn't *real* to her. Wanda grew up, went to university, and became a high school biology teacher. Despite her dark-haired beauty, she remained single, but she wasn't an old-maid schoolteacher; she was vibrant and fun, and her students loved her.

Wanda made a trip to California to see an aunt and uncle in 1975 and fell totally in love with America. She longed to stay in the United States, and she was willing to work at any job so she *could* remain. She answered a want ad in a Palo Alto paper, an ad for a housekeeper. The position was far beneath her educational and cultural background, but it was a start.

The gentleman advertising for household help was Samuel Lewis Touchstone, a.k.a. Robert Lewis Preston, age fifty-eight, a very wealthy real estate entrepreneur in the San Jose area. Touchstone apparently liked Wanda's credentials. He also stared with approval at the slender, high-cheekboned Wanda as he interviewed her. She was hired.

It wasn't surprising that Lew Touchstone's interest in the pretty Pole soon turned to more than that of an employer for an employee; he didn't want to lose her company when her temporary visa ran out. The simplest solution would have been for him to marry her. That wasn't possible, however, because Lew Touchstone was already legally married. But he did have an unmarried son, Ron Touchstone, who lived in Texas. Lew prevailed upon his son to go through a civil ceremony with Wanda, and a "paper only" marriage took place in 1976. There is no evidence that Wanda ever lived with the younger Touchstone, but their marriage was legal and it allowed her to stay in the United States while Lew Touchstone untangled himself from his current wife. When that was accomplished, Wanda was divorced from Ron Touchstone in March 1977.

In May 1977, the now-single Lew Touchstone and Wanda moved from San Jose, California, to Redmond, Washington, where Lew built them a wonderfully lavish house. Wanda had expected that she and Lew would get married right away, now that all the legal impedimenta were out of the way, but Lew found it more romantic for them to simply live together. He recalled the summer of 1977 as a "rather happy" time.

But Wanda wanted to get married. Lew recalled that he wasn't too anxious to move into a third marriage after having gone through two previous liaisons that ended in divorce. He said, too, that he was concerned about their twenty-six-year age difference, and feared that any marriage might end in divorce with a messy fight over property. It would be *his* property, his extensive land holdings and contracts, because Wanda owned nothing beyond her clothes.

Lew Touchstone remembered that it was Wanda who suggested a prenuptial agreement where what was his before marriage would remain his and what was hers would remain hers. Affidavits filed by Wanda indicated that it was Lew who wanted the agreement.

They were unable to reach a compromise, however, and the possibility that they would marry seemed remote. Wanda returned to Poland in August 1977, a little disillusioned with her relationship with Lew Touchstone. They were never going to be able to make it work. He expected an "old country" wife, and she was a modern and intelligent woman, an equal partner, she hoped, for a husband. A month later Lew followed her to Poland and the couple discussed reconciliation, but nothing came of it, and he went back to America alone. Still, Lew Touchstone couldn't forget the woman he'd lived with for two years; he went back to Poland again in February 1978, and this time the couple decided to get married. Was it true love? Who knows? Marriages are made for all manner of reasons. Some of them work, and some of them fail miserably. In light of later events, it would seem that the marriage between Lew and Wanda was not made in heaven.

Wanda flew back to America in April, 1978, and she and Lew were married in Carson City, Nevada, on May 19, 1978. On August 1 she signed the prenuptial agreement that released Lew from granting her any of his property in case of divorce. Because she was not yet fluent in English, the wording of an agreement Lew asked her to sign was impossible for Wanda to understand. She signed it, believing that she could trust her new husband and that he would not have asked her to sign a paper that was unfair.

They seemed to get along well enough for the first year of their marriage. Lew says he gave Wanda $3,000 from one of his land sales "to show her that I loved her and was going to try to make her happy." He also presented her with a diamond ring worth almost $17,000, plus two other diamond rings of lesser—but considerable—value. Even before the marriage, Lew Touchstone had added a fifth car to his stable of vehicles, a Chevrolet El Camino pickup. He told Wanda that it was her car.

By late 1979 the honeymoon phase of their relationship was over and the marriage was in deep trouble.

Lew was clearly disappointed that the compliant young woman from Poland was uninterested in being only a housewife, dedicated to caring for him and their home; Wanda was, of course, a woman of some intellect and yearned to study for an advanced degree in microbiology. First she attended a vocational school where she became considerably more adept with the English language. She was then admitted to the University of Washington to study microbiology, and she planned to have her degree by December 1980. Her commute across the floating bridges of Lake Washington to the university and her need to study didn't leave her as much time for Lew as he wanted.

At least that was what Lew would claim in the

divorce action. According to his affidavits, Wanda didn't cook for him, and they ate together only when he took her out to dinner. He had placed his original ad seeking a good Polish cook, something to remind him of his own early days. She had cooked for him when he employed her, but now that he had married her, she had no time for making kielbasa and rich stews and fancy breads. Lew complained that Wanda did only her own laundry and refused to wash the sheets from his bed. It was *his* bed alone; they had separate bedrooms. All in all, there wasn't much togetherness.

Wanda confided in letters to friends and relatives that her elderly husband was stingy, and she referred to him as a "boor" and an "old goat." She was angry because he kept taking her diamond rings back and he wanted his El Camino back, too. Whether the chicken or the egg came first is hard to determine in retrospect. Lew wanted a housekeeper, bed partner, and full-time companion, and he felt Wanda had broken her premarital promises. Wanda had apparently wanted a protector in a strange country, a college education, a companion, and had expected that they would share whatever wealth evolved through their years together.

Each had made a bad bargain.

There is no evidence that Wanda was unfaithful to Lew before she moved out in April 1980 and began divorce proceedings. She wasn't greedy in the least in her requests from him. She asked only for enough money to pay her tuition at the university and for maintenance in the amount of $600 a month. Lew Touchstone could have afforded many times that amount. Wanda also wanted her $17,000 wedding-engagement ring back. Lew had taken it away in their last argument. Wanda said her husband was "quite wealthy" and that their home in Redmond was worth well over $100,000. (In 1993 that property would be worth close to half a million dollars.)

Wanda felt Lew wanted a divorce because he was about to close a real estate deal that would net him a huge amount of money and he didn't want to risk having to share any profits with her. In fact, Wanda thought Lew was due to get almost a million dollars from his current sale. Beyond that, he would still have property in Washington and California that was worth a great deal. She listed other assets as a Caterpillar tractor and heavy equipment used in building homes.

Their parting had not been amicable, and Wanda was afraid of her estranged husband. She asked the judge for a restraining order against Lew, saying he had been violent with her before and that she feared what he might do to her now that she was asking for something for herself.

Whatever his wealth may have been, it was surely considerable; Lew Touchstone refused to list his assets or even state his income in his divorce action.

It was an untenable situation for Wanda Touchstone. She wanted to divorce Lew, but if she did, she faced deportation. Her attorney advised her to ask only for a legal separation for two years. After that, she could divorce Touchstone and remain in the country legally. Lew wanted out. Maybe.

Lew agreed through his attorney to provide maintenance for Wanda in the amount of $400 a month until December 1980. He grudgingly let her take the El Camino with her when she moved into the bachelor apartment near the university.

Some who knew them say that Lew wanted Wanda back and that he tried to court her again. He was over sixty and she was still in her early thirties. It wasn't likely he would find another woman as beautiful or as young as Wanda. He had gone through so much to make himself available to be with her, and he took the sting of her rejection badly.

But Wanda, who had written to relatives in the old country only two months after the wedding, saying, "I can't stand him anymore," certainly didn't want to go back. Once she moved to the U. District, her life became full and exciting. She was welcomed into Seattle's Polish community, where she danced the dances of her youth and ate the food familiar to her. She also met a tall, handsome bearded man who had come from Poland several years before, John Sophronski.*

John was as gentle as Lew had been aggressive, and he cared for her. They spent time together at parties in the Polish community, and they picnicked on the shores of Lake Washington. They may have begun to fall in love—but time was short.

Once she was on her own, with all the time in the world to study the demanding courses in microbiology, Wanda's progress toward her degree accelerated, and she learned she would graduate at the end of the summer quarter, 1980. With her degree, she would be able to support herself. She planned a vacation and looked at larger apartments. She was happy, not only for herself but for her sister in Sweden who had just given birth to a son.

Wanda hadn't the faintest notion that on that day in August someone was stalking her—stalking her with a specific purpose in mind: murder. As unlikely a target for execution as Wanda Touchstone was, her stalker would prove even more implausible. Even in such a chaotic event as murder, there are certain patterns of behavior that a good homicide detective can usually expect. That would not be true in this case.

The first call for help shrilled in on the 911 line at 2:15 P.M. on August 11. Patrol Sergeant Doug Fritschy was the initial officer on the scene as his patrol car, blue lights whirling, pulled to a stop in front of a walled-in parking lot between 5218 and 5214 University Way N.E. Officers Linda Whitt and Paul Gracy arrived just behind him. The three responding officers were led into the parking lot by Leon Orwitz,* the owner of an insurance company whose offices edged one side of the lot.

"There," he said in a panic. "The injured woman's over there. I found her on the ground with blood coming out of a hole in her neck. Couldn't get a pulse."

A slender dark-haired woman dressed in a blue skirt, red-and-blue-striped blouse, and white sandals lay motionless on the hot asphalt paving. She had fallen between a blue El Camino pickup and a white Valiant, and her blood had pooled beneath her and then made a meandering scarlet path down a slight incline.

Paramedics from Medic 16 were preparing to remove the woman to the hospital, but they shook their heads as they answered Sergeant Fritschy's unspoken question.

"No pulse. She's comatose. Looks like a brain wound."

As the medic's rig went screaming off toward Harborview Medical Center, the officers were joined by a crew from the Crimes Against Persons Unit in downtown Seattle: Captain John Leitch, Lieutenant Ernie Bisset, Sergeant Jerry Yates, and Detectives Danny Engle, Billy Baughman, Dick Steiner, Al Lima, and J. E. Lundin—all of whom would try to make some sense out of the scene.

The area of the parking lot was immediately cordoned off from the crowd of onlookers with the familiar yellow tape that police carry. Detectives used syringes to draw blood samples from the red pools, which were already beginning to coagulate in the hot sun. One expended slug had been located under the Valiant and given to Sergeant Fritschy, who retained it for evidence.

The driver's door of the El Camino was open, as if the occupant had intended to step out for just a moment. There was a woman's purse on the front seat.

Detectives Lima and Lundin began interviewing four witnesses at the scene. One of them was Orwitz, the insurance broker. He was able to identify the injured woman easily enough; she had just left his place of business.

"Her name is Wanda Touchstone," he said. "She had an appointment with my wife to talk about car insurance. She came in about five minutes after two. While she was giving my wife some info for the policy, I stepped out to the lot—that's my car in the first stall there—to get some papers."

Orwitz said he opened his car door and caught sight of a woman standing near the El Camino. "She just stared at me." He remembered that the woman was a blond, and fairly short and slim.

Wanda Touchstone had headed for the lot as Orwitz went back to his office. He was inside only a moment when he and his wife heard a bang, a pause, and then two more bangs.

"I thought it was a muffler, but my wife said it sounded like shots. I ran out and I saw the woman I'd seen before walking out of the lot. I almost said hi, but I didn't. I didn't see anything, and I went back inside."

Mere moments had passed.

Suddenly two women had come bursting into the agency, screaming, "Someone's been shot!" The women, university students, were also repeating a license number over and over: "UKN-524."

Leaving his wife to call 911, Orwitz ran to the lot and found Wanda behind her car, bleeding and unresponsive.

Lima and Lundin talked next to the young female witnesses, Nell Boles* and Jan Winn.* They said they had been walking past the opening to the parking lot when they heard shots and then saw a small woman in a long gray-blue dress come rushing out. "She was bent over, and she was clutching something like a black purse. She walked down the block and got into a red car," Winn said. "I wrote down the license number."

Detective Al Lima had Jan Winn initial the scrap of paper with the license number on it, and then he initialed it and dated it before retaining it for evidence.

Detectives Danny Engle and Billy Baughman were searching the El Camino. The purse left on the seat contained identification papers for Wanda Preston (Touchstone also used Preston as a surname), $38.93 in coin and currency, and the usual makeup articles most women carry. It was bagged to be checked for prints.

Nell Boles and Jan Winn had to have come very close to being eyewitnesses, and they fought to retain their composure as the investigators urged them to remember all they could. Nell Boles said she had definitely heard the victim scream.

"Then I saw this woman hurrying out. She was about five three, 115 pounds, and she had blond hair—rolled up, with a pink and white scarf tied under her chin. She might be in her mid-thirties. It just happened so fast."

The license number of the suspect's car was fed into the Department of Motor Vehicles computers by Detective Gary Fowler, and the hit came up quickly. The car was a red Datsun 200 SX, and the legal owner was the Hertz Rent-a-Car corporation. Fowler phoned the Hertz branch at Sea-Tac Airport and learned that car had been rented to a Cynthia Mahler the day before. The woman had presented a California driver's license and a credit card for identification at the time she picked up the car.

"She told us that her local address would be at the Motel 6," the Hertz representative told Fowler.

Wanda Touchstone was, for all intents and purposes, dead when the medics delivered her to the

Harborview emergency entrance, and the surgery that followed was fruitless.

But why? Who would shoot a woman who was just going about her daily errands? Her purse wasn't rifled; nothing seemed to be missing. And yet from Orwitz's statement, it seemed that the killer had been waiting beside Wanda's car when she left his office—waiting to shoot her. And the person he had seen moments before the shooting was a woman.

Detectives Billy Baughman and Danny Engle, who would be given chief responsibility for the Touchstone homicide, were about to be plunged into the strangest case of their careers, a case that would set legal precedents in Washington State.

An all-points bulletin was broadcast during that late afternoon of August 11, asking every lawman in Seattle to be on the lookout for a red Datsun with license plate UKN-524, probably driven by a petite blond woman. The news of the Touchstone murder hit the media almost as fast, and citizens, too, were asked to look for the car.

In the meantime the streets of Seattle's north end were alive with patrol cars. It isn't often that detectives are fortunate enough to get witnesses with enough presence of mind to jot down the license number of a murder suspect, and every officer on the Seattle force wanted to be sure the red Datsun didn't slip through their web.

Nick Costos,* a purchasing agent for a firm in the north end, was listening to the radio that afternoon about 4:15 as he waited to pick up his wife after work on Stoneway Avenue North. Idly twisting the dial, he heard a news broadcast about the shooting and heard that the police were looking for the Datsun with UKN-524 on its plates, driven by a blond female. Something made him glance at his rearview mirror, and he immediately tensed, dumbfounded. No, it was too much of a coincidence. He saw the right car, with the right license plate, coming up behind him. Only the car was being driven by a girl with long dark hair. In fact, she reminded him of his ex-wife, the same luxuriant black hair curling over her shoulders.

In an instant the car had passed, and Costos sprinted into his wife's office and called 911. "I just saw that car you're looking for!" he said. "The red Datsun's going south on Stoneway!"

Officer Robert Boling heard the new information as he patrolled just west of the Wallingford Precinct; he was only blocks away. He searched through alleys and found the red Datsun at 4:35. It was parked in the lot of a convenience store at 3939 Stoneway North.

The car was empty.

It looked as if the woman suspect had remained within a few miles of the shooting, perhaps circling the area again and again for two hours. But she certainly wasn't in or around the rented Datsun now.

Mary Moran,* a secretary at the University of Washington, was on vacation that bloody Monday, and she hadn't heard anything about the shooting near the U. As she sat in the King's Row cocktail lounge at 3935 Stoneway North, sipping a scotch and water and playing gin rummy with a friend, she was completely unaware of the patrol cars parked near the red Datsun at the convenience store just next door.

The temperature outside was creeping toward 80 degrees, and the back door of the lounge was propped open to create a hint of breeze. Mary Moran glanced out into the glaring August light and did a double take. She saw a tiny dark-haired woman in slacks and a white blouse trying to shinny over the cyclone fence that separated the restaurant property from the row of homes beyond. The fence was almost as tall as the woman, and the petite brunette was having difficulty getting over it.

Ms. Moran thought to herself, That's really silly. The drop on the other side of the fence is about ten feet. She's going to get a big surprise if she makes it to the top of the fence.

The woman finally made it and disappeared from view. Mary Moran didn't hear any yowl of pain or see the woman again, and she turned back to her card game. A few minutes later an officer came into the lounge and asked patrons if they'd seen anything unusual.

"I did," Moran volunteered. "I just saw a tiny little woman scale that fence back there. And I'll bet she landed with a thud on the other side." She described the woman she had seen.

Weird. The detectives had started out looking for a blond woman in a long blue-gray dress, and now they were searching for a woman with long dark hair wearing slacks. But then, good sense might dictate that someone who had just pulled off an execution might have doffed her outer garments and her wig and stashed them someplace. Or was it a woman at all? Maybe they were looking for a midget with a number of wigs at his disposal. Maybe he was really blond and he was now wearing a dark wig.

Things began to happen rapidly. At 5:55, Detective Jim Parks of the Port of Seattle Police called to say that the Hertz rental booth at Sea-Tac Airport had Cynthia Mahler on the phone. "She's calling to tell them somebody stole the car she rented last night."

The Hertz clerk was instructed to keep Mahler on the line, but she had rung off, the officers learned.

Seattle detectives John Nordlund and John Boren were dispatched to the airport to keep an eye on the Hertz booth and to find out if anyone matching the description of the suspect had made reservations to fly out of Seattle. Of course, they had a choice of descriptions: female, blond, tiny, in a long gray-blue dress; or female, petite, long dark hair, dark slacks, white blouse. Their quarry probably wasn't male; the Hertz people would have picked up a deep voice on the phone.

Boren and Nordlund picked up the car rental agreement from Hertz and then checked the manifests of flights coming up from California. The car renter's driver's license gave a Hayward address. The only female flying alone from Oakland on United's Flight 468—which had landed at Sea-Tac just before Cynthia Mahler picked up the Datsun at Hertz—*and* giving a home address in Hayward, California, was a K. Adams. Boren and Nordlund raced to the United reservations desk.

"You have a Cynthia Mahler or a K. Adams booked for any flights out tonight?" Boren asked.

The clerk shook his head and then glanced at the computer. "Wait a minute! It's just coming up now. Kristine Adams, booked for the nine P.M. flight—293 —to Oakland–San Francisco. She'll have to pick up her ticket by eight or eight-thirty."

Luck was still running with the police. But the two detectives didn't know if they were going to see a blonde, a brunette, or a redhead boarding the plane. If the woman had worn disguises before, she might well do it again. They had a little time to spare before Kristine Adams showed up for boarding, and they returned to the Hertz counter.

The clerk who had rented the car to Cynthia Mahler the night before remembered her. "She had a prepaid travel voucher from a travel agency in Fremont, California. We require a current driver's license for I.D., and she had one from California. The voucher was in the name of Mahler, and the name on the license was Marler, but I just figured the computer missed on a letter."

"She was alone?"

"Well, I don't know. There was a man standing behind her, and when she got the keys to the Datsun, he said something like, 'I see we finally got our car.' But she didn't say anything to him."

The Hertz supervisor who had taken the call from Cynthia Marler, or Mahler, an hour earlier—the call where she reported her rental car stolen—said that the woman said she'd already called the police and that the police had told her to inform Hertz. "She said she left it outside a restaurant, and when she came out it was gone."

The Hertz clerk said she would recognize Cynthia Mahler/Marler–Kristine Adams if she saw her again, and went with Detectives Boren and Nordlund to the north concourse, where passengers would soon board the 9:00 P.M. flight to Oakland. She watched the passengers as they moved toward the reservations check-in point, and suddenly indicated a tiny, very beautiful woman with long black hair. The woman wore slacks and a brown tweed jacket and carried a red overnight case.

"That's her," she whispered. "That's the woman who rented the Datsun last night."

The detectives waited until all passengers had boarded, and then moved swiftly down the jetway and onto the plane. The flight attendant pointed toward the wanted woman. Kristine Adams was already engaged in animated conversation with the male passenger beside her, and the man seemed delighted to have such a lovely seatmate for the flight south.

The brunette beauty's laugh was cut short as Detective John Boren leaned over the seat behind her and clapped handcuffs on her slender wrists. She looked up in amazement as he said quietly, "You're under arrest on suspicion of murder."

Her seat companion's mouth fell open. The woman accompanied Boren and Nordlund off the plane meekly enough, half smiling, as if a ridiculous mistake had been made. As they exited, they read her rights under *Miranda*, and she nodded. There was little conversation as they waited to pick up the suitcase she had checked aboard and then drove to police headquarters in downtown Seattle.

She looked like anything but a hit woman. She barely reached five feet and couldn't have weighed more than 95 pounds. But every pound was arranged in the right spot. The woman was gorgeous.

And very, very annoyed.

She gave her name as Cynthia Ellen Marler, born May 2, 1952, and said she had grown up in Hayward and still lived there. She said she had come to Seattle for a brief vacation to visit a brother-in-law, just to get away from the burden of mothering her three children, age four, five, and twelve, for a day or so.

"Why did you fly up here under the name K. Adams?" Nordlund asked.

"A friend—Milos Panich*—booked my reservations and bought my ticket under that name," she replied, "and so I just left it that way."

Asked about the man who had been with her when she checked out the car from Hertz, Cynthia said he was someone named Felix,* a man she had met on the plane. She had offered to give him a lift to his destination in the north end.

Cynthia and Felix had a few drinks, and then she had checked into the Villa Del Mar Motel at 3938 Aurora Avenue North.

"The maid woke me about ten the next morning, and I had breakfast at a family restaurant down the street."

Cynthia Marler said she had left her keys in the Datsun while she ate and had gone out to find that the car had been stolen. She had called her friend Milos Panich in California, and he had told her to call the police. Cynthia said that Panich had also told her that one of her children was ill, and she had decided to go back to California that afternoon. She never had contacted her brother-in-law. Her visit to Seattle had lasted a little less than twenty-four hours.

Cynthia had not had enough money for a return ticket, so she had phoned Steffi Panich,* Milos's wife, who said she'd wire $160 at once through Western Union. "I was going to fly back under my own name, but I decided I might as well stick with Kristine Adams."

Cynthia had checked out of the Villa Del Mar late in the afternoon and taxied to Western Union, where she picked up the money wired by the Paniches. She had the cabbie take her to Sea-Tac Airport to board the flight to San Francisco.

The pretty suspect was incredulous that anyone might accuse her of the murder of Wanda Touchstone, whom she had never even heard of. She was adamant that she was merely a tired mother seeking a few days' surcease from the burden of child care. She was booked into the King County Jail on suspicion of murder.

The investigation would continue. Detectives Billy Baughman and Danny Engle arrived for work early the next morning and began to disentangle the convoluted case. Having learned through the victim's attorney that Wanda Preston-Touchstone was separated from her husband, Lew Touchstone–Robert Preston, they obtained Touchstone's address in Kirkland, a suburb north of Seattle.

If Touchstone was overcome with grief when the two detectives informed him that his estranged wife had been murdered, he hid his feelings well. In fact, Lew Touchstone refused to come to the medical examiner's office to identify her body until he could arrange to have his attorney accompany him.

After identifying Wanda's body, Touchstone grudgingly answered some questions for Engle and Baughman. He said he had spent Sunday, August 10, with Wanda and that they had a very pleasant day. He had met her at a hotel, and they had taken a ferry across Elliott Bay to Bainbridge Island. With the sea gulls calling and the summer breeze, it had been a lovely trip. Wanda had been affectionate, and they had held hands. Encouraged, he had asked her to come back to him, but she had refused. Still, it had been a good day and he was left feeling hopeful about their future. Wanda had been in good spirits when he left her at the hotel at 6:00 P.M.

On the day that Wanda was killed, Touchstone said he had checked into a plastic surgeon's office where he underwent a partial face-lift. He said he had spent the night at a convalescent home, doped up with pain pills, completely unaware that anything had happened to his estranged bride.

Touchstone said he didn't know any of Wanda's new friends; he suspected that she might be dating someone, but he didn't know who it might be.

In checking Lew Touchstone's background, Danny Engle and Billy Baughman did come up with one rather interesting fact. Milos Panich, the man who had paid for Cynthia Marler's trip to Seattle, was married to Lew's daughter, Steffi. The California couple now owned a farm in the Napa Valley that had once belonged to Lew, and they reportedly had interests in an auto body shop business. It seemed unlikely, then, that Cynthia had never even heard of Lew's wife.

A check into Cynthia Marler's background also elicited some facts that cast some shadows on the picture of Cynthia as a simple housewife and mother. The twenty-eight-year-old suspect had a rap sheet going back to 1971. She had been arrested on a variety of charges, including burglary, kidnapping, receiving stolen property (credit cards), theft and forgery (credit cards), conspiracy, driving while intoxicated, and reckless driving. Her husband was presently serving time for bank robbery in prison at Terminal Island, California.

Cynthia Marler had clearly talked to detectives before, even though she had pretended to be shocked that Engle and Baughman considered her involved in any way in a crime.

Detective Billy Baughman inventoried the contents of Cynthia Marler's purse. He found a key ring with two keys wired on to the ring itself, the Hertz rental agreement, an address book, a black date book with the notation for Sunday, August 10, reading, "Try for the 11th," and a piece of paper with the name Felix Misha and an address and phone number on it, $102.10 in currency and coin, and a note signed "Milos," that said, "Don't call me until I call you . . . and that will be never."

Engle and Baughman called Felix Misha,* wondering just what part he might play in this increasingly bizarre case. Misha, a tall, thin man with a wispy little mustache, said he was a concert violinist and lounge performer. He seemed genuinely aghast when he learned what had happened to the pretty woman he'd met on the plane.

"We talked on the way up, and she offered to give me a ride when she picked up her rental car. She didn't know the Seattle area, and I was going to point out some addresses to her."

One of the addresses that had interested Cynthia Marler was that of the apartment house where Wanda Touchstone lived. Misha said that Cynthia had parked beyond the apartment house entrance and told him she would be back in a short while. She went into the lobby while Misha watched, and was back within a few minutes.

"We had a couple of drinks," Misha said, "and I wrote down my address, and she wrote down hers and her husband's and gave it to me."

It was clear that the nervous musician had no closer ties with the case than a chance meeting with the suspect.

Detectives John Boatman and Mike Tando had canvassed Wanda's apartment house—with negative results. No one had seen or heard anything out of the ordinary on or before the day of her death. Her apartment seemed undisturbed; it was messy, but only the clutter one might expect in the home of a woman devoted to study. Notebooks, textbooks on biology and anatomy, and other school materials were scattered around. But there was no indication at all that any violence had taken place there.

By Lew Touchstone's own statement, Wanda had met him away from her apartment on the day before her death and had returned home alone. She didn't live to see the next day out.

Dr. John Eisele, the King County medical examiner, performed the autopsy on the body of Wanda Touchstone. The five-foot-four-inch, 121-pound woman had received two major injuries: both execution-style gunshot wounds. The first was an entry wound two and a half inches behind the right ear canal opening. That bullet entered the skull, passed through the brain, and hit the left side of the skull before ricocheting forward. The bullet was recovered, but there was no way to determine how far the gun barrel had been from Wanda's head; either the gun had been some distance away or her hair had filtered out all the barrel debris.

The second wound was an entrance wound on the left side of the neck. The skin surrounding the bullet hole was stippled with powder, indicating that the killer had held the gun one or two inches away. This bullet transversed the trachea, shattering the bone, passed through the jugular vein, broke Wanda's lower right jaw, and exited through the right cheek.

Ugly wounds. Fatal wounds.

Dr. Eisele found other injuries that were somewhat puzzling; Wanda Touchstone's body bore a number of scrapes and bruises. Large areas of skin had been abraded and contused on her right shoulder, left upper leg, inner left thigh, lower back, and right buttock. It almost looked as if someone had beaten Wanda Touchstone during the last day, or few days, of her life. The bruising was not consistent with someone falling to the pavement after being shot.

Frank Lee, firearms examiner for the Washington State Patrol Crime Lab, examined the recovered bullet under a microscope. He found its class and characteristics (the marks left on a bullet as it exits a gun barrel—lands and grooves, right-hand twist, and so forth) consistent with firing from a .38 caliber Smith & Wesson.

But there was no gun for comparison. The death gun was probably resting on the bottom of one of the many waterways in the north end of Seattle. Even so, the case against Cynthia Marler was tightening. Detectives Baughman and Engle took the key ring found in the suspect's purse with them when they returned to Wanda Touchstone's apartment house. It was a lockout apartment where, for the occupants' security, the common front door leading into the lobby could be opened only with a key provided to tenants.

One of the two keys wired onto the key ring slipped into the lockout, and the door swung open: Cynthia Marler had had in her possession a key to Wanda's apartment house. The second key was tried in the lock of Wanda's apartment itself. It did not fit. But a talk with the manager brought forth the information that Wanda had recently had the locks to her apartment changed and had added a dead bolt.

On the night Cynthia arrived in Seattle, Felix Misha had accompanied her to Wanda's address, and he had seen her gain entrance to the lobby easily. Baughman and Engle wondered if she had not planned to kill Wanda that night—with her new acquaintance waiting in the car. If she had, her plans would have been thwarted when she attempted to insert the second key into the apartment door. That key would not have worked.

That might explain the entry in Cynthia's date book on Sunday "Try for the 11th?" Had Cynthia planned to follow her unsuspecting quarry the next day until she had a second chance?

The impounded Hertz rental car was processed, but there was nothing at all in it to indicate who had driven it—no clothes, no wigs, and certainly no gun or ammunition.

The room Cynthia Marler had rented at the Villa Del Mar had been thoroughly cleaned by maids before detectives could get to it, and nothing of evidentiary value was found. The maids were interviewed and said they had found nothing in the room beyond some tourist brochures. Detectives Gary Fowler and Danny Melton had the Dumpster behind the motel loaded into a Seattle disposal truck, and the contents were spilled onto a clean area in a disposal lot where the two detectives pawed through it—an onerous and monumental task that netted nothing connected with the murder of Wanda Touchstone.

A friend of Wanda Touchstone's, who had been writing a joint term paper with her at the university, came forward and said she had met Wanda in her apartment parking lot the morning of August 11, and Wanda had worn a huge diamond ring. "I commented on it because I'd worked for a jeweler, and I could see that it was more than a carat. She just said the ring had been part of her marriage."

The ring was not on the victim's finger when she was shot a few hours later. It wasn't in her apartment either.

Detectives Engle and Baughman itemized the contents of the red overnight case Cynthia Marler had carried onto the plane where she was arrested, along with the suitcase she had checked. They wondered what a woman might take with her as she embarked on an overnight trip to commit a murder. The luggage was packed with what an average woman might take on a short vacation: makeup, a hair dryer, extra clothes (but no blue-gray dress), shoes, lingerie. There was a cross and a rosary. There was a paperback book, *Blood-letters and Bad Men,* one of a series about infamous criminals.

They found Cynthia Marler's parole papers from an earlier incarceration. And they found a wig, a blondish brown wig styled in short tight curls. There was a silk scarf, too—pink, blue, and white.

Was this wig responsible for the witnesses' description of a blond woman with a scarf, who had hurried away from the death site? Baughman and Engle thought so. She probably had stripped off the oversized dull blue dress and thrown it away during her flight. The wig would have fit in her purse. That explained why some witnesses had seen the blonde in the baggy dress and another had seen a trim woman in slacks whose hair was long and black.

And they were more convinced when Nell Boles, Jan Winn, and Mary Moran picked Cynthia Marler from a lineup of several women. This was the woman Boles and Winn had seen leaving the parking lot after the shooting. This was also the woman Moran had seen trying to scale a fence next door to where the rental Datsun was abandoned.

Working with King County Deputy Prosecuting Attorney David R. Lord, the two detectives agreed that there was enough evidence to file a first-degree murder charge against Cynthia Marler in the death of Wanda Touchstone, but they didn't feel they had the whole story. There was a chance that Cynthia might cooperate and implicate others in a plot against Wanda—*if* she was offered a plea bargain. Second-degree murder charges would mean far less prison time than first-degree, and Lord made the decision to allow Cynthia to plead guilty to second-degree murder if her allegations led to charges against others.

The case made brief headlines in Seattle, and then the media forgot about it; there were new crimes to write about. Baughman, Engle, and Lord didn't forget about it, though. Engle made many trips to California to verify information. He found the travel agent who had booked Marler's flight to Seattle and issued the voucher for the rental car. She said the trip was paid for by Steffi Panich—Lew Touchstone's daughter—who had asked for a receipt.

Cynthia Marler waited in jail. The other people close to Marler and the victim were not eager to discuss the case. Neither of the Touchstones, father or son, had much to say, nor did the Panichs.

As the weeks stretched out and Cynthia began to realize that she probably *was* headed for prison, she began to talk with Dan Engle. Rather, she began to fence with him. She had promised to reveal the whole plot behind Wanda's death, but she was adept at double-talk. This was a woman who was used to conning people, and Engle knew it. Nevertheless, he gambled that when push came to shove, Cynthia would save her own skin. For a while it looked as though she was going to.

Dan Engle and FBI Special Agent Brian Braun traveled to Pleasanton, California, to talk with Cynthia's husband, Jim. He had worked for Milos Panich before he went into prison, and he hoped to have a job in Panich's auto body shop when he was released. But this was his *wife*, the mother of his children. If she was taking the fall for someone higher up, she would go to prison for a long, long time. Engle and Braun asked Marler if he'd be willing to wear a wire the next time Milos or Steffi Panich came to visit.

Marler agreed to be wired, although he didn't seem very enthusiastic about it. Whether he was afraid of Panich or more concerned about his own future than his wife's, the body wire exercise was disappointing. Milos Panich came to visit all right, but Marler was doing everything he could to garble the transmission of their voices.

"We had told him to stay as close as he could to the door," Engle recalled, "so we could hear what they said, but he wandered back by the vending machines. It was so noisy we could only hear about ten percent of their conversation."

James Marler was walking the narrow edge of a knife. He wanted out of prison—so he didn't want to flat-out refuse to help a homicide detective and an FBI agent, but he was obviously standing so far away that his body wire sent out only static, the sound of bottles clunking down in the pop machine, and an occasional complete sentence.

Next, Dan Engle tried to talk to Cynthia again. She was the one who was in immediate danger of facing a murder conviction. If she cooperated, prosecutor David Lord would take that into account. Cynthia smiled and laughed and appeared to be willing to go halfway. Engle tried not to acknowledge that he saw a certain blankness in her eyes, the eyes of a woman who was lying.

Finally she agreed to call Milos Panich on a phone in the Seattle Homicide Unit's offices, a phone that was wired to record the conversation. It could have been the break in the case that would have let Engle and Baughman reel in two, maybe three or four more suspects in the plot to kill Wanda.

But it wasn't. Cynthia's conversation with Milos Panich was about as damaging to him as a call between two people gossiping. It seemed to Engle that caution oozed from Panich's voice and everything he said. Even Cynthia sounded stilted and rehearsed.

"Something was fishy," Engle said. "We suspected she had already called Panich from jail earlier and told him to be careful what he said when she called him later. She had been double-talking all along."

When prosecutor David Lord heard about the phone call, he said, "That's it. The deal's off entirely." Marler's cooperation had produced no substantive evidence against Panich.

Cynthia Marler would be charged with first-degree murder.

Wanda Touchstone earned her degree in microbiology; the University of Washington awarded it to her posthumously. Her grief-stricken sister arrived from Sweden to take the degree back with her, along with Wanda's clothing and a few other possessions. She expected to find Wanda's prized diamond ring, but it wasn't where she thought she would find it.

Where was it? If Lew Touchstone was the true instigator of Wanda's execution, it would have been easy for him to give her the expensive diamond ring on Sunday; he would have gotten it back on Monday when Wanda was shot.

Wanda's sister had hoped to take the body back with her to be buried in Poland, but she could not afford to transport it. She told reporters that Lew Touchstone would not pay the expense. Lew's attorney said he'd offered to pay half and that his sister-in-law had refused.

The sister returned to Sweden without Wanda's body, and Wanda was buried in a Bellevue, Washington, cemetery far from her native land.

If the public and press had forgotten about the Touchstone-Marler case, they were fully aware of it with headlines in late February. Superior Court Judge Richard Ishikawa took an unprecedented legal action. As the pretrial legal hearing opened, Judge Ishikawa barred the press and public from that hearing. When the media are barred, headlines scream. And they did.

John Henry Browne, who had advised Ted Bundy in 1975 when Browne worked for the King County Public Defender's Office, had become one of the top three criminal defense attorneys in Seattle. He represented Cynthia Marler. Pitted against him for the state would be King County Deputy Prosecutor David Lord. Worthy adversaries, just the two of them, walking carefully through a case fraught with legal technicalities. They concurred with Judge Ishikawa's decision to close and seal the pretrial hearing while the media screamed "Foul!" and the public's interest was titillated.

Cynthia Marler's part in the murder of Wanda Touchstone had allegedly been observed by eyewitnesses. It was the possibility that she was not the instigator of the execution-style murder that raised so many questions. Nonetheless, the pretrial hearing remained closed despite the pleas of lawyers from Seattle's newspapers. When the trial itself opened, TV and still cameras were allowed into the courtroom; they would pool the footage that resulted. The press bench was filled with reporters.

Who *was* Cynthia Marler?

She was certainly the camera's darling, posing constantly, directing her smile into the lens. The defendant was so photogenic that it seemed impossible to get a bad shot of her, and she made the papers almost every day of the trial. Cynthia was so tiny that spectators murmured that she certainly didn't *look* like a killer. She wore filmy white long-sleeved blouses, draped slacks, and high-heeled shoes with dainty straps across her slender ankles. As she was led into the courtroom, her wrists were encircled with specially made cuffs; her arms were too small for anything beyond a child-size measurement.

Cynthia joked with her female guard whenever court recessed, and she puffed continually on Camel cigarettes. She seemed ultimately confident, as if she had never considered that she might be convicted, as if she was only the focal point of some legal mix-up. She had thrown away her chance for a lesser charge, and yet she still seemed to expect someone to save her.

The jury consisted of nine women and three men, with two female alternates. Would the women feel sympathy for this child-woman on trial for first-degree murder, or would they judge her more objectively than a jury of men, who might have been taken with her beauty?

The motive for the murder of Wanda Touchstone was foremost in the minds of the spectators and the press, and prosecutor Lord put Detective Danny Engle on the stand—out of the jurors' hearing—to testify as to detectives' suppositions on why Wanda had died. Engle, who had lived, breathed, and slept the Marler case for months, revealed that Lew Touchstone was once considered a suspect in the case. "If we were going to talk to him about the case today," Engle said, "we'd read him his rights under *Miranda* before questioning him."

Engle said that Lew Touchstone's daughter, Steffi, and her husband, Milos Panich, had been investigated, too. Although Milos Panich admitted he paid for Cynthia's plane ticket and car rental, he said it was just a favor for her. The Panichs had not set foot in Washington State since the crime.

Lew Touchstone and his son, Ron (Wanda's first husband, a proxy spouse), were called to the witness stand to testify. They refused to answer any questions at all. Lew went first. He refused to answer such seemingly innocuous questions as "Do you have a daughter named Steffi who was married to Milos Panich?" and "How were you notified of your wife's death?" and "Did you identify the body?"

Lew read from a white card in his hand: "I decline to answer on grounds of the Fifth Amendment of the U.S. Constitution and similar provisions of the Washington State Constitution."

Son Ron followed, intoning the same Fifth Amendment response to all questions.

Judge Ishikawa ruled that Lew Touchstone would be allowed to exercise his constitutional rights under the Fifth Amendment, but that Ron Touchstone, who had never been a suspect in the bizarre murder, had no grounds for taking the Fifth. Resolute, Ron Touchstone still refused to answer any questions and was sentenced to jail for the duration of the trial. Lew and Ron stormed past strobe lights and cameras, covering their faces as they left the courtroom.

As the lengthy trial began, David Lord presented witness after witness, eliciting the information uncovered by Detectives Engle and Baughman. The case had unfolded like a movie mystery. There were the almost-eyewitnesses to the execution of the pretty Pole, the woman who had seen a petite, dark-haired woman trying to scale the fence, the man who had spotted the rented Datsun and alerted police, the pathologist, the firearms expert, the travel agent who had sold the plane ticket to Steffi Panich, the Hertz employees, the Western Union clerk who had handed $160 over to Cynthia Marler, Felix Misha, the apprehensive musician who had gone to Wanda's apartment house with Cynthia the night before the killing, and the detectives. On and on, they took the stand, painting a clearer and clearer picture of the defendant as a woman who had allegedly quite calmly traveled 900 miles to shoot another woman whom she had never known.

Invariably in murder trials the defendant looks away as the defense lawyer examines gruesome photos of the victim, taken after autopsy. Cynthia Marler did not. She studied them intently.

John Henry Browne was good. He was quick, alert, incisive, asking all the right questions on cross. But the answers he needed weren't there. If anyone could have gotten an acquittal for a client, Browne could, but the case against Cynthia Marler was as solid as cement.

There was more of a sense of things *not* said in that courtroom than of things said aloud. Questions danced around the surface of what lay beneath. At one point, Danny Engle read a translation of an ad that appeared in a Polish newspaper—*Courier Polski,* published in Warsaw. It was dated October 30, 1980, a little more than two months after Wanda Touchstone fell dead. Wanda's relatives had mailed it to Engle: "Man from America desires contact with lady around 35 years old. Knows English. Interested in house and family. Send offer to Mr. Lew Touchstone. . . ."

Wanda was gone, but Lew Touchstone apparently was determined to replace her with a mirror image, another Polish woman in her mid-thirties—but one who would stay at home with him and treat him as lord and master of the house. He had even gone to the expense and pain of having a face-lift to look more youthful. Unfortunately, he had disobeyed every instruction his doctor had given him, and his health had suffered.

After much legal maneuvering, Susan Zydak, a King County prosecutor's paralegal, was allowed to take the stand and testify regarding an interview she had witnessed between David Lord and Lew Touchstone. As the jury watched, enthralled, she diagrammed the complicated relationships among and between Lew Touchstone, Ron Touchstone, Wanda Touchstone, Steffi Panich, Milos Panich, and Cynthia Marler. For the first time, they realized that Cynthia had been sent to Seattle by the son-in-law of the victim's husband.

Incredibly, the reason Cynthia Marler might have traveled so far to shoot Wanda Touchstone was never touched upon. Money? A likely supposition. Cynthia had been living on welfare with her three children while her husband served out his sentence for bank robbery. Lew Touchstone had a bundle of money. Milos Panich apparently had enough to foot Cynthia's "vacation" away from her children.

There was no evidence that Cynthia even *knew* Wanda. No evidence that she had any reason to hate her enough to kill her. A payoff seemed a likely reason to kill, but no evidence of a payoff surfaced during her trial.

When the Western Union representative testified, he stated that a still camera routinely took photos of people picking up wired money. Even here the case was bizarre. The number noted for the "Kristine Adams" money order was 8896. But no photo was found. Then Western Union figured that the number might have been upside down; maybe the number was 9688. They checked their files again. No photo. Finally they realized there had been no film in the camera.

Through it all, Cynthia Marler remained the coquettish beauty, smiling at her attorney and whispering in his ear, posing for the cameras. Although she looked soft in photographs, in person she occasionally looked as hard as steel. Her eyebrows were plucked to a thin line, and her acne scars were hidden with makeup. This was a woman who had obviously led a rugged life.

Would John Henry Browne put Cynthia on the stand? Would he take the chance of opening her up to cross-examination by Lord? No. Cynthia never told her story.

Browne called only one defense witness: Cynthia's brother-in-law, the man she said she'd come to Seattle to visit. She had never contacted him. He said that he and Cynthia were "estranged," that he had not seen her since 1977. However, Browne elicited the information that it would not be unusual for family members to just drop in on each other without notice. The witness smiled at Cynthia as he admitted, "We've had a beef from time to time," and she smiled back thinly.

And then it was over. The defense had lasted at most ten minutes.

It was March 10, 1981. Time for final arguments to begin.

David Lord rose to address the jury for the state. Layer by layer he built the case again from the beginning, starting with the travel arrangements for "K. Adams" to fly to Seattle. Her travel schedule was devastating to the defendant when it was first introduced; it was more devastating now as Lord's summary added bricks to the wall of probable guilt that rose around the beautiful defendant.

Lord described the petite Marler as a "cold-blooded, ruthless killer." He suggested that Cynthia's motive was a very old one: money.

John Henry Browne argued that he should be able to mention Lew Touchstone in his final argument, just as he had in his opening remarks. Browne placed the suspicion directly on Lew Touchstone who, he alleged, "had a motive to have his wife killed," the motive of a wealthy man who lived in a community-property state and was facing a divorce settlement.

David Lord felt that if Browne was allowed to mention the elusive Touchstone again, then Lord should be allowed to tell the jury why Touchstone had not testified—that he had refused on Fifth Amendment grounds, suggesting that his statements might incriminate him. Judge Ishikawa ruled that Browne could voice his thoughts on Lew Touchstone in final arguments but that he could not tell the jury why Touchstone had not taken the witness stand.

The attorney for the defense gave a philosophical argument, hitting on the essential ingredient in a first-degree murder conviction—reasonable doubt— telling the jury that it was incumbent on the state to present a case that proves the defendant guilty beyond a reasonable doubt of premeditated murder. He submitted there was still a great deal of reasonable doubt.

Browne's voice rose as he said, *"I* don't have to make sense out of anything. And if you think I do, then let's give up right now. I don't have to prove anything. He [Lord] has got to make sense out of [his case]."* Browne was aggressive. "Our theory in this case is very simple: *prove it."*

And then Browne raised some questions that he hoped would make the jurors wonder if they had absolute proof that Cynthia Marler had committed murder. If Cynthia had carried out a well-formed plan to kill, he asked, "Why rent a car under your own name? Why get rid of a gun, but keep a wig, and keep the keys to the victim's apartment? Why have someone make reservations for a murder trip through a travel agency? Why arrive in Seattle with no money? Not enough money to even get back home? . . . You cannot make soup from the *shadow* of a chicken. You cannot find a person guilty beyond a reasonable doubt because of *questions."*

Browne listed seven reasonable doubts he had gleaned from the state's version of the Marler case. He

found the identification of Cynthia Marler faulty—
the witnesses had been confused in their descriptions
of the person seen leaving the crime scene. He suggested that the defendant might have been set up to be
in the parking lot, seen by witnesses while the real
killer escaped. He suggested that Marler had no
motive to kill Wanda Touchstone. He brought out the
lack of evidence in the case. "Where is *Mr. Touchstone?* What kind of guns does *Mr. Touchstone* have?
What about the bruises all over Wanda Touchstone's
body?"

Browne continued with his list, hitting again and
again on the elusive Lew Touchstone. (He had the
advantage here, since Lord was not allowed to tell the
jury that Touchstone was refusing to testify by taking
the Fifth, and Lord could not explain Lew Touchstone's absence.)

Why were Cynthia's hands free of nitrate traces
when they were swabbed some hours after the murder? Browne did not explain to the jury that the
simple washing of one's hands can remove traces of
nitrate or that smoking a cigarette or urinating can
leave nitrate traces on hands.

Browne felt that there was time for a second person
to have left the parking lot *before* the witness saw a
woman rushing from the shooting scene. *"Time . . .
time."* He questioned later witnesses' ability to accurately estimate the time they'd seen the dark-haired
woman driving the red car and scaling the fence.

Browne's last "reasonable doubt" concerned common sense. He insisted common sense would dictate
that no high-priced "hit lady" would leave such a
well-marked trail behind her with plane tickets, car
rentals, wired money, and taxis.

His scattershot technique hit the jury so rapidly
that several of them were blinking. Questions.
Questions—and then his repeated statement, "I don't
have to explain anything; I don't have to prove
anything." The young defense attorney was good; he

had taken a case with evidence so damning that few attorneys would even have tried. The state and prosecutor Lord had Cynthia Marler so locked into Wanda Touchstone's execution that the press bench was making book the jury would be back within an hour of the start of deliberation, yet Browne was pulling questions out of the air.

It was an either-or situation. Either Cynthia hadn't done it or she had to have been the klutziest, sloppiest hit lady ever to sashay into Seattle.

David Lord made his final statements, stressing that Cynthia Marler—however inadequate she might have been as a paid killer—had done it, and she had done it for money, that her movements between August 8 and August 11 were far too meaningful to be mere coincidence.

The jury went out. One hour. Two. Six. Several reporters paid off on their lost wagers. It was to take ten hours of deliberation before they returned and informed Judge Ishikawa that they had reached a verdict. For the first time, Cynthia Marler seemed to have lost her bravado; she appeared to realize that she might not be acquitted after all. Jury foreman Robert Toigo read the verdict. The jury had found her guilty of first-degree murder.

The raven-haired beauty bowed her head and wept softly, as John Henry Browne leaned over to comfort her.

The foreman told the press later that the jury had spent the better part of two days going over "each and every piece" of evidence. He said one juror had fought a lonely fight for acquittal right up to the last minute. He admitted that the jurors had been confused, that they could not understand certain elements of the case. That was to be expected; Lew Touchstone, and his daughter, Steffi, her husband, Milos Panich, had been mentioned—but never produced. One possible motive for Wanda's death was the bitterness surrounding her divorce from Touchstone—but that was only one. Touchstone was more than wealthy enough to support an ex-wife without diminishing his lifestyle.

On March 26, 1981, Cynthia Marler was led once again into Judge Ishikawa's courtroom. She was no longer dressed in a delicate blouse, tailored slacks, and high heels; now she wore jail coveralls and sandals. She was sentenced to life in prison, with a recommendation of a twenty-five-year minimum. She murmured that she'd like to serve her time in California so she could see her children, but Cynthia Marler would serve out her term in the women's prison at Purdy, Washington.

Cynthia, the woman who had brought a rosary with her when she came to Seattle to kill Wanda Touchstone, grew angry after she heard her sentence. She balked at having her fingerprints taken in the courtroom, and her attorney had to urge her to accede. The television cameras now caught the other side of her personality—the bitter, hostile, tough Cynthia.

Her children would have no mother for perhaps twenty-five years. They had no father, either; he was serving time for bank robbery.

When the proceedings finally ended, a tall bearded man rose sadly and walked out of the courtroom. John Sophronski had seen the trial through to the finish, staring at the pretty little woman who had taken Wanda away from him. Court deputies had seen him wince during the trial, seen him clench his fists, and they had worried about what he might do. But he never said a word or made a move toward Cynthia.

The questions remained—at least officially. Detectives had been told—but were constrained from revealing—that Cynthia Marler *had* been promised payment once Wanda Touchstone was dead. The monetary amount was reportedly $3,000. As a further enticement, Marler had been assured that the title to a 1976 Chevrolet pickup truck would be put in her name. If a price could be put on a human life, Wanda Touchstone's had gone cheap. Cynthia had also been promised support if anything went wrong. Detectives believed that she never expected to go to prison, that she was convinced that those who wanted Wanda dead were so powerful that they could save her. Perhaps that was why she played games with the police and the prosecutor's office; had she *trusted* in the manipulators behind the death plot?

Cynthia took her punishment alone. She probably was behind bars at the Washington State Women's Corrections Center at Purdy before she realized that nobody *was* coming to her rescue. At that point she was undoubtedly afraid to come forward and point her finger, at least publically. She had children on the outside. She kept her mouth shut.

For the moment.

Lew Touchstone was free, but he was a frightened man who often called the very detectives who had questioned him, asking them for protection. He was afraid that he might be the target of violence at any moment. He never was. He lives in relative obscurity with an unlisted phone number.

Cynthia Marler filed her first appeal in mid-1982. She claimed that the state had extracted a pretrial confession from her but then reneged on its promise to reduce the charges against her if her allegations resulted in charges against others. Prior to her trial, she had told prosecutors that Lew Touchstone's son-in-law, Milos Panich, had hired her to kill Wanda Touchstone and offered her $3,000 to do so. Cynthia's husband, James Marler, had allegedly been present when the offer was made. Cynthia said that Panich financed her trip to Seattle, rented her a car, and provided a photo of Wanda, a gun and ammunition, and even the keys and plans to Wanda's apartment. Cynthia also said that Panich had asked her to return to California with the diamond ring that Wanda wore.

The state had given Cynthia "use immunity," which meant the prosecution could not use these statements against her at trial. In addition, Cynthia's statements about her role as a hired killer and her husband James's implication of Milos Panich had been sealed in court records on Judge Ishikawa's orders. It took a suit by the *Seattle Times* and the *Seattle Post-Intelligencer* before that information was published, *after* the trial.

On appeal, Cynthia's new lawyer, Julie Kelser, asked the question, "Why have two men literally gotten away with murder?" King County Deputy Prosecutor William Downing accused Kelser of "Monday morning quarterbacking"; the case was more than a year old. He said the prosecution had not had sufficient evidence to charge either Touchstone or Panich.

On July 12, 1982, the State Court of Appeals affirmed Cynthia Marler's murder-for-hire conviction. The court ruled that the state had acted in good faith and had not reneged on its agreement with Cynthia Marler: it had fully investigated her statements but found no basis for charging the two men with the crime.

While Cynthia continued her life sentence for the crime of murder, there may have been others who walked free——but on egg shells, still waiting for an ax to fall.

And if it did not fall fatally, it certainly hovered menacingly in July 1986, when Cynthia again appealed her conviction for first-degree murder to the State Court of Appeals. She asked that she be released from prison based in part on her claim that one of her attorneys had a conflict of interest at the time of her trial, because he had been paid by what a news story described as "a possible co-defendant in the case," Milos Panich.

It was a most convoluted argument. The same attorney Cynthia now blamed for her incarceration was the lawyer who had negotiated a potential plea bargain for second-degree murder. For her to have received the lesser charge, she would have had to implicate Panich. Her inability to furnish sufficient evidence for the state to charge Panich, however, resulted in the heavier charge.

The appeals court decreed that her trial attorney had clearly been on Cynthia Marler's side and again rejected her bid to be released from prison.

In the end, it was Cynthia Marler's own lack of credibility that did her in. According to Deputy Prosecutor Bill Downing, her statements implicating others were too weak to use. Cynthia had failed a lie detector test and her "trustworthiness" was highly suspect. And the state found no new evidence that warranted charging others with the crime. There is, of course, no statute of limitations on murder.

Detectives proved the most important facet of their case: beautiful, petite Cynthia Marler cold-bloodedly fired two bullets into Wanda Touchstone's head and neck on August 11, 1980, and ended forever the marriage that should never have begun.

Twelve years after her conviction, Cynthia Marler remains incarcerated in the Washington State Women's Corrections Center at Purdy. The usual life term, with time off for good behavior, is thirteen years and four months in Washington State. Cynthia Marler has not been particularly cooperative while in prison, and guards call her "a tough one." She is forty-one now, her children are nearly grown, and the life she left behind has disintegrated with years and distance.

No one will ever really know why Wanda had to die. All of her secrets died with her. All but one.

Her killer took her life—but not her diamond ring. The disappearance of Wanda's diamond ring had puzzled detectives for a long time. The mystery was solved when Wanda's sister came upon it, stuck in the tow of Wanda's panty hose. Wanda might have begun to trust her ex-husband a little more after their happy Sunday together, but not enough that she didn't find it necessary to hide the ring she had just stolen back.

The Runaway

When I began my research into the inexplicable disappearance of a young teenager in Washington State, I was hesitant about approaching her family. I had always been timid about intruding on the grief of survivors of crime victims, but that changed when I met Doreen Hanson. My interview with her resulted in my membership in the Families and Friends of Victims of Violent Crimes and Missing Persons support group. Over the next seventeen years, I would meet scores of extremely brave people—survivors who were not content with the status quo and who worked tirelessly to change the system. Washington State's victims' group was one of the forerunners of such groups all over America. If their own loved ones were gone forever—and most of them were—"Families and Friends" strove to protect other people's children. I found them a most extraordinary group, and I made lasting friendships. Many years ago, when I began writing true crime articles, I agonized over my realization that I was making my living from other people's tragedies. The mothers, fathers, sisters, brothers, and grandparents in "Families and Friends" taught me that their stories had to be told, but that any writer who did so must always remember the victims too. Doreen, Janna's mother, was my first contact, and she taught me to fight for crime victims—even if the only thing I could do was to keep their memories alive.

The bleak search for thirteen-year-old Janna Hanson began on Thursday morning, December 26, 1974, in a little town north of Seattle, Washington. The Christmas just past had been an especially happy one for Janna. Her family had made it through some bad times, but they had finally come full circle and they were happy again. Janna's mother, Doreen Hanson, had divorced the father of her four daughters in the late sixties. And then in 1970 they were getting along so well that they talked of getting back together. It was not to be; Janna's father died of a sudden heart attack that year. He was only forty-one. When their father died, Gail Hanson was nineteen, the twins, Penny and Pamela, were seventeen, and Janna, the baby, was nine.

Their father's death was a blow to all the Hanson girls, but their grief had softened with the years. And this Christmas of 1974 had been good. The comfortable apartment Doreen and Janna shared had overflowed with all the people Janna loved best: her mom and her beautiful big sisters, her baby nephew, Derek. Her Grandma Hanson had traveled hundreds of miles to be with them.

Janna was as blond as her sisters, caught somewhere between childhood and womanhood. Her older sisters occasionally modeled, and Janna showed every indication that she would be as beautiful as they were. She had received almost all the presents she had asked for, but that wasn't nearly as important as just being with her family. The Hansons were—and are—a very close family.

Anyone who knew her at all well knew that Janna Hanson would never have run away. And yet, a day after Christmas, it seemed that she had been swallowed up into some other dimension, simply vanishing into infinity.

Doreen Hanson was about to enter the saddest, most frustrating period of her life. Again and again, for months, she would find her gut feelings dismissed by authorities who insisted that her daughter had run away. That was the obvious answer when one considered the legions of runaway teens in the sixties and seventies; it was incomprehensible to Doreen Hanson.

Janna Hanson had promised a good friend that she would check on the girl's family's mobile home, which sat on the grounds of the Nile Country Club, a sprawling compound near Janna's Mountlake Terrace, Washington, home. Her friend's family was away on vacation. Janna had given her friend some plants for Christmas and had promised to water them faithfully every day. She also was given the responsibility of leaving a water tap turned on just enough so that an unseasonable cold snap wouldn't freeze the trailer's water lines.

That Thursday just after Christmas, Janna left her apartment shortly after 8:30 A.M. She wanted to finish her chores early because she and her mother were due at her older sister Gail's home by noon to pick up Derek. Janna was going to be his official baby-sitter, and she was thrilled about that. Gail and her husband were flying to Alaska for a week-long fishing trip. Janna adored her nephew and was looking forward to caring for him. Unlike many teenagers, Janna Hanson

CAMPBELL'S REVENGE

Renae Wicklund, a beautiful drum majorette in high school in Jamestown, North Dakota. After graduation she moved to the West, where she found great happiness and stark tragedy.

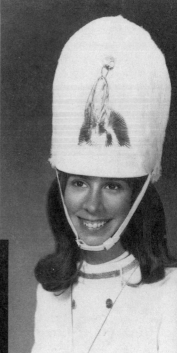

Shannah Wicklund was too young to remember the first time the huge red-haired man came to her house.

CAMPBELL'S REVENGE

Snohomish County detective Joe Belinc worked tirelessly to track down the killer of Shannah and Renae Wicklund and Barbara Hendrickson. *(Ann Rule)*

Washington State patrolmen leading Charles Campbell to the awaiting squad car that would take him to Snohomish County Superior Court, where his 1989 death warrant was issued. *(Drew Perine)*

THE HIT PERSON

Petite and beautiful
Cynthia Marler, who
stood trial for an
unthinkable crime.
(Leslie Rule)

Seattle homicide
detective Dan Engle
during the trial of
Cynthia Marler. He
worked for months to
connect her to the
inexplicable murder of
Wanda Touchstone.
(Leslie Rule)

THE RUNAWAY

Doreen Hanson holding a picture of her thirteen-year-old daughter, Janna. When Janna vanished, local police said that she was a runaway, but her mother was filled with dread. It took almost a year for detectives to discover the truth. (Ann Rule)

A few days after Christmas 1974, Janna Hanson walked onto the grounds of the Nile Country Club (entrance shown here) and disappeared. But the answer lay here all along. (Ann Rule)

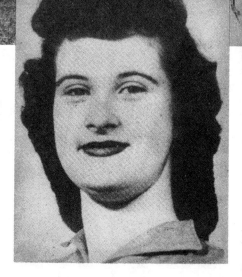

The hut where
Richard Marquette
lived in 1961
was the site of the
murder of Joan
Caudle.

REHABILITATION OF A MONSTER

Jim Byrnes, detective lieutenant in the Marion County sheriff's department, tracked down Richard Marquette for the second time, in 1975.

Richard Marquette was returned to the Oregon State Penitentiary after his second conviction for sadistic murder.

MOLLY'S MURDER

Molly McClure was a much-loved golden girl. Her killer left minute evidence that led straight to him.
(Ann Rule)

MOLLY'S MURDER

Seattle police homicide detective Rudy Sutlovich (above) was the "tall" half of the brilliant investigative team that tracked down Molly's killer. He and homicide detective Hank Gruber (below), the other half of the team, will always remember Molly, even though they never knew her while she was alive. *(Ann Rule)*

was completely reliable about being where she was supposed to be on time.

It was a typical December day in the Northwest—overcast and chilly—when Janna left her home. She wore jeans, a white long-sleeved top, a short, hooded navy blue coat, and a rust and brown knitted scarf. The scarf was a Christmas present from her Grandma Hanson.

It was possible to reach the Nile Country Club by going the long way around on paved streets, but most of the youngsters in the neighborhood took a well-worn shortcut from the apartment building. The path meandered through a thick stand of fir trees and some Scotch broom and eventually led directly into the plush country club grounds near the shores of Lake Ballinger. The path came out close to her friend's mobile home. On any other day, the woods probably would have been full of neighborhood kids, but they could sleep late during Christmas vacation; on December 26, Janna was all alone as she trudged through the lowering trees.

Later, the only thing that her mother could be positive about was that Janna *had* reached the trailer safely. The walk along the shortcut path would have taken her about twenty minutes. Between 9:00 and 9:30 Janna placed a phone call from the mobile home to a school friend. His mother said he was still asleep, and Janna said she would call back later.

But Janna did not answer the phone in the mobile home when Doreen Hanson called there at 10:40 A.M. It had begun to rain heavily, and her mother wanted to be sure that Janna did not attempt to walk home in the deluge. Doreen intended to pick Janna up at the mobile home at 11:20, and she didn't want Janna to walk through the storm if she happened to finish early. The phone rang endlessly. As she listened to the repeated ringing of the phone, Doreen Hanson became a little concerned, perhaps with the kind of second sense mothers possess. She tried to reason that Janna might be hesitant to answer a phone in someone else's home.

Doreen Hanson arrived at the trailer at 11:20, just as she and Janna had agreed earlier. She knocked on the door, but there was no response. She listened for the sound of a television blaring or a radio—*something*—inside that might be drowning out her knock. She could hear nothing but the rain thundering down on the trailer's metal roof. Doreen knocked louder, pounding heavily so anyone inside couldn't miss hearing her. Still no one responded.

"I went back and sat in the car, and I thought, Well, maybe she's vacuuming and she can't hear me knock, or she can't hear me because of the rain," Doreen remembers. "So I honked the car horn. She still didn't come out. I think I knew even then that I would never see Janna again."

Most mothers have it—the visceral sense that something is wrong with their children. Good detectives pay attention; those who go strictly by policy and the odds may overlook what is chillingly clear from the very beginning of a case of disappearance. It would be a very long time before attention was paid to Doreen Hanson.

Suddenly Doreen was aware of how isolated the mobile home was—at least at the moment. There seemed to be no one around, not even the maintenance personnel of the golf course. Janna's mother grew frightened. If Janna had been an irresponsible teenager, she might only have been chagrined. But she was calling for a girl who always was on time or, if she couldn't be, always called home to explain why.

The relationship between Doreen Hanson and her youngest daughter was particularly close because Janna was eight years younger than her twin sisters. Since the death of her father, it had been Janna and Doreen against the world. Although she was very popular with her peers, Janna and her mother shared many things for just the two of them. They had recently gone on a crash diet together, and the slightly pudgy teenager had emerged a glowing young woman who looked closer to seventeen than to thirteen.

Doreen Hanson shivered, and it had nothing to do with the bleak rain and keening wind. She remembered that she had seen a Mountlake Terrace Police patrol car parked near a nearby convenience store, so she drove out of the country club. The police unit was still parked where she had seen it. Officer Donald Lyle listened politely as Doreen told him of her concern for Janna and furnished him with a picture from her wallet of her newly slender, blue-eyed blond daughter.

The teenager had only been missing two hours at most. Lyle made an obligatory sweep of the neighborhood. Doreen Hanson drove to the home of one of Janna's best friends, who lived nearby. She didn't really believe Janna had gone there instead of waiting at the mobile home, but she couldn't think of anyplace else to look. Janna's friend was concerned, too, when Doreen explained the reason for her visit, and the two of them hurried back to the shortcut through the woods, hoping that Doreen's concern was the result only of missed connections. Doreen forced herself to believe that they would meet Janna coming the other way along the path; she concentrated so hard that she could almost see her. But she didn't.

As they walked, Doreen Hanson really saw the trail for the first time. She grew more worried when she realized how isolated the kids' shortcut was as it plunged into a black hole of clustered trees and continued on, shut off from the light of day. If Janna had fallen and been hurt in these woods, no one could have heard her cry for help.

But there was no sign at all of Janna in the darkness of the trees. If she had walked this way three hours earlier, there was no way of telling it now.

Doreen drove back to the mobile home, where she was met by other Mountlake Terrace officers. She explained that she didn't have a key to the trailer, and the officers had already learned that the key kept in the possession of maintenance men had been lost.

"Break in," Doreen Hanson told the skeptical police. "I will take responsibility for any damage."

The officers kicked at the lock with full force, and the front door swung open. The group moved quickly through the large mobile home. Janna wasn't there. But she had been there; her house key and the key to the trailer lay on the drainboard. A light was on in one bedroom, and there was a bag of garbage just outside the back door. It was damp but not sodden, as it would have been if it had been sitting there overnight. It was obvious that Janna had begun to clean the trailer, and something had interrupted her; a few dishes bearing the residue of chili sat in the sink. She had not finished her work. Why? In three hours she would have had plenty of time to do the dishes and vacuum.

Nothing was out of place or knocked over; there was no sign of a struggle in the trailer, and that made Doreen feel a little better—but not much. It didn't make sense that Janna had voluntarily walked away from the mobile home, leaving her house keys and the keys to the trailer behind. And she wasn't the kind of girl to leave a job half done.

Doreen went over everything that had happened since they had awakened that morning, as if she could rearrange this scene and somehow make it all right. She fought to keep her panic down. It had been only three hours—closer to four now. Periodically she dialed her own phone number, hoping to hear Janna's voice.

The vast manicured grounds of the country club were deserted. There had been nothing they could connect to Janna on the path she would have taken back home. Where had she gone?

If Janna had been a small child, forces would have

been mobilized at once to look for her. But police have to make judgments about teenagers who disappear. The vast majority of missing young people come home within twenty-four hours. In any police jurisdiction in America, a widespread search for vanished adults and teenagers is rarely begun until that period has passed. That is policy. That is the widely used rule of thumb. And sometimes it is tragically wrong. Each instance is different, however. If there is evidence of foul play, the police make a judgment call.

Janna's mother and family could not wait twenty-four hours. Just sitting at home waiting for the phone to ring was agonizing. Doreen Hanson actually found herself hoping that Janna *was* a runaway, although she could not imagine why her daughter would do such a thing. She searched her mind for some quarrel, some disagreement, that might have made Janna want to leave, but there was nothing more than a slight difference of opinion on a trip Janna had wanted to take to Bremerton on a ferryboat. No, that was long since forgotten. She was grasping at anything. Doreen had already raised three girls, and she knew teenagers. She knew that she could trust Janna's good sense—*if* Janna was in a position to make a decision.

While one member of the family remained at home by the phone, Doreen Hanson and Janna's sisters, other relatives, and friends looked for her. They fanned out over the Nile Country Club golf course hunting for some trace of her. Doreen talked with Ken Burke, one of the greenskeepers. He told her not to worry, that youngsters often ran away. He had had some experience in that department, he assured her, and his own kids had always came back.

But Janna didn't.

The Christmas decorations at home, the cookies she had made, her presents, were only sad reminders that Janna wasn't there. Despite Doreen Hanson's objections, Janna Hanson's name and description were entered in statewide computers on December 27 as a runaway.

But was she? Janna had taken no clothing, no makeup, no extra money. Her school principal described her as a well-adjusted, happy student. Her close friends didn't believe she would run away. Rumors started, as they always did, sparked by casual acquaintances and even strangers, rumors that said Janna had hinted that she might run away. They were like cotton candy, evaporating because there was no substance to them.

When 1974 passed into 1975 there was no celebration of the New Year at the Hanson apartment. Doreen was certain by then that something terrible had happened to Janna, but there was no place else for her to look. She arranged to have bulletins bearing Janna's picture posted all over the area in the hope that someone might have seen her daughter.

Mountlake Terrace police, still officially listing Janna as a runaway, sent teletypes to law enforcement agencies in the thirteen western states. Doreen detested having Janna listed as a runaway, but she went along with whatever it might take to keep her disappearance in the public eye.

There *were* people who claimed to have seen Janna alive and well. They were positive it was Janna they had seen. One report came in from Lynnwood, another from Renton. But every attempt to follow up the sightings ended in failure. Janna Hanson's disappearance was becoming like an urban folktale. When police or her mother tried to find the *source* of the sighting, it was always "a friend of my cousin's next-door neighbor" or "Somebody who works down at the K mart heard a customer say . . ." There was no way to get to the source. There was never the last link in the chain. Each person contacted always had new names, and they all ended in frustration.

A casual friend was positive that she had seen Janna

at a roller-skating rink. No one else had. As the posters bearing Janna's smiling likeness proliferated all along the West Coast, calls came in from as far away as Santa Barbara, California. One frightening report said that young girls were being hired to be go-go girls in Alaska in an operation that was really a front for white slavery and that Janna had been one of them. Doreen Hanson was packed and ready to fly north when that rumor, too, turned out to be valueless.

In February, divers from the Snohomish County Search and Rescue Unit, led by Sergeant John Taylor, probed the depths of Lake Ballinger for Janna's body. They found junked cars, golf balls, and every other kind of debris, but they did not find Janna Hanson. Doreen had steeled herself for a tragic discovery in the bottom of the lake, but Janna wasn't there.

On February 27 one of Doreen's former neighbors —who was unaware that Janna was missing—passed a blond girl on a downtown Seattle street and was so sure it was Janna that she nodded and said hi to the teenager she had known for years. It was weeks before she found out that Janna had disappeared. The neighbor was contrite as she talked to Doreen Hanson. Had she seen a look-alike—or Janna?

One of the oddest sightings was reported by the brother of a private investigator. He told police that he had talked to a pretty blond girl at his girlfriend's house. He had assumed she was older, and she seemed to be a good friend of his girlfriend. The girl had worn a bathrobe at the time he met her, and she had told him that she had twin sisters—as Janna did—and that she wanted to be a model, as the twins were. When he was shown a picture of Janna Hanson, he swore that was the girl he had seen. Police tracked down the girl.

It was not Janna.

One ominous development came when the family who owned the mobile home returned. As the mother of the household caught up on the washing, she gathered up a bundle of blue jeans. It was only when she started to iron one pair of jeans that she realized they didn't belong to her daughter. They were Janna's —the jeans she had worn the morning she disappeared. If Janna had slipped out of those jeans because they had gotten soaked that rainy morning, what had she put on instead? No clothes were missing from the mobile home.

The Hansons had a friend who knew a psychic in Portland, Oregon, who reportedly had incredible extrasensory powers. The psychic asked Doreen to assemble a sealed paper sack containing some of Janna's possessions. What harm could it do? Doreen asked herself. She gathered a few things, and her friend placed a phone call to the seer, keeping the sack nearby as they talked. He didn't tell Doreen what the psychic had said. It would only have made her endless vigil more difficult. The psychic had "seen" Janna in an area with trees, a pond, and fallen logs. She was almost certain that Janna was dead. If not dead, she was a great distance away from home.

It might well be true, but how could police isolate one area with trees, a pond, and fallen logs in the state of Washington? The whole state was rife with similar spots. The trouble with psychics and police investigations was that psychics frequently spoke in general terms while detectives needed something specific and precise—like a license plate, an address, a Social Security number, or a fingerprint—and in Janna's case, they had nothing at all.

Doreen didn't tell anyone beyond her other daughters, but she sometimes felt that Janna was trying to tell her something. Although she did not hear footsteps approaching, she sometimes heard someone knocking at her apartment door. When she opened it, there was no one there. The weeks had become months, and she had gone through such agony that she wondered if she was only hoping that Janna was trying to get through to her. It wasn't until a friend heard the phantom knocking that Doreen trusted her own ears.

Janna's new Christmas ski equipment, never used, remained in the Hanson apartment as the skiing season came and went. Unbelievably, *eight* months had passed without one scintilla of solid information about Janna Hanson. It was the summer of 1975, and there still was no more information about the blond teenager's whereabouts than there had been the day she vanished, despite the hundreds of teletypes sent, the scores of interviews with her friends and school-mates, and the fact that her mother never stopped searching for her.

Not really believing that Janna was out there—that she had run away from home over some slight that Doreen had not known about—Doreen went on television, trying once again to reach her missing daughter or someone who might know where she was. Doreen reported that Janna's older sister had a new baby. If Janna knew that and *could* come home, Doreen knew she would. But there were no letters, no phone calls—not even the hollow knock on the front door.

Janna still was missing.

They found Janna Hanson on Sunday, August 3, 1975. The rural community of Maltby is about thirteen miles east of Mountlake Terrace. Close by, there was a large commune, whose members had joined together to operate a farm that would supply most of their simple needs and where they could shut out a world that marched to a different drummer. One of the residents of the commune took a walk on that Sunday afternoon and passed a large cherry tree on his way to an access road. It was a pleasant day, and he noticed nothing unusual until he returned along the same path sometime later. A human skull rested beneath the tree, on top of the earth, almost as if it had been placed there so that it could be discovered.

The man picked up the skull, carried it to the commune farmhouse, and called the Snohomish County Sheriff's Office.

The skull might well have belonged to any of several missing persons in the Northwest. All during 1974, beautiful young women had vanished inexplicably until their number totaled nine. Six of them had been found—four identified by their skulls alone—and three still were missing: Janna, Georgeann Hawkins from the University of Washington, and Donna Manson from Olympia. The person who had murdered the girls, however, remained a mystery. Janna Hanson's disappearance had not fit into the pattern of the other missing girls'. She was much younger than they were.

Lawmen from several jurisdictions converged on the tranquil farm where the skull had been found, and dental charts soon established absolutely that the remains found were those of Janna Hanson, the little girl who had vanished almost eight months before. For Doreen Hanson and her family, the long search was over and the last vestige of hope was gone. The agony of not knowing was replaced with a searing sense of loss.

The task of putting the fragmented case together fell to Snohomish County investigators. There was still the possibility that Janna had run away, perhaps joined the commune, and died either naturally or some other way during the months she had been missing—but that was highly unlikely. Good detectives always view a body discovery by beginning with the supposition that they are dealing with a homicide. From there they proceed to suicide, to accidental death, and, only after they have eliminated everything else, to death by natural causes. They are trained to expect the worst.

Snohomish County detective Sergeant Doug Fraser directed the search of the area, aided by Detectives

Doug Engelbretson and Ben Duncan and a huge crew
of search and rescue personnel. Only Janna's skull had
been found. The officers reasoned it probably had
been dragged to its resting place beneath the trees by
one of the two hunting dogs belonging to the commune. Somewhere in the dense woods and swamp
there might be other clues.

The skull bore traces of cedar and swamp cabbage.
"We're looking for a swampy area," Fraser suggested.
"Someplace with cedar trees, swamp cabbage, perhaps even underwater. Look for a depression in the
ground, away from the light."

Unknowingly he was directing his detectives to find
a spot very like the area described by the Oregon
psychic months before.

It was a big order. The area was gridded into
sections a quarter of a mile square, and search and
rescue officers from Snohomish County, Marysville,
and Alderwood Manor, along with the King County
police, literally sifted the ground cover in the grid
areas.

It was not an easy search. Included in the grid
pattern was a teenage parking spot, a deserted cemetery dating back perhaps a hundred years, and a cattle
burial ground, plus thick woods and rolling
pastureland.

Deputy Ron Cooper and his wife drove the back
roads in his four-wheel-drive vehicle. After many
passes, he found an area that seemed to match the
criteria Sergeant Fraser had laid down: cedar trees,
swamp area, and a depression in the ground. It was
three-tenths of a mile from the tree where the skull
was found.

Engelbretson and Duncan joined Cooper there and
searched the ground on their hands and knees. They
found a wristwatch, earrings, a pair of inside-out knee
stockings, bits of cloth, a pair of panties, and some
human bones.

Janna Hanson had lain there, in that quiet woods,

for all the long months that her family and police had searched for her. Physical anthropologists from the Smithsonian Institution would confirm that Janna had been dead since shortly after she vanished.

But how and why she had died were burning questions that had to be answered. And who had brought Janna to the lonely place thirteen miles from the mobile home on the golf course and on the edge of a hippie commune? Snohomish County detectives knew they would be working at a distinct disadvantage. The optimum time for solving a homicide is in the first twenty-four hours after it has occurred. The probability of successful case closure decreases with every day that passes. And Fraser and his crew had to go back eight months and start from the beginning.

They began by questioning the seven families in the commune where Janna had been found. For a week, two hundred searchers had learned about the land; now detectives would learn about the humans who lived there. In the seventies, police and hippies were considered natural enemies, but Fraser and his detectives later spoke of the members of the communal 150-acre farm as "beautiful." The young people who lived off the verdant land did everything they could to cooperate with the investigation. But they knew very little.

They couldn't recall seeing any suspicious vehicle in the area in December of 1974. They did know that a chain that blocked a way leading into the area where the dead girl's remains were found had been mysteriously cut late in December.

One member of their group had left during the year, but he was described as a "loner" who moved on whenever he felt hemmed in by people. He had never shown any tendency toward violence; he was a gentle soul who needed quiet and space.

Detectives checked the police files for any individuals in the Maltby area with records of sex offenses. They came up with two men who had been convicted of rape in the past, but when they traced the whereabouts of the men on December 26, they found they had solid alibis: one was dead drunk in the county jail, and the other had been seen at work the whole day.

By August 25, 1975, Fraser, Duncan, and Engelbretson agreed that everything led right back to the Nile Country Club. They were convinced that Janna had met her killer there.

"We're going to take the old investigation and work right through it again from the beginning," Fraser told co-workers. "Somewhere there's the key that will tell us what happened to Janna."

The officers reread statements made by the two employees of the Nile Country Club who had been working on the day after Christmas: thirty-eight-year-old Kenneth Burke and sixty-five-year-old Sven Torgersen.* Burke was still employed as a greenskeeper, but Torgersen had retired in January. According to their statements, neither man had seen Janna that morning. Burke recalled that he had arrived at work about 6:30 A.M. on December 26. He had taken the key to the trailer from the drawer in the maintenance shack and used it to open the mobile home so that he could check the water lines at 6:55 A.M. Then he had put the key back in the drawer and gone out to check the greens and clear away debris from the storm of the night before. Burke had walked the greens instead of using a cart. He stated he hadn't seen Janna at all that morning.

Later, of course, when the Mountlake Terrace police asked him for the keys to the trailer, he hadn't been able to find them. No one but Burke and Torgersen had had access to the keys.

According to Burke, he had started to replace some trailer steps at the mobile home later, but he had mashed his finger and given it up. That would have been about 10:30 A.M., he estimated. He said he hadn't heard the phone ringing inside, even though Doreen Hanson called Janna at 10:30.

The men usually worked within sight of each other,

but on that day—from 11:00 A.M. to 1:00 P.M.—Burke said he hadn't seen Sven Torgersen. He had been eating his lunch. The men's workday had ended at 3:00 P.M.

The Snohomish County detective team next looked at Sven Torgersen's statement about December 26. His account of the day concurred fairly closely with that of his partner. They had come to work before 7:00 A.M. Burke had checked the mobile home and returned the keys. Torgersen's account said he had taken the key later to use the bathroom at the trailer, but he had dropped it on the way there underneath the steps of the maintenance shed. He had not been able to find it right away, but he had found it after the police had left. Too late—they had already kicked open the trailer door. Evidently the two greenskeepers had been separated often during the day; they had been checking separate golf-course areas and had eaten lunch alone.

Fraser tapped the case file in front of him. "There are two things that bother me. This Torgersen saying he lost the key under the steps. If he knew where he lost it, why didn't he just fish down there and get it when the police needed it to open the trailer?"

"And the mail," Duncan cut in. "Burke says he picked up the mail for the trailer, and the report shows that there were some letters inside . . . some damp letters. It couldn't have been the mail from the day before Christmas. That would have been dry by the twenty-sixth. And he couldn't have picked up the mail at seven A.M. when he said he went inside the trailer. The mail isn't delivered that early."

"Right. That's the second thing that doesn't fit," Fraser agreed. "Somebody with a key went back inside that mobile home after the mail was delivered— which would put Burke there the same time Janna was supposed to be there."

On October 2, the Snohomish County detectives interviewed Ken Burke again. He recalled the day of

December 26, 1974, well. He agreed that he and Torgersen were the only employees who had access to the trailer keys. He had been on vacation from December 2 to December 23, so he had not known that Janna was supposed to check the trailer, and he had checked it each day as usual. He didn't think there was any reason for Torgersen to go inside the trailer.

Ken Burke said he noticed the bedroom light was on in the trailer when he checked the pipes at 6:45 A.M. on December 26. He said there were no dishes in the sink. He didn't see any keys by the sink. His recall of time had changed ever so slightly. Was it deliberate? Did it matter? Janna wasn't there until 8:40 A.M.

Burke had been very cool as he started to talk with the detectives, but he became increasingly agitated as the conversation continued. There was a reason for that; he told them he had served time in Leavenworth prison for something that had happened while he was in the service in Korea.

They didn't press him. They could check that out themselves. Besides, Ken Burke had some theories of his own to offer about a possible suspect. He told the Snohomish County investigators that there had been a strange young man around the golf course—Rick Ames,* who earned a living as an itinerant golf ball diver. Ames traveled around the area scooping up lost balls in water traps. He was nineteen and, according to Burke, had "a dirty mind and was always after girls." Burke described the youth as six feet five inches tall; he wore size 13 shoes and had bright red hair. Burke thought Ames had been around the Nile Country Club course during December of 1974.

"Shouldn't be difficult to spot," Engelbretson commented dryly as the detectives drove back to their office in Everett.

Further checking proved that there was a Rick Ames who dived for balls in golf course ponds around the state and that he had been in Mountlake Terrace. But not on December 26. Duncan and Engelbretson traced his meanderings by interviewing a dozen acquaintances of the golf ball diver. He had been in the area before Christmas, but then he had gone to Vancouver, Washington, 200 miles south. They verified that he had been on a train on the critical day. Nevertheless, they located him and gave him a polygraph examination. He passed easily.

Ken Burke was contacted again on September 11. They told him that they wanted to talk further with Sven Torgersen, and Burke pulled out a picture postcard that bore the retired man's address in Arizona. "You'll have to travel a bit to talk to Sven. He's down there living the good life."

Duncan and Fraser studied the man before them. Burke—five feet eleven inches tall, 155 pounds—did not present a formidable image. He spoke with a slight southern drawl as he fielded their questions. He was a garrulous man, and he seemed to want to explain his prison sentence.

So they let him.

Burke told them that he had fought in the Korean War and had been threatened by his first sergeant. He'd believed the man meant it, so he had lain in wait for the sergeant when he was on guard duty. "I shot him five times with a forty-five," he said.

Amazingly, the sergeant had survived, but Burke said the corporal of the guard had been hit by a stray bullet and died. Burke said he had been convicted and sent to Leavenworth in the 1950s. He said he had been paroled in 1967 and remained on active parole until 1972. Ken Burke was clearly panicked at the thought of going back to prison. He talked too much, and he seemed to embroider his stories with too much detail. The detectives knew he was too young to have been in the Korean War. They doubted his whole story. He was hiding something.

Burke had said that nineteen-year-old Rick Ames was a womanizer. The detectives had heard much the same story about Burke from the redheaded golf ball collector. Ames had said that Burke made weird comments about girls and that he personally "would never trust" the greenskeeper around a girl.

The time had come to give a lie detector test to Ken Burke. He agreed to appear at the sheriff's office on September 25 for the polygraph examination. He did show up, but he had taken so many tranquilizers that the machine's leads might well have been connected to a department store mannequin. A new appointment was set for September 30.

The Snohomish County detectives felt that Ken Burke had lied about his activities on December 26. Among the things that bothered them were the lost key, the mail in the trailer, his claim that he hadn't seen Janna that day, and his insistence that he hadn't heard the phone ring at 10:30 when he supposedly was working on the steps just outside the mobile home. The investigators had looked at those steps and found them far too heavy for any one man to move; there was no way he could even have attempted to place them at the trailer door by himself. He would have ruined his back and had the hernia to end all hernias if he had.

The Snohomish County detectives had interviewed almost two hundred people in the Janna Hanson case, but they kept coming back to Burke. He did not avoid them, and although he was apprised of his constitutional rights before each conversation, he said he did not want a lawyer. He almost seemed to enjoy jousting with them, but his nerves always began to betray him when the conversation got too specific about Janna.

On September 30, Ken Burke showed up again to take a polygraph test. But this time he was so distraught that he could not even be linked up to the machine. He broke into tears and said, "I don't want to go back in a cage."

Burke told the detectives that he often thought

about violence and death, but he didn't know why. He said he often thought about killing those closest to him, even though he loved them.

"Sometimes I think about killing people . . . all people . . . just beating their heads," he said.

Taken aback, the detectives let him talk. Words spilled out of him like lava long under pressure in a volcano. Burke recalled that he had killed his cat by beating it to death. As a teenager he had cut off his dog's head because he wanted to make a plaster cast of it. The detectives stared at him.

"Did you kill Janna?" one of the investigators asked quietly.

"I don't think so."

Asked if he'd ever had any treatment for his emotional problems, Ken Burke replied that he had "only Mickey Mouse games with ink spots in prison." Then the suspect pleaded, "Please help me." Fraser and Duncan immediately arranged for an appointment for Burke at a mental health clinic. They also consulted with a psychiatrist, outlining what they had heard, and were told that their suspect might very well be dangerous to the public and, for that matter, to himself.

The detectives were in an untenable position. They could not force Burke to accept treatment, nor did they have enough physical evidence to arrest him on a murder charge. On October 2, they talked with him again. Again he refused to have a lawyer present. Once again they retraced that long-ago stormy day after Christmas.

Burke said he ate his lunch—a sandwich—early that day, from 10:30 to 11:00, in the maintenance shed. In this latest version he said he went to the mobile home at 11:00 to fix the steps, but stopped after he mashed his thumb. He said he was having pains from an operation done three weeks earlier and that he went home to lie down until 1:00. When he returned to the country club at 1:00, he saw the police personnel around the mobile home.

He was "almost positive" that he hadn't hurt Janna. He went on to say that he got an urge to kill about once a month, but he usually "drove it off." He remembered an incident that had occurred years earlier at Fort Gordon, Georgia, where he had hitched a ride with a motorist and then attacked him with brass knuckles. "I tossed him in the palms and drove off. I never heard of him again."

Ken Burke's obsession with violence had gripped him for over twenty years. He recalled almost killing his father when he was seventeen; he had aimed a loaded gun at the sleeping man and started to squeeze the trigger when his father groaned and turned over. That had frightened Ken and he fled. Another time, he said, a young employee had "sassed" him, and Burke had headed for him with a hammer. "I smashed a bench with the hammer instead," he said.

Fraser and Duncan stopped the interview and took Burke to a hospital for a psychiatric evaluation. He was diagnosed as having a mild "situational depression" because of his involvement in a homicide investigation and his fear of returning to prison. He was not diagnosed as psychotic—crazy. Burke seemed calmer when they took him home.

On October 10, Ben Duncan was successful in placing a phone call to Sven Torgersen. Torgersen repeated much of what he had said ten months before. He said Burke had come back about 7:00 A.M. after checking the trailer. The two of them went out to clear debris, but they weren't together. He said Ken ate lunch at 9:45 while he himself went to a nearby shopping center. When he returned at 10:30, Burke was gone. Sven said he took the trailer key from the drawer just before the police got there and then he lost it. Later, Burke complained of pain and went home.

Asked what kind of tires were on Burke's car

(Mountlake Terrace officer Lyle had noted snow tire tracks directly behind the trailer when he arrived on the morning of December 26), Sven said "snow tires."

"Did Burke ever talk about sex?" Duncan asked.

"Men always talk about sex some when they get together."

"Mr. Torgersen," Duncan said, "we've given polygraphs to almost everyone else. Would you be willing to take one if I can arrange it with the Phoenix police department?"

There was a long pause, then Torgersen blurted, "Well . . . about that key . . ."

"Yes."

"Well, that wasn't exactly the way it happened. When the officers asked for the key, I just stood there like a fool. I never took it, and I never had it. I guess I just made it up out of embarrassment."

Duncan's long frustration at getting vague answers broke through as he said, "Who the hell had it?"

Torgersen didn't know. "Somebody must have found it," he said. "I lied and said it was lost so I wouldn't look like an ass. Ken Burke turned it in the day after because he said he didn't want any more to do with that trailer."

On October 16, Duncan and Engelbretson talked with Ken Burke at the Nile Country Club. Burke was angry when he heard that Sven Torgersen said that he had the key on December 27. He said the key probably was in the drawer the whole time after he'd put it there early on the morning of December 26. In this new—and once again different—statement, Burke claimed that he had driven a motor scooter up to the back door of the mobile home and that it had left the wide tire marks.

He said he hadn't seen the damp garbage sack, but that Mountlake Terrace police officers had told him about it. His questioners knew that the Mountlake Terrace cops had never told him that. It was information they had all deliberately held back so they could eliminate chronic confessors.

"*Anybody* could have had a key made for that trailer," Burke insisted. He had a ready explanation for every discrepancy mentioned, but sweat beaded on his forehead as he talked with the two detectives.

On the evening of October 16 the man who had convinced a psychiatrist that he was essentially sane did something aberrant. He had given his last version of his whereabouts on the day Janna Hanson vanished. Ken Burke was found dead of a self-inflicted bullet wound in the head. He left a note disclaiming any guilt in the death of Janna Hanson. The death weapon was a .25-caliber automatic, a gun he had told friends he had "thrown in the bay" many months earlier. It was a Colt with the serial numbers filed off.

Any information that Ken Burke had about Janna Hanson's death died with him. But the investigation was not over. Duncan flew to Phoenix and observed a polygraph examination administered to Sven Torgersen. It proved the old man was telling the truth when he said he had never seen Janna Hanson and didn't know her. But he admitted he had lied about some of the occurrences of December 26.

"The first part of the morning went just like I said," Torgersen told Duncan. "But I didn't tell you that Ken left later and took the scooter. He came up from the mobile home area and told me I should go to lunch early." Torgersen described Burke as "awful nervous" and said his co-worker just sat in the maintenance shed a little after 10:30 and shook his head back and forth. When Torgersen came back from lunch shortly before 11:30, he found that Burke was gone. A little while later Ken Burke came walking up the hill from the trailer complaining of "pains." He left the country club grounds and didn't come back until one o'clock that afternoon.

Torgersen had lied about the sequence of events

because neither man had spent much time working that day, and Torgersen was afraid they would be in trouble with the golf course management.

The investigators theorized that Ken Burke had come upon Janna Hanson as she cleaned her friend's mobile home that morning. From their countless sessions with him, they were aware of the strength of his compulsion to kill. The pictures in their minds were chilling, but they knew they were right. Burke must have forced Janna to his car, parked at the back door. There had been no struggle in the trailer.

Janna's resting place in the cedar forest was a half hour's drive from the country club in midday traffic. Burke could have strangled Janna with her own scarf, hidden her body, and returned to the golf course by one o'clock.

Doreen Hanson was finally able to tell the public what she had always believed: Janna was never a runaway. She was probably already dead when her mother went looking for her at 11:20 on the morning of December 26, 1974. There was no way she could go home again to the family she loved.

Janna Hanson's memorial service at the Richmond Beach Congregational Church on August 21, 1975, was marked not by grief but by joy for the happy girl she had been.

Doreen Hanson was active for many years in Family and Friends of Missing Persons and Victims of Violent Crimes.

The Rehabilitation
of a Monster

Whenever I present a seminar or lecture or appear on a radio or television talk show, there is one question I always expect: "Do you believe in the death penalty?" Before I researched the following case, my answer was no. I began true crime writing as the complete social worker. I believed that anyone could be rehabilitated if he or she was only given love and kindness and made to feel valued. But I learned that some human beings have no compassion, no empathy, and no desire whatsoever to change. And why should they change? They are quite content the way things are. And the way things are for them is that they have an obsessive drive to take what they want, when they want it, without a backward glance at the suffering and death they cause.

Since I wrote about the killer in the following story, I have come upon his counterparts again and again. They all make wonderful prisoners; they are compliant, charming, and cooperative. They are almost always handsome—or beautiful—and intelligent. The people they interact with want to like them. And the charismatic sadistic sociopaths count on that. They will go along with the prison program and never give one clue about what they are really thinking.

Of course they won't reveal what is inside. They want to get out of prison. And too many of them do.

My answer then is yes. I do support the death penalty

441

in certain instances. When a killer's first crimes are marked by such cruelty that the mass of men must turn away from the details, I don't believe he deserves a second chance. If life in prison literally meant *life in prison, I would be against the death penalty. But a life sentence rarely results in life in prison, and I prefer to give the benefit of the doubt to innocent victims yet to be rather than to a proven sadistic killer.*

Salem is the capital of Oregon, a beautiful city in a beautiful state. Even in December, roses bloom along the parking strips of most streets. In the spring, Salem's cherry trees are frothy pink with blossoms, and there are rhododendrons, azaleas, daffodils, and the fragrant satin florets of daphne everywhere. The huge statue of the golden pioneer towers majestically above the Oregon State Capitol beckoning new settlers. Ever since the days of the *real* pioneers, thousands upon thousands of people have come to Oregon seeking a fresh start, a new life in a faraway place. Some accomplish their dreams; some have only sought out a geographical solution to their troubles, unaware that they have brought worry and failure right along with them.

Salem is in Marion, County, where all but one of Oregon's state institutions are located: the state prison, the state mental hospital, the home for the developmentally disabled, and the girls' training school—a euphemism for "reform school." Only the boys' training school is located outside the capital county. Many of the "graduates" of these institution stay on in Salem, living in a section of the city that locals call "Felony Flats." Even so, Salem does not have a markedly high incidence of crime, but when there are crimes in Salem and in Marion County, many of them are bizarre, sensational, and complicated.

Fishing should have been better than it was on that early spring afternoon of April 19, 1975. The fisherman decided to try one more spot in the slough near the Brown's Island Sanitary Landfill southeast of Salem. He had moved to a stony bank beneath a wooden bridge and was preparing to drop his line again when his eyes fixed on what appeared to be parts of a department store mannequin floating among the reeds in the shallows at the west side of the bridge. There was some clothing drifting there, too, and a white towel.

When the fisherman looked more closely at the mannequin's legs, however, he drew back in horror. He could see skeletal ball joints at the tops of the limbs that were undulating slowly in the water. Half aloud, he murmured, "Dummies don't have no ball joints. . . ."

All thoughts of fishing gone now, the man ran to his car and headed for a telephone. In his panicked rush, he couldn't find a phone booth right away, and he decided to go directly to Salem Police headquarters to report his gruesome find.

Salem officer R. Richie responded and soon verified that there were indeed human remains in the slough —but he noted that the area was in Marion County Sheriff Jim Heenan's jurisdiction. Marion County Sergeant Ronald Beodigheimer was dispatched at 4:14 on that Saturday afternoon, the first of a phalanx of investigators to rush to the scene: Chief of Detectives Lieutenant James Byrnes, Detective Lieutenant Kilburn McCoy, Detectives Larry Lord and Dave Kominek, Corporal Dave McMullen, Detectives Ron Martin, Carl Bramlett, and Lieutenant Ken Keuscher.

Marion County District Attorney Gary Gortmaker,

known throughout Oregon's thirty-six counties as the definitive policemen's D.A., joined the investigators, as he always did.

Many of the detectives at the Brown's Island site had worked scores of homicides, but none of them had ever seen anything like the horrendous mass of human tissue that floated in the slough. Clearly, it had been a woman: two breasts bobbed near the surface. Her head, arms, legs, torso, and unidentifiable pieces of flesh were there too—all dissected as neatly as if they had never been part of an intact human form. As if the desecration of the body by amputation were not enough, the butcher who had done this had scored the limbs with a sharp instrument, laying the flesh open to the bone in wavering vertical cuts.

They made no attempt to remove the fragmented corpse from the water until the Oregon State medical examiner, Dr. William Brady, arrived from Portland. The dapper pathologist walked a circumscribed path to the edge of the slough, waded in, and pulled the torso onto the bank. It, too, had been slashed and mutilated. The breasts, of course, were nearby in the water; the genitals were completely missing, excised with gynecological thoroughness.

Strangely, only the woman's head was free of the savage mutilation. Her eyes were closed and incongruously peaceful. Her complexion was dark, suggesting Spanish, Indian, or perhaps black origin. Her eyebrows were carefully plucked and arched, her lips full. Even drenched with the muddy water of the slough, the victim's hair was still very curly and dark—more brown than black.

The investigators fished the clothing from the water. All of it seemed to be female apparel: blue slacks, a blue and gray plaid jacket top, a white sweater, panties, a girdle, and a Playtex bra cut through the middle in the front. The hook panel from the back was missing. There were shoes—black leather sling-backs with a medium heel. The clothing was tasteful, well coordinated, and handmade by a seamstress of considerable skill.

The towel was white, utilitarian—probably from a motel—and it bore distinct bloodstains, as did a flowered pillowcase.

There was one distinctly male item in the slough: a mateless sock, grayish white with a band of red at the ankle—the kind of sock a man might wear to work in the woods or to go hunting. Maybe the sock was a mistake, caught up accidentally as the killer reached into a drawer or cupboard for something to wrap his gruesome handiwork in.

Chief of Detectives Jim Byrnes took color photographs of every phase of the crime-scene investigation; there would be 120 shots when he finished, an awesome photographic record of the most sadistic homicide ever uncovered in Marion County.

The investigators worked as rapidly as they could without eliminating any of the painstakingly tedious steps of a thorough crime-scene probe. As they performed their tasks, the April afternoon sun began to deepen into twilight and they knew that precious physical evidence could drift away or sink into the silt at the bottom of the slough.

Evidently the killer had expected that the body parts and clothing would sink; perhaps he was unaware that the slough was only two or three feet deep where it passed beneath the bridge. The fact that they had not sunk might be the one advantage the detectives had.

But that was the *only* point in their favor. Identification of the victim was going to be difficult. Fingerprints were out; her hands had been so severely flayed that her fingertips were virtually destroyed. There were no rings, no jewelry at all beyond the broken strands of silver chain that had once been a necklace. Most disappointing of all, there was no purse that might have held a driver's license, a ticket stub, a scribbled note that could give a clue to who the fragmented lady before them had been.

The body parts were removed from the scene at 8:30 P.M.—more than four hours after the investigators had reached the Brown's Island location—and taken to Golden's Mortuary in Salem for further examination by Dr. Brady and Deputy Medical Examiner Roy Patten.

According to the pathologists, the woman had been thirty to forty years old, a nonsmoker, probably a nondrinker, five feet two to five feet four inches tall, and had weighed 145 to 165 pounds. She had borne at least one child, and she suffered from gall bladder disease. There was no way to tell if she had been raped; her external and internal genitalia were completely gone, excised by the knife of what could only be a madman. The right nipple was also cut away. "He knew what he was doing," the pathologist commented quietly.

It was almost as if Jack the Ripper were still alive. The pathologists' findings were frighteningly similar to those found in London ninety years earlier.

The woman had been dead twenty-four to thirty-six hours, not from the incredible knife wounds but from manual strangulation. The intact hyoid bone at the back of her throat eliminated strangulation by ligature, and her eyes, cheeks, heart, and lungs were all dotted with the characteristic petechiae—the small burst blood vessels—of strangulation.

The victim's nails were strangely mutilated too; some had been deliberately pulled loose, while others were broken. Her face was very scarred, but they were old scars, long healed, indicating that she had suffered terrible beatings in the past.

Chief Byrnes took pictures of the dead woman's face, Polaroids that would be hand-carried at once to every law agency in the area. Other copies were rushed to the Salem *Statesman Journal* so that they could be published in the early editions Sunday morning. Later, at midnight, there would be a debriefing of investigative personnel, but no sleep; the enormity of the crime had changed night into day for the Marion County detectives.

Kilburn McCoy and Jim Byrnes checked missing persons reports that had come in the previous day; they found none that matched the description of the nameless victim. But then, she was an adult female, dead only a short time; it was quite possible that no one had seen fit to report her missing.

The second break in the mutilation slaying came in the form of a phone call to Marion County headquarters at 11:30 Sunday morning. The man who called had just read his Sunday paper. He said, "That woman—the dead woman—I can't be sure, but she looks like a woman I hired to do some sewing for me. She advertised as a seamstress, and she was very good. She was a white woman, but very dark-complected, and she had several scars on her face. She said she was from North or South Carolina. Her name was Betty Wilson. I've got her phone number. Would that help?"

Chief Byrnes told the caller that it most assuredly would.

The number was a listing in Scio, a hamlet in neighboring Linn County. Byrnes called the number and asked for Betty. The woman said she was Betty Wilson's sister—but Betty was not at home. Then Jim Byrnes explained who he was and the sister asked, "Oh, is this about the missing persons report? I just filed it at the Linn County Sheriff's Office. Betty hasn't been home since Friday night."

Tactfully, Byrnes asked the woman if she would come to Salem and attempt to make an identification of the victim. She agreed, and, by 11:00 P.M. that Sunday, the identity of the dismembered woman in the slough was confirmed. She was thirty-five-year-old

Betty Lucille Wilson, late of Fayetteville, North Carolina.

Much irony may be found in murder: Betty Wilson was a woman who had spent her life looking for love and security, and she had suffered mightily in her thirty-five years. She had come to the place of her cruel death because she had run away from a life of abuse. Escaping that, she had met an even worse fate.

Betty was one of seventeen brothers and sisters. She married at sixteen and over the next nine years had seven children of her own. When she died, those children were eighteen, seventeen, sixteen, fifteen, fourteen, thirteen, and nine—all of them in foster homes in the South.

There was never much money in the household although Betty had tried to help with piecework sewing jobs. The family had lived in an old bus at the edge of a city dump in Fayetteville with none of the facilities that constitute a proper home. And Betty Wilson had claimed that she had been beaten by her husband, not once but often—which accounted for the old scars on her face; at one point, she said she had been beaten so severely that she was blinded for five days.

Betty Wilson had made her own last desperate bid for freedom in January of 1975. Her sister and family had driven away from a visit in Fayetteville and had gone many miles west when Betty popped up from the backseat. She was a stowaway, a very frightened stowaway, who begged to be allowed to go to Scio with them because she wanted to start a new life.

Betty was welcomed. Her sister's family had a lovely home, and there would be a room for her. She promised to support herself as soon as she could as a seamstress. She hoped to get situated securely enough so that she could send for her children.

Investigators Byrnes and McCoy were shown the room Betty Wilson occupied in her sister's home. She had pitifully few belongings—one suitcase, a few clothes, and some personal papers. She had made the clothes herself. "Betty could make a complete outfit in a day," her sister said sadly. "She could turn a few dollars' worth of material into a seventy-five-dollar outfit."

Betty Wilson was not a bar hopper or a party girl. She had been married since she was hardly more than a child. She didn't smoke, seldom drank more than a beer or two, and her sister said she had received no phone calls except those from sewing customers. Betty had filed for divorce from her husband through the legal aid office in Linn County.

Betty had been out at night only once since January. The second time was the evening of April 18. On that Friday evening just past, Betty's niece—who was fond of her aunt—had invited her to go along on a date. The trio planned to go to the Pepper Tree restaurant in Salem. They would have dinner and dance to the combo there. Betty loved to dance. She was thrilled to be invited and had dressed in a new blue pantsuit she'd made for herself.

Right from the start things had gone wrong. Betty's niece, who had just turned twenty, was not allowed into the Pepper Tree because she was underage. Betty had been so disappointed that the niece and her date suggested that she stay and dance for a while. They would come back and pick her up around 11:00 P.M.

"And did you?" Jim Byrnes asked the young couple.

"I went back in," the youth answered. "I could only go up to the velvet rope they had strung up there. They said they already had 250 people inside and the fire marshal wouldn't allow more. I stood there until Betty saw me and came over. She said she was having such a good time that she didn't want to leave then—said she'd meet us later at a friend's apartment in Stayton."

Questioned further, the niece's boyfriend said that there had been a man standing behind Betty who might possibly have been with her. He recalled that the man had dark hair and was about five feet ten inches tall.

"Anyway, I went back out to the car and told my girl that Betty wanted to stay. She said, 'No way. Mom will kill me. I'm supposed to look after Betty.' We couldn't find a place to park right away. When we went back, we couldn't find Betty."

The young couple looked for Betty Wilson, drove around, and notified the friend in Stayton that Betty would be coming there. But she didn't. At 3:00 A.M. they gave up and went home.

While this interview was going on, Oregon State Police technicians and divers searched the banks and waters of the slough for evidence that might show up in the light of day. They found more human tissue and, oddly, a profusion of lollipop sticks.

Lieutenants Byrnes and McCoy headed for the Pepper Tree. Maybe the missing clues to Betty Wilson's disappearance could be found there. The club was flamboyantly and expensively decorated in shades of red, from its flocked wallpaper to its padded bar and thick carpeting. It was the kind of restaurant that drew both couples and singles, always well patronized, especially on weekends. It was not a pickup spot, but strangers did feel free to dance together and "ladies' choice" dances were a regular feature.

The two detectives found the staff of twelve gathered to talk with them. The managers, bartenders, and cocktail waitresses were cooperative, searching their memories for recollections of Betty Wilson and any men she might have danced with on the previous Friday night. But it wasn't easy; there had been 250 human beings inside the Pepper Tree, dancing, drinking, and listening to the blaring rock ensemble. But several *did* recall the woman in the blue pantsuit, principally because of her pronounced southern accent. She had joined two younger women at a table first and then moved to the bar.

The barmaid in her section remembered, "She seemed to be having a good time. She had a few beers. Maybe she switched to Harvey Wallbangers later . . . I'm not sure. She paid for her drinks with a lot of change she had in her purse. She left unexpectedly. You know, people at the bar usually say good-bye or something, but she was just *gone.*"

Lieutenant McCoy stood at the padded barstool where the victim had sat and looked directly along the bar. Anyone sitting there would be in eye contact with the occupant of a stool five seats away along the curving bar. The investigators talked to the bartender in that section. Who had been sitting there? A lot of people—but he remembered one man who came into the club occasionally, a man who had mentioned he had a problem with alcohol and was on an Antabuse program (the drug when ingested concurrently with alcohol makes a person violently ill).

"This guy could handle a beer or two, though, if he spaced it out with straight water."

The bartender didn't know the man's name, but said he was middle-aged and came in three or four times a week. He *did* remember the woman down the bar who had picked up her purse and coat and joined the man after a ladies' choice number. He had not seen them leave together.

How were they going to isolate one average-looking middle-aged man out of 250 people? They had no proof that he had even left the Pepper Tree with Betty Wilson.

Jim Byrnes wondered if Betty Wilson's husband—the man who she said had beat her—hated her enough to follow her 3,000 miles across the country to finish the job. He contacted Chief of Detectives Major Kiser in Fayetteville, North Carolina, and asked for a verification of Wilson's whereabouts during the essential time period. Kiser reported back that Wilson had punched in at his job on April 17 and 18 and was seen by a deputy who knew him well in Fayetteville at 8:00

A.M. on Saturday, April 19. There was no way he could have been in Oregon when his estranged wife was killed and dismembered.

The Marion County detectives had now gone almost thirty-six hours without sleep, and Betty Wilson's killer was almost as much of a mystery as he had been to begin with. They interviewed local residents who lived near the wooden bridge over the slough. A farmer recalled seeing a white International pickup parked there about 10:00 A.M. on the morning of April 19. He hadn't even bothered to look at the license number because the man was obviously a fisherman.

Several teenagers came forward and said their car had been stuck in mud near the bridge at 11:00 P.M. on Saturday. They hadn't seen the body in the water, but then, they hadn't looked in the water.

The tire and shoe prints Jim Byrnes had photographed at the slough bank proved useless as evidence; the ground was too gravelly to show clear demarcations.

On Sunday, April 20, detectives talked to employees in the office on the sanitary landfill dump. Perhaps they had seen the vehicle that had carried Betty Wilson's body parts to the slough. And there they found the kind of lead a detective dreams of. The personnel at the dump explained that every vehicle coming into the landfill must stop, pay, and give the name of the driver. "We have a receipt for every vehicle," one employee said. "Customers who are not on a regular contract get the original, and we keep the carbon."

The detectives asked to see the records for the early morning of April 19. The first three entries were before 7:45 A.M. when the day shift employee came on. Two were regular customers, truckers who routinely dumped large loads of trash in the landfill.

"This third one, the one with the 'sixty-nine Ford

pickup-camper, was a stranger," the early morning man recalled. "I asked for his name, and he said, 'You'll never be able to spell it.' Here it is."

The investigators studied the slip. The name was Marzuette, and it was indeed unusual. Returning to the sheriff's office, they checked phone books for twelve surrounding communities and didn't come up with even one Marzuette. There was a man with a name similar to Marzuette—a man whom Detective Chief Jim Byrnes remembered only too well. He'd had occasion, as a rookie patrolman in Beaverton, Oregon, fourteen years earlier, to participate in one of the biggest manhunts in the Northwest. The man he had stalked then through the woods and brush of the Portland suburb was Richard Laurence Marquette, twenty-six, a murderer whose crime was so savage that any law enforcement officer who heard about him would never forget him.

Chief Byrnes had thought of Marquette frequently during the Wilson investigation, but it had seemed almost too pat. He hadn't wanted to focus on Marquette merely because he *seemed* right, and thereby blind himself to other possibilities. Tunnel vision in a homicide investigation could be dangerous.

Now, while thumbing through the Salem directory to see if the name Marquette was there, Byrnes thought back to the events of 1961.

It had begun on Thursday, June 8, 1961, with quiet horror. A Portland, Oregon, housewife noticed that her dog had brought home a paper bag, probably after prowling the neighbors' garbage cans. Exasperated, she called the animal over and pried the bag from its mouth. As the dog's teeth lost their grip, the bag came open and something rolled out on the grass.

It was a foot—a human foot—carefully severed at the ankle. She had to force herself to look at it. It was undoubtedly a woman's foot, petite in size, with bright red toenails.

Portland Police Chief of Detectives Byron Shields

and a crew of homicide detectives were dispatched at once in answer to the woman's frantic report. Arriving and examining the foot, they agreed it was human, and they noted it had come from a body that had not yet undergone any decomposition. Even as they looked at the gruesome find, the dog scampered off again. Following the animal, they found a second package. This one contained a human hand, amputated just as neatly as the foot.

The Portland detectives called for help from uniformed patrolmen, and the area around the complainant's home was searched. There was another hand and a femur; the thigh had been boned as neatly as a haunch of beef. None of the body parts had been buried, all had been bled almost dry, and all were fresh; the pathologist, Dr. William Lehman, felt that the woman who had been dismembered had not been dead for longer than forty-eight hours. He promised detectives he would roll the fingers of the hands for prints as soon as possible.

"There is something else that might help in identification," Lehman commented. "The third and fourth toes are webbed; the cleft of the skin there is very shallow. Someone close to the victim may have noticed that."

While officers combed the neighborhood's garbage cans, vacant lots, empty houses, and thousands of other spots where a killer could hide the grisly packages, the disembodied hands were rolled for prints. Unfortunately, only a thumb and three fingers gave clear prints; the other fingerprints had been mutilated beyond recognition.

At that time—decades before computerized fingerprint matching—the FBI kept single prints on file only in the cases of the most-wanted criminals. Without a full set of prints, Portland detectives could not hope for a quick identification via the good prints—but they *could* serve to confirm identity of a victim whose prints were already known.

The detectives found no more body pieces, even though search dogs, Explorer Scouts, and jail trusties had been called upon to enlarge the sweep around the quiet Portland neighborhood.

Where the rest of the dissected woman was, and *who* she was, no one knew. Given the sketchy remains the pathologist had to work with, the supposition was that the victim was a young female, probably brunette, with fair skin, who wore a size seven shoe.

A check of missing persons records in Portland and vicinity showed that four youngish women had been reported missing in the previous week. Shields concentrated on those who had disappeared during the forty-eight hours prior to the morning of June 8. Unless the body parts had been refrigerated, they could not have belonged to anyone missing before Monday, June 5.

The first was a sixteen-year-old girl, June Freese.* She was an orphan who had moved in with an aunt two years earlier. It was hardly a surprise that the combination of a stormy teenager and a spinster who had lived alone for years had not worked. The aunt told detectives that June had threatened to run away to California many times in the past. Now, in the first week of June, with school out, it appeared that the girl had carried out her threat.

"She took her clothes, jewelry, and she had a little money. I've checked her friends, and they haven't seen her at all. I'm afraid she tried to hitchhike and someone terrible picked her up," the aunt confided fearfully.

Asked if her niece had any webbing between her toes, the relative could recall none. A check of the shoes left behind in June's closet showed them to be a good size smaller than the severed foot.

The second missing report had been filed by the husband of a Portland woman, twenty-four-year-old Joan Caudle. Her husband told the investigators that she had gone out Monday evening, June 5, to do some Father's Day shopping. The sheet-metal worker said he'd stayed home to baby-sit with their two small children. "Joan had over a hundred dollars in cash with her; I'd cashed my paycheck Saturday night, and she had most of it."

He said he had not reported his wife missing for two days because he figured she had stayed away for reasons of her own. Her mother had been very ill and was, in fact, dying. It had hit Joan hard. If she needed some time to control her emotions, he understood.

But now he was becoming frightened. He'd called her relatives and friends, but none of them had seen or heard from his pretty wife. As far as he could tell, Joan hadn't even called the hospital to check on her mother's condition.

Joan's husband couldn't say whether she had webbed toes; the Portland detectives were realizing that the toes of a loved one were not something the average person even noticed. "This is one time I wish we had a witness who was a foot fetishist," one officer commented sardonically.

The shoes in Joan Caudle's closet were size seven. That made her a "possible"—although a good 40 percent of the women in Portland wore the same size.

The third missing person report was about a thirty-year-old Beaverton, Oregon, secretary who hadn't shown up for work on Monday morning. She was quickly eliminated as a possible victim; she was back home by the time detectives called. She'd taken an unexpected trip with her estranged husband in an attempt to patch up the marriage. It hadn't worked, and she had come back to file for divorce. It had never occurred to her that anyone would report her missing.

Alma Jean Stromberg,* a nineteen-year-old farm girl, was the final missing person the detectives scrutinized. Alma Jean had been gone from her home just outside Portland for a week. Her mother said there had been a family quarrel. "She wanted to work and buy clothes," the woman said tearfully, "and her dad said she should stay on the farm and do chores and he'd see she got all the clothes she needed. . . . I pleaded with her not to go, and then I said, 'Go ahead, but at least write to me and let me know where you're at.' But she didn't. She was mad at me too."

Alma Jean wore a size seven shoe, but her mother said she had never painted her toenails. "Of course, I don't know what she'd do once she got away from her dad. He was awful strict with her."

Despite the widespread search for more body parts, none had turned up. The Portland detectives now believed that the parcels found had been tossed from a passing car. They were going to have to try to identify the dead woman with what they had.

Pathologist Lehman had done more thorough examinations on the foot and hands. He explained that they were completely free of blood in the veins and arteries.

"You don't mean the body was embalmed?" Shields asked. "It isn't a buried body dug up and hacked to pieces?"

Lehman shook his head. He explained that the body had been drained of blood immediately after the victim was dead—not unlike what a hunter or butcher would do. Somewhere—wherever the woman had been slain—there had to be a tremendous amount of human blood. Perhaps that was where they would find the rest of the victim's body.

The three missing women had never had their fingerprints taken, but there was one way to solve that problem. Technicians went to the women's homes and asked for items of personal use that the women had touched—hairbrushes, cologne bottles, compacts. In addition, they dusted countertops and doorjambs for latent prints.

Charles Hamilton, supervisor of the I.D. Bureau,

compared the latents raised with the prints he'd rolled from the disembodied hand. The process was very precise and very difficult. The prints from the women's homes were old and smudged, and the delineations on the whorls and ridges of the prints from the severed hand were not as clear as Hamilton would have liked. Just as it seemed the probe had come to another of a series of dead ends, Hamilton rushed into Shields's office shouting, "We've got her!"

"Who . . . which . . . ?" Shields asked.

"Mrs. Caudle. There are more than enough comparison points on one of the prints out of her home and one finger from the hand. There's no doubt that the dead woman is Joan Caudle."

The police broke the news to Joan's distraught husband. He nodded his head as if they had only confirmed what he already dreaded. "I knew something had happened to her," he said. "Her mother died, you know, and when Joan didn't come to the funeral, I figured she had to be dead. She never would have missed her own mother's funeral."

Now detectives could home in on the activities of one woman. They asked Joan Caudle's husband to go over again the events of Monday, June 5. He was their prime suspect, although he didn't know it. The spouse is always the first suspect detectives look at.

"Well, it's like I said," the husband explained. "The stores were open Monday night, and Joan went out to get Father's Day presents. She called me around nine and said she'd be a little bit late."

Joan Caudle had not been driving a car; she would have come home by bus or taxi.

"Would your wife have stopped at a bar or a cocktail lounge after shopping?"

"She might have; it wasn't anything she did often, but she was so uptight about her mother being sick and all. Yes, she might have stopped for one drink."

It was a ticklish question, but the detectives had to

explore another possibility. Did Joan Caudle's husband have any reason to think that his wife might have been seeing another man?

"No. I'm sure she wasn't. She was here with the kids all day, and she took good care of them. And I was home every night. Even if she wanted another man, there was no time when she could have met him . . . and she just wasn't like that."

What had happened to Joan Caudle between the nine o'clock call home on Monday night and the awful discoveries of Thursday morning? Her husband gave the detectives a photograph of his wife. They could see she had been a very pretty woman who stared clear-eyed into the camera, smiling slightly. She had dark hair, turned under in a pageboy. It was a good picture, and she had obviously been attractive enough so that anyone seeing her would have been likely to remember her. The picture was distributed to Portland papers and it appeared in the evening editions with a request for information.

The next afternoon, a Multnomah County jail matron called Chief Shields and said there was a young woman in her section who wanted to talk to the detectives about Joan Caudle. "She claims she saw her Monday—the fifth. It may be a bid for attention or she may be trying to work a deal, but I think you'd better see what she has to say."

The woman was very thin with Titian hair and milky skin dusted with freckles. She had clearly seen better days. Her rap sheet listed a dozen arrests for drunk and disorderly, but she was sober now and she did indeed have information for the Portland detectives. She had staked herself out on a bar stool in a lounge in southwest Portland on the Monday night Joan Caudle disappeared. The redhead said she had charmed another bar patron into paying the tab for a succession of double scotches.

"He's been around before," she said, "but the other

times I seen him he looked crummy—you know, greasy clothes, dirty fingernails, the whole bit. But Monday night he looked pretty good, all slicked up. So I figure, let him buy me a couple slugs and we'll see what happens."

Investigators Shields and Tennant waited for her to get to the point. She obviously enjoyed her moment at center stage and wouldn't be rushed.

"Anyway, so me and Dick—that's all he said his name was—were hitting it off fine . . . until she walks in. You know, the one in the paper, the one they say got chopped up. He takes one look at her and it's good-bye time." She shivered slightly and lit another cigarette. "I was burned up then, but I guess I'm lucky. It could have been me."

"You're sure it was Joan Caudle? You're sure of the picture?"

"I'm sure. I looked her over good, like women do, to see what she had that I didn't. She was younger, and I'll have to admit she was pretty. I'd never seen her before in the place, and I hang out there a lot."

"And this Dick—you say he comes in regular, too?"

"Pretty regular. He's about twenty-five—say, six feet tall, 175 pounds, light brown curly hair, blue eyes. Not bad looking."

"What did he say to you?"

"The usual. He called me 'dear,' and he told me I had soft brown eyes like a deer. Pretty corny, and I told him so—but that's what you have to put up with in a bar. They all like to think they're poets."

At the mention of the word "deer," both detectives winced. They remembered Dr. Lehman's statement that the killer had butchered the body and boned it out the way a hunter would cut up a deer.

Pressed to give a clearer description of Dick, the redhead concentrated hard, closing her eyes, then said abruptly, "Hey! How about this? He was young, but I'd swear he had false teeth. He seemed to be having trouble with them. You could hear them click when he talked."

This proved to be the one detail that struck a spark of recognition in the bartender of the lounge. He recalled a young man who complained that he'd had to have all his teeth pulled. "I don't know his name, but the fellow over at the service station does."

"Sure," the attendant said when he was questioned minutes later. "That's got to be Dick Marquette. He works over in the auto wrecking yard." He gave the address.

While one team of detectives headed for the wrecking yard, another tracked down other customers of the bar. Several recalled that the missing woman had been in the bar on Monday night, and they also remembered that she'd been with a man called Dick.

"It was real strange," one patron recalled. "She came in alone, and then this fellow joined her. They were playing the Where-do-I-know-you-from? game and they thought they'd gone to high school together, but it turned out they'd both gone to the same grade school—hadn't seen each other in fifteen years. When they left, I heard him tell her that he didn't have a car but he said, 'We can walk.'"

At the wrecking yard, a worker said Richard L. Marquette had been employed there but that he hadn't shown up after Thursday, June 8. Then he added, "He's still got his pay coming."

Marquette's employee records listed an address in the neighborhood where the body parts had been discovered. There the Portland investigators found a two-room house surrounded by a yard grown high with weeds and littered with trash. The structure had only one door and one window, and both were shut tight.

They knocked on the door, not really expecting an answer, and they got none. They found that the flimsy door was unlocked. As it swung open, a cloying stench rushed out, a smell familiar to any officer who has worked homicides: the odor of death, long neglected in summer heat.

Inside, the detectives found a black sweater identical to one Joan Caudle had worn when she left on her shopping trip. Nearby they found some bloodstained lingerie.

One detective opened the door to an old refrigerator, its motor laboring in the closed heat of the house. He drew back instinctively as he saw that the compartment was jammed with packages wrapped in newspaper. It looked like a quarter of beef cut and wrapped. But it wasn't. Dr. Lehman's analysis confirmed that the macabre packages were human flesh, bled and butchered just as the first body parts had been. The head was still missing.

A murder warrant was quickly issued for Richard Marquette. His stunned neighbors described him as a rather shy, quiet bachelor who always had a friendly greeting for everyone. In an era long before the term "serial murderer" was even coined, the missing Richard Marquette drew the same accolades that all notorious killers seem to get: "He was the nicest guy you would ever want to know. Real quiet. He never bothered anyone, and he always lent a helping hand if you needed it."

On June 19, 1961, the FBI joined the hunt. Then Governor Mark Hatfield called the Caudle murder "the most heinous crime in Oregon history" and asked the FBI to take an unprecedented step and make Marquette Number 11 on the Ten Most Wanted List. The FBI agreed that this should be done, and Marquette's picture went up on a federal flier on June 29.

That very afternoon a real estate salesman in Santa Maria, California, was talking with a clerk in the office of a local credit bureau when the flier arrived. "Hey, we just got your picture in," the clerk joked.

The salesman did a double take and exclaimed, "I *know* that guy! He's working out at the old airfield. My partner and I picked him up hitching and we got him a job."

It was a rare bit of luck for law enforcement. FBI agents arrested a nonresistant Marquette at a salvage shop the next day. At first he made feeble attempts to deny the mutilation murder, but suddenly he blurted, "I was out of my head—dead drunk. That was the first time I'd seen her since grade school. . . . I didn't know her married name. I was drunk at the time, just sitting there. I don't know who picked who up."

He said he had taken Joan Caudle to his home, where she allegedly agreed to sexual relations. There was no way to tell if that was true or a fabrication on Marquette's part. From everything the Portland detectives had found out about Joan Caudle, the suspect's version of the evening sounded unbelievable. But he was the only one alive to remember. Marquette said he had sex with Caudle. After a second act of intercourse, he then choked her in a struggle. "I woke up the next morning and saw her there—dead. I panicked."

Since he had no car to use to get rid of the body of his old schoolmate, Marquette said he dragged her corpse into the shower and dismembered it. He wrapped up all the pieces but the head, which he threw into the Willamette River near the Ross Island Bridge. Detectives later recovered it there, snagged in some brush and rotting timbers at the shoreline.

Richard Marquette's trial began on November 28, 1961. Jurors saw a young man who looked as clean-cut as a divinity student. He was actually quite handsome, and he had an almost shy demeanor. He had been charged with felony murder because the prosecution believed Joan Caudle had been murdered either during a rape or a rape attempt.

After two weeks of testimony, the jury deliberated twelve hours and returned a verdict of guilty of first-degree murder, with a recommendation for mercy. Richard Marquette received a life sentence, but he would not face an executioner. Oregon citizens relaxed in their belief that Marquette would be locked up forever. His picture appeared in the *Oregonian* a few more times as the coverage of the shocking case wound down, and then people forgot about him.

And so Richard Marquette was transported forty-seven miles to the Oregon State Prison in Salem. For eleven years he was a model prisoner. His incredible crime had long since faded from the headlines, and there was barely a ripple made when Marquette was released to parole on January 5, 1973.

Marion County Detective Chief Jim Byrnes was one of the few people who knew that Richard Marquette was out. He made it a practice to know whether most of the individuals convicted of brutal homicides in his part of the state were in or out of prison. Given the merry-go-round of arrest, conviction, prison, and parole, it sometime seemed as though prisoners went in the front door and out the back door of the Oregon State Prison. Actually, the average "life term" was about ten years.

Byrnes had heard that Marquette was working as a plumber's apprentice for a very reputable Salem firm and living in a trailer park but he didn't know the paroled murderer's exact location. As he moved his finger along the reverse directory for mobile home parks, he found what he needed. There was a trailer court at 1865 Highway Avenue, Number 1. And that trailer park was only about 300 yards, diagonally across the street, from the Pepper Tree! Byrnes checked with the manager and verified that Richard Marquette lived there in the mobile home park.

It was 4:30 in the afternoon of April 21, 1975, when the Marion County detectives drove into Marquette's trailer park in an unmarked car. No one answered their knocks on his trailer door, and there were no sounds inside. Detective Larry Lord was staked out across the street to watch for Marquette's arrival. The probers hoped there *would* be an arrival; the last time publicity on a dismembered woman had hit the news media, the suspect had taken off.

At 6:12 P.M. Lord alerted Byrnes and McCoy that Richard Marquette had pulled up in a 1969 Ford pickup-camper. "He's sweeping out his trailer," Lord said. "You'd better hurry."

Byrnes called D.A. Gortmaker and alerted him that they would probably be needing a search warrant, and then he and McCoy drove at once to the trailer park. Marquette was almost forty now, fourteen years older than when Jim Byrnes had last tracked him. He wondered if he would recognize him. Lord pointed toward a man who stood in the doorway of his trailer. He had a mop in his hand, and he leaned on it as he chatted easily with a neighbor.

Marquette's physical appearance had changed a great deal in the years since Joan Caudle was killed. He looked older; the youthful face was gone, and he was gaunt and weathered.

But he appeared eminently relaxed as Jim Byrnes approached him and said, "I understand you're expecting us."

"No." Marquette smiled. "I wasn't."

"Well, we'd like to talk with you, if your friend will excuse us."

Still Marquette remained calm. Asked about his knowledge of Betty Wilson's murder, he said he'd heard something about it on the radio, but that was all he knew.

Byrnes asked him if he minded if they looked around. Marquette didn't demur. He gave both verbal and written consent to search, but the detectives wanted to be absolutely sure that there would be no legal loopholes; they knew the search warrant for probable cause was on its way. The two detectives and the murder suspect talked casually as they waited.

Byrnes studied Marquette for any signs of anxiety or concern, and he found none.

With the search warrant in hand, the investigators moved into the small mobile home. While the meticulous search was being carried out, Marquette leaned easily against his pickup, arms folded across his chest. He was as friendly and cooperative as a man with nothing to hide had every right to be. He seemed almost oblivious to the search, and if they had expected him to follow them and peer over their shoulders, they were mistaken. Byrnes was beginning to think his hunch had been wrong and that it was only a coincidence that Marquette, a known sadistic psychopath, lived so close to the Pepper Tree.

And then he saw something that told him his suspect did indeed have things to hide. Byrnes spotted the characteristic dark mahogany stains of dried blood on the doorsill and on the hot water tap. A pair of Jockey shorts with a faint pinkish stain hung on the shower rod in the bathroom, and there was a matching stain on a pair of jeans.

Just outside the front steps, Byrnes leaned down and picked up a torn fingernail. Byrnes later commented, "A fingernail was even better than a fingerprint for means of identification. The ridges matched, the torn edges matched—even the hangnails and cuticles matched."

That nail had probably been swept out, unseen by Marquette, just before the detectives arrived.

The Marion County detectives actually vacuumed the yard outside Marquette's trailer, and then they sealed the whole vacuum bag into an evidence container so that the debris could be sorted out and evaluated.

Detective Jan Cummings spotted something glittering in the sparse grass, something the vacuum cleaner had not caught. It was a broken strand of silver chain, and it would prove microscopically identical to the other strands found in the slough with the body parts.

Also swept out by the suspect's broom was the missing hook panel from the Playtex bra found with Betty Wilson's body.

And here, just as they had at the site of floating body parts, the detectives found a profusion of lollipop sticks. They had no idea what use Marquette made of them—and it didn't matter. They were one more link between the suspect and the victim. The police had come hoping for just one or two pieces of physical evidence, and they had struck a bonanza.

The searchers pried up a floor register and found a portion of clothing that didn't seem to fit the case— not then. It was the crotch of a woman's panties. All of Betty Wilson's undergarments had been found, and they were all intact.

Jim Byrnes walked out to the pickup where Marquette waited. Finally Marquette had lost some of his nonchalance as he watched officers emerge again and again from his trailer with sealed and labeled plastic bags containing evidence. He had been taken out to a restaurant for supper as the evening progressed, and although he ate heartily and chatted amiably with his escorts, the pressure was obviously beginning to build. Suddenly Marquette blurted to Jim Byrnes: "I wish I could live it all over again."

"Live *what* all over?"

Marquette hesitated and then replied, "Oh, the last twelve to fourteen years of my life." That seemed an odd response since he had spent the last fourteen years inside the prison walls.

Byrnes advised Richard Marquette of his rights under *Miranda,* and the suspect nodded that he understood—but he still wanted to talk.

"You did go to the dump on Saturday morning?" Byrnes asked.

"Yeah, I went. I had some trash to get rid of."

"How do you account for the blood we found in your trailer?"

"That's not blood."

Marquette was obviously torn between his compulsion to confess and his desire to be free.

Asked about his activities on Friday evening, he said he had gone to the Pepper Tree and had a few beers. "I'm on that Antabuse program," he told Byrne, "but I can beat it if I have a beer, throw up, and then get back to drinking." Marquette also admitted to having used amphetamines—speed.

He remembered that he had stayed at the Pepper Tree lounge until about 10:00 P.M. and then gone back to his trailer and fallen asleep on the couch. When he awakened, it was six in the morning and he made his early trip to the landfill to dump a load of siding.

Quietly Byrnes asked the important question of all, "Did you kill Betty Wilson?"

"No! No, I'm clean!" Marquette insisted.

But if ever a man was *not* clean—of murder, sadism, and unbelievable cruelty—it was Richard Marquette. At 2:30 A.M. he was placed under arrest on suspicion of first-degree murder and booked into the Marion County Jail.

As he was undressed preparatory to getting regulation jail coveralls, the detectives noted many small cuts and nicks on his body that had just begun to heal. But these cuts could never have accounted for the amount of blood found in his trailer. Oddly, both he and Betty Wilson turned out to have the same comparatively rare blood type: O Negative.

"There was a time span of fifty-five hours and fifteen minutes from the moment Betty Wilson was found until Marquette was arrested," Byrnes says. "Our team of detectives worked one stretch of forty-seven hours and thirty minutes without sleep."

Predictably, most of Marquette's neighbors were aghast when they heard he had been arrested for the incredibly vicious homicide. They said he had been a perfect neighbor. If someone needed help—a lawn mowed, a trailer leveled, anything—he was right there to assist. He had seemed like such a gentle man, devoted to his pet cats—so much so that he had built them a ramp up to the kitchen window so that they could get in out of the weather when he wasn't home.

Byrnes did talk to one rather insouciant neighborhood girl who came to visit Marquette just before he was arrested. She confided that she been "a little turned off" at first when she heard about his prison time. "I heard he killed his wife. That's not too freaky, but then I heard he cut her up . . . and I figured, 'Wow, that's a whole different trip!'"

It was that, even though the rumor she had heard was only half right.

While searching the trailer, the detectives found leather-working tools—the very best, worth $1,500—and many professionally executed leather items, including elaborate pistol holsters.

Jim Byrnes tried to trace his suspect's life as far back as possible. He wasn't surprised at what he found; Richard Marquette was almost a textbook case. He was the product of a broken home and had known many father substitutes, none of whom particularly cared to have him around. At the same time, he had been abnormally dependent upon his mother. In his teens, Richard Marquette had served in Korea in the army—ironically, as a military policeman. He was honorably discharged on October 22, 1953.

Up to that point, his relations with women appeared to have followed a normal pattern. He had become engaged (by mail) to a young woman, but when he came back to the States he found that she had married someone else. Nevertheless, she invited Marquette over to dinner while her husband was away. She later charged her ex-lover with attempted rape, although the charges were dropped after he convincingly insisted that she had invited him into her bedroom.

His pattern of violence had begun to emerge. Marquette always claimed that his victims had seduced him, that he was not responsible for the arguments that inevitably followed. He could not bear to have women reject him.

It had been that way, he said, with Joan Caudle.

Something similar had happened before Betty Wilson encountered the ultimate wrong man. Marquette had been going with a divorcée since the first part of 1975. The relationship had progressed to the point that they were considering marriage, and then the woman had broken off with him, for what inexplicable reason he could not say. He had not seen her for two weeks before he was arrested for the murder of Betty Wilson.

Had he taken out his rage and frustration on Betty Wilson?

Richard Marquette had *seemed* to be all right after his release from prison to a halfway house. He had managed completely normal sexual relationships with at least two women. But when the woman he wanted to marry turned away from him, he had reverted to type.

Early in May 1975 Marquette's court-appointed attorneys announced that their client was willing to make a statement concerning the death of Betty Wilson. Marquette agreed to be taped and televised as he talked to detectives.

Yes, he had met Betty Wilson at the Pepper Tree and invited the pathetically lonely woman back to his trailer. According to Marquette, Betty had been willing to engage in some physical closeness and he had begun to make love to her on his living room couch. He had taken off her blouse and sweater and was working on her bra when she resisted. Betty Wilson was from a strict religious background. She had probably snapped back to reality and the fact that she was about to have intercourse with a complete stranger. Or maybe she had never permitted him willingly to remove any of her clothing. At any rate, Richard Marquette said she had tried to sit up and put her clothing back on. And he, of all men, could not stand to have a woman fight him.

"I choked her until she was quiet."

At that point Betty Wilson had certainly recognized that she had made a terrible misjudgment. Marquette looked into the sheriff's department's cameras as he described how she had pleaded for her life. "She told me she would go ahead with what I wanted—if I just wouldn't hurt her."

But it was much too late for that. He recalled putting more force behind his powerful hands as he choked Betty until she was dead.

The scenario might have been lifted from the original murder script of 1961. It was clear to those who questioned Marquette that sadistic and murderous sex was much more exciting to him than consensual intercourse. This time, of course, Marquette had a more than adequate vehicle to get rid of a body, and *still* he decided to cut his victim into sections. It was part of his obsession, although he would not admit that. Clinically, he explained that the vertical scoring of the limbs was done to hasten blood loss. Marquette insisted that he had no formal training in butchery, nor was he a hunter—yet he had managed to sever the legs and arms just at the joints.

Early on Saturday morning, with what was left of Betty Wilson wrapped in the towel and pillowcase, he had headed for the landfill. He dumped her purse there to be buried under tons of garbage, and placed the body in the slough, thinking it would sink like a stone.

This confession itself was more than most men—even trained lawmen—could stomach, but there was more. Marquette said he had killed still another woman in mid-1974 shortly after his release from prison. He didn't know her name or anything about her. He figured nobody had even missed her because he'd never heard anything more about her. Was this the woman whose panty crotch was found hidden in Marquette's trailer register? He would not say.

As he talked, Jim Byrnes recognized that the M.O. in 1974 was chillingly similar to that of Marquette's other two known murders. He had picked up his anonymous victim in Dubious Dudley's bar in Salem, brought her home for sex, and according to Marquette, she too had backed down at the last moment. And she too had been strangled, dismembered, and disposed of.

Marquette agreed to lead detectives to the spot where he had left the 1974 victim. On June 13 Jim Byrnes and Kilburn McCoy, along with members of the Marion County D.A.'s staff and the suspect's lawyers, traveled to the lonely, rugged area near the Roaring River Rest Stop alongside the Clackamas River. There the admitted three-time mutilation killer pointed out two graves a half mile apart. Approximately three feet below the ground they found the skeletal parts of the unfortunate lady from Dubious Dudley's. There was no clothing, no jewelry, to help in identification. Worst of all, there was no head at all. Dental records would have been the only positive means to find out who she was; fingertips and other soft tissue had long since decomposed.

She remains today simply Jane Doe, a tragic victim of a predatory killer.

Richard Marquette, faced with overpowering physical and circumstantial evidence against him, pleaded guilty to the crime of murder. On May 30, 1975, he was convicted and sentenced to prison for life. And this time, life *meant* life. Marquette is almost sixty years old and his name rarely comes up in the press. But should he ever be considered for parole, Jim Byrnes, who is now a private investigator in Salem, will remind the parole board and the public of Richard Marquette's crimes.

Molly's Murder

"Molly's Murder" *stands out in my memory for a number of reasons. When I was twenty-one and a Seattle police officer, I lived in an economy apartment whose yard backed up to the same alley Molly Ann McClure's apartment building did. Had we been born into the same generation, we would have been neighbors, ridden the same bus each morning and worked across the street from each other in downtown Seattle. There were, however, twenty-five years between us, so we were never* true *neighbors. Still, as I wrote about this case, I remembered being very young and very confident in my first apartment, and I felt a kinship with a young woman I never knew.*

Molly McClure's death was remarkable not only because of its senseless, stark tragedy but also because it was solved with a combination of the most sophisticated forensic science and good old-fashioned seat-of-the-pants police work by two of the best detectives I ever met: Hank Gruber and Rudy Sutlovich of the Seattle Homicide Unit.

By the time Molly Ann McClure moved to Seattle's Eastlake neighborhood, the world—and the neighborhood—had changed. Eastlake Avenue used to be the main route between downtown Seattle and the University of Washington district. By 1986, when Molly moved there, the I-5 Freeway with its multiple lanes of north and south traffic bypassed Eastlake. The neighborhood was in transition, along with most of the streets that ran parallel to Eastlake. Twenty-eight-year-old Molly found an apartment on Franklin Avenue East. There was an apartment building or two and then some private homes: a bungalow from the 1920s or a pseudo-Norman from the late thirties. Homogenous. The street was so narrow that cars parked on both sides allow only enough room for one vehicle to navigate at a time. Molly saw it would be quiet; there wasn't room for hot-rodders to race.

She could walk to the bus in three minutes, to the little corner store in two minutes. She could be at work in twenty minutes or so. Lake Union, edged to capacity with quaint-funky or half-million-dollar houseboats, was three blocks west. There were many trendy ethnic cafés and yuppie taverns down on Eastlake, ever changing in ownership and national derivation. It was the perfect neighborhood for a young career woman.

Molly Ann McClure was three weeks away from her twenty-ninth birthday when she died, a lovely, laughing golden girl who had made her parents proud, who had brightened the lives of an untold number of friends. Molly seemed the least likely person to become a murder victim. She was too good, too careful, too alive.

None of that mattered, of course. Killers choose their prey with hearts as cold as winter rain, their minds full of lust and avarice; they are not concerned with the pain they cause.

Molly McClure grew up in the perfect family of the fifties. Jean and Warren McClure of the Clyde Hill section of Bellevue, Washington, had three daughters and one son, all of them wanted, all loved. Jean was a kindergarten teacher and Warren an engineer. All of their children attended the Bellevue First Presbyterian Church Sunday school, and when they were older, they went to church camp at Seabeck on Hood Canal. When Molly was in college, she worked summers at the Seabeck camp. She was petite; she never grew much over five feet. Still, she was amazingly strong. Her camp counselors remember Molly as the only girl who could heft a mattress and carry it to her cabin all by herself. If any young woman had the strength and guts to fight off an attacker, it would have been Molly . . . if she had any warning.

It is well nigh impossible to find a picture of Molly McClure where she is not smiling. In most of the shots, she is hugging a friend, giggling in the midst of a group. She was bubbly, laughing, strong, and smart. A natural winner.

Molly graduated from Bellevue High School in 1975. She attended the University of Washington in nearby Seattle first, where she pledged Alpha Chi Omega. Her sorority sisters elected her president a few years later. Molly was a young woman who focused on a goal and headed straight for it. She was intrigued with a career in hotel management, and Washington State University in Pullman, 300 miles east of Seattle, is known for its hotel program. She transferred to WSU and graduated with a degree in hotel and restaurant management in 1982.

Many of Molly's friends got married right after graduation, but Molly made up her mind to put off serious personal commitments until she was thirty. She was a rarity in the 1980s. Molly was a virgin, and she would die a virgin, unconscious and blessedly unaware of what her killer did to her.

When you are in your mid-twenties, time seems endless, with years enough and more to fit in all your hopes and dreams. First Molly would build a firm foundation under her career. Then she would marry and have babies.

Like any rookie in the corporate world, Molly went where the jobs were. She was accepted into the prestigious management program of the Westin Hotel chain. Her first job was as front office manager for the Westin Oaks in Houston. She was promoted then to assistant manager of the Westin Hotel at Tabor Center in Denver. The jobs were excellent, but the cities where Molly worked had crime rates that made Seattle seem as safe as a Sunday School picnic. In a bad year, Houston homicide detectives sometimes worked a thousand murders, twenty times Seattle's average year. Denver's violent crime statistics showed that the mile-high city had more rapes per capita during the time Molly lived there than almost any city in America.

Although her family worried, Molly survived Houston and Denver unscathed. And then with a tragic synchronicity, Molly moved back to Seattle on November 1, 1985—just weeks before her killer was due to be released from the federal prison on McNeil Island, Washington.

Molly had been offered a great job as a hotel restaurant consultant with Laventhol & Horwath, a

ANN RULE

certified public accounting firm. Delighted to be heading back to her family and hometown, she stored her furniture in Denver, with instructions that she would send for it as soon as she found an apartment in Seattle.

The man who returned from the penitentiary had slimmer prospects. But he always had an ace in the hole. He was a man who lived off women . . . in one way or another. Indulged and pampered by his women, he could turn surly when he did not get his way. Nevertheless, he held a fascination for women that belied his average appearance. Female relatives supported him; girlfriends let him live in while they paid the rent. To make ends meet, he was not averse to committing a burglary or two . . . or three. He was from a world a million light-years away from Molly McClure's.

Molly's job with the accounting firm was in downtown Seattle, in a soaring skyscraper kitty-korner from Seattle Police Headquarters. She looked for an apartment beyond the downtown area but not way out in the suburbs. She had close relatives living near Eastlake Avenue. When Molly found the apartment on Franklin Avenue East, she considered that a plus. Her aunt and cousins would be only four blocks away.

The apartment seemed a real find. The rent was only $350 for a two bedroom unit in a four-plex built in the fifties of Roman brick and cedar. The building looked neat and sturdy. Rhododendrons and camellias and evergreen trees had grown up high around the windows, allowing a sense of privacy. The vacant apartment was the lower unit on the north side of the building, 2358 East Franklin.

A careful renter, Molly called on one or two of the tenants in the other units, but nobody had complaints about the building. Sure, the owner was a little slow in making repairs, but for $350 rent in such a great neighborhood, that was a minor concern. She grabbed the apartment and moved in on Thanksgiving morning, 1985. Her furniture wouldn't arrive for three weeks, but she was willing to rough it until then.

Molly's apartment had been painted, but the metal casement windows were slightly sprung, letting cold air and Seattle's winter dampness in, and there was putty missing. Molly put a piece of cardboard up in the cracked bathroom window. Her dad, a Boeing engineer for almost forty years, dropped by several times to fix things—plumbing, electricity, and the refrigerator, which had a noisy motor.

Warren McClure was concerned because Molly's front porch light didn't work, so he bought a fixture and came over the first Saturday in January to install it. He was standing on a chair tinkering with it when one of the upstairs neighbors walked by and said hi. Molly was a little embarrassed; she didn't know the man's name, but her dad just reached out and shook hands. The men introduced themselves, and Molly went back inside.

In the short time she had lived there, Molly knew only vaguely who the other tenants were. The downstairs apartment that shared a common wall with hers was rented by a single man, a letter carrier. Right over her apartment was where the man—she found out his name was Kvay—lived with his girlfriend. A middle-aged career woman lived in the south upstairs unit. All of them seemed pleasant, and nodded and smiled when she passed them.

Molly was very busy during the first part of January. She loved her new job, and she concentrated on familiarizing herself with it. When her furniture arrived from Denver, she arranged it and added some plants and pictures to make the apartment homey. She had chosen the larger bedroom in the rear of the apartment for herself and slept in a queen-size bed she'd bought at a bargain price when the Westin remodeled its rooms and replaced the beds. The smaller bedroom became a kind of junk room. She had her childhood single bed there, a desk, her bicycle, her ironing board, books, files—everything that overflowed the other rooms.

Molly had an aversion to cats, and she sprayed her windowsills and porch with a substance guaranteed to discourage them. She didn't care if other people kept them as pets; she simply preferred not to have them prowling around her apartment. She vacuumed out the heating ducts to rid her apartment of dust and paint odors that blasted out whenever she turned on the heat. She left the vent covers off because she planned to vacuum them again.

Molly wasn't dating anyone special; she often spent her evenings at home alone or with relatives and girlfriends. She had to be up by six on weekdays, and in January, darkness settles over Seattle before 5:00 P.M. She was in a long flannel granny gown by nine on many nights, watching TV while rain pelted against the windows.

It was pitch dark at 4:00 A.M. on Thursday, January 16, when Molly's neighbor, Jack Crowley—the letter carrier—woke to hear someone pounding on his door. Half asleep, he stumbled to the door, but when he got there, he realized the knocking was not at his door but at Molly's. He stood behind his closed door and listened to voices only two feet away. He recognized one as Molly's and the other as a male's. Molly didn't sound upset, and the conversation was short. Crowley heard Molly's door shut, and he went back to bed to catch another forty winks. When he thought about it later, he was a little puzzled; his new neighbor never made any noise. No parties. No stereo creeping through his walls. Who would be knocking on her door at four in the morning?

Molly got to work shortly before 8:30 A.M. She seemed a little upset when she told her boss, Andy Olson, that she'd been awakened very early by one of her neighbors who was concerned about her safety.

"He said he was out jogging, and he saw somebody

trying to get in my front window," she said. "Luckily, he chased him away."

Molly hadn't been too worried at first. She was drowsy and she had gone back to bed until her alarm sounded at six. But as she was leaving her apartment, she saw that some putty had been partially chipped away from her window frame. That jolted her.

Olson heard her calling someone about renter's insurance and took her aside, saying firmly, "Forget the insurance. First, you call the police."

She promised him that she would do that before evening. Molly worked a full day, her worry about the aborted burglary lessening with the rush of business. But when she returned home it was dark again, a storm was beginning to kick up, and a long, scary night loomed ahead.

Molly McClure was in no way a dependent, frightened woman. She was the type who took action. First she contacted Jack Crowley next door. She went over at six to tell him about the attempted break-in. She showed him the marks on her window, remarking how fortunate it was that Kvay Knight, who lived upstairs with Sondra Hill,* had come back from his morning run just in time to scare the man away.

"We exchanged phone numbers," Crowley recalled later. "And we agreed to leave extra lights on. She was concerned, but she wasn't hysterical."

Molly wanted to be sure all the neighbors were alerted. Kvay Knight already knew about the problem, of course. Molly was sure he had told Sondra. Besides, there were two of them and they lived upstairs. She would have to warn Dora Lang,* too; she knew Dora better than any of the other tenants; they sometimes had coffee together. Dora was also a woman living alone, although her unit seemed more secure because her windows weren't on the ground floor.

Molly called the Seattle Police department at 7:00 P.M. to report the would-be burglar. She didn't call on the 911 line, and she said that it wasn't imperative that an officer respond at once. It was 9:00 when Officer Gary Kuenzi appeared at her door. Shortly before Kuenzi got there, Molly had glanced out to see that Kvay Knight was picking up his mail just outside her front door, and she had invited him in to offer his impressions of the prowler to the police officer.

Kuenzi usually worked as a K-9 officer, but he was working patrol that night of January 16, 1986. He stepped inside Molly's apartment, and she pointed toward a man sitting with his back to the officer. Kuenzi wondered why the man hadn't turned around when he entered, but shrugged the thought off; a lot of people weren't crazy about policemen.

"Kvay saw him," Molly said. "I didn't. Kvay frightened him off and then woke me to warn me."

Molly's guest introduced himself as Sherwood "Kvay" Knight. He was a muscular black man of medium height. He explained to Kuenzi that he'd been jogging around 4:30 A.M. when he'd seen a figure bent over Molly's front window. The man had spotted Knight and sprinted off.

"He was either white or maybe Oriental," Knight said. "I'd say five feet six, maybe 140 pounds. He had on a black coat and blue jeans. . . . I didn't see his face, only black hair."

Kuenzi walked around the apartment living room, inspecting the windows. He suggested that Molly put screws in the handles of the front window. Idly, he noted that the apartment was neat and clean. He didn't check the bedroom.

He asked Molly if there was anyone she was afraid of. Old boyfriends? Someone who might have bothered her or come on too strong? She shook her head, but she said she'd heard that the previous tenant had had a "boyfriend problem."

Kuenzi spent about twenty minutes on the call—checking out the premises and warning Molly about safety measures. Kvay Knight was still in the apartment when Kuenzi left.

Molly had called her aunt that morning to tell her about the break-in, and she called again after Kuenzi left. "I offered to send one of my sons up to sleep there, but Molly said that she wasn't afraid," her aunt recalled. "She just wanted to be sure I didn't tell her parents, because she didn't want to worry them. She *was* concerned enough that she wanted to move. We agreed that we'd go out Saturday and look for another apartment."

Molly called out to Dora Lang to alert her when she saw Dora come home from work late in the evening. "I offered to let her sleep here," Lang recalled later. "It makes me sad that she didn't come stay with me. . . . She said, 'If you hear screams, come rescue me'—but no one heard a peep."

No one did. Dora watched the late news that night and then went to bed at 11:30. The storm that had begun as an average January downpour turned into a violent windstorm that woke Dora Lang. "That building was rocking on its foundations—it was horrible, frightening." Lang got up between seven and seven-thirty, and everything was quiet. The storm had passed.

In the apartment next door to Molly's, Jack Crowley had fallen asleep in his living room in front of the TV. The wind woke him up about midnight, and he moved to the bedroom. He slept through the night and got up at 5:00 A.M. He left for work at 6:00 and was surprised to see that Molly's porch light was off. Odd—since they'd agreed to leave extra lights on.

Dora Lang went to work a little later.

Sondra Hill hadn't gone to work on Thursday. She'd had the flu for days and still felt terrible. Besides that, the storm had started the arthritis in her knees aching. She was only thirty, but she could already predict storms in her knees. She'd been up and down all night long, taking aspirin, rubbing her throbbing knees. Kvay had slept on the couch so that he wouldn't bother her.

The second time Sondra got up, she let her cat out. She saw that Kvay had fallen asleep with the television set on. That irritated her.

Hill's alarm was set for 5:40 A.M. When it sounded, she reached over to turn it off and heard the outside door close. She assumed it was Kvay going out to jog.

At the offices of Laventhol & Horwath, Andy Olson glanced at his clock nervously. Molly was late, and that wasn't like Molly. He called her apartment, but the phone rang hollow and endless. Well, he could rationalize that. The storm had been a bad one, and she had been worried about the prowler too, so it was more than likely that she'd gone to stay the night with relatives. But nine o'clock passed. And nine-fifteen passed. And Molly didn't rush in with breathless apologies.

Olson thought about getting in his car and driving by Molly's place, but he knew she'd filed a police report on the attempted break-in, so he called the police and asked for assistance. It is a common call heard over Seattle police radios: "Check on the welfare of . . ."

Officer Harry J. Burke, with twenty-two years on the force, was working Edward sector that morning, just as he had since 1976. He knew those streets in the north end of Capitol Hill as well as he knew the floor plan of his own house. Burke was working first watch—3:30 A.M. to 11:30 A.M. Burke was "Edward 3" that morning.

Six-year veteran Charlotte Thomas had been a community service officer before becoming a patrolman. She was "Edward 4." She had gotten the "possible burglar in neighborhood" information at roll call at 3:30 A.M. Thomas had taken a swing by the 2300 block of Franklin Ave. East just before dawn. Everything looked all right. There was a light on one of the lower-unit porches. There was a streetlight right outside the four-plex. The whole block was sleeping, quiet. Thomas didn't see a living soul.

Hours later, when Burke caught the "welfare check" call, Thomas called Radio and said she would back him as she was familiar with the situation. They pulled up across from the four-plex, one patrol unit behind the other. The sun was bright now. The storm had swept everything gloomy away in its fury.

Officer Burke walked to the front door of 2358. He knocked, and the two officers waited. The drapes were pulled. He knocked again. No answer. Burke pounded on the door with the butt of his flashlight, and still no one responded. They walked around the building, but all the drapes and curtains in Molly McClure's apartment were pulled tight, and they could not see in. It was difficult to get close to the windows anyway; the dark, waxy leaves of rhododendrons and prickly holly bushes blocked their way. From a cop's point of view, the shrubbery was a hazard: the bushes would provide cover for a voyeur or a prowler.

The two patrol officers walked into the area beneath the outdoor stairway that led to the second-floor apartment on the north side. Burke clambered up onto a stair rail and tried to jiggle a side window lock loose, but the rail gave way under the stocky officer. He went back to the front door and knocked again.

But no one answered.

Burke advised Radio that he was going to try to enter the apartment. Radio said Molly's bedroom was reported to be at the back of the unit. Burke and Thomas couldn't budge that window—it was out of alignment and stuck—so Burke tried the side window. He had noted that it was stuck closed but it wasn't locked. Standing on a lawn chair, he wiggled and rattled the window until it finally slid loose.

Burke boosted himself up from the lawn chair and stepped on a rhododendron limb. He called into the apartment three times: "Police!"

It was too quiet inside.

Before he so much as touched the window, Burke looked at the wide white windowsill. He saw the print of a large shoe, the tread of a man's athletic shoe, and felt a chill. Carefully avoiding the print, he literally tumbled into the room, landing on a single bed. He could see he was in a spare room, used as a storage area.

Burke helped Officer Thomas in through the window, warning her away from the footprint. There was a pervasive hush in the apartment, somehow louder than noise. They moved cautiously out into the hall. With the drapes shutting out sun, the only light was from a little table lamp next to the couch. The living room was neat—and empty.

Burke covered Thomas as they headed down the hall toward the back of the unit, the female officer opening the doors of the long closet on their left. Charlotte Thomas peered into the bathroom at the end of the corridor on the left side and saw a dark shape behind the shower curtain. Unconsciously holding her breath, Thomas pulled the curtain aside.

A long bath towel hung there.

She stepped across the hall to the master bedroom, with Burke still covering her. There was a still figure on the bed. Charlotte Thomas thought first, *It looks like a mannequin.* But of course it wasn't. It was Molly McClure. Thomas wasn't sure if she said it out loud or only thought it: "Oh, my God."

The girl on the bed wore a blue flannel nightgown and lay facedown and diagonally across the bed, her face hidden by shiny light brown hair. She was partially covered with a pink blanket, but they could see that her hands were tied behind her.

Charlotte Thomas leaned over and gently touched Molly's carotid artery, seeking vainly for a pulse in her neck. She found none, and the flesh she touched was already cooling.

Despite her training, Thomas was momentarily

overcome with emotion and she stepped out into the hall. "She's dead. She's in there dead," she whispered to Burke.

"I had to force myself to go back in the room," Thomas would testify later. "I saw a silver flashlight on the floor, and some papers on the bed. At first I thought that maybe it was a suicide note."

But when the officer picked them up, she saw that one slip of paper bore the address of Colonial Penn, an insurance company. The other listed the names and phone numbers of the tenants in the other units of the four-plex. Numbers for Molly to call for help in an emergency.

Too late.

Charlotte Thomas and Harry Burke lifted the pink blanket slightly. They could see a ligature of some kind around the victim's neck.

Burke called for homicide detectives and the King County medical examiner from his patrol car, and then he and Thomas secured the scene.

They had seen that all the heating vents were uncovered, and they wondered if somehow drugs might be involved; furnace vents were a favorite place for dopers to stash their drugs. But that thought warred with everything else they had seen in the apartment. Neat and clean, with plants and books. A young woman sleeping—alone—in a flannel nightie.

Detective Sergeant Don Cameron and Detectives Gail Richardson and Gene Ramirez responded to the East Franklin address at 10:40 that morning. According to the Homicide Unit's rotation schedule, the next detectives up for a murder case were Hank Gruber and Rudy Sutlovich. They were due in court that morning, but they were notified to respond to the McClure apartment as soon as they could get there.

Molly McClure lay facedown on the bed, her legs spread wide, her nightgown pulled high over her buttocks, which were stained with blood. Her hands were tied behind her with a cord cut from an electrical appliance (which proved to be her electric blanket control). Her head was turned to the right. When Medical Examiner Donald Reay, accompanied by forensic pathologists Corrine Fligner and Eric Keisel arrived at 11:40, they determined on their initial examination that Molly had been strangled by ligature—and probably manually, too. Her panties had been forced into her mouth until only a slight bit of cloth protruded, a cruel gag that probably had contributed to death by suffocation. A khaki wool sock was tied around her neck.

She had bled slightly from the back of her head, three linear cuts from some manner of blunt instrument. Reay found them consistent with a "striking force," which had probably stunned Molly or knocked her unconscious but would not have been fatal.

Rigor mortis, the stiffening of the joints that begins shortly after death, was well under way. In violent death, rigor is often accelerated. Lividity, a reddish purple staining that occurs when blood sinks to the lowest portions of the body, can be seen first a half hour to two hours after death and is usually fixed by six to eight hours. It, too, was evident as the investigators began their probe into Molly McClure's murder. Time of death is difficult to fix using body temperature when strangulation has occurred; rather than dropping, it tends to rise. Molly's core body temperature, using the liver as source, wavered between 99 and 101 degrees at noon, at least six hours after her death.

And the time of her death might prove to be vital in Molly's case.

Hank Gruber, nineteen years a cop, sixteen-and-a-half years a detective, with seven and a half of those in homicide, was notified at home and arrived at the scene a little after noon. His partner, Rudy Sutlovich, arrived about the same time. They were briefed by the officers present.

"Burglaries are very obvious," Gruber explains. "There's nothing subtle about a burglary. They dump the stuff all out and paw through it."

The motive here didn't look like burglary. Everywhere the detective pair looked, they saw something that any self-respecting burglar would have taken: television set, portable stereo, jewelry, Molly's purse hanging on her bedroom door. The drawers hadn't been dumped out the way a burglar would have done. The place was tidy. No, someone had come in and found Molly asleep, either because he knew she'd be there or because he broke in and found her. But why would he break in—if he didn't intend to burglarize?

Unless he intended to rape. And he knew Molly was in there alone.

The investigation had begun, and no detective who saw what had been done to Molly McClure was going to let go of it until the killer was convicted. Rudy Sutlovich tried to put into words how they felt: "There are some people who just shouldn't be murdered. . . . No, that's not what I mean. No one should be murdered. But with someone like Molly—and we have some other cases where the victims were just good, wholesome, sweet young girls—it shouldn't have happened. And then we have to go out and tell their parents what happened, how it happened, because they want to know. And we go, and we see the pain. . . . Molly McClure was one of those special cases. We'll never forget her."

Not likely. Hank Gruber and Rudy Sutlovich both have daughters.

Richardson and Ramirez had carefully gathered up possible evidence, bagging it and labeling it: the pink sheet, the mattress cover, a beige silk pillow, the two notes, a hair they found clutched in Molly's right hand, and a second hair caught in the wristband of the watch on her left arm.

In the bathroom, the detectives found a curling iron with its cord cut, but the cord was out next to the phone. Whatever purpose the killer had in mind for that, he had not used it. There was a bloodied tampon in the toilet. There were two pennies on the bathroom floor. The detectives took those, too, not sure what they meant—if anything. Better to take too much, including items of no evidentiary value, than to take too little. The crime scene would never be intact again.

Gruber asked if there had been forced entry, and Richardson said they couldn't be sure. He showed Hank the window in the smaller bedroom and the footprint on the sill. The whole case could turn on that one print, and Gruber wasn't going to take any chances. He was a man who has been known to cut out parts of walls and lug them into the evidence room—just in case. Gruber decided to remove the entire sill and wrap it safely in brown paper.

The chair that Harry Burke had used to get into Molly's apartment had been right there under the outside steps to the second floor. Neighbors said the chair had been there for a long time. Oddly, the front window—where Kvay Knight had seen the prowler the morning before—hadn't been disturbed at all. There was no sign that someone had forced his way in on a second try.

The killer had to have left by the window in the small bedroom. The front door was still dead-bolted when officers arrived; the killer could not have gotten out without a key. All the keys Molly had were quickly accounted for. The shoe print on the spare room windowsill was pointed *into* the room, as it would have been if a person had backed out of the window.

Knowing about the previous break-in attempt, learning how intelligent and cautious Molly McClure had been, Sutlovich and Gruber could not believe that she wouldn't have checked all her windows and doors on Thursday night. "No, it's got to be somebody she knows," they concluded.

To this day the detective partners feel that Molly's

killer managed to talk his way into her apartment, using one ruse or another, that he came in through the front door and exited through the window so that he would not be seen after her murder.

Gruber looked into the purse hanging from a knob in Molly's bedroom. With tweezers he opened it and fished around carefully. He saw numerous credit cards and a little cash. It looked as if the killer hadn't even seen it there on the knob.

The detectives searched the apartment for the weapon used to inflict the wounds on Molly's head, but they couldn't find anything with a narrow, curving, blunt edge that matched. Nor did they find blood in any other area of the apartment.

Sutlovich worked the scene all afternoon while Gruber testified in their current court case. That night and the next, the two detectives worked in the quiet rooms until after midnight. They believed the answer was close, so close that they couldn't *see* it, or couldn't recognize it. Each night when they left, they activated a Varda alarm, which would sound in all the patrol cars in Edward sector if anyone tried to enter the premises.

Hank Gruber and Rudy Sutlovich spoke with twenty-seven-year-old Kvay Knight at Sondra Hill's apartment on that first Friday night. They took a taped statement from him as he tried to remember everything he could about the prowler he'd seen on Thursday morning. He stressed that he wanted to help; he'd called Sergeant Don Cameron to offer whatever help he could. He had told Officer Kuenzi what he remembered about Thursday night—the night right before the murder—and then he'd stayed for a while visiting with Molly. He was trying as hard as he could to bring back something, anything, that might pinpoint the "burglar" for the detectives.

Gruber asked Knight if he was familiar with Molly's apartment, and he said that he had only been in the living room. Like the other tenants in the four-plex, he had heard no cries for help, no screams or sounds of a struggle during the night.

On Saturday, January 18, Knight stopped by Molly's apartment as Gruber and Sutlovich continued their day-long crime-scene search. He had remembered that he *had* been a little beyond the living room.

"Molly was afraid of spiders," he explained, "and she asked me to look down some of the heating vents to see if there were any down there. I used her flashlight."

Ahh. That was one question answered. The silver flashlight. It had belonged to Molly. It had been dusted for prints by I.D. Technician Marcia Jackson, but none appeared. Most of the prints Marcia found in the apartment were Molly's or "unusables," because they were fragmented or smudged. On the pictures in the living room and on a drawer in the bedroom she found some clear prints that she could not match either to Molly or her family. But then, it had only been a few weeks since movers had carried Molly's things in from their van. The investigative task was monumental; so many people had moved through Molly's apartment, both before and after she moved in, many of them strangers.

Kvay Knight told Hank Gruber that he hadn't planned to be in Molly's apartment on Thursday night, but she had asked him to come in and wait to talk to the police. He estimated he had stayed perhaps half an hour after Kuenzi left. They had talked mostly about cooking; she'd recommended a recipe and then loaned him one of her cookbooks so he could try it.

Dr. Eric Kiesel performed Molly McClure's autopsy on Monday, January 20, with Rudy Sutlovich and Hank Gruber in attendance. Kiesel found that Molly had succumbed to strangulation by asphyxia, both by ligature and manually. She had also been suffocated when her panties were jammed into her mouth, pushing her tongue to the back of her throat.

Molly had been raped, and there was slight tearing and bruising to the labia minora, the inner folds of the female genitalia. But the man who deserved no luck had been given some. Molly had been menstruating, and the semen found in her vaginal vault was mixed with menstrual flow. The semen was Type O. But Molly's blood was Type O, too. That didn't necessarily mean the killer had won; there were some very sophisticated tests that could be done on blood enzymes and subgroupings.

And there was more physical evidence, so minute that a layman would never have considered it evidence: a pill of lint removed from Molly's buttocks, a tobacco flake under the fingernail of a woman who detested smoking, a black hair from the inner portion of her left thigh, fibers caught in Molly's hand, bright blue fibers found under the pillowcase on Molly's bed, a pubic hair lifted from the panties used as a gag. There were eighteen strands or fragments of hair in all.

What did they all mean? Even a decade earlier, most of that almost infinitesimal evidence might have been part of an insoluble puzzle. However, with rapid advances in forensic science, the criminalists at the Western Washington State Patrol Crime Lab might now be able to winnow out the script of a crime from those washes of blood, semen, fibers, hairs, pills of lint. Chesterine Cwiklik is a criminalist who knows as much about hair and fiber analysis as anyone in America. Enjoying the almost impossible challenge, she went to work on the evidence that Gruber and Sutlovich had given her.

One thing was already quite obvious to the two detectives. The dark spiraling hair found on Molly's thigh at autopsy appeared to belong to someone from the black race. Chesterine would have to verify that, but Gruber and Sutlovich were already sure themselves.

The two Seattle detectives believed from the beginning that Molly had known her killer, if only casually, and that there had been no break-in. They wondered if Molly had black friends in her social circle who might have visited her.

No. Her family and friends were positive she wasn't dating a black man and currently had no black female friends. She hadn't mentioned anything about new friends; she hadn't really been back in Seattle long enough to meet new friends. Her boss said the same thing. Olson's group in the hospitality section of the company was small, and they knew each other well. Andy Olson had never seen Molly with a black man—or woman, for that matter. Neither had she ever voiced any prejudice toward other races. Indeed, Molly had a heart big enough to welcome anyone she met. Moreover, she trusted people—perhaps too much.

While evidence was being evaluated and theories explored, Molly McClure's memorial service was held at the Bellevue First Presbyterian Church that Monday evening. More than six hundred mourners packed the church and overflowed outside. Seattle newspapers published pictures of Molly, all of them, of course, smiling. She looked like a younger version of her mother. She was quite beautiful with big eyes and almost cherubic cheeks.

Warren and Jean McClure received scores of letters about Molly—from people they had known for years, from people in Molly's life, and from complete strangers who had read about their loss. They had no idea just how many lives she had touched and, in doing so, enhanced.

* * *

Jack Crowley could not bear to live in his apartment after Molly was killed; he spent only one more night there, and then he moved out, unable to shake the thought that Molly had been strangled to death on the other side of the wall and he hadn't even heard her cry out for help. *Why* hadn't he heard her? The storm, maybe. Maybe she had not had a *chance* to scream.

Rudy Sutlovich and Hank Gruber figured that Molly had been dead before 6:00 or 7:00 A.M. That was the simplest riddle to solve. If her alarm had gone off, she would have been up and getting ready for work. The shower walls had been dry, and the coffee-pot hadn't been started. Molly was found in bed in her nightgown. And the degree of rigor and lividity in her body when detectives arrived after 10:00 suggested that she had almost certainly been killed four or five hours earlier.

Gruber and Sutlovich kept coming back to one glaring fact. The only black man the detective team could connect to Molly was Sherwood "Kvay" Knight, who lived right upstairs. But he had knocked on her door to warn her once. Why would he hurt her? He had seemed more than sincere in trying to help catch her killer.

There *was* something that niggled at the two detectives. Although they hadn't yet mentioned it to him, Hank and Rudy knew about Knight's past, and it was not particularly savory. He had a record that made him a less than desirable neighbor. He had just been released from prison on a burglary conviction. He had been convicted of robbing a video store clerk after he'd tied her hands behind her with an electric cord. He wasn't the law-abiding citizen he was trying to portray. They learned that Kvay Knight had also been questioned about a rape case that occurred in Snohomish County, Washington, in December of 1984 and that he had been released for lack of evidence. An unsolved murder case in that same county bore a marked resemblance to the M.O. used in Molly McClure's death.

Knight often used the alias "Billy Williams." Rudy Sutlovich and Hank Gruber, by nature and profession suspicious men, began to see Knight's "rescue" of Molly on January 16 from a different angle.

"Suppose," Sutlovich began, "suppose he saw Molly around, found her attractive, which she certainly was, and he wanted to check out her habits. When he knocked on her door at four or four-thirty A.M., he could have found out a number of things. Number one: Jack Crowley said he heard knocking for a long time before she came to the door, so Kvay knew she was a sound sleeper. Molly told her aunt that she'd had trouble waking up when he knocked. Two: he found out she lived alone. Three: that she slept alone. Four: she normally was home—and asleep—at that hour of the morning."

There were still a lot of pieces missing. Kvay Knight lived with a most attractive woman. It would have been foolhardy of him to attack the woman who lived right downstairs—especially after he'd talked to a Seattle policeman only hours before the murder.

Or might he have counted on the investigators coming to that conclusion? Had he figured if he committed a murder almost literally right under the Seattle Police Department's noses, they would never believe he could be so stupid?

Rudy Sutlovich had done most of the interviewing of Sondra Hill. Hill, a legal secretary, had lived in the four-plex for four and a half years. Until six months earlier, she had lived in the unit right next to Molly's, which had the same floor plan, only mirror-imaged. In June of 1985 she'd moved into the upper apartment over Molly's, and Jack Crowley had moved into her old place.

Sondra said she had known Kvay Knight since February of 1979, and they had dated for six years.

When he got out of prison after serving fifteen months, he had moved in with her and registered for classes at North Seattle Community College. Because he wasn't working, Sondra and one of Kvay's female relatives supported him. He had started classes in January and had an eight o'clock on Monday, Wednesday, and Friday and a nine o'clock on Tuesday and Thursday. Because he had no vehicle, Kvay had to take a circuitous bus route to get to his classes. Although his destination was north, he first had to take a southbound bus downtown and then catch a bus that would take him north again.

As far as Sondra Hill knew, Kvay had gone to school on Thursday, and then he had come home, fixed supper for her, and left to visit relatives. At 10:30 Thursday night, when he came back to the apartment they shared, he told Sondra about talking with the officer and then visiting with Molly. Kvay had been a little surprised that Molly had even called the police, Sondra said, because he told her Molly had laughed and hadn't believed him when he told her about the prowler early that morning.

Sondra and Kvay had watched the end of "20/20" and some of the eleven o'clock news. Then they had an argument, she told Sutlovich and Gruber.

"What did you argue about?" Gruber asked.

"He wanted to have sex, but I felt too lousy to be interested." She said Kvay had been grumpy and gone to sleep on the couch. Since it was a cold night, he had pulled a sleeping bag over himself, and she had added a blue afghan she had crocheted.

Sondra said she had been up half a dozen times during the night. She had heard the front door slam at 5:40, just after her alarm went off. She assumed it was Kvay going out jogging. He had suddenly become serious about running, she said, going out in the very early morning hours for two or three hours of exercise.

About twenty minutes after Sondra heard the door slam, she had heard a loud "staticky sound" coming from Molly's apartment below. That was really the only unusual aspect of the whole night; Sondra had never heard any sounds from Molly's unit before.

Although she felt rotten, Sondra nevertheless had decided to go to work. She got up, showered, and put on her makeup. She didn't hear Kvay come back, but when she went out to the kitchen at 7:10, he was there, with his hand in the refrigerator. He had smelled sweaty, she remembered, as if he had been jogging hard. He gulped down some juice and told her he was late for school.

"What was he wearing?" Sutlovich asked.

"Black cotton slacks and a gray Husky Rose Bowl sweatshirt—the same thing he had on the night before. And running shoes."

He hadn't paused to take a shower—just grabbed his notebooks and knapsack and left.

Sondra had left for work at 8:00 A.M. It was much later in the day when she received a phone call from her landlord telling her that Molly had been murdered.

Sondra Hill had been terribly afraid after that. She gave notice to the landlord that she was moving out on February 1. Even so, she had new locks installed on her apartment door for the two weeks she stayed. She wasn't fearful when Kvay was home—but he was gone so much, especially in the dark hours before dawn.

She told Rudy Sutlovich that she remembered Kvay had been in a tearing hurry the morning of January 17 because he was late for school.

As Sutlovich and Hank Gruber canvassed the neighborhood to see if anyone remembered something—anything—that was different on the morning after Molly died, they talked to Susan Stroum,* who lived in the apartment building next door. Kvay had given her the same impression that he was in a great hurry. Stroum was a woman of precise habit, and she unfailingly left for work between 7:20

and 7:25. On the morning of January 17 she had seen Knight as they walked between the buildings at precisely 7:25. She recognized Kvay; he'd lived with Sondra on and off for years. They both turned and headed south.

Susan Stroum had crossed the street, prepared to turn at East Lynn Street, and Knight continued on Franklin.

The detectives checked at North Seattle Community College and learned Kvay Knight wasn't going to school; he hadn't shown up for more than three or four classes all term. He was supposed to be taking data processing and office functions, but the college records showed he had last attended a class on January 10. Sondra didn't know that, and neither did his mother, who was giving him money.

One thing was clear. Sherwood "Kvay" Knight was a liar and a mooch. But was he a killer? And if he was, could Hank Gruber and Rudy Sutlovich prove it?

Sutlovich and Gruber felt the frustration of having to move at an agonizingly slow pace. At the crime lab, Chesterine Cwiklik and John Brown worked on the fiber and hair evidence and on the shoe print. That was really all they had. Most of the evidence couldn't even be seen by the naked eye.

The detectives returned to question Sondra Hill and Kvay Knight again—and again. With each visit they were less welcome. Kvay Knight, who had been so anxious to "help" the police, was growing surly. And so was Sondra. Hank Gruber told Kvay that he and Rudy were positive that the killer was black because of the distinctive pubic hair found during the postmortem. They needed to eliminate any innocent black males who had been around her. Knight's face betrayed shock when he heard this. No, he certainly would not want to take a polygraph test without talking to an attorney, he blurted. Why should an innocent man be subjected to such a thing?

When the detectives knocked on Sondra Hill's door on January 22 and asked for Knight, she was sarcastic. "No, he's not here. You wanta come in and look?"

On January 24, a week after Molly McClure's murder, Gruber, Sutlovich, Detective Duane Homan, and Detective Gail Richardson went to Sondra Hill's apartment to execute a search warrant. It was a search warrant based more on the gut-level hunches of two experienced detectives than on anything else.

"We spent two hours on the phone with one assistant D.A.," Gruber remembers. "Then a long time with another one. We worked over that affidavit and hand-carried it to a Judge Phil Killien. We finally convinced him. It was one A.M. when we got a search warrant signed."

Before seven o'clock the next morning, Hank and Rudy were at Sondra Hill's front door while their fellow detectives covered the back. As they had hoped, they literally caught Kvay Knight with his pants down—or rather, off.

He answered the door in long johns, shorts, and a T-shirt. It was apparent they had awakened him. The four detectives had no intention of arresting Knight at this point; they merely wanted to obtain hair, blood, and saliva samples and articles of his clothing, and to search Hill's apartment. In order to obtain blood samples, they had to take Kvay downtown to the crime lab, where the needed samples could be obtained.

A most indignant Kvay Knight was arrested—but only for investigation; they knew they couldn't hold him for more than seventy-two hours. Even if the lab should one day be able to match the hairs and fibers they had to head, temple, and pubic hair from the suspect, it might take weeks. But it was necessary to *get* those hairs, and Kvay Knight had been so adamant in refusing to voluntarily give up those samples that they had to arrest him in order to pluck his hair and draw a few test tubes of blood.

During the search, they took Knight's Husky sweat-shirt, a pair of black slacks hanging over a chair, and a second pair of black slacks they found soaking in a plastic tub. They simply picked up tub, water and all. Knight wanted to wear his tennis shoes, but Hank Gruber suggested he wear another pair; Gruber wanted *those* shoes to compare with the print left on Molly's windowsill. They also took hairs they found in Sondra Hill's bathtub and in the trap underneath the stopper.

Neither Sutlovich nor Gruber wanted to balance a tub of cold, soapy water on his knees for the ride to headquarters, so they flipped for it.

Sutlovich lost. At six feet seven, he already had enough trouble fitting his long legs into a car; now he had to hold a lapful of sloshing gray water to boot. Gruber drove, grinning at his partner's dilemma.

Gruber had more to grin about than the sight of Sutlovich balancing the tub. This was the impossible case, with nothing to go on but a few pills of hair and lint, a faded footprint. But now, suddenly, it looked as though things might be turning around.

Kvay Knight gave up his blood, hair, and saliva, served his forty-eight hours, and was released.

But Chesterine Cwiklik was finding more and more trace evidence that matched. Cwiklik's specialty is akin to unraveling a puzzle, both figuratively and literally. A postgraduate student in organic chemistry, she specializes in microscopy, using a microscope to investigate very small items and to enlarge them for comparison and matching. Cwiklik was in charge of the microanalysis section of the State Patrol Crime Lab. And when she testified, she spoke of what she had discovered from those minuscule bits of fiber and lint.

A fiber is anything that is long and thin; fibers can be plastic, metal, cotton. Clothing is either *synthetic,* as in the ubiquitous polyester, or *natural,* as in jute, hemp, or cotton. The most common animal fiber is wool. With the exception of carpet fibers, most fibers are thinner than a human hair.

Once Cwiklik had a fiber, there were innumerable procedures she could choose to evaluate it. She often used a spinneret—a disk with holes of different shapes that separated and differentiated fibers. She could test for luster—a manufacturer's treatment of a surface. She could detect the differences in dye and in the stages of dyeing. She could make a "glass sandwich" with a fiber or hair fixed in a transparent mounting medium, and then gaze at it with a polarizing comparison microscope that magnified it 800 times.

Rudy Sutlovich and Hank Gruber had presented Chesterine with 237 pieces of trace evidence. It would take her weeks—months, even—to test it all. She looked at the detectives and said, "Which is the most important?"

"The stuff that was closest to the body."

And so she had begun. The black fibers found on Molly McClure's hand, buttocks, and nightgown matched microscopically the fibers from the black pants the detectives had found soaking in the plastic tub. The lint and hair pill removed from Molly's buttock contained fibers and hairs very similar to those in the pill that came from the crotch of Knight's pants; each tiny ball had cat hair mingled in it.

Cwiklik took the pant fibers several steps forward. She magnified them 1,110 times and looked at them through the polarizing comparison microscope. And there they were, each side of the screen indistinguishable from the other.

Chesterine Cwiklik knew that every human being collects bits and pieces of the world he or she lives in. Every person picks up debris—fibers, hairs, dirt—common to his or her surroundings. "Molly's environment, for instance, had rose-red and purple fibers, paint chips, natural fibers—no cat hair," she explained to Gruber and Sutlovich. "Upstairs, in Ms.

Hill's apartment, there were synthetic fibers, oranges, browns, blue and green, tobacco flakes, and a great number of cat hairs."

When the fiber profile of one household intrudes into another, vital trace evidence is transferred. Molly detested cats, but someone had brought cat hairs into her bed. Molly's pillowcase bore fibers that were microscopically similar to the afghan Sondra Hill had crocheted in many shades of dark blue and white, fibers with a distinctive twist—a continual *S,* thermally bonded. There was nothing at all in Molly's apartment with those colors.

Kvay Knight had slept under that blue and white afghan the night before Molly was killed. He denied ever having been in her bedroom. But he had left signs. For Chesterine Cwiklik, it was as if the killer had signed his name and left it next to his victim.

Hair microscopically indistinguishable from Kvay Knight's was found: on Molly's left wrist, on her mattress, on her pillowcase, on her buttocks, in her pubic hair, on her inner thigh, on her sheet, in the ligature that had been used to strangle her, in the panty gag. Sondra Hill's hair—picked up in her apartment and transported—was also found in Molly's bedding. Molly's hair was found on the sole of Knight's shoes, on the blanket that Knight stood on when he removed his clothes during the search warrant, and in Knight's tub.

Good. But was it enough to convince a jury? Hair and fiber testimony is hard for the layman to understand. And it isn't absolute; it is only highly *probable* evidence.

When a case relies upon trace evidence and circumstantial evidence, the more ammunition from the lab, the better. Each "very probable" match raises the percentage of likelihood. John Brown worked over the shoe print. The pattern of the sole *could* very well have come from Knight's right sports shoe; the size was right, too, but the sole was quite common and there were no distinctive marks of wear or damage. It had rained at 2:00 A.M., but if Knight had come down from upstairs he would have stepped on only a small patch of damp earth and would not have had appreciable mud on his shoes.

The tobacco flake under Molly's nail was foreign; she didn't smoke. She hated to be around smokers, and no one smoked in her apartment out of consideration for her. The minute speck matched tobacco particles on Knight's Husky sweatshirt.

George K. Chan, an expert in biochemistry and a criminalist at the State Patrol Crime Lab, took over the testing of body fluids found at the crime scene and during the execution of the search warrant. Tremendous strides are being made in isolating blood and other body fluids, matching them to a single source. All human beings have genetic markers in tissue, blood, and body fluids. ABO typing can be done on bloodstains, and genetic markers can be isolated from blood groups, enzymes, proteins, antigens, and RH factors. Miraculous silent testimony can be extracted from blood, saliva, semen, sweat, mucus, and tears.

Over 80 percent of humans are "secretors"; their blood type can be determined from body fluids. Tests showed that both Molly McClure and Kvay Knight were Type O secretors. Chan had a problem right away, of course, when he tried to work with the vaginal swab containing Molly's menstrual blood and the semen from her rapist-killer. Both were Type O. But he knew he could do further, more probing tests.

When Chan examined the Husky sweatshirt that Kvay Knight had worn to bed on the night of the murder and when he left the next morning, the criminalist found three patches of dried blood *inside* the waistband. The sweatshirt had not been washed in the week between the murder and the search warrant. Undoubtedly Knight had no idea the blood was there.

Now the most delicate testing began. Chan determined that the dried blood was Type O. But Knight had no cuts or abrasions on his body. He had not bled. Only Molly had bled.

Chan's tests had to go beyond blood type, and he began a search for other genetic markers. The white, black, red, and yellow races tend to have certain Gm (Gamma) and Km (Kappa) markers. Even with "genetic drift" brought about by the co-mingling of the races, the signal flags remain. For instance, in Caucasians, a Gm count of 3,11 occurs in 44 percent; a Km of 3 occurs in 86 percent. In the black race, 3 is most unusual in Gm, but a 1,11 combination is common.

If a black man should bleed on his own shirt, he would almost surely leave blood with a Gm reading including an 11 but not a 3. As Gary Harmer, a forensic serologist, explained, "If you have oranges, apples, and grapes, and mix them and test them, you will get only a mixture of oranges, apples, and grapes; there will be no bananas."

The chart resulting from the test of the three bloodstains and the blood from Molly McClure and Kvay Knight looked like this:

	GM	KM
Victim (Molly)	3,11	3
Suspect (Kvay)	1,11,28	1,3
Sweatshirt	3,11	3
	3,11	3
	3,11	

Chan found *only* Caucasian genetic markers in the Type O blood dried on the inside of Kvay Knight's sweatshirt. Unknowingly, Knight had carried Molly's blood around next to his skin for a week. Had he washed the sweatshirt, the critical evidence would have been lost, but apparently he never saw the faint bloodstains, and they were almost miraculously preserved.

As Gary Harmer explained, "The bloodstains on

the waistband of the shirt *could* have come from Molly McClure, but they could *not* have come from Sherwood 'Kvay' Knight."

No test yet had exonerated Kvay Knight, and the results—taken together—were building a higher and higher mountain of evidence all the time.

Molly's father was going about the sad task of closing out her bank accounts. He received her bank statement from Great Western Savings and Loan, which included all transactions she had made with her bank exchange card on an automatic teller machine. As McClure ran his eyes over the figures for the period between January 15 and February 15, he froze. *Someone had made two withdrawals from Molly's account on the morning of January 17.* It could not have been Molly; she was already dead. Moreover, Molly had only rarely used the card; she wrote checks. The withdrawals were for $100 each at 7:34 and 7:35 A.M. on January 17. The transactions were made at a Seattle First banking facility on Eastlake—only blocks south of Molly's apartment!

Warren McClure called Gruber and Sutlovich immediately.

Whatever the killer's original motive had been—rape or burglary—he had accomplished both.

At first, the detectives thought they had finally found something that would be easy to trace back to Molly's killer. Some 25 percent of the cash machines in Seattle were equipped with cameras to record the image of the person withdrawing money. But this ATM had no camera. Indeed, the bank machine was located in a facility that kept only records; it had once been a full-service bank, but was no longer. However, the money machine was still there. Whoever used it had to *know* it was there; there were no signs to mark it.

Hank Gruber and Rudy Sutlovich went to the four-plex on Franklin with a stopwatch. They would try to time a reenactment of Molly's killer's actions just after her murder. Okay, Susan Stroum had seen Kvay Knight leaving his apartment and heading south —in a hell of a hurry—at around 7:25 A.M. Gruber would have to walk it; Rudy Sutlovich's legs were so long that one of his strides equaled two of an average man's, so they couldn't get an accurate time reading from Rudy. With Sutlovich holding the watch, Hank Gruber walked the eight blocks from Molly's apartment to the cash machine.

Nine minutes. Again and again, it worked out the same. If Kvay Knight had left walking south in a hurry, Molly's cash card in his pocket, at 7:25 A.M., he would have reached the machine at 7:34 A.M.

The exact time the first $100 was withdrawn.

Then he would have had to wait a minute and withdraw the next $100.

Hank and Rudy wondered how Kvay Knight would have known the machine was there. That puzzle was solved easily. Sondra Hill admitted that she had a card that was honored at the ATM, a card that had expired only two months before the murder. Her lover would have known about the machine hidden behind what looked like a simple office building rather than a bank.

Taken individually, the blocks of evidence were not overwhelming. Combined, they defied credibility. Hank Gruber and Rudy Sutlovich believed as they had never believed anything else that Sherwood "Kvay" Knight had killed Molly McClure.

And he was getting away.

Sondra and Kvay moved out of their apartment on the first of February. Sondra went home to her parents, and Kvay was swallowed up in the mean streets of the Central District of Seattle. He was a smooth talker, persuasive and slick, and he had friends who would shelter him for a day or so before he moved on. He and Sondra kept in touch, and she was standing behind him, refusing to believe he was guilty of anything more than skipping school.

But Sutlovich and Gruber could not catch up with Kvay. He was as elusive as the wind. He surfaced here and here and here, and then he was gone again.

The detective team had become close to Jean and Warren McClure, a friendship that would last long after their investigation was over, and they wanted to be able to say, "We have your daughter's killer, and he's going to trial." But they couldn't do that. When Rudy and Hank visited Molly's family, they had to tell them that now that they had enough evidence to arrest Kvay, he had disappeared.

"But don't worry," Gruber said confidently. "Finding people is the easiest part of our job. We'll get the arrest warrant, and we'll find him."

Once they were back in their car, Rudy turned to Hank, puzzled. "What was all that about? You and I both know that finding people is the *hardest* part of our job! We're never gonna find that guy. He's gone!"

"Have faith," Gruber said. "We'll find him."

King County Senior Deputy Prosecutor Becky Roe requested bail of $250,000 when she filed affidavits on April 18, 1986, charging Sherwood "Kvay" Knight with aggravated first-degree murder. The charges were based on circumstantial and trace evidence. Roe was willing to gamble on conviction.

Knight hadn't waited around to be arrested. Rudy Sutlovich and Hank Gruber believed, however, that he was still in the Seattle area. They had a lot of places to look for their cagey suspect. They sat on stakeouts for three days, watching Knight's friends' houses.

And still their quarry eluded them.

But the news of the murder charges had been in Seattle papers, and two casual acquaintances spotted Knight sitting in a car near the Boeing Plant on East Marginal Way with a young man. Kvay was busy selling "merchandise" to the driver and didn't notice he was being observed. The acquaintances had no particular loyalty to Knight and were as repulsed by the crime he was charged with as the rest of Seattle was. They called the police.

By the time Sutlovich and Gruber arrived, the Boeing plant was ending a shift, and traffic was jammed in every direction. Finally something had come easy for the stubborn detectives. They found their suspect sitting in a police car in the middle of a traffic jam. Sherwood Kvay Knight had been arrested and handcuffed by Seattle Police Officer Al Thompson.

In October 1986, Kvay Knight went on trial in Superior Court Judge Terrence Carroll's courtroom. The twelve jurors and two alternates—six men, eight women—gazed inscrutably at the now mild-looking young man in the gray-blue suit. He didn't look very strong; he looked slender and meek. His hair was cut in a modified Afro. His two public defenders sat beside him, patting him on the shoulder, leaning over to hold whispered conferences.

All across the first two rows of the gallery, Molly McClure's family and friends packed the wooden benches. They watched and listened to horrific testimony with quiet dignity, their tear-brimmed eyes the only sign that they were far more than casual court observers. Reporters came and went, but they did not stay all day. It was not a *big* story. Jean McClure murmured, "We didn't expect reporters at all. We're just an average family who lost our daughter. We're not front page."

Only to Hank Gruber and Rudy Sutlovich. To prosecutors Becky Roe and Dan Kinerk, too, Molly McClure's death was no average case. Outside the courtroom, the October sun shone and jackhammers tore up Third Avenue as workers opened up the street for an underground bus tunnel. Inside, the courtroom hushed as a 11-by-14-inch photograph of Molly in her blue nightgown, dead, was tacked up on a display board. There is no dignity in murder; it is so important to convict the guilty that the jurors *have* to see the horror.

Testimony continued for days. Sondra Hill, looking beautiful—but pale—stared down at her ex-lover as she described the night and morning of January 16–17. Molly's family and her boss testified. And the forensic experts patiently explained what all the hairs and fibers and blood meant.

Sherwood "Kvay" Knight did not testify in his own defense. As the trial progressed, he slouched down in his seat at the defense table farther and farther as if he knew things were not going well for him.

They were not.

On October 10, the jury deliberated only two and a half hours before returning with a verdict of guilty. Becky Roe and Dan Kinerk had not asked for the death penalty. On November 3, Judge Carroll imposed the mandatory sentence: life in prison without possibility of parole. Knight stood with his hands behind him. As television cameras whirred and reporters stuck microphones in his face, he declined to make a statement.

Kvay Knight was soon swallowed up in Washington's penal system.

Kvay Knight's conviction was faint comfort to Molly McClure's family, but it put an end to one phase of their grief. "She had a sparkle about her," her aunt remarked quietly. "I don't think she had an enemy in the world. If you knew her, you loved her."

Molly Ann McClure will never be forgotten. So many gifts were given in her memory. The Molly McClure Memorial Scholarship for the College of Business and Economics at Washington State University and the Molly Ann McClure Leadership Scholarship in Alpha Chi Omega are both perpetually endowed. A tree was planted in Molly's memory in Marymoor Park in Redmond, Washington. There is a hand-carved lectern in the Fellowship Hall of

Bellevue's First Presbyterian Church, and Molly's name appears in three spots in the monument at the entrance to the Downtown Park in Bellevue.

In July 1986 her parents had taken her ashes to the beach at Seaview on the Long Beach peninsula, which juts out into the Pacific Ocean off Washington's southwestern state line. "We spread her ashes, with our tears, at the water's edge. It was a favorite place of hers where she spent so many happy times with her good friends . . . and we felt she might have wanted to be returned to that place."

Jean and Warren McClure have kept their last communication from their lost daughter, a short note on pink note paper, sent two days before she died. It included a car payment and said,

1/86

Mom and Dad,

Don't know when I'll come over to drop this off. Thought you'd rather have it sooner than later.

Dad, thanks a lot for spending your time working on the outside light. It's working great.

See you one of these days. . . .

They never did.

The #1 *New York Times* bestselling author

ANN RULE

EMPTY PROMISES

Ann Rule's Crime Files: Vol. 6

POCKET
BOOKS

2059